# FIRE & STEAM

# FIRE & STEAM

# A New History *of the* Railways *in* Britain

## CHRISTIAN WOLMAR

Atlantic Books
London

First published in Great Britain in hardback in 2007 by Atlantic Books,
an imprint of Grove Atlantic Ltd.

9 8 7 6 5 4 3 2

A CIP catalogue record for this book is available from the British Library.

978 1 84354 629 0

1851 railway network map © Jeff Edwards
All other maps © Mark Rolfe Technical Art

Printed in Great Britain

Atlantic Books
An imprint of Grove Atlantic Ltd
Ormond House
26–27 Boswell Street
London
WC1N 3JZ

*Dedicated to my wonderful children, Molly Brooks, Pascoe Sabido and Misha MccGwire, even though they think I am a mad trainspotter, and to the Railway Children, the charity that helps less fortunate children around the world (www.railwaychildren.org.uk).*

# CONTENTS

List of Maps and Illustrations                                        viii

Preface                                                                 xi

Acknowledgements                                                        xv

Maps                                                                    xvi

Introduction: Why Railways?                                              1

1   The First Railway                                    21

2   Getting the Railway Habit                            43

3   Joining Up Britain                                   60

4   Changing Britain                                     75

5   Railways Everywhere                                  87

6   The Big Companies: Great But Not Necessarily Good    108

7   The Agatha Christie Railway                          122

8   Danger and Exploitation on the Tracks                146

9   Speeding to Danger                                   164

10  The Only Way to Get There                                 181

11  Fighting Together – Reluctantly                           206

12  Compromise – The Big Four                                 229

13  And Then There Was One                                    253

14  An Undeserved Reputation                                  269

15  The Future is Rail                                        300

Notes                                                                   319

Further Reading                                                         339

Index                                                                   345

# LIST OF MAPS AND ILLUSTRATIONS

## MAPS

1. The railway network in Great Britain in 1851.
2. The railway network in north-east England in 1907.
3. The railway network in north-east Scotland in 1947 and 2007.

## ILLUSTRATIONS

1. Lithograph commemorating the opening of the Stockton & Darlington Railway, 1825. National Railway Museum.
2. The opening of the Liverpool & Manchester Railway, 1830. National Railway Museum.
3. 'The Pleasures of the Rail-Road', 1831. National Railway Museum.
4. Caricature of John Bull, 1836. Hulton Archive/Getty Images.
5. Railway carriage classes, 1837. Hulton Archive/Getty Images.
6. Ladies ticket, 1840. National Railway Museum.
7. Open carriages crossing the Bridgwater Canal, 1830s. Milepost 92½.
8. Bristol Temple Meads station, 1846. Milepost 92½.
9. 'Battle of the Gauges', 1846. Milepost 92½.
10. 'Unemployed Horses', *c.* 1850. Hulton Archive/Getty Images.
11. Brunel and Stephenson, 1857. National Railway Museum.
12. Primrose Hill Tunnel, *c.* 1840. Milepost 92½.
13. Construction of St Pancras, 1868. Milepost 92½.
14. Tay Bridge disaster, 1879. Milepost 92½.
15. Construction of the Forth Railway Bridge, 1880s. G. W. Wilson Collection, Aberdeen Library.
16. 'Modern Advertising', 1874. Milepost 92½.
17. Wealthy rail passengers, 1876. National Railway Museum.
18. 'Summer and Winter Resorts' poster, 1897. National Railway Museum.
19. Locomotives on the Highland Railway, 1890s. Milepost 92½.

20. Midland Railway porters unloading milk, 1890. National Railway Museum.

21. Train driver, 1907. Hulton-Deutsch Collection/Corbis.

22. Women railway workers, 1917. National Railway Museum.

23. Ambulance train, *c.* 1915. Imperial War Museum.

24. Accident at Penistone, south Yorkshire, 1916. Arthur Trevena Collection.

25. Strike-breaking staff and volunteers, 1926. National Railway Museum.

26. Southern Railway poster, 1926. Milepost 92½.

27. Interior of a London, Midland & Scottish refreshment car, 1920s. Milepost 92½.

28. 'Take Me By The Flying Scotsman' poster, 1932. Milepost 92½.

29. 'So Swiftly Home' poster, 1932. National Railway Museum.

30. A4 Pacific locomotives, *c.* 1938. Milepost 92½.

31. Post Office carriage, 1935. National Railway Museum.

32. Repair gang, 1940. Bert Hardy/Picture Post/Getty Images.

33. Evacuees, *c.* 1940. Fox Photos/Getty Images.

34. 'Food, Shells and Fuel Must Come First' poster, 1940. National Railway Museum.

35. Breakdown crew, 1943. Harry Todd/Fox Photos/Hulton Archive/Getty Images.

36. Miners waiting for a train, 1950s. Milepost 92½.

37. Holidaymakers queuing at Waterloo, 1946. Fox Photos/Getty Images.

38. British Railways' coat of arms, 1950s. Milepost 92½.

39. Diesel train, 1960s. Milepost 92½.

40. Train liveries, mid-1990s. Milepost 92½.

41. 'Intercity Sleepers' poster, 1985. National Railway Museum.

42. Norwich station, 2006. ATOC/Paul Bigland.

43. Eurostar train at St Pancras, 2007. London & Continental Railways/TROIKA.

# PREFACE

There was a great temptation to write a nostalgic book about the railways. The smell of oil and steam emanating from the massive Princess engines in the Willesden depot and the more compact Kings and Castles in Old Oak Common just down the road is still with me. And so is the memory of the policeman who shouted 'Oi, you' and chased me around the back of the Willesden depot but lost out when I proved more nimble at jumping over the fence. My childhood is full of such tales as trainspotting was my escape from my mother's overcleaned flat in Kensington. My journeys with Mr Potter's Locospotters Club to places as far afield as Birmingham and Glasgow were the highpoints of my early years, even when I ended up in casualty to get a piece of grit removed after I had ignored the injunction not to stick my head out of the window when being hauled by a Merchant Navy-class engine.

However, this book is not it. And my trainspotting days ended when I became interested in girls. There is so much more to the railways than that vague nostalgic ache felt by many people my age, which leads thousands of people to flock to preserved railways across the country for steam galas every summer weekend. The railways deserve a wider appraisal, one which celebrates their achievement in opening up the world in an unprecedented way. The railways turned the Industrial Revolution into a social revolution that had an impact far beyond the routes where the tracks took the trains.

This book tries to do something which few writers – and certainly none recently – have attempted before: to put the history of the railways encompassing both their construction and their social impact in one easy-to-read volume. The railways constitute a fantastic story which has often been told only by those obsessed with particular aspects of the system, individual lines or even specific types of locomotives. This book seeks to do more than that – to provide an overview of the invention and development of this wonderful system that changed the lives of everyone in the nineteenth century and continues to play a vital role in the economies of many countries in the world nearly two centuries after the first tracks were laid.

Of necessity that has meant omissions. Of the fifty famous railwaymen listed in a book of that title, there is no mention in my book of around half of them. There is, in other words, no attempt to be comprehensive. There are more than 25,000 titles listed in George Ottley's *Bibliography of British Railway History*, and this book is only 125,000 words long, necessitating a difficult selection of the parts of the history to include. Most importantly, I have made no attempt to give anything other than a cursory explanation of the technological aspects of the railway, many of which require books in themselves (and, indeed, have them). Nevertheless, I hope this book gives enough information to demonstrate that the railways were an invention that was unique in its impact, arguably far greater than any other previous technological development apart, possibly, from the wheel itself.

The choice of what to include has, therefore, been very difficult. After the introductory chapter on the prehistory of the railways, the obvious main starting point in Chapter 1 is the Liverpool & Manchester Railway, a far more significant milestone than the oft-quoted Stockton & Darlington. The Liverpool & Manchester was conceived as a freight railway but in fact developed its passenger business far more quickly, demonstrating the huge latent demand for travel which, it seems, nearly two hundred years later we have yet to satisfy. Trains started the transport revolution that was later picked up by cars and planes, and the success of the Liverpool & Manchester ensured that the railways spread rapidly throughout Britain and, indeed, the world. As Chapters 3 and 4 show, the railways took barely two decades to reach all but the most remote parts of the United Kingdom.

But the railways were not just about enabling people and goods to get around more cheaply and rapidly than ever before. There are so many facets of modern life that they did influence, it is almost easier to list those that they didn't. This book focuses far more on all these developments than on the technological advances which made them possible. Chapter 4 shows that by the 1850s people were flocking to the trains, taking advantage of guaranteed cheap third-class fares or the numerous excursion trains which gave them the first taste of the seaside. The railways enabled them to sample fish and chips in their home town as well as by the sea, and ensured that towns no longer had to have cows cluttering up the streets and the basements in order to obtain fresh milk. The railways changed the way business was conducted (Chapter 5), leading to the creation of the firm as we know it today; railway companies were, for a time, the biggest commercial concerns in the world.

While initially there was resistance in many rural areas to the advent of the railway, and some towns lost out as a result (Northampton is a tragic example, cited in Chapter 3), by the 1860s virtually every town, village and hamlet was clamouring to be connected to this growing machine (Chapter 7). Throughout the book I have tried to describe what travelling on the railway was like, as in the early days it must have been a pretty grim experience, without heating, lavatories, food or adequate lighting. Gradually the situation improved, as did safety (Chapter 8), but at a pace that was rather too leisurely. The railways became universally used and enjoyed a brief heyday (Chapter 9) before the war intervened.

All through the book, too, I have emphasized the political aspects of the railway and the role of the state – rarely benign and often, frankly, obstructive. Nowhere was this difficult relationship demonstrated better than by the two world wars (Chapters 11 and 13) where the railways' magnificent contribution to the war effort was inadequately rewarded by government.

While many histories of the railways concentrate on the Victorian period of development and growth, I felt it important to celebrate the role of the railways throughout more recent history too. The interwar period of the Big Four is often perceived as another heyday (Chapter 12) but perhaps the PR was better than the reality. And the reverse is arguably true for the story of British Railways, which was wrongly blamed for many of the calumnies inflicted upon it (Chapter 14). The privatization of the railways (about which I have written in *On the Wrong Line* (2005), is covered in the last chapter, which also predicts that this nineteenth-century invention has a strong role to play in the twenty-first century.

I realize, too, that some of the information is patchy. There is more detail, for example, on the construction of the Forth Bridge and Settle to Carlisle railway than on the Severn tunnel or the West Highland line, but that is inevitable given the space constraints. For some people, this book will be a taster to explore the rich literature of railway history; for others it will be all they want to know about it, and indeed perhaps a little too much. The book, therefore, is a myriad of compromises between information overload and conciseness, and I am sure many people will dispute my choices and wonder why I have taken the narrative down some strange branch lines, but hopefully that will not detract from getting as much enjoyment from reading it as I have had from writing it.

Christian Wolmar
January 2007

# ACKNOWLEDGEMENTS

I owe considerable thanks to those who read the draft and commented on it. Tony Telford did a fantastic job working on the draft, both saving me from errors borne of ignorance and adding ideas that greatly improve the book, and I cannot express my gratitude to him enough. John Fowler contributed greatly, too, in ensuring that there were no major omissions and Nigel Harris picked up numerous errors. Phil Kelly's advice was very helpful, and thanks are due, too, to Jon Shaw, Stan Hall, Pip Dunn, Toby Streeter, Rupert Brennan-Brown, Mike Walton, Roger Ford and Mike Horne, all of whom made very helpful suggestions. My partner, Deborah Maby, read the proofs with a practised eye. I am also extremely grateful to my agent, Andrew Lownie, without whom this project would not have happened, and, of course, Toby Mundy and Sarah Norman at my publishers. Colin Nash and Colin Garratt at the railway photographic agency, Milepost 92½, were extremely helpful and generous in finding and providing photographs. The errors, naturally, are mine, and please advise me of them. I can be contacted through my website, www.christianwolmar. co.uk, or via the publishers. There will, hopefully, be further editions and therefore I invite comments and suggestions. Enjoy the journey.

The railway network in 1851: 6,100 route miles across Great Britain.

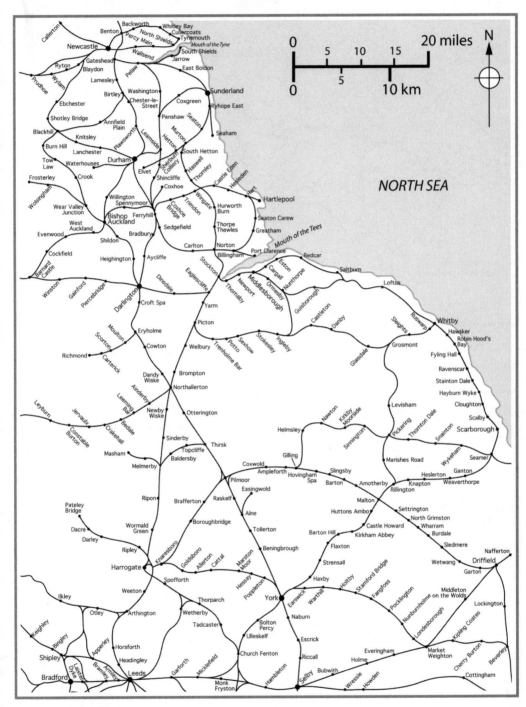

The railway network in its heyday in 1907: 19,500 route miles across Great Britain. Detail of north-east England.

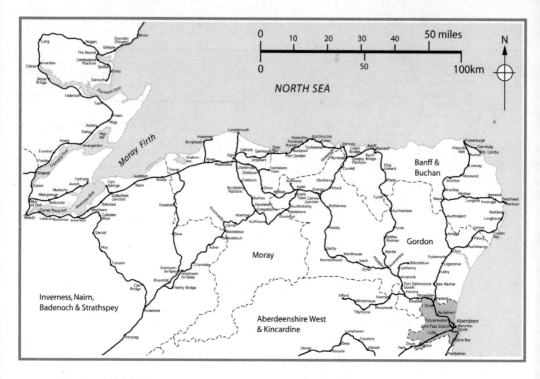

The death of the branch line: The railway network in north-east Scotland in 1947 (above) and 2007 (below).

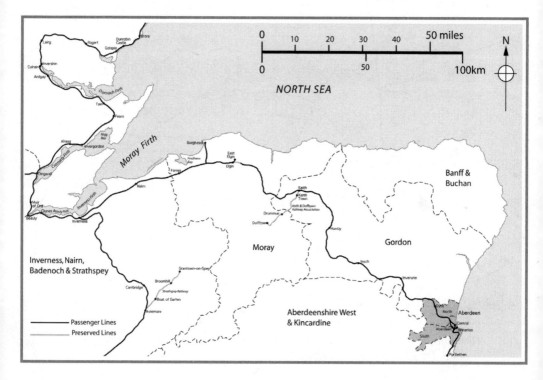

# FIRE & STEAM

# WHY RAILWAYS?

One of the least known facts about Louis XIV is that he had a railway in his back garden. The Sun King used to entertain his guests by giving them a go on the *Roulette*, a kind of roller-coaster built in the gardens of Marly near Versailles in 1691. It was a carved and gilded carriage on wheels that thundered down a 250-metre wooden track into the valley, and, thanks to its momentum, up the other side. The passengers would enter the sumptuous carriage from a small building in the classical style that could lay claim to being the world's first railway station. Then three bewigged valets would push the coach to the top of the incline, giving the overdressed aristocrats a frisson as it whooshed like a toboggan down the hill.

There were other, rather more prosaic railways in the seventeenth century, too, mostly serving mines. Indeed, there had been 'tramways' or 'wagon ways' (often spelt 'waggon ways') for hundreds of years. The notion of putting goods in wagons that were hauled by people or animals along tracks built into the road is so old that there are even suggestions that the ancient Greeks used them for dragging boats across the Isthmus of Corinth. In Britain, the history of these wagon ways stretches back at least to the sixteenth century when, in the darkness of coal and mineral mines, crude wooden rails were used to support the wheels of the heavy loaded wagons and help guide them up to the surface. The logical extension of the concept was to run the rails out of the mine to the nearest waterway where the ore or coal could be loaded directly onto barges, and as early as 1660 there were nine such wagon ways on Tyneside alone, and several others in the Midlands.[1] By the end of the seventeenth century, the tramways were so widespread in the north-east of England that they became known as 'Newcastle Roads'.

These inventions preceded the railway age. They were nothing like the pioneering and revolutionary invention which finally emerged in the first half of the nineteenth century with the opening of the Liverpool & Manchester Railway in 1830, and, as a prelude, the Stockton & Darlington in 1825, five years earlier. As with all such innovations, the advent of the railways was rooted in a series of technological, economic and political changes that stretched back decades, even centuries. Each component of a railway required not only an inventor to think up the initial idea, but several others to improve on the concept through trial and error and experimentation. These developments were not linear; there were a lot of dead ends, technologies that did not work and ideas that were simply not practical. Heroic failures are a sad but necessary part of that process and for every James Watt or George Stephenson who is remembered today, there are countless other unknowns, who together may have made a substantial contribution to the invention of the biggest 'machine' of all, the rail network.

It was not only knowledge and technology that were needed to create a railway. There was the baser requirement of capital – lots of it – that would enable engineers to turn this plethora of inventions and concepts into an effective transport system. The brave investors who raised the vast amounts required to build a railway were taking a plunge in the dark by putting their money into an unknown concept and it was not really until the beginning of the nineteenth century, with the Industrial Revolution in full swing, that such funds became available. Then there was the difficult matter of harnessing a better source of power than the legs and backs of men and beasts. It was, of course, steam that was to make the concept of rail travel feasible. The first engines driven by steam were probably devised by John Newcomen,[2] an eighteenth-century ironmaster from Devon, although in the previous century, a French scientist, Denis Papin, had already recognized that a piston contained within a cylinder was a potential way of exploiting the power of steam. Newcomen used the improved version of smelting iron that had recently been invented and developed the idea into working engines that could be used to pump water from mines. His invention was crucial in keeping the tin and copper ore industry viable in Cornwall, since all the mines had reached a depth at which they were permanently flooded and existing water-power pumps were insufficient to drain them. By 1733, when Newcomen's patents ran out, he had produced more than sixty engines. Other builders in Britain manufactured 300 during the next fifty years, exporting them to countries such as the USA, Germany and Spain. One was even purchased to drive the fountains for Prince von Schwarzenberg's palace in Vienna.

Working in the second half of the eighteenth century, James Watt made steam commercially viable by improving the efficiency of engines, and adapting them for a wide variety of purposes. Boulton & Watt, his partnership with the Birmingham manufacturer Matthew Boulton, became the most important builder of steam engines in the world, providing the power for the world's first steam-powered boat, the *Charlotte Dundas*, and 'orders flooded in for engines to drive sugar mills in the West Indies, cotton mills in America, flour mills in Europe and many other applications'.[3] Boulton & Watt had cornered the market by registering a patent which effectively gave them a monopoly on all steam engine development until the end of the eighteenth century. Steam power quickly became commonplace in the nineteenth century: by the time the concept of the Liverpool & Manchester railway was being actively developed in the mid-1820s, Manchester alone had the staggering number of 30,000 steam-powered looms.[4]

However, putting the engines on wheels and getting such a contraption to haul wagons presented a host of new problems. There had been several unsuccessful attempts to develop a steam locomotive, starting with Nicholas Cugnot's *fardier*[5] in Paris in 1769, which was declared a danger to the public when it hit a wall and overturned. It gets mentioned in motor car histories as, arguably, the world's first automobile. Several devices to run on roads were built in the late eighteenth century but none met with any success due to technical limitations or their sheer weight on the poor surfaces.

It is Richard Trevithick, a Cornishman, who has the strongest claim to the much-disputed accolade of 'father' of the railway steam locomotive. Whereas Boulton & Watt had insisted on building only low-powered engines, Trevithick developed the concept of using high-pressure steam, from which he could obtain more power in proportion to the weight of the engine and this opened up the possibility of exploiting his other notion, making the device mobile. Rather than developing power for static wheels, these engines could provide the energy to move themselves. His first effort was a model steam locomotive built in 1800 and a year later he produced the world's first successful steam 'road carriage'. It was, though, to be short-lived. Trevithick had not devised a proper steering mechanism and on the way to parade the machine to the local gentry, it plunged into a ditch. The assorted party went off to drown their sorrows in the pub, forgetting to douse the fire under the boiler. The resulting explosion presumably cut short their drinking session.

Despite such mishaps, Trevithick built an improved steam engine in 1802 and took the crucial next step of putting it on rails at Coalbrookdale, an iron works in Shropshire,[6] which not only obviated the need for steering but also provided a more stable base than the road. Rails, too, had progressed from the simple wooden planks of the seventeenth century by strapping iron to the wood. L-shaped rails were developed to keep the wheels aligned, but the crucial idea of putting a flange all around the wheel – a lip to prevent derailment – only began to be developed in the late eighteenth century. In 1803, travelling on these crude early rails, Trevithick's engine managed to haul wagons weighing nine tons at a speed of five miles an hour at another iron works, Pen-y-Darren in Wales. This was certainly a world first even if the locomotive proved too heavy for the primitive rails and was soon converted into a stationary engine.

This suggests the answer to a fundamental question about the history of the railways: why did these iron roads (as they are called in every language other than English) evolve and spread across the United Kingdom and the rest of the world some sixty years before self-propelled vehicles, what we now call motor cars? The main reason was that the roads were awful. The well-engineered highways built by the Romans had been allowed to decline for more than 1,000 years and it was only in the early eighteenth century that any attempts at maintaining trunk roads properly began. The old system of making parishes responsible for the maintenance of roads, even major through routes, within their area, with free labour having to be supplied annually by the parish folk, was replaced by a network of Turnpike Trusts, groups of local people who would maintain a road in return for the payment of a toll by anyone using it. By 1820, virtually all trunk routes and many cross-country roads came within this system which led to great improvements. For example, the journey between London and Edinburgh took less than two days compared with a fortnight a century previously. Exeter could be reached from London in seventeen and a half hours, an average speed of 10 mph, and for a brief period, with the introduction of the mail coach in 1784, stagecoaches enjoyed a heyday thanks to the network of rapidly improving roads, catering to the small minority who could afford such travel.

This progress had been made possible as a result of the improvement in road-building methods developed by pioneers such as Thomas Telford and John Macadam. Telford tried to build sturdy – and consequently expensive – roads which, he hoped, would be able to take the weight of steam locomotives on metal wheels trundling up and down. However, it was Macadam's lighter techniques that became almost universally accepted and his success meant that a network of decent paved roads extended quickly and relatively cheaply around the country.

The wider question of why the railways dominated land transport for the rest of the nineteenth century is rather more complex. Steam locomotives for use on roads continued to be developed but were hampered by the heavy tolls charged for using turnpikes – sometimes up to fifteen times the cost of a horse-drawn vehicle – precisely because the road owners recognized that they caused far more damage to the surface. Moreover, the Locomotive Act of 1865, popularly known as the Red Flag Act, killed off any hope of road vehicles rivalling railways as it set a speed limit of 4 mph in rural areas and 2 mph in towns and required a man with a red flag to walk sixty yards ahead of each vehicle warning horse-riders and pedestrians of the approach of a self-propelled machine.

However, it was more than the simple opposition of the turnpike owners and legislators to these embryonic cars that prevented them from posing any serious challenge to the railways until the end of the nineteenth century. The answer lies in the technology. Britain may have been the world leader in developing steam coaches, several decades ahead of any rival, but these vehicles were simply not good enough to compete with railways. Quite simply, rails could bear a much heavier weight and locomotives required little springing because they travelled on a hard, smooth surface. The development of flanged wheels meant there was no need for steering[7] and the design of the axles ensured there was no requirement for differential boxes[8] to cope with curves. Moreover, steam locomotives on rails could pull a number of carriages and wagons, which would be impossible for a road carriage due to the sharp gradients and curves.

A road carriage, in contrast, had to be light enough to spare the surface while having to carry all the paraphernalia of its own machinery in addition to the passengers or freight, all crammed into the same vehicle and perhaps, at most, one trailer. Steam road carriages 'were lacking, despite all efforts, in a number of technical respects'.[9] Designers had to try to make simultaneous major improvements in steering, suspension, transmission, boiler and engine. Not surprisingly, they failed.

Since technology was at the root of this failure, it may well be that had the pneumatic tyre or the internal combustion engine been developed just that bit earlier, history might have been very different. Given, too, legislation which favoured roads rather than imposing restrictions such as the Red Flag Act, then we might never have had the railways at all. Or at least their rapid expansion would have been stymied. It was partly happenstance that gave railways their technological advantages: the use of rails happened to fit perfectly with the available traction technology and this, fortuitously, gave the railways almost a century of domination across the world.

At the time of the opening of the Liverpool & Manchester railway in 1830, there were more than 1,000 turnpike companies in England, which maintained 20,000 miles of road. Stagecoach travel had reached its peak and was now an industry employing more than 30,000 people – a significant number, but less than a tenth of the workforce the railways would require thirty years hence – carrying both passengers and mail. For the rich there was an efficient but expensive network of post chaises which radiated out from the London Post Office to various provincial centres. Both the stagecoach services and the roads on which they ran would begin to decline from 1840 as railways achieved their stranglehold. By the early days of the nineteenth century, there were already some transport undertakings which called themselves 'railways', mostly developments of the 'waggon ways', and their principal function was to take heavy material from mines and quarries to the nearest navigable waterway as that was the cheapest form of haulage. A horse that could pull one ton on a road could haul a barge carrying a load weighing 25 tons with the same effort.

The first line that could be used by anyone prepared to pay the toll was the Surrey Iron Railway which opened in July 1803 and therefore became the first public railway.[10] It was a freight line serving the industrialized area between Wandsworth and Croydon and was double-tracked throughout to accommodate the heavy traffic. The nine-mile route,[11] which mostly followed the valley of the Wandle, had only a very gentle slope and horses could haul half a dozen wagons, each weighing 3.5 tons, at a speed of 2.5 mph, far more efficiently than any alternative on the road or the river. It was, of course, horse-powered and the developers installed L-shaped rails in order to keep the wagons on the track, since the idea of flanged wheels was still not universally accepted, not least because wagons fitted with them were useless on muddy roads and therefore could not be used off the rails. The promoters had ambitions to extend the line all the way to Portsmouth, some fifty miles away, but eventually managed to build only a few more miles out to Godstone and Merstham.

The first passenger service is widely reckoned[12] to have been on the Swansea & Mumbles[13] Railway built, originally, to connect the docks at Swansea with the mines and quarries at Mumbles five miles away. The wagons were to be pulled by horses, and for a time, remarkably, helped by sails. Interestingly, the Act authorizing the construction of the railway allowed for other forms of power, such as the locomotives developed by Trevithick, who happened to be on good terms with the owners of the line, but they chose to stick with horses. While the Swansea & Mumbles Railway missed out on being the first to use steam power (not introduced on the line until the 1870s), it can lay claim to being the first in the world to carry fare-paying travellers. On its completion in 1806, one of the shareholders of the line, Benjamin French, had the inspired idea to run services for passengers. He bought the rights for a mere £20 (say around £1,200 in today's money) and began operating coaches on the line in March 1807, charging a shilling (5p and equivalent to around £3 today) for the ride.

There is little record of these early journeys. The main surviving account is by a writer, Elizabeth Isabella Spence, who clearly enjoyed her trip in 1808, although it suggests her previous life must have been unexciting: 'I have never spent an afternoon with more delight than the one exploring the romantic scenery at Oystermouth (Mumbles). I was conveyed there in a carriage of singular construction built for the conveniency [sic] of parties who go hence to Oystermouth to spend the day. This car contains twelve persons and is constructed chiefly of iron, its four wheels run on an iron railway by the aid of one horse, and the whole carriage is an easy and light vehicle.'[14] Indeed, it must have been a lot more comfortable than riding in a carriage along the notoriously bumpy roads of the time, although Richard Ayton, who travelled on the line in 1813, disagreed, perhaps because the track had deteriorated by then. He reported that the sixteen-seater carriage made the noise of 'twenty sledge hammers in full play' and described emerging from the experience 'in a state of dizziness and confusion of the sense that it is well if he recovers from it in a week'.[15]

Despite the success of the Mumbles railway, it was nearly two decades before the next notable advance towards anything approaching a modern railway. In the meantime, the idea of railways as an exciting new form of transport was beginning to take hold and the notion that one day, possibly quite soon, there might be a network of 'iron roads' across the country no longer seemed absurd. The nineteenth century was full of people intent on exploiting the new technologies, even if many of the schemes proved fanciful. Some of the projects that did later come to fruition, such as the Metropolitan Railway running under London or the construction of the Crystal Palace, initially seemed as bizarre as many of those heroic failures. Even before the turn of the century, William Jessop, who built the Surrey Iron Railway, had suggested a 'waggon way' between Liverpool and Manchester, and there were many far more ambitious suggestions. Thomas Gray, a native of Leeds who had lived for a time in Brussels, suggested a plan for a network throughout Britain, and indeed Europe, of a 'general iron railway'[16], which received widespread attention, helped by his tireless campaigning. Gray, too, had the prescience to realize that locomotives rather than horses were the obvious power source. Another early proponent of the railways was William James, who in 1808 put forward the idea of a 'general rail-road company' which would have required capital of £1m (rather optimistic given the eventual cost!). While nothing came of that idea, James, who was variously known as a miner, engineer and surveyor, later became one of the pioneers behind plans for the Liverpool & Manchester.

There was even an idea in 1821 for a monorail, promoted by an engineer, Henry Palmer, who suggested that 'a single rail should be supported in the air on stout wooden posts'[17]: two systems based on his idea were actually built during that decade. Little is known about the first, completed in 1822, which linked the Thames with the Royal Victualling Yard in Woolwich, but the second, at Cheshunt, had a grand opening in June 1825 with a specially constructed carriage in the elegant 'barouche' style for passengers. The wagons used to carry bricks from a pit to the Lee Navigation were best described as a pair of panniers strung over a fixed rail at a height of 3ft, hauled by a horse with a tow rope. Since this was not a journey that would ever attract much patronage after the initial opening, it could hardly be called a passenger railway and the barouche carriage, sadly, disappeared.

The origins of the Stockton & Darlington stretch back to the long-standing problems moving coal from pitheads to navigable waterways. The north-east of England, and particularly County Durham, had long been a mining area interspersed with a host of wagon ways that took the coal to water. Transport was always the major component in the cost of coal – except at the pit-head or very close to it – and there were constant efforts to try to reduce that expense through faster or cheaper forms of transport. One particular irritant for the coal owners was the ability of any landowner fortunate enough to be sited between the pit and the nearest river to hold them to ransom by charging 'wayleave', as the rent was called. It was the announcement by the Earl of Strathmore in May 1818 that he intended to build a canal to the Tees from his colliery near Stockton that was to prove the spur for the alternative proposal of a railway line. While Stockton's townspeople were happy with the canal plan, those in neighbouring towns were worried that their own businesses would decline as a result and while initially they campaigned for an alternative canal, they soon started raising support for a railway line instead. By November a committee to promote a railway had been formed which drew up a plan for an 'iron way'. The plan proceeded swiftly and within a couple of months the promoters had prepared a Parliamentary Bill. There was, however, no shortage of objectors, and such opponents were to be the bane of railway developers for the rest of the century. The Stockton & Darlington set the pattern by giving every self-interested Luddite the opportunity to press their case, pushing up the legal bills which were to become a major expense for promoters of railway schemes. In this instance, the two main objectors were Lord Eldon, who was profiting from the extortionate wayleave payments he was getting from pit owners for crossing his land and could not see why it was necessary for the railway to impose compulsory purchases on the land it required; and the Earl of Darlington, later the Duke of Cleveland, who was terribly concerned about his favourite pastime, fox-hunting, being jeopardized. The Bill was rejected in Parliament so the promoters drew up a new route, avoiding the Earl's precious fox holes. This was passed in April 1821 but only thanks to a last-minute loan of £7,000 by the key supporter, Edward Pease, to fulfil the requirement that 80 per cent of the capital should be deposited by the time the Bill was presented to Parliament. Thus the route of the world's first public railway had to be moved to accommodate the pleasures of an Earl. The Industrial Revolution may have been in full swing, but society still had its feudal elements and they were to have a lasting impact on the development of the railway.

Edward Pease and his son Joseph, both Quakers, were the driving force behind the construction of the line and its eventual commercial success. Pease *père* was not only the largest contributor of the £113,000 (around £6.8m today) investment in the railway but also used his network of Quaker friends, particularly bankers in Norwich such as the Barclays and the Gurneys, to raise further funds. Pease was motivated by far more than a desire to make money as he understood the tremendous social benefit for local people that came with the railway's ability to provide cheap coal.

The scheme was ambitious. The Bill authorized the construction of nearly thirty-seven miles of single-line track which was to be a public highway, rather like a turnpike road on rails, open to anyone prepared to carry passengers or freight on payment of a toll (or access charge as it is known today). In reality the line was the 'Stockton to three collieries near Bishop Auckland line via Darlington'[18] since the latter was at the halfway point of the twenty-six-mile main line which then ran towards Bishop Auckland with branches to a couple of other pits. Therefore, the promoters of the Stockton & Darlington Railway were already required to balance the convenience of having branches against the extra expense and complexity of junctions that entailed – which would invariably reduce performance on the main line – a dilemma that would face many of its successors.

With the route settled to the satisfaction of the local gentry, there were still a host of decisions to be made. After all, no one had built or operated such a transport system before. The first concerned the method of traction: should it be the long-established tradition of using horses or the new technology of locomotives? It was the equivalent of the choice in the 1960s between the card index and the computer, and the result was inevitably to be a compromise. There was also the gauge – the distance between the two rails – to be settled upon. It is unlikely that any of the promoters of the railway realized that the decision they were to make over the gauge would determine the size of most of the railways around the world, stretching hundreds of thousands of miles. In fact, what is now called the standard gauge – 4ft 8½ins – had been in use for a long time on many wagon ways, particularly those in the north-east of England. There is an often repeated story that the 4ft 8½in width was determined by the size of the backsides of horses pulling chariots in Roman times, suggesting the horses' rumps determined the width between the wheels of the vehicles that were used on 'rutways' with a gap of 4ft 8ins, however it is really little more than an urban myth, as the Romans did not use chariots much other than in races and their roads were smooth without 'ruts', as can still be seen from the odd surviving section. However, as with all myths, there is just enough truth to keep it going. As far back as in Ancient Persia, grooves were cut into roads to prevent chariots driven by messengers from toppling over mountainsides when going fast around bends, and these are 4ft 8ins apart. Moreover, carts from time immemorial have been built with their wheels around 5ft apart because that suited the dimensions of a horse.

The reason why 4ft 8ins – the half inch was added later – was chosen therefore remains unknown though many of the wagon ways serving the mines for which George Stephenson first developed his locomotives doubtless used that gauge because of its convenience in relation to the size of a horse's rear end. If Pease had been left on his own to sort out the form of traction, his conservative and cautious Quaker instincts would have pushed him towards using horses rather than steam locomotives. However, George Stephenson, eager to be involved in what was by far the biggest railway project to date, turned up on Pease's doorstep in Darlington in April 1821 to argue the case for locomotives.

Stephenson, born in Wylam near Newcastle in 1781, stimulates as much controversy today among railway historians as he did among his peers. While some laud him as the father of the railways, others are ready to pour scorn, suggesting that he merely copied a few good ideas and exploited the skills of others. Even if that were the case, there is no doubt that his role in developing the technology was vital. It is not so much that without Stephenson the railways would not have happened, but rather that they were built earlier and faster as a result of his drive. Given that this self-educated and barely literate man was an obstreperous character who did not suffer fools gladly, it is not surprising that he lives on in history as such a controversial figure. But it is unarguable that he played a vital role in the construction of both the Stockton & Darlington and the Liverpool & Manchester.

Stephenson's meeting with Pease had a rather longer agenda than just the choice of traction. His principal skill may have been as a locomotive engineer but that did not stop him from involving himself in all aspects of railway construction. Pease had been worried about the route selected by the original surveyor, George Overton, and quickly gave Stephenson the task of drawing up an alternative. He produced a far more direct route, knocking three miles off the original scheme which had been designed with meandering bends as tight as those on a country lane, completely unsuitable for a railway. In designing the new route, Stephenson set the standard for future railways, with their long sweeping curves linked by as much plain straight line as possible. But in other aspects, Stephenson was not always right or forward-looking. His choice of wrought iron rather than the more brittle cast iron for the rails was definitely correct (though, for reasons of economy, some cast-iron rails were used, too), but he used very short lengths which made the ride bumpier.[19] Worse, he placed them on heavy stone blocks, whereas the far more stable timber sleepers at right angles to the rails had been used for nearly forty years on some wagon ways. On the question of mechanical versus horsepower, however, Stephenson was unequivocal. He knew locomotives represented the future, but even his ambitions were relatively modest. In 1821 he had written: 'On a long and favourable railway, I would start my engines to run 60 miles a day with from 40 to 60 tons of goods.'[20] It was not long before locomotives would be running several hundred miles in a day.

Trevithick had continued to develop the idea of a steam locomotive on rails for several years after his early failures, most notably with his demonstration of a steam engine with the humorous name of *Catch Me Who Can* on a circular track near the present site of Euston station. The contemporary pictures of the scene show precious few spectators, which may suggest that it was lack of interest that sent Trevithick off to seek his fortune in Peru.

Others, however, were quick to follow in his steps. The north-east was the Silicon Valley of its day, a ferment of ideas with various locomotive engineers devising more effective forms of steam locomotive to suit the growing needs of the colliery owners. There were all sorts of developments, and while some were universally adopted, others were technological dead-ends. One of the latter, using cogged drive wheels, was developed because of concerns about metal wheels having little adhesion on iron rails, the wrong solution for a genuine problem that has continued to dog railways (just like 'leaves on the line'). John Blenkinsop subsequently designed an engine whose cogs meshed with a toothed rail for the Middleton Colliery in 1812, the first steam locomotives to run on a commercial basis. However, while rack and pinion later became a feature of mountain railways, they were not really suitable for running on the flat. Then there were what we now with hindsight perceive as completely crazy ideas, including the *Steam Horse*, which was driven by a series of legs sticking out from the rear like a huge grasshopper which 'walked' the locomotive along. Initially it did not have enough power but, disastrously, when it was rebuilt the new larger boiler exploded on its inaugural run at Nesham's Colliery, killing or maiming fifty-seven people. At the same time, progress was being made on the kind of steam locomotives that, within a couple of decades, would be running up and down railways across Britain. With the help of Timothy Hackworth, whom Stephenson later appointed as resident engineer to the Stockton & Darlington, William Hedley built *Puffing Billy* without using cogs, proving that metal-on-metal contact could offer sufficient adhesion. He later modified his early engines into eight-wheelers to enable them to pull 50-ton loads.

Several of the innovators of this period have some claim to be the 'father of the steam locomotive', an appellation often attributed to Stephenson. In fact, as mentioned above, his real skill was in exploiting other people's ideas; as the *Oxford Companion to British Railway History* puts it, 'the peculiar genius of George Stephenson was that he made it happen'.[21] In 1812 Stephenson became the 'enginewright' at Killingworth Colliery, just north of Newcastle, with the task of building a series of stationary steam engines. But he quickly transferred his energies to locomotives and produced the *Blucher* that could pull 30 tons up a slight gradient at 5 mph in 1814. He built a further three engines for Killingworth and then five for the Hetton colliery line near Sunderland, which were a great improvement. An eight-mile railway was completed by Stephenson in November 1822 which connected the colliery with the river Wear and on the flat sections these 'iron horses', as they were known, could haul seventeen wagons weighing a total of sixty-four tons, more than double the performance of the *Blucher*. Nevertheless, as the pictures show, all these engines were still primitive beasts that frequently broke down, lost steam through every join and battered the tracks which could barely withstand their weight.

Stephenson was appointed as surveyor of the Stockton & Darlington in January 1822 but the directors still needed some persuasion before they would commit themselves wholeheartedly to mechanical horsepower rather than the hay-eating kind. They made visits to Killingworth colliery – since Hetton was not quite complete – and were sufficiently impressed to choose the new technology. However, since this was to be a public railway, open to all comers using whatever form of traction suited them, many of the trains would in fact be horse-drawn.

Building the line was a laborious process. The big railway contractors of the Victorian era had yet to emerge and the work was undertaken by a host of small companies which required close supervision. The main obstacles were the Myers Flat swamp and the Skerne river at Darlington. Stephenson eventually managed to create a firm base on the swamp by filling it with tons of hand-hewn rock but required the help of a local architect who designed a bridge over the river that was eventually built of stone.[22] Despite the length of the railway and ambitious nature of the scheme, the construction proceeded relatively smoothly, and the line was formally opened on 27 September 1825, which was declared a local holiday. It is a mistake to think that because these events took place in obscure northern towns that now boast little more than under-performing football teams, they passed unnoticed. In fact, there was worldwide interest in the development of the Stockton & Darlington Railway with newspapers and technical journals covering every detail. Its fame was born of the recognition that this was the world's first railway to operate steam engines, although most of the haulage in the early years was provided by horses. The crowds clustered around the line on the opening day were also testimony to the fact that people realized this was a 'Big Story' that would have a far wider impact than merely reducing local coal prices, the primary intent of the promoters. The spectators were chary of approaching the steaming locomotive too closely, since they were worried, quite rightly, that the boiler could blow up, a relatively frequent experience in the early days of the railways. Stephenson, ever the self-publicist, put on a show for the opening ride. Driving *Locomotion*, he brushed aside the horseman who had been deputed to lead the procession along the line and raised the steam pressure to reach 12 mph, even 15 mph on a few stretches. He soon outpaced the local riders who had taken to the fields to try to keep up with the train and, after various stops, covered the twelve miles between Darlington and Stockton in three hours.

The railway made a great impression on local onlookers. One recalled: 'The welkin [sky] rang with loud huzzas [applause], while the happy faces of some, the vacant stares of others and the alarm depicted on the countenances of not a few, gave variety to the picture.'[23] That description fairly sums up the mixed reaction to the railway from the public. While overall it was supportive, there were, as ever, detractors. Shortly before the opening, the editor of the local *Tyne Mercury*[24] had thundered: 'what person would ever think of paying anything to be conveyed . . . in something like a coal wagon, upon a dreary wagon-way, and to be dragged, for the greater part of the distance, by a roaring steam engine'. Others expressed fears that the cows in fields next to the railway would be so terrified by horseless carriages hurtling past them that their udders would dry up. Needless to say, these critics were proved wrong. The railway quickly filled up while the cows remained sanguine.

Mostly, though, the benefits were widely understood. The *Newcastle Courant* applauded the venture and correctly stressed its importance by predicting the railway 'will open the London market to the collieries of Durham as well as facilitate the obtaining of fuel to the country along its line'.[25]

At the opening, the line was not entirely complete as some of the branches had not been built and there were few facilities such as sidings and engine sheds. There was, too, a shortage of rolling stock: the company merely owned 'a single locomotive (*Locomotion No. 1*), one passenger carriage and 150 coal wagons'.[26] More were delivered over the next couple of years by Stephenson's company but horses remained the mainstay of the railway. Nevertheless, traffic built up quickly. In the first three months, 10,000 tons of coal were carried on the railway, much of it horse-hauled. The coal was of better quality, as bigger lumps could be carried than on the panniers of pack-horses, and the price had gone down by more than a half: 'At Stockton, [coal] could be profitably sold for 8s 6d (42.5p) per ton, rather than the pre-railway price of 18s (90p) a ton.'[27]

Passengers, too, used the railway. The only coach provided on the first day, aptly called the *Experiment,* was a primitive affair with seats along the side of the interior and was said to resemble a showman's caravan. It went into service being horse-drawn between Stockton and Darlington, a distance of twelve miles, which it covered in two hours, an hour less than Stephenson had done on that opening day, and was soon replaced by more comfortable carriages. But even these, in reality, were little more than old stagecoaches adapted for rail use with flanged wheels, each carrying sixteen passengers. The railway leased out the rights to run the passenger service to various independent operators including, interestingly, two female innkeepers, Jane Scott of the King's Head, Darlington, and Martha Howson, who ran the Black Lion in Stockton. A year after the opening of the line, seven coaches were covering the distance and were being charged 3d per mile by the railway. The horses cantered at 12 mph, sometimes reaching 14 mph, though obviously they were far slower when climbing the inclines or when they tired. Locomotives often fared less well. Although notionally they were faster than horses, as Stephenson had demonstrated on the opening day, they were confined to 5 mph when the track passed through woods because of fears that running them too fast would throw sparks far into the countryside, causing fires. Moreover, the company was fearful of excessive speed, as the directors rightly perceived it meant greater wear on the track, and consequently drivers were fined, even sacked, for this offence. The strict Quaker management encouraged the public to report any speeding or other misdemeanours by the drivers, and directors were known to patrol the line themselves, seeking out miscreants who had to appear before a disciplinary committee to explain their actions.

Although traffic built up well, the first days of the Stockton & Darlington were not profitable, due to the high costs of maintenance and the relatively low charges (which, however, were of great value in stimulating the local economy). The economics of the railway were not helped by the fact that Stephenson was frequently away working on the Liverpool & Manchester and his six locomotives were unreliable, often running out of steam and in need of frequent repairs. Indeed, despite Timothy Hackworth's skill in keeping them working, the railway's directors came close to reverting to an entirely horse-run railway by the second half of 1827. Hackworth then designed a much improved locomotive, the *Royal George*, with six wheels each 4ft in diameter and coupled together and with a more powerful and bigger boiler, that was a great improvement. Robert, Stephenson's son who, it seems, had fallen out with his father and left in 1824 to seek his fortune in South America, returned, and his engineering skills became vital in keeping steam running on the track.

It was not just the unreliability of the locomotives and the slowness of often exhausted horses which made operations on the line chaotic.

Running a train along the Stockton & Darlington was a hazardous and difficult business. A great mistake had been to make it single line, with just four passing loops[28] every mile to allow trains to pass each other. The points were operated by the driver or his assistants, and, with so much, traffic disputes were inevitable when trains met each other far from a loop, rather like cars meeting head-on on small country roads. There was no signalling and there were frequent altercations between drivers over who should be allowed to proceed first, an area of conflict exacerbated by the fact that these men worked for various private companies, rather than all being employed by the railway. The rule was supposed to be that passenger trains would reverse to the nearest loop since the coal trains were far heavier, but passengers did not like these delays and were known to join in fisticuff fights on the side of their driver. This highlights one aspect of the railway that was to prove a mistake and that consequently other railways did not follow – the idea that it should be run like a turnpike road, open to all comers prepared to pay the toll for their carriage wagons or trains, rather than being operated by the owners.

This open access experiment had its roots in the *Zeitgeist* of the early 1820s when the idea of a very pure form of free markets and free trade was in vogue. The old traditions of monopoly companies and guilds working as cartels had been discredited in the previous century by Adam Smith and his ideas were being revived. As one historian of the railways puts it, the Stockton & Darlington was created like a free market in transport: 'Demand would be met by enterprising suppliers; fares would be kept down by competition between carriers; operational costs would be kept down by competition between the aspiring contractors . . . All would be individualism and competition.'[29] That is perhaps putting on too much of an ideological gloss, given that, at the time, there was no other way of running a railway, though the very motto of the railway company – 'At private risk for public service' – seems to encapsulate Adam Smith's philosophy.

Even so, railways do not work well under these conditions. As the regular punch-ups between operators showed, there are simply too many interrelated interests where the need is for cooperation, rather than competition, between different users. The open access regime on the

Stockton & Darlington lasted only until 1833 when the directors took over the running of services which then became all locomotive-hauled. The Liverpool & Manchester, whose promoters were watching events in the north-east with great interest, would not make the same mistake.

The Stockton & Darlington paid a healthy 5 per cent dividend within two years and, more importantly, demonstrated the impact that railways would have in fostering the development of their hinterland. The line was soon extended to Middlesbrough, five miles from Stockton, then a mere hamlet with a few houses and a population of less than 400 scattered in local farms. The railway quickly turned it into a boom town and the population increased fifteen-fold to 6,000 by 1841. Thanks to investment by Pease and his Quaker colleagues, docks were built and it became a major seaport, later acquiring large shipbuilding yards and iron smelting works. Within half a century, tiny Middlesbrough had been transformed into a thriving industrial town with the largest iron-producing centre in the world, thanks to the advent of the railway. Middlesbrough was, therefore, the first example of the railway as a catalyst for economic growth and urban expansion, although sadly this pioneering railway town is ill-served by the railway as it is not on a main line. As the later chapters show, there were to be countless more.

By the late 1850s the Stockton & Darlington was paying an average dividend of 9.5 per cent, better at the time than any railway company in Britain, although by then it was a rather insignificant little operation ripe for merger with its bigger and newer rivals. It retains a place in railway history but the importance of its role remains at issue. On the one hand it could be dismissed as a mere extension of its predecessors, the dozens of little railways that principally ran from mine to waterway and mostly used horses to pull the wagons. Moreover, the railway's reliance on sub-contracting to the extent that it did not even operate its own passenger services bore little relation to later nineteenth-century railways. On the other hand it has been argued that the line 'proved an invaluable testing ground both for the technical development of locomotives and for improvements in track'.[30] The way that the promoters of the railway attracted capital was an early example of the raising of finance through personal networks that 'played a critical role in financing Britain's early industrialisation'. While the Stockton &

Darlington suffered all the disadvantages of being a pioneer, it helped usher in the railway age. That era did not really begin in earnest until five years later with the completion of the Liverpool & Manchester, which has all the appropriate features to back its claim as the world's first railway.

# THE FIRST RAILWAY

It was not by chance that the world's first steam-hauled and twin-tracked railway should have run between Liverpool and Manchester. In 1830 when the line opened with much fanfare and, unluckily, a terrible tragedy, they were two 'world-class cities' of their age. Manchester and its Lancashire hinterland was the centre of the cotton trade while Liverpool had been built up on a rather more sinister industry – slavery – and despite the decline of that trade remained Britain's second most important port, thanks to the burgeoning imports of cotton from the USA. The Liverpool & Manchester represented the start of the railway age – just as it marked a significant advance in the technology – and was far grander in scale and conception than any of its predecessors.

While work had progressed on the Stockton & Darlington, there had been something of a mini railway mania, the first of several over the next few decades, as various enterprising promoters put forward ideas for schemes to criss-cross Britain. Lines worth a total of £22m (about £1.32bn today),[1] an unprecedented amount of capital at the time, including an ambitious scheme for a London–Edinburgh railway, were put forward in 1824–5, though most never got further than a prospectus and a vague scrawl on a map. The publicity around these ideas, however impractical they may have been, helped shape the public climate. Railways began to be seen as a realistic proposition, rather than a mere pipedream, and this was a key factor in helping promoters win over the public and, most vitally, investors, to their schemes.

A line between Liverpool and Manchester was the obvious place to start and the time was ripe for such an investment. The turmoil of the early years of the century, characterized by incessant wars and political instability, had receded and the economic situation was looking brighter with the north-west enjoying particularly rapid growth. The line had everything going for it, given the importance of the two places it would serve and the lack of any decent alternative transport. Liverpool and Manchester were the boom towns of the era: in 1760 Liverpool had a population of 26,000, a few more than Manchester, but by 1824 those numbers had swelled to 135,000 and 150,000 respectively and were still rising. Manchester was rapidly becoming the most important industrial city; as Asa Briggs put it, 'all roads led to Manchester in the 1840s'.[2]

Traffic between the two towns was also growing apace. Trade amounted to 1,000 tons per day[3] and it was the poor and overcrowded condition of the roads and the circuitous canal routes on which goods had to be carried that spurred local merchants to come up with the idea of a railway. Despite losing the slave trade, Liverpool's port was expanding swiftly as it replaced London as the principal landing point for cotton from the United States and eight new docks were opened between 1815 and 1835. By 1824, the port was handling 1,120 bags of cotton every day, 80 per cent of the total imported into Britain. At the other end of the putative railway, there was Manchester and Salford, with their ever-expanding factories and mills. Lancashire's sweatshops were the equivalent of those in western China today, producing the cheapest cloth and exporting it across the world.

But the existing transport links between the two towns were lamentable. There was a continuous scene of chaos on the thirty-six-mile turnpike road, which had been open only since 1760, with hundreds of carts, horse-drawn wagons and pack-horses cluttering up the road. Accidents and obstacles due to bad weather were frequent and for passengers the bumpy and tiring journey in a stagecoach between the city centres was an exhausting five-hour slog.

For freight, there was the alternative of the canals, a journey that took a couple of days at best. The canal network had developed from the mid-eighteenth century, offering a smoother and more reliable alternative to the terrible roads. Liverpool's relatively remote harbour had become well served by a series of canals built since 1750, and by the early nineteenth century there were three rival routes between the two towns. But the canals were far from being an ideal system of transport. As one writer put it, 'heavy winds and storms, frozen surfaces in the winter, shallow water in the summer, and pilferage on the slow circuitous routes'[4] all created problems. Nevertheless, with trade growing and the roads so crowded, the canals had an effective monopoly for heavy goods. Despite the apparent competition between them, the companies that owned them became rich and powerful by charging exorbitant rates to their customers, suggesting there was something of a tacit cartel. Meanwhile, the merchants and businessmen who needed to transport their goods between the two towns were concerned that trade was being strangled by the inefficiency of the transport system, a familiar cry still heard today from the Confederation of British Industry.

It was the Liverpool traders who were most frustrated at the cost and slowness of transport, and who started considering the construction of a railway. The initial driving force was Joseph Sandars, a Liverpool corn merchant and underwriter, who was angered by the transport owners' ever-rising profits and their failure to improve facilities. There had been several earlier proposals for a railway between the two towns but they would have been horse-hauled like the Surrey Iron Railway whose builder, William Jessop, had proposed a wagon way as far back as 1797. He even surveyed the route for a group of Liverpool merchants who had shown some interest in the project but their enthusiasm waned at the prospect of funding such an ambitious scheme. The following year another engineer, Benjamin Outram, had interested a group of Manchester businessmen in an alternative route. A third suggestion came from Thomas Gray, one of the first people to put forward the idea of a national rail network. He proposed that a line between Liverpool and Manchester should be a trial run for the national scheme and wanted the service to be operated with steam locomotives. While none of these schemes really made it on to the drawing board, let alone off it, their very existence sowed the idea of a railway in the minds of the local business class of both towns. All it needed was for someone to set the process in motion. And that required a combination of courage, verging on foolhardiness, and optimism, bordering on naivety.

Sandars had all those qualities and was prepared to invest his money where no one else had dared to venture. As a chronicler of the railway suggests with some irony, Sandars was ambitious and influential but 'had little experience of project management, and less of engineering works, and [was] thus ideally placed to underestimate the vast political, financial and technical turmoil that lay ahead'.[5] In 1821, he met William James, who was something of a jack-of-all-trades having trained as a solicitor but worked as an engineer and, most significantly, as a land speculator draining marshes and supervising property development for the aristocracy. James and Sandars 'set about transforming the country',[6] and in 1822 Sandars paid James £300 to conduct a survey between the two towns in order to prepare a Bill for Parliament.

This was not an easy or indeed a safe assignment given the hostility of the entrenched interests. James's surveying team was attacked by opponents of the scheme, canal owners and local landowners. Even coal miners joined in the attacks, which was odd as their coal would become more valuable once the railway had reduced the cost of transporting it to the towns. James lived in fear of being lynched and hired a local prize-fighter as a bodyguard. Even when the surveyors took to working at night in order to escape the thugs, they were still disturbed by shots fired into the air to scare them off. These men worked for a local landowner, Robert Bradshaw, a ruthless opponent of the railways who had been given control of the Bridgwater canal by the old Duke of Bridgwater, the creator of Britain's first man-made navigable waterway.

This was a battle which extended far beyond the north-west of England. Bradshaw was an important voice at national meetings of canal company delegates, once expelling a hapless soul who made the mistake of admitting he owned a paltry five shares in a railway. The canal companies were powerful and often very profitable; the long boom in canal construction was only just coming to an end. Over the previous sixty years, since the opening of the Bridgwater in 1763, 2,200 miles of canal had been built throughout Britain, providing such an extensive network that there was no place south of Durham that was more than fifteen miles from navigable water. A horse, limited to pulling a ton on a bumpy road, could haul 25 tons in a barge, but canals offered more than great savings in horsepower. Fragile loads like pottery suffered far less risk as waterborne freight than when they were subjected to the jolting of the roads, and the dense but yielding medium of water sustained weighty loads which could not be carried on the roads. For these reasons the artificial waterways spread, growing straighter, wider and deeper as capital and profits furthered their expansion. Bradshaw and his fellows realized that the Liverpool & Manchester Railway was not just a threat to their local interests but would presage a price war between the two methods of transport in which, thanks to speed and flexibility, there could be only one winner.

Not surprisingly given this hostility, William James's survey took longer than expected, delaying the start of the parliamentary process. Moreover, the poor fellow had neglected his other business interests and in the spring of 1824 he was thrown into jail for debt, ending his role in the history of the railways. His job was given to the ubiquitous George Stephenson, who ignored much of the curvy and hilly route that James had devised and went for a more direct line. He faced similar opposition from landowners. As with the Stockton & Darlington, the aristocracy was making life difficult for the railway promoters because the proposed route passed through land owned by two powerful Lords Sefton and Derby. As a result, Stephenson tried to minimize the impact on their estates, which meant he could not always proceed with the best possible alignment.

News of the surveys had reached the local press and a propaganda battle ensued. The canal owners produced leaflets which described in graphic detail the dangers of steam locomotives with their risk of exploding or of setting fire to nearby fields and houses. Stephenson was not averse to using similar dirty tricks and produced a document that misleadingly purported to give Lord Sefton's sanction for his survey.

Despite the need for the odd extra curve to avoid the wrath of their lordships, the eventual route proposed by Stephenson was thirty-one miles, just a mile longer than the crow flies. More significantly, it was five miles fewer than the road and twelve fewer than the shortest of the three canal routes. The downside of such a direct route was that it necessitated a large number of expensive bridges and viaducts, a total of sixty-three or an average of two per mile. As with the Myers Flat swamp which the Stockton & Darlington had to cross, there was also one major natural obstacle, a damp bleak plain called Chat Moss that required an innovative engineering approach to support a railway. Using conventional draining ditches was not feasible because they would simply fill with water, so Stephenson devised the notion of 'floating' the railway embankment on a raft of brushwood and heather, along with vast amounts of spoil from other sections of the railway, a scheme that eventually proved successful despite concerns that the swamp would simply swallow up any amount of earth and gravel tipped into it.

While James, and then Stephenson, were conducting their surveys, Sandars had to ensure that the money was available to finance the construction and operation of the railway. He had formed a wide-ranging committee of local notables, including bankers, merchants, landowners and solicitors. Although they came from both towns, Liverpudlians predominated and the railway would always be regarded primarily as going from the port to the hinterland, rather than the other way around. Its headquarters and the most imposing structures would always be in Liverpool and, when the railway was finally opened, the first train would inevitably depart from the port heading inland.

The committee faced a tricky task. To build the railway, they needed the right to impose compulsory purchase orders on the land, much of which was owned by backward-looking aristocrats or people such as Bradshaw with an interest in canals. To obtain this, they had to promote a parliamentary Bill and overcome the powerful opposition of vested interests, with the inevitable risk of failure. It took pluck to invest in such a groundbreaking venture. The initial estimate was that £300,000 would be required but this was later increased to £510,000 with a contingency for a further £127,000, making a total of £637,000 (which crudely represents about £38m in today's money).[7] Many of the investors were the very merchants who would benefit most from better transport for their goods, but it would be unfair to characterize their motivation as entirely self-interested. They were committed, too, to the notion of progress and modernity, a key characteristic of the progressive members of the moneyed classes and one of the driving forces behind the Industrial Revolution.

Railways were seen as the future, although so were many other new inventions. As one writer puts it, there were a lot of schemes that were to prove far less rewarding than the railways: 'In the 1820s, you could invest in balloon companies which would carry passengers through the London air at forty miles an hour, or in coaching companies which were going to run coaches on relays of bottled gas instead of horses. Or you could lose your money in a railway run by steam.'[8]

In 1824, in an effort to obtain support, the committee issued a prospectus, an eloquent document largely written by Henry Booth, the highly literate company treasurer. The proposal at this stage did not commit the railway exclusively to locomotive haulage but instead suggested that a combination of steam engines, both fixed and moving, as well as cables and horses, would be used. The advantages of the railway were unequivocally stated: it would be more reliable than the canals, which were affected by water shortage in the summer and ice in the winter, and provide a more secure journey for goods which were frequently lost to pilferage during their transhipment to boats and their meandering passage on the water.

The lengthy prospectus was far-sighted in that it stressed the importance of Britain embarking on railway construction before its rivals overseas. The Tsar of Russia, Booth warned darkly, had expressed an interest in the design, and visitors from the United States had become acquainted with much technical detail. The railway, he observed, would stimulate the economy and encourage 'fair competition and free trade'. On the issue of who would use the railway, however, the prospectus was less prescient. It concentrated on freight as the principal purpose of the line, almost ignoring the carriage of passengers to which Booth devoted barely a couple of sentences in the whole document. However, that began to change. In a letter in support of the railway sent to MPs and Lords just before the Bill entered Parliament, Sandars with great foresight anticipated the notion of commuting. While factories no longer needed to be next to rivers, thanks to steam rather than mill power, houses for the workers still had to be within walking distance. But with the railway, Sandars argued, that would no longer be necessary. He was way ahead of his time, as the commuting habit did not develop on any scale until the mid-Victorian period.

It seemed that everything was in place when the Bill was presented to Parliament in February 1825. The arguments were sound, there was support from all the local Chambers of Commerce, and even from their colleagues over the water in Ireland. The national interest was at stake and the existing transport methods were slow and expensive, so what could go wrong? Well, British class interest for a start. The landowners had lined up the best briefs who marshalled their self-interested arguments with great aplomb. Worse, those arrogant barristers would enjoy roasting the self-educated and semi-literate Stephenson when he appeared in the witness box to outline the scheme. Stephenson let himself down by being too vague, having left much of the detailed work to assistants whose competence was, to put it kindly, variable. The sheer nastiness and dishonesty of the attack symbolized a desperate last *cri de coeur* of a class that suspected its days of ruling unchallenged were numbered. As one historian put it, the building of the railways was 'the final battle between two economic systems and two ways of living'.[9] One can imagine the scene. The barristers must have been unable to hide their contempt for the wooden Stephenson with his almost incomprehensible Northumbrian accent and his lack of clarity on detail. He stumbled over basic questions such as the width of the Irwell river where the railway was to cross it, the location of the baseline for all the other height levels (some of which were wildly wrong, thanks again to the incompetence of his assistants), and, most importantly, the method of crossing Chat Moss. After his ordeal, it was little wonder that Stephenson commented ruefully: 'I began to wish for a hole to creep into.'[10]

Misguided the opposition may have been, but that did not stop it being successful. After three months and thirty-seven committee sessions, in May 1825 the MPs killed off the Bill by rejecting its preamble: it could not be proved, as it claimed, that the railway would be of benefit to local people. Thomas Creevey, an MP who had been against the motion throughout, crowed rather prematurely in a letter to his stepdaughter: 'Well, the devil of a railway is strangled at last.'[11] However, Creevey, along with Derby and Sefton, who were said to be ecstatic about the committee's decision, was to be proved wrong rather sooner than expected. Stephenson might have lost the battle but he won the war when a new Bill was drawn up a year later. For a time, though, he was cast off in the wilderness. He was sacked from the Liverpool & Manchester and his place as surveyor was taken by Charles Vignoles, a slender Irishman who had recently carried out an excellent survey of the route between London and Brighton for another putative railway. As with James and many other brave railway pioneers, Vignoles had a varied past in several professions and, like most of them, his career would be punctuated by both great successes and rank failures.

Vignoles was under instruction to reduce further the impact of the line on the aristocrats and their fellow landowners and he even tried to win over Bradshaw by suggesting the canal man should buy shares in the railway. Bradshaw, whose mission for the canals was characterized by his biographer as 'profit extraction to the utmost limit, regardless of the feelings and interests of the users of the canal',[12] was hardly going to fall for that one, and he suggested instead that he became sole owner of the railway. However, not all those with canal interests were as Luddite as Bradshaw since the Marquess of Stafford, the heir to the Duke of Bridgwater, was prevailed upon to become the biggest investor in the railway, buying 1,000 shares at £100 each.

When the new prospectus and Bill were produced, the directors were confident of success. With the canal interests split, the railway's directors weakened the opposition further by promising that land purchase would be at the full market rate and they muddied the water over traction by suggesting that steam locomotives would not be the primary form of power. Nor was there the stumbling Stephenson to face the committee. Instead, Vignoles and George Rennie who, along with his brother John, was in charge of engineering, gave a far better impression, convincingly batting back any difficult questions from the counsel representing the objectors.

Suddenly, it all seemed obvious. Of course the railway project should go ahead; why would anybody object, since it represented progress and offered wealth generation? *The Times*, a good weathervane for the *Zeitgeist*, was suddenly fully supportive and just after the Bill was passed in May 1826 commented: 'The petitioners' faith in their project and their willingness to build in the face of such distress were to attract the admiration of all England and gave the Liverpool & Manchester Railway Company a reputation for courage and persistence.'[13]

The resulting Act may have received the Royal Assent, but the concessions made to opponents meant that the scheme fell short of the fully-fledged railway so desperately needed to provide the two towns with a quick and efficient transport link. Locomotives were not to be used in Liverpool and engines on the rest of the line would have to be fitted with condensers to eliminate smoke. One rule that would become universal was established straightaway: level crossing gates would be closed across the railway and open to road users unless a train was imminent, rather than the other way around. Somehow, the primacy of road users was established right from the outset. While constraining the railway in so many ways, the legislators had also protected themselves against the prospect of excessive profits should the railway be too successful by stipulating that annual dividends could not exceed 10 per cent.

With the Act at last in the bag, the big question was who should build the line? The job was initially offered to the Rennie brothers but their terms, which included keeping Stephenson out of the project, were rejected. Almost inevitably, there was only one man to whom the promoters could turn, the most experienced engineer of the time. So barely a year after his humiliating experience in Parliament, Stephenson returned in triumph, with the dual responsibility for both the civil engineering and the locomotives. Knowing that he was already employed in a similar capacity on the Stockton line, the directors gave him a salary of £800 annually for nine months' work. Stephenson was to be in charge of all aspects of building a thirty-one-mile railway: bridges, tunnels, embankments, cuttings, pumping engines, drainage, stations, earth-moving wagons, track and points. As rail historian Adrian Vaughan says, 'this was a vast field for a man who had dragged himself up by his bootstraps and who had not learned to read until he was eighteen'.[14]

Stephenson, truculent as ever, soon fell out with Vignoles, who promptly resigned, and instead hired Thomas Gooch as his assistant. The whole construction of the railway centred on Stephenson, who became utterly indispensable: it was his vision and his ability to organize projects that brought about a successful conclusion to this unique enterprise. The task facing Stephenson and the team of twenty young acolytes he had hired and trained to prepare the design of the railway was completely unprecedented. The railway was to be a double-track line linking two towns and was a completely different proposition from the Stockton & Darlington or any of the numerous coal and mineral ore railways dotted around the north of England.

Stephenson sketched out broad ideas for all the various aspects of the civil work – bridges, embankments, tunnels, machinery, turntables and so on – and Gooch developed them into working drawings. It is difficult to visualize the practical difficulties they faced in the absence of any modern equipment or communication methods. Even the typewriter had not been invented and every report had to be dictated to assistants and composed by hand. The simple task of sending a message to the other end of the line or one of the many work sites involved despatching couriers on horseback and waiting hours for a response. But Stephenson was tireless. He would work from dawn to dusk, often ending up on some remote part of the railway where he would lodge near by. Although he gave contracts to suppliers to provide rails and other pieces of equipment, he was effectively the main contractor who appointed the assistant engineers. Each of his assistants was responsible for teams of up to 200 men. In later years, the roles of engineers and building contractors would be separated and large companies undertaking the construction of railways would emerge, but for the Liverpool & Manchester Stephenson took on both tasks himself.

The men who carved out the railway – and all those that followed in the next seventy years – were a special breed known as navvies, an abbreviation of 'navigators', for they were the direct descendants of the workers who had built the canals. As Terry Coleman points out in his seminal work on the history of this amazing band of men, not all labourers who worked on the construction of the railways could term themselves a 'navvy': 'They must never be confused with the rabble of steady, common labourers, whom they out-worked, out-drank, out-rioted and despised.'[15] The ordinary labourers would come and go, working on the railway when there was nothing to do in the fields but returning to them at harvest or planting time. In contrast, the navvies were an elite class of worker who could qualify for the appellation only if they fulfilled three criteria: they had to work on the hard tasks, such as tunnelling, excavating or blasting, and not on the easier types of work away from the railway; they had to live together and follow the railway, rather than merely residing at home; and they had to match the eating and drinking habits of their fellows, two pounds of beef and a gallon (eight pints) of beer a day. The agricultural labourers hired from nearby villages could eventually qualify to become navvies but at first they would down tools, exhausted, at three in the afternoon and it would take a year to build up their strength enough to earn a good wage through the piecework system, and cope with the hard living.

The navvies came from all around the UK, but there were particularly large contingents from Scotland, Ireland and the two Rose counties, Lancashire and Yorkshire. They were a proud group of men whose fashions were surprisingly up to date and expensive. They favoured 'moleskin trousers, double-canvas shirts, velveteen square-tailed coats, hobnail boots, gaudy handkerchiefs and white felt hats with the brims turned up'.[16] Their most distinctive feature was a rainbow waistcoat, and they would pay a staggering 15 shillings (75p) for a sealskin cap.

Wages were paid in pubs, encouraging the long drinking bouts that could last for several days and the navvies normally returned to work only once their money had run out. Long-lived navvies were a rarity, with the combination of diet, drinking and danger killing most of them by their forties. And yet their achievements cannot be belittled: between 1822 when work on the Stockton & Darlington started, and the turn of the century, they built 20,000 miles of railway, largely through wielding picks and shovels with the odd barrel of gunpowder to speed things along, often at great risk, and, until the final years of the nineteenth century, without mechanical devices apart from crude lifting gear. Navvies died in their scores on many railway projects, particularly tunnelling, often through sheer carelessness or the fact that they were drunk on the job. Neither their sobriety nor the safety of their work was helped by the fact that some companies refused to hire a man unless he agreed to receive part of his wages in beer.

On the Liverpool & Manchester the most dangerous task was working on the tunnel on the approach to Liverpool and its excavation cost many lives, including the first recorded death of a navvy, reported in gory detail, as was the contemporary style, in the *Liverpool Mercury* on 10 August 1827: 'The poor fellow was in the act of undermining a heavy head of clay, fourteen or fifteen feet high, when the mass fell upon him and literally crushed his bowels out of his body.' Many would die in precisely the same manner because undermining a big chunk of earth to precipitate its collapse was a way of getting more pay through the piece-rate system. It was particularly perilous as any misjudgement or unexpected fault line could lead to disaster.

Progress on the tunnel was hampered by faulty surveying work by both Vignoles and Stephenson's assistants, but Joseph Locke, one of Stephenson's protégés who was to become one of the great railway engineers of the age, managed to sort out the errors. While tunnels were not new, this was the first one in the world to be cut out of the rock and earth under a major town. On its completion in 1829, it was opened as a tourist attraction after its walls had been whitewashed and gas lighting installed. For a shilling, visitors could walk through the tunnel with the sound of a band echoing through the chamber to provide a fairground-type experience and, crucially, help win over the public to the railway itself. This sort of public relations initiative was essential as the railway pioneers needed to improve their image, being still frequently portrayed as rapacious land-grabbers disrupting the established order of things. Which, of course, *inter alia*, they were.

With work progressing well on all the other major obstacles, such as Chat Moss, the deep Olive Mount excavation at the entrance to Liverpool which was needed to keep the track almost level, and the long Sankey viaduct over a deep valley, several key decisions about the operation of the railway had to be made. The gauge had effectively been determined when Stephenson was chosen as engineer since he had already envisaged a national network of railways and therefore there was no doubt that he would use the same 4ft 8½ins as the Stockton & Darlington. But there is more to railway gauges than simply the distance between the two rails. What about the space between the two tracks? Here Stephenson was in uncharted territory as the Liverpool & Manchester was the world's first double-track railway. He opted for the same distance as between the rails – a mistake precipitated by the need to keep the cost of land purchase to a minimum, since it was too narrow and constrained the width of the trains, as well as risking the lives of passengers. Indeed, the narrowness of what is still called the 'six foot'[17] between the two tracks of lines contributed to the death of William Huskisson, the former Cabinet minister famously killed on the day of the opening of the railway (see below).

Another key decision was whether the railway should be an integrated operation – both carrier and operator – or, as with the Stockton & Darlington, it should be managed on the turnpike principle, open to all comers prepared to pay for access. The directors, with their customary thoroughness, set up a committee in February 1828 to discuss the issue, although it is pretty incredible that they had not fully considered and decided on such a crucial matter before. Running a railway was a fiddly business, involving considerable initial capital expenditure on equipment such as wagons and carriages, warehouses and horses and carts, as well as all the logistical complexity of ensuring onward delivery and the bureaucracy of invoicing. Why not leave it to others with long-established working methods such as Pickford's, which was then a flourishing general carrier and is now famous as a removal firm? For a time this sentiment prevailed, but perhaps as the directors became acquainted with the chaotic situation on the Stockton & Darlington they reluctantly agreed to the railway becoming the sole carrier.[18] After all, the railway would receive the entire revenue from its operations rather than merely getting tolls from independent operators.

That decision, which had to be written into a new short Act passed by Parliament, led directly to the next key question: if the railway was going to run all the trains, both for goods and passengers, which method of power should be used? Since there was now no question of contracting out the services, the railway needed to buy the equipment to run the trains itself: locomotives or other forms of traction, such as stationary engines, cables or even horses. Stephenson had long entertained the vision of a national rail network and it was clear that the idea of using horses or cables to run hundreds of miles across the country was fanciful. With steam locomotive technology at last beginning to improve, and the difficulties of using alternative power sources, the answer might have seemed obvious, but there were nevertheless strong counter-arguments at the time.

In fact, promoters of contemporary railway schemes were by no means convinced that steam locomotives were the future. The technology was still novel and there were remarkably few locomotives in use, only around thirty having been built by the time the Stockton & Darlington opened in 1825. Consequently, horses were still seen by many railway directors as the appropriate method of haulage and were used on the most significant new railway built after the completion of the Stockton & Darlington and before the opening of the Liverpool & Manchester – the seventeen-mile Stratford & Moreton, whose principal purpose was to bring coal from the navigable Avon to Moreton-in-Marsh.[19] William James, who was involved in the early stages of the project, favoured using Stephenson's engines, but the directors insisted on equine power, partly because it allowed steeper gradients which reduced the cost of construction. Even more remarkably, the parliamentary Bill for the sixty-two-mile-long Newcastle & Carlisle, which won parliamentary approval in 1829, envisaged the railway to be exclusively horse-drawn and went as far as including a clause that specifically ruled out the use of 'steam locomotives and moveable steam engines'.[20] The thirty-three-mile Cromford and High Peak railway, a virtual contemporary of the Liverpool & Manchester, used a mix of traction methods and was a bizarre hybrid of canal and railway. The railway, authorized in 1825 and opened five years later, was designed to carry minerals and freight but not passengers[21] between two canals across the Peak District. It was built on canal principles with horses being used to pull wagons along the flat sections of track while the nine inclines were worked by stationary steam engines which hauled the wagons up the gradients – the rail equivalent of a flight of locks. Within a couple of years, steam engines had replaced the horses on the flat sections but stationary engines were still used for the inclines which ranged from 1 in 16 to 1 in 7.5, far too steep to be operated by conventional locomotives.[22]

Despite these contemporary examples, directors of the Liverpool & Manchester were not taken in by the short-term advantages of using horses. Apart from the animals' slowness and impracticability, horses were more expensive, despite the lower initial investment required, as the price of fodder was high and their life expectancy, given the arduous nature of the task, low. Indeed, on the Stockton & Darlington, horses were allowed to mount carriages called dandy cars on the downhill sections to give them a rest, but even that did not prolong their working lives beyond a few years. Yet several of the Liverpool & Manchester directors were keen on stationary engines which would pull the trains on long cables, a method which had to be used on the initial section out of Liverpool where, as mentioned previously, locomotives had been banned by the Act authorizing the line. Despite a report prepared by Robert Stephenson, George's son, and Locke, which suggested cable haulage was more expensive, was unable to cope with heavy loads and, of course, was slower, the directors were not convinced. Instead, in April 1829, they decided on a 'beauty contest' of the available steam locomotives to be held six months later on a level 1.5-mile-long section of the track completed at Rainhill, nine miles from Liverpool. The rules were relatively simple, stipulating, for example, a maximum weight of four and a half tons, the need to have a pressure gauge, a maximum boiler pressure of 50 pounds per square inch and a cost not exceeding £550. The locomotives in the trial were required to pull a train of 20 tons at 10 miles per hour on a daily basis and in order to show they could do this, they were required to make ten return trips, a total of thirty miles.

The trials attracted all sorts of madcap concepts. The directors were assailed with ideas from humble self-educated inventors to illustrious professors of philosophy, including devices powered by a fantastic variety of mechanisms ranging from hydrogen gas and high-pressure steam to perfect vacuums and even that ultimate goal, a perpetual motion machine. Carriages which had so little friction they could be hauled by silk thread (but would have been jolly difficult to stop) were proffered, as well as the *Cycloped*, which consisted of a horse operating a treadmill that pulled the wagons. The latter was eliminated straight-away and was, in truth, probably a joke to entertain the crowds. And crowds there were. While the Rainhill trials were very much a real experiment whose result was not predetermined in any way, they were part PR, a way of stimulating interest in the railway. They attracted the imagination of the public and contemporary estimates suggest between ten and fifteen thousand people attended on 6 October 1829, the inaugural day of the event that was to stretch over the following week.

After all the other crazy inventors had been eliminated, there were four realistic contenders who were listed in a programme rather like the runners and riders in a race, but in the event none of Stephenson's three rivals put up a serious challenge since they all failed to complete the course. A couple of his rivals flattered to deceive. The elegant *Novelty*, designed by a Swedish engineer called John Ericsson, was praised as a pretty little engine by the local press but it was little more than a vertical boiler on wheels and after a couple of good runs reaching 28 mph, it started leaking badly and was quickly disqualified, despite attempts to patch it up with cement. *Perseverance*, designed by Timothy Burstall, was quickly withdrawn after its team failed to repair damage incurred in transit to Liverpool and, most humiliatingly, the safety plug in the boiler of Timothy Hackworth's *Sans Pareil* melted in a cloud of steam in full view of the grandstand that had been erected for the spectators.[23]

Stephenson, and in particular his son Robert, had worked hard to improve on the rather unreliable engines used on the Stockton & Darlington. Crucially Robert had developed the multi-tube boiler,[24] a feature that greatly reduced the chances of the engine running out of steam and stalling. Several other improvements were incorporated into the 'premium engine', as it was known before it was given the name that is now famous throughout the world – the *Rocket*.[25]

In the trials, the Rocket performed peerlessly, living up to its name with Stephenson *père* at the controls and Locke as fireman. Back and forth it went over the 1.5-mile track, racking up average speeds of around 14 mph until, on the last leg, he let it loose, presumably as a way of showing all those tomfool lawyers and parliamentarians who had humiliated him how wrong they had been. The engine responded by averaging nearly 30 mph for the final run, demonstrating what good engineering could achieve as well as offering an exciting spectacle to the assembled gentry and peasantry who had never seen anything travel faster on land than a galloping horse or deer. The £500 prize was his, as was a commission to supply another four engines of the same design for the railway within the next three months, an onerous order which he fulfilled successfully bar a few weeks' delay on the delivery of the final locomotive. And bigger and better locomotives were delivered in time for the opening.

*Rocket* is a tiny little engine that now sits rather glumly in London's Science Museum,[26] dwarfed by its far larger successors. But its impact was to be monumental as its success demonstrated the potential of steam locomotives, just as the Wright brothers showed the potential of aircraft with their short flight seventy years later. The *Liverpool*

*Mercury*, which in anticipation of the trials predicted that the railway might 'alter the whole system of our internal communications . . . substituting an agency whose ultimate effects can scarcely be anticipated'[27] was to be proved right. The *Scotsman* was equally enthusiastic, stating pretentiously and clumsily: 'The experiments at Liverpool have established principles which will give a greater impulse to civilisation than it has ever received from any single cause since the Press first opened the gates of knowledge to the human species'.[28]

Meanwhile, the railway had to be completed and opened. Now that the major issues over its operating methods were decided, the only remaining question was how quickly Stephenson could get the line open so that the railway started earning a return for its investors. Sections of the route had been completed and by mid 1829 eminent figures were given rides, even enemies of the railway like the MP Thomas Creevey who had crowed at the defeat of the first Bill. Now he reported that the ordeal of travelling on the railway was 'like flying and it is impossible to divest yourself of the notion of instant death to all upon the least accident happening'.[29] It gave the poor chap a headache which lingered for several days. His fellow campaigner Lord Sefton was apparently 'convinced that some damnable thing must come of it', but poor Creevey confessed that no one else seemed to think so.

Stephenson was intent on showing the power of his new locomotives and took a party of forty passengers over the 'floating' railway on Chat Moss, reaching the amazing speed of 30 mph on the return leg which passengers reported as remarkably comfortable. Trial runs were widely reported locally and, just as today, newspapers sought expert advice to assess the risks. A Doctor Chambers assured potential passengers that there was no cause for alarm even if the train reached 35 mph, and that their eyes would not be damaged by looking at the passing scenery.

The opening was scheduled for 15 September 1830, and by June the trackwork was sufficiently advanced to allow a full rehearsal from Liverpool to Manchester. Stephenson, driving one of his new locomotives, the *Arrow*, took a party of forty including the directors and, just to test the capability of his engine, he added wagons containing stone to give a weight of 39 tons. The journey took a mere two hours, and the return, when the stone was left behind, barely an hour and a half discounting stops. The engineering had proved itself.

Just as with the Stockton & Darlington, the opening of the line was truly a world event, attracting attention from around the globe, and would have gone down in history as a complete success had it not been marred by a tragedy that resulted in the first death of a railway passenger. The opening ceremony was planned as a grand parade, with all the available locomotives and carriages called into action to take the guests to the end of the line and back, watched by the crowds (a contemporary estimate in the *Morning Post* suggested a million, although given this amounted to nearly three times the combined population of the two towns, that appears to be a piece of journalistic licence).

The procession which gathered at the Liverpool end of the line on the morning of Wednesday, 15 September was truly impressive. There were to be no fewer than eight trains, carrying a total of thirty-two carriages, all hauled by a Stephenson locomotive and driven by his engineers. Stephenson, of course, drove the royal train. Well, it was not quite royal, more a VIP carriage, since the monarch had not turned up but the Prime Minister, that old war hero but nevertheless deeply unpopular Tory, the Duke of Wellington, was at the opening. His carriage was certainly fit for a king, as the *Liverpool Courier* enthused: 'The floor [was] 32 feet long by 8 feet wide, supported on eight wheels, partly concealed by a basement [the understructure] ornamented with bold gold mouldings and laurel wreaths, on a ground of crimson cloth; an ornamental gilt balustrade extended round each end of the carriage and united with one of the pillars which supported the roof . . .' and so on. Splendid it may have been, but unfortunately the carriage did not have permanent steps, only temporary ones which could easily be taken up in order to prevent misuse. The procession of trains pulled out of Liverpool one by one and Wellington's, in the lead of course, made good time, reaching Parkside, seventeen miles down the track, in under an hour. As the engine took on water, the notables made the mistake of deciding to stretch their legs, despite prior warnings to stay in the train, and some fifty men got off and began milling around. Huskisson, who had fallen out with Wellington a couple of years previously, went up to him in an effort to make amends and hopefully get reinstated to the Cabinet. He must have thought that as he was a local MP who had supported the railway project his star was in the ascendancy and a chat with the top man would be just the ticket. But as he shook Wellington's hand, a shout went up that an engine was approaching. It was the *Rocket*, driven by Joseph Locke. Most people climbed back on the train or, more sensibly, sought the refuge of the embankment. Huskisson, however, who had a gammy leg and was not very mobile, panicked and ran to the side of the Duke's carriage but, without the benefit of steps, could not clamber up properly.

Poor Locke saw too late that disaster was inevitable. The trains were not fitted with any kind of brake, only the ability to throw the valve gear into reverse, rather as today's aeroplanes use reverse thrust on landing, a process that could take ten seconds to put into effect. Instead of cowering in the space between the tracks where there was easily sufficient room, Huskisson grabbed at the door of the carriage which swung open, tossing him into the path of the *Rocket*. The sickening crunch as his leg shattered under the wheels was heard by all those around; the contemporary account in *The Times* refers to the wheel going over his left thigh and 'squeezing it almost to a jelly' – and it was immediately clear that 'the poor man was mortally wounded'.[30] Stephenson, reacting quickly, said he would take the stricken politician on towards Manchester to seek medical aid as rapidly as possible and thus turned his train into an ambulance. With three doctors tending the dying man, the train reached speeds of 35 mph, which Stephenson, never averse to milking a situation, said later was a world record. The speeding train provided a fantastic spectacle for the crowds, who had no idea of the reason for the urgency. Stephenson dropped Huskisson and two of the doctors at Eccles where they were taken into the vicarage – but to no avail. Despite the arrival of surgeons summoned by Stephenson, Huskisson died in considerable pain at 9 p.m.

The festivities continued largely as planned, including the banquet at the Adelphi Hotel, although the band was cancelled out of respect for poor Huskisson. There had been no doubt that the ceremonies should start and end at Liverpool where the enthusiasm for the railway appeared unalloyed. The quality of life of the working poor was perhaps a trifle better there, and the crowds were wholeheartedly enthusiastic about the new invention, whereas in Manchester contemporary observers noted that the procession was watched 'with looks of sullen or insolent indifference'.[31] Indeed, the welcome in east Lancashire was far from warm. Despite the accident, the organizers had decided that it was prudent to continue the procession across the bridge at the river Irwell, with its huge Doric columns, and terminate at Manchester station, rather than disappoint the thousands lining the path of the railway. However, as the train progressed eastwards, the cheering on occasion degenerated into hooting and even stone-throwing at the carriages. There were clearly two factions among the crowd: those who opposed Wellington, many wearing tricolour cockades – showing their sympathy for the French Revolution – being matched in numbers by supporters who greeted the trains with wild cheers.

At Manchester, the mood of some of the crowd was so hostile that Wellington, who had only gone there reluctantly, remained in the safety of the carriage with his entourage rather than face the protesters, fearing that his presence might trigger another Peterloo, the nearby massacre of anti-Corn Law demonstrators by soldiers eleven years previously. On this historic day for Britain, and in fact the world, the great conqueror of Napoleon was unable to win over his own people and left Manchester defeated by their show of strength.

It was not so much Luddite fear of the machine that had stimulated the crowd's anger but rather a wider antipathy to Wellington's government which, despite the all-too-obvious penury and suffering of large sections of the population, was adamantly resisting any attempts at social reform. The fact that many of the protesters held banners advocating 'Vote by ballot' and 'No to the Corn Laws'[32] suggests that it was not opposition to the railway that had attracted their ire. At the time of the opening, Manchester had no parliamentary representatives, while tiny Newton, through which the line passed, had two, a reflection of the rotten borough system that was in desperate need of reform. The masses were never going to get change from Wellington and perhaps he could be called the railway's first political casualty when, two months later, he resigned in favour of the more reform-minded Earl Grey. Nor did the experience whet Wellington's appetite for rail travel as the old curmudgeon did not venture on the tracks for a further thirteen years, arguing that railways would simply 'encourage the lower classes to travel about' and that the roads, improved by the likes of Macadam, would prevail. They eventually did, of course, but not in the lifetime of the old Duke.

To this day, Huskisson's death continues to mask the true importance of the event by grabbing the headlines. The tragedy was not even reflective of the risks faced by passengers; after all, Huskisson had disobeyed instructions not to leave the train. It is perhaps no coincidence that in Britain the railway authorities have always been far more reluctant to allow people on to the tracks than their foreign counterparts, where it is considered to be of little concern.[33]

The Liverpool & Manchester Railway was never conceived as a self-contained entity, nor as the summit of railway building. Quite the opposite. Even the prospectus published initially for obtaining parliamentary approval envisaged branch lines to the prosperous town of Bolton and the industrial area of St Helens. As Peter Parker, widely regarded as one of the greatest chairmen of British Rail, put it, with a hint of his characteristic mischievous humour, 'the world is a branch line of the pioneering Liverpool Manchester run'.[34] All the elements which made up a 'proper' railway were found for the first time in the Liverpool & Manchester: locomotives hauled passenger and goods trains on a double-tracked railway linking two major towns. It was truly the start of the railway age, but despite its success, rather like the stuttering start of a big steam engine on damp rails, it would take several years before the process of building a national railway network really got under way. In the meantime, the people of the north-west began to get the railway habit.

# TWO

# GETTING THE RAILWAY HABIT

The grand opening ceremony of the Liverpool & Manchester railway, the meticulous engineering skill and the £1m of capital that had gone into the project were still not sufficient to guarantee its success. Far from it. This was an entirely new idea, completely different in scope and ambition from the coal-dominated Stockton & Darlington. Now that the railway was built, would anyone use it?

The answer was unequivocally yes, but not in the way that its promoters envisaged. While the original motivation for its construction had come from Liverpool merchants seeking to reduce the cost and time of transporting their goods, the line would become, unlike its predecessors, primarily a passenger service. The people who flocked to the railway proved to be the mainstay of the business as the goods traffic took longer than expected to build up.

Travelling by train was an utterly novel experience and it is remarkable how many of the customs and practices of rail travel developed in the early days of the Liverpool & Manchester survive to this day. At first, buying a ticket was a major enterprise. For some unaccountable reason, tickets had to be bought a day in advance and passengers had to give their name, address, age, place of birth, occupation and reason for travelling! As one historian of the line suggests, it was 'more a passport than a ticket',[1] but the flocks of passengers arriving to take the train soon put an end to this onerous requirement, with simple tickets bearing the passenger's name being provided instead. All tickets included the reservation of a specific seat, a railway practice that endured for many years until rendered impractical by the sheer number of passengers. On the back of the tickets were heavily printed lines as destination guides to help passengers who were illiterate.

The initial service was fairly unambitious but as it was the world's first regular train service between major towns, predicting demand was all but impossible. There were three first-class trains per day departing from the two termini at 7 a.m., noon and 4 p.m., with room for just under a hundred passengers each paying a fare of 7s (35p) single. Second-class trains, leaving at 8 a.m. and 2 p.m., were introduced a few days later with a fare of 4s (20p), still relatively expensive for the working classes whose wages were often less than £1 per week. Services were added regularly so that by 1835 there were nine daily passenger trains in each direction, as well as various specials. There was, as yet, no notion that the great masses, who had mostly never travelled beyond walking distance from their homes, would be able to use the railway. Third class, designed to accommodate them, would only come a decade later.

However, cannier members of the working class realized that rules are meant to be circumvented. Manchester weavers worked out that they could reduce the time spent carrying their loads to their customers by using the train, but the fare was too high. So groups of three gave their bundles to one of their number to carry on the train until the railway company got wind of this wheeze and restricted passengers to one pack each. The brave weavers challenged the ruling by boycotting the line and eventually the company, eager not to lose their custom, backed down, a rare early victory by passengers in the face of the monopolistic railways.

Anyone with a few bob to spare must have readily paid the extra to sit in first class. While the first-class carriages were mostly fully enclosed and had leather-upholstered seats, second class, until 1834, consisted of benches in open wagons, squeezing four passengers abreast, exposed to the sun and rain and, worse, to the burning sparks and soot from the engine, risking damage to their clothing and even hair. Oddly, a few of the early first-class coaches were left unprotected on the sides but that was soon changed when too many smart and expensive clothes were ruined by the fiery emissions of the engine. As with the Stockton &

Darlington, the first-class carriages, which had three compartments taking six people each, still looked like stagecoach bodies and appeared rather unstable as they were perched on two sets of wheels mounted close together. Not surprisingly, the journey was pretty bumpy, not just due to the weakness of the springs and the vagaries of the track, but because the carriages were linked by simple chains which meant that nothing prevented them hitting each other as the train accelerated or slowed down. To cushion the blows, the seats in first class, which were separated by armrests, had strong leather mufflers for the head but this was not enough to stop the well-to-do from complaining loudly.

Nevertheless, they were well treated, pampered even, by today's standards. Omnibus connections, horse-drawn, of course, to the city centre were available gratis at both ends of the journey, and porters were on hand at the stations to carry their bags. Tips were expressly forbidden on pain of dismissal of the poor porter, which must have been a difficult rule to enforce since travellers on stagecoaches were in the habit of paying regular tips to ensure a comfortable seat or a safe place to put their luggage. And the porters, who were paid a trifling couple of shillings a day (one passenger's fare would easily cover that), could certainly have done with the extra cash.

Here again, the Liverpool & Manchester was establishing a tradition that would prove durable: the employment of a tightly controlled workforce that was expected to be loyal. The workers were uniformed and had to submit to military-style discipline with the company issuing 'orders of the day' early every morning. They could be sacked instantly for any serious transgressions or, for more minor offences, have their wages docked with 'fines'. In contrast, as experienced railwaymen began to be sought by other companies, they had to give three months' notice if they wanted to leave, a rule designed to prevent poaching. Selection of employees was haphazard, often through word of mouth or friendship, with ex-military men particularly sought after, and training was non-existent. The hours were long, often between sixteen and eighteen hours per day for six days a week; so long, in fact, that they were later seen as a safety problem which needed to be addressed by legislation (see Chapter 10). In compensation, the wages were high with railway labourers receiving twice the pay of their equivalents on the farms. The drivers, enginemen as they were known, quickly established themselves as an elite of the manual workforce, earning as much as £2 per week, and developed that independence of spirit necessitated by the difficult task of keeping these complicated and frequently misbehaving engines running smoothly. There were injunctions not to run too fast, as witnessed by the fate of one Simon Fenwick who in 1832 found himself at a disciplinary hearing for having completed the journey in 68 minutes, rather than the two hours recommended by Stephenson as a measure to limit wear and tear of the track and locomotives. There was, too, an officer class, the clerks and managers who worked in offices wearing white shirts and suits, but even they started out, as lads, on a mere 5s (25p) per week.

The permanent nature of the job in contrast to the transience of most comparable unskilled or semi-skilled work, the decent wages, the uniform and the respect earned by working for a service that was at the cutting edge of technology all contributed to a burgeoning sense of corporate loyalty and dedication that no other industry or business has ever managed before or since. The railways were special and everyone seemed to sense it right from the beginning. For its part, the railway company may have been a hard taskmaster, but the directors saw themselves as responsible employers with an almost feudal attitude towards their staff, which manifested itself in the provision of various benefits within the bounds of what was deemed acceptable to the shareholders. For example, the Liverpool & Manchester pioneered the concept of railway cottages rented cheaply to its employees, a tradition that continued right into the twentieth century. Moreover, while the railway was quick to levy fines, the company also paid bonuses to its 'servants' for accident-free records, long service and good conduct, money which it was under no obligation to disburse. The railway even supported employees who were absent from work through injury or illness, but, by contrast, did not consider itself liable for those killed on duty, although discretionary sums were normally paid out. This policy reflected the strong laissez-faire ideology of the time tempered with moral obligations towards the workforce. This combination of harshness and compassion created an ethos that placed great stress on the maintenance of continuity of service, and the huge pride in being a railwayman, summed up in the often used slogan: 'the train must go through'.

Indeed, sticking to the timetable was another rule established right from the outset. If at all possible, late starting was to be avoided, even though at first no timings were offered for intermediate stations or even arrival at the final terminus because of concerns over the reliability of the locomotives and other vagaries such as the weather, the stops to be made (the trains called at each of the twenty intermediate stations on the route only by request) and mishaps such as animals on the line or gatemen absenting themselves. People getting on the train along the way had to make an informed guess about when it might arrive, a situation that still exists at some of the network's more remote stations.

These early stations were not pleasant places to wait, consisting merely of a gate on to the track, with no raised platform and no shelter and it was a decade before these basic facilities began to be provided. Certainly it was not worth waiting for a train on a Sunday as no services started from either terminus between 10 a.m. and 4 p.m. This had been a contentious issue among the directors, some of whom were reluctant to allow any Sunday services at all in line with the strong Sabbatarian traditions in nearby Wales and in Scotland. The partial timetable was a compromise that ensured the operation of the trains did not clash with church services and established a pattern followed later by other railway companies. While most ran some Sunday trains, several companies, especially in Scotland, closed down entirely. The trend even extended to the London Underground with the Metropolitan Railway incorporating a 'church interval' into its services when it opened in 1863, a practice that continued as late as 1909. In the 1860s companies began to notice that services appeared to be little used on the Sabbath and withdrew them to save money. Special Sunday working arrangements appear to be a British phenomenon, as European countries, even those with far more devout populations, largely run the same service seven days a week.

There were other hazards involved in taking the train. The interior of the coaches remained unlit until 1834 and even then only one compartment of each first-class carriage was provided with a single oil lamp, a major fire hazard given that the coaches were wooden. Smoking, however, posed no such risk since it was banned in first class even if the other passengers acquiesced. However, the railway company could hardly stop people in second class from lighting up, given that they were effectively in the open air, but as the accommodation gradually improved and became fully enclosed by 1840, a similar restriction was imposed. While the early railway companies mostly followed suit, arguing that smoking was a fire risk, more and more began to allow it as longer journeys became possible. In 1868, remarkably, Parliament legislated to force companies to provide smoking carriages, even on the Underground railway in London. Smoking policy has now come full circle on the railways as the last modern train operator to allow it, Scotrail (and then only for its sleeper services), imposed a ban in October 2005, leaving the whole network smoke-free once again.

But it was the passengers who caused the most trouble. 'Twas ever thus. Given the rapid rise in numbers, with upwards of 2,000 people soon using the line daily, the scenes at the station resembled those still common on the Indian sub-continent today, with crowds of passengers, meeters and greeters as well as assorted sightseers and pedlars crammed into a small space. Gates were hastily erected and manned by unwavering porters to prevent latecomers delaying the departure of the train, or worse, trying to jump on after it had started moving. To speed the process along, the first trains were sent off with a bugle sound, a stagecoach tradition, but by 1832 this was replaced by a large bell rung five minutes before departure.

Many of the bad habits had been inherited from stagecoach travel. It might have seemed unnecessary to warn passengers not to travel on the roof, but how were they to know they could be hit by a bridge? Why should they not put their heads out of the window when the train was moving as they always had done on stagecoaches? They were an undisciplined bunch who had to be educated in the railway's ways. But the worst were the rich. After all, most of the first-class passengers were used to being conveyed in their own carriages whose coachman would be at their beck and call. Was it not a bit presumptuous for these rough railwaymen to seek to shepherd them aboard when they were deep in conversation with their fellow gentlemen? The well-to-do would also tend to hop off at intermediate stations or water-stops to stretch their legs, a seemingly harmless aspiration for passengers who had been cooped up in a small compartment for hours on end, but a habit which the railway staff had to break in order to maintain punctuality. While for most rules were rules, there was clearly a secret list of VIPs who were sufficiently notable to keep the train waiting, since one of the early excuses for late running was that the train had been 'waiting for important people'.[2]

While the risks of riding on the roof quickly appeared all too obvious, the most difficult habit to break was the tendency for passengers to jump off the train before it had stopped, a dangerous practice which resulted in deaths on British railways right up to 2005 when the last slam-door trains were finally taken out of service.[3] People were unaware that the speed of trains was so much greater than on the ponderous stagecoaches to which they were accustomed and, worse, many were tempted to leap off while the train was at full speed if the track happened to go near their ultimate destination. To prevent passengers taking this risk, the railway company started locking its passengers in, but this created another hazard, the possibility of being trapped in the event of a fire.[4]

The indiscipline of many early railway passengers quickly demonstrated to the company the need to draw up a set of rules and regulations. These were given statutory backing and became the by-laws familiar to all passengers forced to while away the wait for a train by perusing platform notices. From the outset, the railways had the status of a quasi-state and it was no coincidence that the staff who looked after the track, and later the signals, were initially called policemen.

There was, in fact, no signalling whatsoever at the beginning. Trains were controlled on a time interval basis – in other words, they were prevented from leaving until a set number of minutes had elapsed since the departure of the previous train. Policemen would be sited at key points along the line – surely the second loneliest job on the planet after lighthouse keeper – and were instructed to give a 'Stop' signal if a train had passed within the last ten minutes, a 'Caution' if more than ten but fewer than seventeen minutes had elapsed, or otherwise a sign to proceed. If a train broke down, the policeman was supposed to run back a mile down the track to protect the train from oncoming traffic by showing a hand signal. If the other track were blocked, the crew were supposed to build a warning fire on the track with their coals to alert other trains, a practice that did little for the condition of the sleepers. This system of signalling was adopted by all early railways and was only improved once its limitations became all too apparent.

To alert people on the line, some early trains on the Liverpool & Manchester had buglers sitting atop the first carriage (despite the injunctions for passengers not to travel on the roof), but steam whistles were soon fitted to locomotives and at night trains had a large lantern as a headlamp. At the back, there was a red bull's eye reflector, and later a tail lamp whose purpose was to show the train was complete. Signalmen knew that a train without one probably meant there were loose wagons on the track.

Mishaps included an accident at Rainhill in 1832 where one train ran into another in thick fog, killing a passenger and injuring several others; and another four years later, when an axle broke, sending the carriage down an embankment but surprisingly resulting in no fatalities among the locked-in passengers. Most deaths and injuries, however, were due to passengers' own mistakes or foolishness, often occasioned by drunkenness. One man tried to walk on the rail as if it were a tightrope and, fatally, did not notice a train coming up behind him. Similarly, in 1833, three passengers walked up and down the line impatiently waiting for their service, failing to see a train approaching in the other direction which killed them. Others died or were injured while standing up in the uncovered carriages or jumping off the train while in motion or, as still happens regularly today, trespassing on the tracks. There was even the odd bit of hooliganism, with people throwing stones or leaving timbers on the line, a phenomenon which, again, survives to this day. Railways require a high level of societal trust to function because they cannot be protected against all such attacks and fortunately, for the most part, the people of Lancashire welcomed the railway and therefore desisted from threatening its safety.

Given these various incidents, the oft-quoted claim by the management in 1838 that only two passengers had lost their lives on the railway was being rather economical with the truth. Nevertheless, the railway could not be considered as particularly hazardous, especially at a time when life generally was far more perilous for the average citizen than it is today. From the beginning trains were a relatively safe form of transport, especially when compared with stagecoaches which were being driven ever faster along the roads in a vain attempt to compete.

The railway presented far more danger for the staff than for passengers and the rate of fatalities reached carnage proportions by the end of the century. Throughout the history of the railways, workers have borne the brunt of the steady death toll, although it is the major passenger accidents that attract attention. The early railways had to find the safest working practices by a process of trial and error, but this was cold comfort to those who were killed during the learning process. The technology, too, was obviously experimental and required continuous improvement and modification. Early boilers were a particular danger and even though they were fitted with safety valves, they were wont to explode occasionally. This happened to Stephenson's *Patentee* in an incident that killed the driver and the fireman. Another constant danger for enginemen was having to get on and off the footplate during shunting operations to give hand signals and deal with couplings. One early victim was a fireman on the *Mercury* whose head was crushed between the vehicles when he was uncoupling the wagon attached to the engine. But, as ever, the greatest number of fatalities was caused by mistakes or sloppiness, often occasioned by tiredness as a result of those long working hours. The biggest risk in the early days was the failure of policemen to position the points correctly, leading to derailments. In one incident at St Helens Junction, wrongly set points resulted in the collision of two locomotives and the death of an engineman. Other derailments came about because the policeman simply dozed off, leading to prosecutions and even jail sentences. Another unlucky driver was killed when his engine hit a plank left on the line by workmen who had sat on it to eat their tea. These incidents, which all occurred in the first decade of operations, would be repeated time and time again over the next 150 years of railway operations.

On the whole, though, the railways were safe, particularly for those who used them sensibly and were sober. A good safety record was crucial in helping people overcome their natural fear of travelling faster than anyone had ever done before. Had there been a major accident in the early years, such as a derailment or collision causing many casualties, the consequent boom in railway development might well have been stymied: 'for every one convinced of the value of new railway schemes, there was an extremist who saw only a vision of passengers maimed or suffocated, horses bolting and vegetables refusing to grow'.[4]

Despite the many primitive aspects of the service and the odd mishap, the journey delighted most of those who took the train. For such a male-dominated business, it is surprising to find that the best early chronicler is the highly literate and long-lived actress Fanny Kemble. Travelling as a guest of the company a couple of weeks before the official opening, when she was barely twenty-one, she was entranced with the railway and even with the gruff George Stephenson whom she described as 'a master' whom she was 'horribly in love with', a playful bit of artistic licence. In a long letter to a friend, she describes her fascination with the machine, driven inevitably by Stephenson himself: 'You can't imagine how strange it seemed to be journeying on thus, without any visible cause of progress other than the magical machine, with its flying white breath and rhythmical, unvarying pace, between these rocky walls [she obviously left Liverpool through the Olive Mount cutting] which are already clothed with moss and ferns and grass; and when I reflected that these great masses of stone had been cut asunder to allow our passage thus far below the surface of the earth, I felt as if no fairy tale was ever half so wonderful as what I saw. Bridges were thrown from side to side across the top of these cliffs, and the people looking down upon us from them seemed like pigmies standing in the sky.'[5]

She then traverses Chat Moss 'on which no human foot could tread without sinking and yet it bore the road which bore us'. Showing her extensive knowledge of the history of the line, she recalls 'this had been the great stumbling block in the minds of the committee of the House of Commons; but Mr Stephenson has succeeded in overcoming it . . . we passed over at the rate of five and twenty miles an hour, and saw the stagnant swamp water trembling on the surface of the soil on either side of us.' Stephenson takes her down to the bottom of the Sankey viaduct so that she can admire the grand structure with its nine arches and he clearly he caught her attention, as she points out that his explanations of the workings of the railway were 'peculiar and original' but that 'although his accent indicates strongly his north-country birth, his language has not the slightest touch of vulgarity or coarseness'.

Stephenson must have purred at the reception he got from this attractive young woman, just fresh from playing Juliet, compared with the roasting he had been given by the parliamentarians just five years previously. On the way back, as Stephenson was wont to do, he opened up the regulator and the engine raced up to 35 mph, 'swifter than a bird flies' and, Kemble adds, 'you cannot conceive what the sensation of cutting the air was; the motion is as smooth as possible . . . when I closed my eyes, this sensation of flying was quite delightful and strange beyond description'. Yet, she stresses, she felt 'not the slightest fear' as the 'brave little she-dragon flew on'.

Kemble's description may be more artfully written than other contemporary reports but they were almost all equally enthusiastic. Yet there was still criticism from the odd self-interested curmudgeon like Creevey, representing the canal owners and stagecoach companies whose fears and opposition to the railway had proved well founded. The canal companies had tried to pre-empt the railway's arrival by cutting rates and improving the waterway as soon as the first Bill had been published. But nothing proved the case for the railway better than their subsequent behaviour. The Bridgwater Canal Company, which had reduced its tolls by 18d (7.5p) per ton in anticipation of the advent of the railway, restored its old level of charges as soon as the first Bill was defeated. It was an own goal, since the second prospectus for the railway exposed this example of monopoly exploitation and promised that the railway would reduce the price of coal by 2 shillings (10p) per ton, to the benefit of local citizens. The canal, which had delivered a fantastic 40 per cent rate of return to the Duke of Bridgwater for many years, would never do so again. Once the railway was completed, it was forced into cutting its rates permanently by a third. Nevertheless, for a time there was room for both methods of transport and the canal would remain profitable for many years.

As for the stagecoaches, within three months of the opening of the Liverpool & Manchester, over half the twenty-six on the route had ceased running, though of course there was still the rest of the country to serve. Indeed, the number of stagecoaches nationally peaked in the mid-1830s, and only began their inevitable decline when the railways started to spread across the country. In response to the competition from the new railway, the surviving stagecoach owners slashed their fares to 10s inside and 5s outside, but even that was not competetive with the train, and all but one had stopped operating by 1832. In truth, the railway had done much more than merely poach passengers from the stagecoaches. The figures for passenger numbers show that the railway had developed its own market simply by making travel so much pleasanter, faster and cheaper. In 1830 the stagecoaches had a capacity of around 700 passengers per day, whereas in the three years between 1831 and 1833 the railway averaged 1,100 passengers daily. The Liverpool & Manchester was to the 1830s what the easyJet phenomenon is today, fulfilling a latent demand to travel at affordable prices.

The rapid demise of canals and stagecoaches, which were themselves relatively new forms of travel, demonstrated how the Industrial Revolution was accelerating the rate of social change. Indeed, the railways were the greatest product of the Revolution, and its major driver. Even though, as Nicholas Faith[6] points out, more miles of canals than railways were built in the ensuing decade, this was the most rapid example of obsolescence the world had so far seen: the railways would rapidly do to stagecoaches and canals what muskets had done to the longbow.

Others who expected to suffer from the railway found themselves profiting from it. Innkeepers were worried about the loss of stagecoach business and obviously those catering on remote stretches of highway solely for stagecoach passengers went out of business quickly. However, as always, innovation and new technology created opportunities as well as losses. Hostelries close to intermediate stops on the railway found that passengers were all too willing to use up the time with a drink or two. They even began to offer onboard services – a 'serving wench' was spotted soon after the opening at the Patricroft halt selling drinks and cigars from a tray to first-class passengers.

Given the Liverpool & Manchester's instant popularity, it is hardly surprising that the railway was profitable from the outset. By the end of 1830, just three and a half months after opening, the railway paid shareholders an immediate dividend of £2 per £100 share. The directors clearly hoped to grant shareholders almost the maximum allowable under the Act, which had restricted annual dividends to a maximum of 10 per cent. In the decade and a half of independent operation, until the line's merger with the Grand Junction in 1845, shareholders received an average of 9.5 per cent annually, amounting to almost two and a half times the price of their shares. Not a bad investment in a period of little inflation.

Many future railways would be equally useful and well patronised, but would never attain the profitability of the Liverpool & Manchester because of the higher costs of construction or because they did not serve large agglomerations separated by such short distances. Today, once the high capital cost of building and maintaining the infrastructure is taken into account, there are barely any profitable railways in the world due to competition from road transport.[7]

Receipts from passengers ran at twice the level from goods during the first few years, which was more a reflection of the railway's success in attracting people to use the line than the absence of freight. It was perhaps the Rainhill trials where people were able to experience the excitement of speed for the first time and, as a consequence, the real potential of the railway, which was the turning point. In fact, because of a shortage of locomotives, the directors allowed passenger trains, with the occasional freight wagon attached, only during the first couple of months of operation. Stephenson had been unable to keep up with the demand for more locomotives, and catering for passengers was seen as the best way of building up patronage quickly. The first goods train ran in early December 1830, hauling cotton, oatmeal and malt to Manchester. Soon, the whole assortment of goods that were to become familiar on the railway were being carried on the Liverpool & Manchester, ranging from oil, spice, coffee and tobacco heading from the port to clothes, salt and Staffordshire pottery destined for the docks. By the spring of 1831, 150 tons of goods were being carried daily and in 1835 four times that level. Mail was carried right from the beginning under an agreement with the General Post Office – the start of a long tradition – and livestock, much of it from Ireland, was soon being transported in specially designed trucks. The carriage of pigs in their new wagons attracted the rather apt comment from the *Liverpool Times* that their accommodation 'is a much handsomer and more commodious vehicle than those in which His Majesty's liege subjects were accustomed to travel fifty years ago'.[8]

While putative railway promoters around the country were looking at the Liverpool & Manchester's figures with great interest, there was no immediate rush to follow suit. For the most part, promoters were waiting to see whether the initial rush of enthusiasm for taking the train would be maintained. The early 1830s were a time of political uncertainty. In the towns, workers were becoming increasingly dissatisfied with their dreadful conditions, while in the rural areas the rising numbers of labourers were being displaced by new technology such as threshing machines and were starting to protest. The pressure for the Reform Bill was reaching a head and there were major riots in Bristol and Nottingham, all of which created an atmosphere that was hardly conducive to investment in long-term projects.

Nevertheless several railways were being developed in conjunction with the Liverpool & Manchester. The eight-mile-long Bolton & Leigh had been completed in 1828 and effectively became the first branch line of the Liverpool & Manchester when it was linked via a third railway, the 2.5-mile-long Kenyon & Leigh, in 1831. On the other side of the tracks, heading south, the five-mile Warrington & Newton opened that year too, as the first stage of the long railway to Birmingham. The Stephensons, who seemed to throw up odd bits of railway in their spare time, were involved in the construction of all three of these smaller Lancashire lines. These railways were, however, separate entities, demonstrating in microcosm the complexity created by the unplanned and haphazard development of the railways that was to continue throughout much of the century. While the Liverpool & Manchester was clearly the largest concern, its directors still had to thrash out deals with the other railways over their running rights and other matters such as use of equipment and the condition of their locomotives. By the end of the 1830s, other nearby towns such as Wigan, Preston, St Helens and Runcorn had been connected to the railway, greatly boosting its usage but also increasing the complexity of administration and operations.

In various parts of the country, odd little stubs of lines had already been approved or were under construction by the time of the opening of the Liverpool & Manchester. The longest was another coal railway, linking the mines of Swannington and Coalville with Leicester, and the chief engineer was the twenty-nine-year-old Robert Stephenson. The railway, which carried both passengers and freight, was, at sixteen miles, half the length of the Liverpool & Manchester, and opened in 1832, a mere two years after it was authorized by Parliament. Fortunately, Stephenson senior insisted that it should be designed to his preferred 4ft 8½ins gauge, which meant that it could later easily become part of the extensive Midland Railway. A similar railway, to cater for the burgeoning cotton industry in Leeds and to provide traders with a better transport route for their goods to the port of Hull, was the Leeds & Selby, completed in 1834. These new lines, however, were limited in scope and largely catered for established freight routes rather than being perceived as part of a major nationwide network.

Around the whole of the UK, various pioneering railways were opening in a haphazard way, determined by the ability of local promoters and the availability of capital. New short lines opened in 1831 in Edinburgh and Dundee, both operated by cables and horses, showing that the lessons of the Liverpool & Manchester had still not been learnt. Glasgow's first railway, the Garnkirk & Glasgow, was operated by steam engines that had no cab for the driver and fireman, also opened that year. There was, too, the Dublin & Kingstown, the first railway in Ireland. However, England still had barely 100 miles of line by 1836: this included some strange little sections of railway such as that linking Whitstable and Canterbury in Kent and the first part of the much more significant Newcastle & Carlisle line, which had belatedly decided to adopt steam technology.

But why did the obscure little towns of Bodmin and Wadebridge in Cornwall get a railway before London? While in the capital building a railway would inevitably be a major undertaking, in provincial areas there was scope for individual enterprise to bear fruit quickly. In Cornwall, an enterprising local landowner, Sir William Molesworth, realized that it was the best way of carrying the limey sea sand from Wadebridge, which was much in demand further up the valley of the river Camel for use as fertilizer, and commissioned a survey. The single-track railway, built to the standard gauge, opened in 1834, funded largely by local shareholders who had put up the £35,000 capital. The seven-mile line, which boasted a couple of small branches, also carried passengers. Most notably, three excursion trains to Bodmin transported a total of 1,100 passengers to view the public execution of the Lightfoot brothers for murder in 1840.[9] Similar local efforts would generate countless more small railways and, later, branch lines for the rest of the nineteenth century (see Chapter 7).

At last London got a railway in 1836 when the first part of the London & Greenwich opened to the public. It marked a radical departure from all the earlier railways, being built in an already developed area with the idea of catering for nascent commuter traffic. Moreover, the railway faced the added disadvantage of having to compete with the well-established boat traffic on the Thames. Like their predecessors, the promoters had to face down the pessimists, such as the *Quarterly Review*, which commented: 'Can anything be more palpably ridiculous than the prospect held out of locomotives travelling twice as fast as stage coaches . . . we will back Old Father Thames against the Greenwich railway for any sum.'[10]

The 3.5 mile railway was a remarkable achievement, built on top of 878 large arches to avoid using up land and interfering with the busy street pattern below. An amazing 60 million bricks were used in the construction of the line which took five years to build. The 400 navvies working on the line used more than 100,000 bricks per day, causing a shortage for other construction activity in London. That run of arches remains the longest in Britain and the construction method set a trend in London, which eventually acquired twenty five miles of these railways in the sky, and in several other cities. Initially the London & Greenwich directors hoped that people would be persuaded to rent the arches for housing but were soon dissuaded of this notion, a decision for which the capital's scrapyard dealers and car breakers have been grateful ever since.[11]

It was a stunningly ambitious scheme that cost nearly £1m, virtually the same as the Liverpool & Manchester which was nine times longer. For operational reasons, involving the shared use of the line out of

London, in 1850 the London & Greenwich started running trains on the right-hand side, a little curio since it is the only British railway ever to do so (and the practice continued until 1901). As ever with new rail lines, the London & Greenwich was opened with great fanfare, special trains, speeches by notables, a brass band (provided by the Scots Fusiliers) and the inevitable banquet. Although the railway was the first to be devoted solely to passenger transport, its developers still did not dare commit themselves entirely to the concept and hedged their bets by building a 'pedestrian boulevard' alongside the railway, charging users a penny toll. To allay passenger fears about the dangers of travelling on top of the endless viaduct, the trains were designed with a special low centre of gravity to reduce the risks of toppling over the 4½-foot parapet walls. However, fears must have been overcome as the railway was soon joined by the London & Croydon, with a separate station alongside at London Bridge. Passenger numbers built up rapidly with 1,500 people per day using the railway and the 'boulevard' was quickly replaced by additional tracks. Nevertheless, the line struggled to make a profit until a much wider network of suburban services built up in south London in the 1850s to cater for the growing job market in the city centre of London.

While all these lines were pioneers in one way or another, helping to establish the viability of the railway concept, the big project in the offing was the construction of the main line railways which still form the spine of the network today. Because of the political uncertainties in the early 1830s and the sheer scale of the task, it would be eight years before another major new railway would join together two major conurbations like the Liverpool & Manchester Railway. Then there would be two in quick succession, first the Grand Junction and then the London & Birmingham. They would both be grander in scale and scope than anything that had come before and would involve their promoters and builders in overcoming much greater obstacles than their predecessors had faced.

# THREE

# JOINING UP BRITAIN

With the opening of the London & Greenwich in 1836, the story moves further south. There were good reasons why the early railways had been developed in the north: not only was the demand for better transport great, but that was also where the liquid capital, the enterprise and the engineering skills could all be found. However, with the success of the Liverpool & Manchester, the potential benefits of railways to the rest of Britain became too obvious to ignore and groups of promoters formed in major towns across the country. While it had become clear that Britain was to get a national rail network, its precise nature and routes would be thrashed out in the rather archaic and chaotic parliamentary process. Parliament would set rules for these new companies, restricting them in various ways, but would not initiate the creation of any railway; neither would the government, which showed no interest in determining where the railways would go, let alone planning a network. This was in marked contrast to other European countries where the state played a far more active part in the process. In Belgium, the only country where the railways developed as quickly, after the first line opened in 1835, the government laid out the shape of the network with four main lines departing from a central hub and funded their construction.[1]

But at least the financing of schemes had been made easier. Until 1826, only the Bank of England was accorded joint stock status, in other words, allowed to have a multitude of investors underpinning its financial activities. Other banks were until then restricted to the amount of capital that could be raised by six people, but once the regulation had been removed several banks operating on the joint stock principle quickly emerged. Moreover, railway companies had a privileged position in relation to other enterprises. Until 1860, they were the only type of companies that could raise capital from more than five people, a restriction imposed on manufacturers following the South Sea Bubble collapse in the eighteenth century. This ensured that the railway companies were the most favoured alternative investment to government stocks. While, at best, the latter yielded 4 per cent, people with a bit of spare cash saw that the Liverpool & Manchester was paying dividends of just under 10 per cent. Crucially, too, railway investors were protected right from the beginning by limited liability – in other words, they could not be held responsible for any losses beyond the amount they had already paid for their shares.

With the creation of a more accessible banking system and the return of a stable political climate, the railway promoters began pushing their schemes once again. The eventual passage of the Reform Act of 1832 had given the vote to a quarter of a million more people, and this important measure began the move towards a democratic society, a process that was speeded up by the arrival of the railways. The feeling that society was changing, coinciding with a brief period of bright economic prospects, encouraged the development of a succession of major new railway projects on a far grander scale than the Liverpool & Manchester. Between 1833 and 1836, a series of Bills were passed by Parliament that were to lay the foundations of the main line network.

The most important were two railways which, though promoted separately, were always envisaged as a joint operation and eventually created a line that ran from London through Birmingham and on to Liverpool and Manchester. The southern part was the London & Birmingham, a 112-mile railway from Euston through Watford, Rugby and Coventry to Birmingham. There it was to meet the 78-mile Grand Junction which ran through Staffordshire to join the Liverpool & Manchester at a junction near Warrington. Again, the Stephensons were ubiquitous. George was the chief engineer for both projects but in practice Joseph Locke did most of the work on the Grand Junction and Robert Stephenson was responsible for the London & Birmingham. The combined two railways were to be six times longer than the Liverpool & Manchester and therefore far more expensive to build, but from the outset the financial case was very strong since the two railways would link up the four major conurbations in the country. Raising the money, therefore, was not the biggest obstacle faced by the promoters; rather, it was the forces of reaction, the landowners and canal owners with their vested interests.

The first attempt at a Bill for the railway between the two Lancashire towns and Birmingham collapsed when the government fell over the failure to push through the Reform Bill. When the Bill for the Grand Junction returned to Parliament, the usual opponents argued strongly against its authorization but surprisingly those who stood to gain so obviously from the cheaper and quicker transport – the Staffordshire iron and pottery makers – jumped on the bandwagon and tried to extract their tuppennyworth, demanding exorbitant sums for land as well as compensation for disturbance. Opposition may have been boosted by the fact that the Grand Junction was a project initiated from the north end of the line, without the involvement of any prominent Birmingham or even Midlands investors, and therefore the local benefits were not immediately apparent. Remarkably, a key objector was James Watt, none other than the son of the great steam-engine pioneer and the owner, thanks to his father's legacy, of considerable canal interests. He lived in Aston Hall and refused to cede any of his land to the railway company. Reluctant to force a confrontation in Parliament with such a powerful opponent, the company was obliged to reroute the line around the estate to connect with the London & Birmingham at Curzon Street in a station alongside the Grand Junction's terminus. This was a far less convenient arrangement since it made through-running of trains impossible, and forced passengers to suffer the hassle of changing trains at Birmingham. Moreover, the station was a mile away from the city centre, a journey that cost a shilling in a hackney cab. It was replaced in the 1840s by New Street station, which did allow through-running but Curzon Street's impressive classical façade survives to this day.[2]

Opposition to the London & Birmingham Railway was also widespread and an earlier version of that scheme had been rejected by Parliament. As with the Liverpool & Manchester, much survey work had to be done under cover of darkness to avoid attracting the attention of landowners and their often violent servants. Robert Stephenson described the kind of attitude he had to contend with when he met a 'courtly, fine-looking old gentleman, of very stately manner'. This was a certain Sir Astley Cooper, an eminent surgeon and the owner of land at Berkhamsted in Hertfordshire, through which the railway had to pass. The old doctor called the scheme 'preposterous in the extreme' and could not understand why 'our estates' had to be 'cut up in all directions for the purpose of making an unnecessary road'. Why, he concluded, if 'this sort of thing be permitted to go on, you will in a very few years destroy the *noblesse*'.[3]

There was really only one way to counter this sort of opposition: buy it off. Railway promoters realized that to push their schemes through Parliament they had to simply open their chequebooks and bear the pain. Between them, the Grand Junction and the London & Birmingham paid more than £700,000 in payments to the landowners to acquire what in effect were narrow slivers of land used, if at all, for agriculture. This enormous sum represented a fifth of the two railways' combined initial share capital of £3.5m.

Work on the two railways started very soon after authorization. The Grand Junction involved four major viaducts and a two-mile cutting at Preston Brook which also required the construction of an aqueduct to carry the canal over the railway.[4] The most impressive of the new structures was the Dutton viaduct over the river Weaver, which is nearly 500 yards long, a distance covered by twenty red sandstone arches that reach sixty-five feet above the river. It took 700 men two years to build, without the loss of a single life. The projects for major structures on the line were undertaken separately and simultaneously by a variety of contractors, since the scale of the railway had put an end to the notion that Stephenson or his fellow engineers could both organize and oversee the work themselves without the intermediary of a contractor. It was to be the start of a boom period for railway contractors, one of whom, Thomas Brassey, became the greatest and most efficient of all (see Chapter 6). Brassey completed the Penkridge viaduct in Staffordshire on time and on budget. Indeed, the cost had been greatly reduced with Brassey's agreement, when Joseph Locke had spotted that the viaduct had originally been greatly overpriced relative to the cost of others on the line.

The construction of the Grand Junction was a great engineering success, thanks to Locke's skills as he, rather than Stephenson, saw the scheme through. However, it was the London & Birmingham that was to catch the public imagination and attract the plaudits. Partly that was because the construction of the railway meant that, at last, London would have a main line railway which immediately opened up large swathes of the country to travellers from the capital. It was also the scale of the task which had impressed people, along with the magnificence of the engineering. Apart from the initial mile out of Euston which, as at Liverpool station, was operated by a cable system because of the 1 in 70 incline,[5] Robert Stephenson created a virtually level railway all the way to Birmingham. Aware that the line would be heavily used as soon as it was completed, Stephenson designed the route for ease of operation but that meant spending extra sums on nine tunnels and three long deep cuttings. It was a stupendous engineering achievement, created in five years by, at its peak, 20,000 workers. The Victorians themselves had difficulty in grasping the scale of the task and one contemporary writer, Peter Lecount,[6] worked out that it outstripped the achievement of the construction of the Great Pyramid at Giza. He calculated, laboriously, that while the pyramid only required the raising of 15,733 million cubic feet by one foot, to build the railway required lifting 25,000 million cubic feet, two thirds more and, moreover, the task was undertaken in just five years, a quarter of the time it took to build the pyramid. The precise figures may be rather fanciful, but such calculations demonstrate that the building of the railways was by far the biggest construction feat of modern times and arguably the greatest in human history. The London & Birmingham ensured Robert Stephenson's lifelong reputation as the most renowned railway builder in the world and while the work was carried out by contractors, Stephenson himself was reckoned to have walked the length of the line twenty times during the five years of construction. Even he could not prevent the occasional disaster, most tellingly at Watford, where a group of navvies was killed during the tunnelling when the gravelly ground gave way.

The London & Birmingham opened in sections – with stagecoach connections linking train journeys at either end while the Kilsby tunnel was being completed – and through-running along the whole line started in June 1838. The journey between the two cities took six hours as the locomotives commissioned by the railway were rather under-powered for the task and had to be changed at regular intervals. There were surprisingly few intermediate stops, partly because the aim of the railway was long-distance travel, rather than serving the villages – which had yet to become suburbs – on the outskirts of London. The first station was Harrow, eleven miles out of London, and it was many years before the development of any closer to the centre of the capital. These early railways made little effort to serve even quite sizeable towns that were near the line as the promoters were interested in rapid connections between the main conurbations. Thus on the Grand Junction line, Walsall, Wolverhampton and Northwich were simply ignored even though they were all under five miles from the railway.

The inaugural one-way fares between London and Birmingham were £1 10s (£1.50, or around £100 adjusted for inflation) in first class, and £1 (£67) in second. Dogs were an outrageous 10s, though you could put a two-wheel carriage on a wagon for a mere £1 17s (horses extra!), rather like the car sleeper services still widely used in Europe. The additional 10s for first class must have definitely been worth the money given the primitive conditions of second class, which still had open wagons for a journey that was three times longer than that on the Liverpool & Manchester. These high fares suggest that the railway companies were still making no attempt to serve the working classes for whom a pound would easily represent a week's wages or more. They enabled the wealthier middle classes to live far away from their work and to flee the unpleasant centres of cities more easily, while not offering any such opportunity for the poor. However, as we see later, with the advent of cheap fares both for workers and leisure travellers, the railways did become a catalyst for wider social change and even some *rapprochement* between the classes.

Despite the high fares, the ride on these long journeys was not necessarily enjoyable. The author of an early guide to train travel, Francis Coghlan, may have been trying to be helpful in advising second-class passengers where to sit in their 'wagons', but after reading his advice they might well have decided to stick to the stagecoach or pay the extra for first class where 'all the seats [are] alike . . . comfortably fitted up': 'Get as far from the engine as possible – for three reasons: first, should an explosion take place, you may happily get off with the loss of an arm or a leg' whereas nearer 'you would probably be smashed to smithereens'. Secondly, he continues, 'the vibration is very much diminished' and third, 'always sit with your back towards the engine . . . to avoid being chilled by a cold current of air which passes through these open wagons and also saves you from being nearly blinded by the small cinders which escape through the funnel'.[7] Perhaps this explains why first-class carriages are always those furthest from the direction of travel at London termini.

Coghlan goes on to explain how once passengers were aboard their carriages, having been helped up by a 'stone platform, protected from the weather by a light handsome shed', and the ticket offices were closed, the train was at last ready to depart. The porters and police then had to push the train, 'which was attached to a thick rope worked by a [stationary] steam engine' for two hundred yards before the line would become taut and drag the train up the incline to Camden where it was attached to a locomotive. The slope is still there, of course, and was an operational hazard, frequently causing wheelslip to engines starting off from the platforms. I remember vividly as a child seeing the stuttering of the huge wheels on the massive Duchess locomotives before they could get a grip on wet rails, and wheelslip remains a problem even on today's railway.

The rather unwieldy process of using ropes, which continued until 1844 when locomotives were deemed to be sufficiently strong to climb the incline under their own steam, rather diminished the grandeur of Euston station. The station entrance was a Doric portico, a clear statement of the importance of the railway, and within a few years a great hall built in a classical style with a sweeping double flight of stairs leading to upstairs offices was added.[8] Euston would retain its status as the sole 'gateway to the north' until the completion of the rival Great Northern in 1852 with its King's Cross terminus. With the opening of the Birmingham & Derby Junction Railway, which connected with the London & Birmingham at Rugby and then went on to join the North Midland Railway, both Stephenson *père* enterprises, passengers could also reach various Midland towns and, indeed, travel all the way to Leeds from Euston by 1840. Within a decade of the completion of the two railways, they had merged – together with the successful Trent Valley railway which bypassed Birmingham (used today as the main route for trains between London and Liverpool, Manchester and Glasgow) – to form what later became the biggest railway company and, for a time, the largest business concern in the world, the London & North Western Railway.

The third major Bill passed in the busy parliamentary period of the mid-1830s authorized another of Britain's major railways, the Great Western, which, right from the beginning, established a monopoly over a large swathe of the country. At last this was a railway with which the Stephensons had little connection and only because of an abortive attempt to run it into Euston. The moving spirit behind the railway was Isambard Kingdom Brunel, whose grand name showed remarkable prescience on the part of his father, Marc, a French emigré and himself a notable engineer. Brunel vies with the younger Stephenson for the title of the greatest railway engineer and, apart from his achievements on the railway, he designed the Clifton Suspension Bridge in Bristol, three large steamships and much else. Unlike his engineering contemporaries who tended to be self-taught and often rather eclectic in their backgrounds, Brunel had received a formal training in engineering as an apprentice, initially in France and then working on the first tunnel beneath the Thames, under the tutelage of his father who designed it. Brunel's self-confidence and drive would have been called arrogance in anyone less talented but his achievement in creating the Great Western railway, known fondly to its supporters as God's Wonderful Railway (its detractors later called it the 'Great Way Round'), speaks for itself.

Brunel came early to the project. The idea of a railway between London and Bristol, at the time the nation's most important port, had been mooted as far back as 1824 but it was not until January 1833 that a group of Bristol businessmen formed a committee to take action on the project. The first idea had been to follow the route of the rather windy coach road (the present A4), but Brunel, who learnt of the scheme, rushed to Bristol to argue the case for a much more ambitious project. Indeed, Brunel was not going to have any old railway built by the cheapest contractor to minimum standards. No, he was going to have the best railway, so perfect that rivals would never venture on to its territory through fear of being outshone by its excellence.

Sometimes pure chutzpah pays off and by a majority of just one the committee appointed Brunel as surveyor even though he had little experience on railways, having previously failed to obtain a similar post he had sought from the Newcastle & Carlisle Railway. The committee was rewarded with what one railway historian calls 'a masterpiece of strategic planning . . . with easy gradients which would pass over a summit at Swindon half the height of that at Marlborough [on the coach road route]'.[9]

There were the usual parliamentary struggles. While the landowners again extracted every penny they could, receiving £750,000 in compensation, the most fanciful objection expressed in the forty days of parliamentary hearings came from John Keate, the headmaster of Eton College. He suggested that London's riff-raff would travel to the town and ruin its college and, worse, that the scholars would be tempted to travel into the capital, where they would fall into 'degrading dissipation'. For some reason, he was even worried that the railway would result in an 'increase in floods' that would endanger the life of the boys. Such nonsense could easily be dismissed but Brunel's initial idea of having the terminus at Vauxhall Bridge fell foul of various landowners with parks on the fringes of London and the first Bill had to be dropped. It was replaced with a scheme that would have gone to Euston and was accepted by Parliament, but following a dispute over the gauge with Robert Stephenson, the eventual project with a grand terminus at Paddington received parliamentary assent. The railway was, indeed, 'Wonderful'. Not only were there few gradients, but on the principle that expense should not be spared in seeking perfection, Brunel decorated stations, tunnel mouths and viaducts playfully with all kinds of mock castles, using an eclectic range of classical, Tudor and Jacobean styles. The two most difficult structures, the Maidenhead Bridge with its flat arches, at the time the widest in the world, and the 1.75-mile-long Box tunnel near Bath, were both great achievements in their own right.

There was more in this desire to create an elegant railway than just engineering showmanship. The railways were a tremendous imposition on the British countryside, unprecedented in scale and extent, and they needed to blend into the environment. The railway pioneers like Brunel realized the importance of winning over the public and to have merely built structures such as bridges and viaducts in the cheapest and most shoddy way would certainly have alienated the more affluent and influential section of the population whose support they needed. Railway stations, too, were designed on a far grander scale than the size of their location might have required in order to appease and flatter local interests. With few exceptions, these railways enhanced the local landscape, rather than destroyed it, unlike the roads and airports of the twentieth century. As Michael Robbins comments, 'the railway etches in fresh detail to the scene. It rarely jars and usually pleases.'[10] That is in no small measure due to its great early builders.

It is hardly surprising that Brunel's engineering brilliance has survived the passing of time and his designs have proved robust, but that does not mean he was always right. His decision to go for a different gauge from any other railway was to prove one of the great blunders of railway history. It was born of the same self-confidence that resulted in Brunel's masterpieces and since so many of his ideas proved to be successful, it was a brave man who stood up to him. Virtually all the railways authorized up to that point had been built to Stephenson's favoured 4ft 8½ins but to Brunel, ever the perfectionist, that was not good enough. He had once ridden on the Liverpool & Manchester and had found it wanting because he could not draw freehand circles and lines in his notebook due to the bumpy ride. He vowed to create a railway on which 'we shall be able to take our coffee and write whilst going noiselessly and smoothly at 45 mph'.[11] He rather forgot about the coffee bit, and train refreshment services would have to wait until long after his death – the first dining cars were introduced in 1879 – but he pressed ahead with his choice of gauge, which was to be 7ft,[12] half as wide again as Stephenson's 'standard' gauge.

Brunel was also concerned with safety, having seen steam locomotives derail and concluded that their centre of gravity was far too high. To lower it meant putting the bottom of the boiler between the main frames, and consequently the wheels had to be further apart. Brunel did not underestimate the inconvenience of creating this new gauge but was foolhardy enough to believe that his would prevail over the others and that the older railways would end up having to fall into line with the Great Western. He was to be proved wrong, at great cost to the company, as his decision not only increased the expense of building the railway but after he died resulted in the need for conversion initially to mixed, and later to standard, gauge.

The choice of gauge was no mere technical detail. It meant that no through trains would be able to proceed on to another company's tracks once the limits of GWR's own territory were reached, causing great inconvenience to passengers who were forced to swap trains. Brunel had rather airily told his directors that passengers would simply be able to walk from one train to the other while their luggage would be conveyed mechanically, though he omitted to outline the nature of the device to be used, which presumably was some notion of a primitive conveyor belt. In the event, nothing emerged and the resultant chaos with hordes of porters and passengers struggling to manhandle luggage from one end of the platform to the other at Gloucester were highlighted in a famous *Punch* cartoon.

At first, given the railway was largely self-contained, the Great Western's separate gauge did not create too many problems, but as various railways interwove its network, the situation became increasingly intolerable. Bizarrely, Brunel had not really taken advantage of the opportunities afforded by his wider gauge, which was supposed to allow a better quality of ride for his passengers: the carriages he ordered were barely an improvement on those of other railways. Brunel appeared to have misunderstood the key issue: it was not so much the distance between the wheels, but the overall width of the carriage, which in practice was not much greater on the Great Western because platforms and bridges had been built closer to the tracks than on other railways.

Parliament finally resolved the gauge issue in 1846 through a commission which decided, after hearing at great length evidence from proponents of both gauges, that all future railways should be 4ft 8½ins. Gradually the Great Western installed an extra rail to enable mixed gauge running and eventually converted fully to the standard gauge in May 1892 (see Chapter 9), marking the end of Brunel's failed experiment.

Brunel made another, less well-known mistake, but one that would also cause great stress to the railway's directors long after his death in 1859. Inevitably, during construction, costs soared: the original estimate had been £2.5m but running to Paddington, further into London, and building that superb terminal had added £1m. With other additional costs, notably difficulties with the Box tunnel, the total bill came to more than £6m. Consequently Brunel was under great financial pressure and during the construction of Swindon station and works, he agreed to a deal with the contractors, a pair of brothers called Rigby, that was to compromise the efficient running of the railway. The Rigbys agreed to build the station and the housing for the workers at their own expense, in return for the rents and a lease on the station refreshment rooms, with the obligation that Great Western stop all trains there for ten minutes for the next hundred years and refrain from offering alternative catering! There was the exceptional very fast train which only stopped for a minute, but mostly, for half a century, trains made unnecessarily lengthy stops at Swindon until in 1895 the company bought itself out of that disadvantageous contract.

Brunel was always seeking innovation and that led him to pursue one of the many technological dead-ends that were all too prevalent given the inventiveness of the Victorians and their readiness to experiment. He undertook the survey for the fifty-three-mile South Devon railway from Exeter to Plymouth, and decided that the railway, which opened in 1847, should be powered by stationary engines and pneumatic power by creating a vacuum in a tube between the rails that would pull the train along. There had been a couple of other such experiments, but 'they were a brilliant near miss'.[13] To seal the vacuum, leather flaps and grease were used but the results were always unsatisfactory. Although the often-repeated tale that rats ate the flaps is now accepted as a myth, the vacuum was impossible to maintain and the railway reverted after barely a year to using conventional locomotives. Brunel's failed experiment cost the company £500,000.

All this is being a bit tough on Brunel. He had created a veritable speedway that enabled the company to run the world's fastest train services, and his legacy, in terms of structures, is arguably the greatest of any railway engineer. Brunel was fortunate in that he had an equally brilliant mechanical engineer, Daniel Gooch, younger brother of Thomas Gooch, Stephenson's assistant on the Liverpool & Manchester, who was the company's locomotive superintendent from its creation until 1864. Gooch developed several types of engines for the broad gauge railway that enhanced the company's reputation for reliability, although it was not long before the Great Western's reputation as the country's fastest railway was superseded.

The fourth major railway to be constructed in this busy period of the mid-1830s was the London & Southampton, which soon became the London & South Western. Southampton was an odd choice of destination for the first railway to run southwards out of London and its history demonstrates how the decisions of the railway companies about their routes were already having a profound impact on the economies of the regions they served. The contrast between two towns with sports teams nicknamed 'The Saints' illustrates this neatly. Northampton, which was already the prosperous centre of the country's shoe industry, did not get a railway early on, but Southampton, which at the time was a sleepy little seaside resort greatly dwarfed by neighbouring Portsmouth, did. That was the fault of Northampton's Luddite inhabitants.

The town would have been on the most direct route for the London & Birmingham, but its inhabitants were so adamantly opposed to the railway that Robert Stephenson was forced to choose a more expensive alignment, necessitating an extra tunnel at Kilsby, nearly a mile and a half long and costing £300,000. The opening of the line was also delayed because of the huge amount of sandy wet soil that had to be pumped out. The opposition had been spurred on by the gentry and in particular the long-established local shoemakers who were apparently worried that smoke from the railways would discolour their sheep. Indeed, wherever the railway went there were similar concerns about cattle being put off their feed, horses bolting wildly into rivers or even vegetables failing to flourish.

However, it was not long before Northampton's residents changed their minds, presumably noting the absence of discoloured sheep, and the town's movers and shakers began pressing hard for a branch from the main line, which was eventually completed in 1845. Still, it meant that Northampton suffered from being off the main line and to this day has a far inferior service than, say, Rugby, which is on it.

In many other places, the effect of the railway was much more immediate and several towns were actually created by the arrival of the railway. Crewe was a hamlet of just a few houses, rather like Middlesbrough, until it became the junction of three railways: the Chester & Crewe, the Manchester & Birmingham and the Grand Junction, which also established its main locomotive and carriage works there. Within a few years, there were 800 people living at Crewe in 200 houses, and by 1871 the town had 40,000 inhabitants with virtually the entire male population employed at the works. The local football club, Crewe Alexandra, is still nicknamed 'the Railwaymen'. Swindon, on the Great Western, was also a tiny hamlet before the arrival of the railway, which was followed soon afterwards by the massive workshops that were to be the town's principal employer until well after the Second World War.

Southampton was chosen as the southern terminus of the first main line south of London because local interests had promoted it effectively, even though it was by no means the obvious choice. For a time the railway – exploiting its monopoly by charging high rates for a poor service – did not help it grow. In 1892, however, the London & South Western railway, having seen the huge potential of the port, bought Southampton Docks and was instrumental in building up a vast transatlantic passenger and freight trade. The promoters of the London & Southampton made the mistake of not appointing Stephenson or any of his acolytes like Joseph Locke, and instead chose Frank Giles, an experienced engineer but a poor organizer, who did not manage to keep control of his contractors. Eventually he was replaced by Locke, who designed a fine railway, straight and with very slight gradients, still considered essential at the time, given concerns about the inability of locomotives to handle inclines.[14] Because of Giles's failings, progress was far slower than on other, more ambitious projects to the north. By 1839, five years after work had started, only the first forty-seven miles, from London to Basingstoke, had been opened. At the same time, a branch line to Portsmouth, a far more substantial port at the time, was given the go-ahead, but it went to Gosport on the wrong side of the harbour, necessitating a ferry trip across the water. While the burgesses of Portsmouth had to put up with an inadequate service, they could not tolerate the idea of being a branch off the London & Southampton and insisted the name be changed to London & South Western. The line finally reached Southampton in 1840 and Gosport the following year.

The railways were still largely being funded by the great burgeoning industries of the north, whose entrepreneurs contributed a substantial part of the investment in all these schemes apart from the Great Western. Remarkably, even the London & Southampton obtained 40 per cent of its initial capital from Manchester business interests. As for the London & Birmingham, more of the money came from Lancashire and Cheshire than from the two cities which gave the railway its name, and Lancashire capital was prominent in funding railways as diverse as the small Canterbury & Whitstable and the Great Western as well as projects in Edinburgh, Glasgow and Dublin.

By the end of the 1830s, then, the railways had established themselves. Trains hauled by steam locomotives were accepted as the dominant new form of technology of the age, having beaten off alternatives that ranged from steam road vehicles and balloons to atmospheric and cable railways. The imagination of the public had been caught and investors began to be lured by a series of stock exchanges that popped up in places as diverse as Halifax, Leicester and Bradford. The railways had begun their long spread across Britain, but it was to be a stuttering process, with times of rapid expansion alternating with periods of little or no construction.

# FOUR

# CHANGING BRITAIN

By 1843, just thirteen years after the opening of the Liverpool & Manchester, Britain had the makings of a railway network. The year was a notable one because it marked the end of the first phase of construction and the start of a brief hiatus before the railway mania of the second half of the decade began. There was, too, a lull in activity by the promoters. Once again, times were bad, both economically and politically, following a severe depression in trade caused by a series of failed harvests and the terrible Irish potato famine.

There were also genuine doubts about whether Britain needed any more railways. A long article in the literary magazine the *Athenaeum* in May 1843 argued that several million pounds had been wasted in building parallel railways, such as the Midland Counties and the Birmingham & Derby, which both ran north out of Birmingham. It questioned whether both 'the Manchester and Sheffield, and the Manchester and Leeds should have been made as separate railways' and advocated that the government should have determined the structure of the railway network, as in Belgium, thus preventing this sort of duplication.

The *Athenaeum* article might have had a point had it been written twenty-five years later, when, as we shall see, many unnecessary and uneconomic railways were laid, but at the time the magazine was simply plain wrong. In 1843, there were 1,800 miles of railway open for traffic, a sharp rise from the 250 miles in 1838 but still less than a tenth of the eventual high point reached in the Edwardian period.

Even though there were still large gaps in the network, the railway system offered the population the ability to move around the country in a way that had never been possible before and most of the main lines in use today had begun to be built. Passengers could travel from London to Birmingham and then on to Liverpool and Manchester, and there were now branches that stretched to Chester, Lancaster and Leeds; and to the east they could reach Hull and Darlington, albeit by a pretty circuitous route. In broad terms, the West Coast main line had been largely developed, but the East Coast had not even been started, and there were no connections through the hilly border country between England and Scotland. South of the Thames, the South Eastern was open to Folkestone, the Brighton line was complete and the South Western ran through to Southampton and Gosport, but much of the huge complex of lines in suburban south London and the south-east had yet to be built. In the east, quite remarkably, the Eastern Counties railway opened its Norwich to Ely and Cambridge railway in one stage in 1845 and later that year started running all the way between Norwich and London. Two rival railway companies, the Northern & Eastern, and the Eastern Counties, were setting out from London and both lines would eventually reach Cambridge (which explains why even today there are trains to the great university city from both Liverpool Street and King's Cross stations). These eastern railways were, however, venturing into sparsely populated country, which meant they would always struggle for profits, at least until the spread of the London suburbs eastwards in the final quarter of the nineteenth century.

There was, too, a scattering of railway lines that had no connection with any part of the growing network, some just a few miles long like the Bodmin & Wadebridge, but others quite substantial, notably the Newcastle & Carlisle. Even where lines appeared to be linked on the map, they might not be physically connected and, as in Birmingham, serving different stations quite far apart. There were a couple of short lines in Ireland; Scotland's two main cities, Edinburgh and Glasgow, were connected and there were various local lines around Dundee. Wales had only the Chester & Holyhead railway along the north coast, and a few very short lines, leaving the Principality without any effective railway communication.

Train travel was very slow by modern standards but, of course, amazingly quick compared with any contemporary alternative. It was not so much the potential speed of the locomotives that pushed up journey

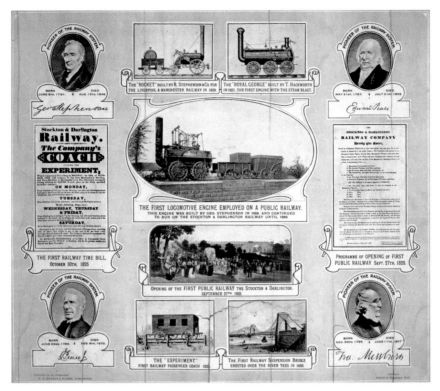

A lithograph commemorating the fiftieth anniversary of the opening in 1825 of the Stockton & Darlington Railway, with images of George Stephenson and his *Locomotion* engine, as well as later developments such as the first railway suspension bridge.

The opening of the Liverpool & Manchester Railway in 1830 attracted enormous local and worldwide interest.

Early opposition to the railway was widespread, as shown in this satirical cartoon by Henry Hughes from 1831, which illustrates concerns about the dangers of this new form of transport.

This caricature of John Bull drunkenly accepting numerous proposals for railway bills was published in 1836 during one of several periods of excessive speculation in railways.

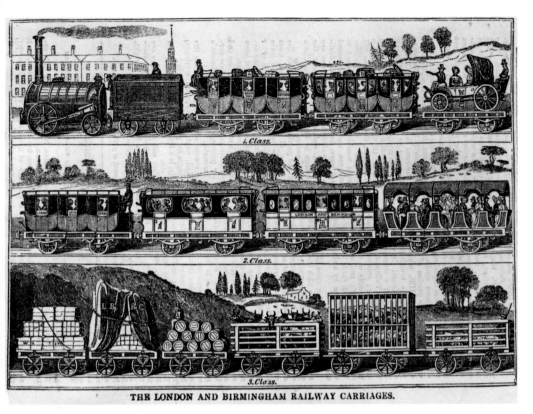

THE LONDON AND BIRMINGHAM RAILWAY CARRIAGES.

The class divide: illustration from the *Mirror* in 1837 portraying the three types of carriages on the new London & Birmingham Railway.

Ladies ticket from 1840: women were often offered the opportunity to sit in their own compartments in the early days of rail travel. Ladies' compartments continued to exist until the 1960s.

A view of open carriages crossing the Bridgwater Canal on the Liverpool & Manchester Railway in the 1830s. The gauge looks rather wide but is in fact the standard 4ft 8ins used across nearly all the railway network at this time, apart from on the lines of the Great Western.

Bristol Temple Meads station in 1846 before platforms became the norm.

An illustration from the *Illustrated London News* highlighting the difficulties caused at Gloucester station, which for many years in the mid-nineteenth century was the meeting point of railways operating different gauges. Passengers travelling between Bristol and Birmingham had to change trains, creating delay and scenes of chaos.

A satirical cartoon from 1850 suggesting possible alternative forms of employment for horses made redundant by the advent of the railway.

The railway greats: Brunel (far right) and Robert Stephenson (seated left) with colleagues at the launch of Brunel's SS Great Eastern in 1857.

In an effort to make the railways more acceptable to the public, the early engineers would often add embellishments to structures such as bridges and tunnels. This surprisingly rural scene from around 1840 is the entrance of the Primrose Hill Tunnel near Camden Town in north London on the London & Birmingham Railway built by Robert Stephenson.

The construction of St Pancras station as published in the *Illustrated London News* on 15 February 1868. The recently-built tunnel roof on which the men are standing in the foreground is the top of the world's first underground railway, the Metropolitan.

The Tay Bridge disaster of 1879 killed seventy-five people and remains to this day the worst railway accident caused by structural failure.

Construction of the iconic Forth Bridge, built between 1883 and 1890, which considerably shortened rail journeys between Edinburgh and Fife, Perth, Aberdeen and the north of Scotland.

This lithograph by Alfred Concanen from 1874 illustrates how the railway companies soon found an extra source of revenue by selling space on their walls for advertising anything from sherry to medical remedies.

Early railway companies also earned income by offering luxury rail tours to wealthy passengers. Here, a seventeen-strong party accompanied by two maid-servants, a cook and a steward are setting out from St Pancras in 1876 on a twenty-six day excursion around Britain. The trip took in Scotland, the newly built and very scenic Settle to Carlisle line and the West Country.

times, but their constant need for water and the necessity of making lengthy stops for refreshments and for what we now call 'comfort breaks'. Express and through trains on the main lines were timed to run at between 20 and 30 mph, including stops, and journeys around Britain were rather akin to long-haul aeroplane trips today. The first train to Liverpool, for example, left Euston at 6 a.m. and reached its destination, after changing at Birmingham, at 4 p.m., an average for the 210 miles of 26 mph. The hardy passenger could reach Darlington from London, having gone by a roundabout route which involved changes at Birmingham, Derby and York, by 7 p.m., a thirteen-hour marathon compared with a journey of under two and a half hours today.

All the information on these lengthy trips and every other railway journey could be found in Bradshaw's, the railway timetable. This was first printed as a monthly publication in 1842 by George Bradshaw and quickly established itself as the only guide that set out all scheduled rail services in the country. It was notoriously difficult to use because the publishers had no editorial control; the companies simply provided the list of services in a non-standardized way, with countless incomprehensible notes and annotations. Nevertheless, despite later imitators like ABC and the information produced by the railways themselves, Bradshaw's survived until 1961, well after nationalization. It was then replaced by British Rail's own timetable, which was continued by Railtrack and Network Rail, and only ceased to be published in paper form after 2007, replaced by the web and the excellent National Rail Enquiry Service.

According to Bradshaw, the fastest trains in the 1840s were, by far, on the Great Western. For example, by October 1852 the company was running an express service from Oxford to London in sixty-eight minutes at an average speed of 55 mph and, most impressively, it had one daily express to and from Exeter which, as it was exempt from the ten-minute refreshment stop at Swindon, averaged a very commendable 43 mph for the 193-mile journey. Brunel argued this was a justification for his broad gauge but in fact these speeds were soon to be matched and bettered on standard gauge main lines.

Of course these were the scheduled times and there was no Passenger's Charter – John Major's invention – to assess the actual reliability of the trains in relation to the timetable. The Victorians were as wont to moan about train delays as we are today, though most of the timetables had a lot of slack[1] which meant that time could easily be made up. This was especially true for the few trains that were earmarked solely for third-class passengers, which averaged far less than 20 mph. However, the lot of these passengers was greatly improved by the Railway Regulation Act of 1844, brought in by William Gladstone, who was President of the Board of Trade.

Amazingly, given contemporary suspicion of state interference, Gladstone's principal ambition was to regulate and even nationalize the railways, and the original draft of the Bill he presented to Parliament would have given the government a powerful range of controls over the management and working of train services, including the idea of eventually nationalizing them. However, the howls of protest from the railway owners led to the Bill being watered down. A partial notion of nationalization was retained, with the government having the right to take over new railways, but this power, which came into force in 1865, was never actually exercised – though of course the whole industry would be taken into public hands some eighty years later.[2] Crucially for poorer passengers, Gladstone's Act required the train companies to guarantee at least one train per day on every line, running at a minimum speed of 12 mph and with a fare of not more than 1d (0.42p) per mile. Notionally these parliamentary trains, as they became known, had to be provided only by new companies, but in practice all the existing railways quickly fell into line, even if some, like the Great Western, did their utmost to make the services unattractive by scheduling them for the early hours of the morning. For example, the first train out of Paddington to the West Country for many years was the parliamentary train departing at 6 a.m. Some railways, notably the Great Western, Manchester & Leeds and the Edinburgh & Glasgow, resorted briefly to operating fourth-class trains with open-sided wagons but eventually the success of third class made the railways realize it was in their commercial interest to provide these cheap services. Within five years, more than 50 per cent of passengers were paying the third-class fares of a penny per mile.

There were other bargains to be had as well. While the numerous changes of train required for a long journey resulted partly from the existence of so many different companies, passengers could also benefit from the competition when there were alternative routes. Derby had a grand station served by three companies, two of which ran trains down to Rugby by different routes. As the railway historian Jack Simmons put it, 'Cut-throat competition is a mere stale phrase to describe the vigour of the rivalry between the two companies. For three glorious years, the traveller made merry at their expense as stage by stage they cut their rates, each trying to secure his patronage by the cheapness and alleged superior convenience of its trains.'[3] As Simmons points out, this was commercial suicide and the services were eventually amalgamated in 1844 into the Midland Railway.

The other source of cheap travel was the excursion train, filled to the brim with holidaymakers and therefore, like charter flights today, very cheap to run. As far back as the early days of the Liverpool & Manchester various groups began hiring carriages or full trains for special events. The first recorded group was an outing of 150 Sunday school teachers who, soon after the opening of the line, hired a train of second-class coaches for a return trip from Liverpool to Manchester. Special trains were run during the Whitsun holiday week and other public holidays, and parties of racegoers travelled to the course at Newton near Manchester. Indeed, trips to the races were a particularly early source of railway traffic: in 1840, 24,000 people were ferried by rail between Glasgow and Paisley for a two-day race meeting.

Vice and virtue seemed to compete equally for railway traffic and it was the latter which, most famously, stimulated Thomas Cook to organize an excursion for the short journey between Leicester and Loughborough. Its purpose was to take people to a 'temperance fête', which may have sounded unexciting but attracted no fewer than 500 trippers. The price was a shilling, which included food and was the start of a business that would, by 1872, offer around-the-world trips taking 212 days at a cost of £210. Cook's short trip to Loughborough was reputedly the first one organized by a travel agent rather than by the passengers themselves and the excursion business took off from that point, becoming an important source of revenue for the railways. These excursions gave birth to what became known as 'monster trains', massively long and hauled by several locomotives, rather like those interminably long trains that carry freight across the United States today. An excursion from Leeds to Hull, organized by the Leeds Institute, took 1,250 passengers in forty carriages and another on the same route in 1844 reportedly carried 6,600 passengers in 240 carriages, hauled by nine locomotives[4]. Further south, the trains were slightly more modest. In the same year, 1,710 went in forty-six carriages from London to Brighton for the day on an August Sunday, with a further 300 being left behind. For the more adventurous, the South Eastern railway organized the first of seven trips that year by rail and steamship to Boulogne in May 1844, which carried a total of more than 2,000 people.

By 1850, in just one August holiday week, more than 200,000 people left Manchester by excursion train. The importance of this phenomenon went far beyond merely giving the masses a day out. It was helping to inculcate the railway habit in millions of people who would not have travelled otherwise. As one early commentator put it: 'Men who but a few years since scarcely crossed the precincts of the county in which they were born, and knew as little of the general features of the land of their birth as they did the topography of the moon, now unhesitatingly avail themselves of the means of communication that are afforded.'[5] Moreover, these excursions grew into the mass seaside-holiday business which previously had been the preserve of the rich; the railways began to make great efforts to serve towns with a strip of beach or a few pleasant coastal views that could be observed from the train. In 1840, Fleetwood, for example, a new port where 'summer bathing' was on offer, became the first seaside venue when it was connected to the Preston & Wyre railway, and, more significantly, the following year a branch from the Great Western reached Weston-super-Mare, already an established resort. Scarborough followed in 1845, and between 1846 and 1849 a further fourteen resorts were joined to the rail network by branch lines, including Blackpool, Eastbourne and Torquay. Going to the seaside became a welcome release for huge swathes of the population stuck in their factories working long hours in slave-like conditions and, of course, for many these trips provided a first-ever glimpse of the sea.

At the other end of the social scale, Queen Victoria began to travel on the railways. Prince Albert, her beloved husband, had started using the

Great Western regularly but the Queen appeared rather reluctant to use trains at first. Eventually, urged on by the press, her first journey was from Windsor to London in June 1842, an event which 'opened up a new chapter in the history of the British monarchy'.[6] It gave Victoria the opportunity, for the first time, to show herself to the public at large. For centuries, sovereigns had largely been confined to the capital or at best to coach rides conducted at a fast pace to avoid adoring or possibly hostile crowds, but with the advent of rail travel, this changed completely. 'The monarchy now became a physical reality to many people, not merely an institution.'[7] The Queen's new ability to travel influenced her choice of holiday home as she bought the secluded country estate at Balmoral, which remains a favourite of the present Queen. The castle is 600 miles from London and was realistically reachable only by train, though initially it required a long coach journey from Aberdeen, which had been connected to the railway network soon after she bought the estate, in 1850. The royal entourage must have been rather relieved when a branch line was built to Ballater, nine miles from the castle, in 1866 but apparently the Queen did not want the railway to reach any nearer to her estate so that commoners would desist from visiting it.[8]

There was some public disquiet at the young monarch travelling on what was seen as a risky form of transport. In France, the briefly reinstated King Louis Philippe was barred by his ministers from travelling from Paris to Rouen in July 1843 because it was considered not sufficiently 'secure'.[9] The British royal family may have begun to use the trains but they were rather nervous passengers. Neither the Queen nor Albert liked travelling at speed and he was in the habit of telling conductors on the Great Western 'not quite so fast, Mr Conductor, if you please'.[10] Victoria then banned any train on which she was travelling from exceeding 40 mph, even if delays caused her to be behind schedule, and protested vehemently when this order was ignored. This insistence on slow travel created even more difficulties for the poor rail companies who had to draw up special train timetables, which were discussed at great length by railway managers in order that the royal train could be accommodated on the network, a task made more complicated by the fact that her long journeys invariably took in several different companies' lines. For the trips to Balmoral, there was the further difficulty that the Queen, with her vast entourage, had to endure the palaver of changing trains because of Brunel's different gauge.

As average speeds on routine services rose and the use of lines intensified, royal trains caused severe delays to other travellers. There were strict rules to minimize risk to royalty: no trains, except those carrying (the royal!) mail were allowed to travel in the opposite direction and a pilot locomotive had to be sent fifteen minutes ahead, rather like a royal food taster, to test the track and check for any danger. Arrangements became even more complex when in the later years of the century Irish terrorists began to pose a genuine threat and the routing had to be kept secret. The tradition of special royal carriages was quickly established: the first vehicle was provided by her local operator, Great Western, in 1840 and the London & Birmingham commissioned a couple more coaches two years later. They all ran on just four wheels, ensuring a rather bumpy ride, which perhaps explains the Queen's dislike of speed, although it was still an improvement on the fast-travelling coach and horses which she had used previously.

Royal trains may have been the ultimate form of personal transport but it was not uncommon for rich people to charter their own 'special' if they fancied a day out. They would turn up, usually with their huge retinue, unannounced at a station, demanding that the railway provide a train immediately together with a crew, since self-drive hire was not an option. This hiring arrangement was so common that the rail companies even published set rates which were around 5 shillings per mile (25p) for a single journey and half as much again for a return one, in addition to the normal, presumably first-class, fare. Moreover, those who could afford it were able to make up their own timetable. The *Edinburgh Chronicle*[11] reported that a gentleman needing to get to Glasgow from Edinburgh missed the 9 o'clock train and commandeered a special engine which started half an hour later, which 'overtook the train at Falkirk at 10 past 10 o'clock, running the 23 miles in 40 minutes, 15 minutes of which was occupied in stopping at three of the stations'. Why this chap's personal train had to stop at the intervening stations is not explained, although probably it was because there was no proper signalling system, and presumably he was charged royally for his indulgence by the Edinburgh & Glasgow Railway. But if you were in a rush, there was no better way to travel. The man who trained the horses of Lord Eglinton, a great racehorse enthusiast of the time, chartered a special from Manchester to Liverpool in order not to miss a race and the train covered the thirty miles in just forty minutes.

The military, too, were quick to spot the potential of the railways, both to quell riots and, in the event of war, to transport troops to ports. The Liverpool & Manchester quickly won a contract from the government to carry soldiers and their baggage. It even allowed women 'belonging to the regiment' to be conveyed free of charge, provided there was no more than one woman for every ten men. Officer class only, therefore. As early as the Chartist disturbances of the late 1830s, the government used the railways to transport troops around the country.

The mail was another source of revenue. Since the Liverpool & Manchester had established the idea that mail could be carried by train (see Chapter 2), other railways quickly followed suit. On its opening in 1837, the Grand Junction became part of a new postal service allowing mail to be transported by coach from London to Birmingham and then by rail to Liverpool. The government may have been reluctant to involve itself in the planning of the railways, but it quickly realized that the postal service would be transformed by using the network and passed legislation requiring the railways to carry the mail, as directed by the Postmaster General. Rail companies were even required to provide carriages exclusively for conveying mail and even sorting letters while in transit; the railways were left only with the power to negotiate a fair price for the arrangement. The tone of the legislation was rather out of keeping with the usual government attitude of laissez-faire towards the railways but was illustrative of the relationship between the two.

Rowland Hill introduced his penny post for a half-ounce (14 gm) item in 1840, opening up the postal service to anyone who could afford the relatively modest charge, and the railways quickly became a vital part of the Post Office distribution system. By 1842, 1,400 miles of railway, operated by forty different companies, were carrying mail. Special coaches, laid out as travelling post offices in which mail could be sorted on the move, had been introduced on the combined railway route that stretched from London to the Liverpool & Manchester, and quite rapidly these TPOs, as they became known, were travelling around the whole main line rail network and survived until the start of the twenty-first century.

It was not only the government that saw the enormous potential of these iron tentacles gradually extending around the country. Interestingly, while the railways had been conceived principally to handle goods, freight earned only a small proportion of their income on most lines in the early days. In 1843, the Great Western, for example, was collecting £13,000 per week from passengers, more than four times the £3,000 it obtained from freight. On the London & Birmingham the ratio was five to one and on others it was even greater. Broadly, the further north the greater the proportion of receipts from goods being transported, with the Newcastle & Carlisle earning twice as much from freight than passengers, hardly surprising given the need to transport locally produced coal and the paucity of population. In a world which had been so immobile, the railways were truly creating a social revolution. As The Times put it, 'thirty years ago not one countryman in one hundred had seen the metropolis. There is now scarcely one in the same number who has not spent the day there.'[12] While many travellers had been displaced from the turnpikes, the railways generated much of their own business, ranging from the leisure travellers on a day out and people visiting their relatives to commercial travellers and landowners going about their business. In other words, not much different from today's passengers.

The impact of the goods business on the railways was no less an important factor in changing economic patterns and stimulating growth. The opportunities created for new freight flows invariably disrupted traditional markets, creating new opportunities and destroying long-established businesses. A Cheshire farmer was reported as no longer producing cheese because he could supply the Liverpool market with fresh milk, arriving, at the end of a forty-three-mile journey, at 8.30 in the morning. Wet fish could be delivered fresh in Midlands towns like Birmingham or Derby, which enabled fish and chip shops to start offering their wares throughout the country, where previously the dish had been confined to seaside towns. In Darlington, now connected with the line to London, a new trade had been created. According to the *Great Northern Advertiser*,[13] 'vast numbers of sheep have been slaughtered by the Darlington butchers and have been sent *per* railway to London'. The local 'butter wives', too, were gratified to find that a London dealer had come up to buy 2,000 pounds (900 kg) of their produce, instantly pushing up the price by tuppence per pound. The railway was also a far better way for farmers to take their cattle to market than driving them along roads, which took days, resulting in serious weight loss. A Norfolk farmer reported that as soon as the Eastern Counties railway was opened, he sent his cattle to Smithfield on the train, a journey that took twelve hours rather than a fortnight during which they lost three guineas (63 shillings) in value.

Already by the early 1840s, the advantages of having a rail connection were widely understood and the arrival of the railway was generally seen as beneficial to local people. On the opening of the North Midland railway in 1840, which brought York within easy reach of the capital, the *Sheffield and Rotherham Independent* with an eye to Roses rivalry commented: 'The completion of this vast undertaking which has at last made Yorkshire a sharer in the great advantage of railway communication that Lancashire has for some years enjoyed is no ordinary event. It opens to a million and a half Yorkshiremen a mode of communication with the Midland Counties and the metropolis, such as twenty years ago would have been ridiculed as a Utopian chimera.'[14]

Yet many people and businesses did lose out. Take the village of Hounslow, a dozen miles from the centre of London and a major staging post where 2,000 horses used to be kept in the various inns. By 1842, a local paper reported that in the 'formerly flourishing village of Hounslow . . . so great is the general depreciation of property on account of the transfer of traffic to the railway that at one of the chief inns there was an inscription "new milk and cream sold here"'.[15] The cattle dealers in Southall in Middlesex, barely six miles from London, complained that as more stock could be brought in from further afield by the railway, their prices had been forced down. Maidenhead, further west, had also suffered greatly with the main hostelry, The Bear, once a flourishing inn, closing its doors. In Reading, the Michaelmas Fair traders had suffered: 'When the dairymen had their cheese brought up the old road, they used to load the wagons home with brooms; but now, since the mode of conveyance is changed to the railway, it does not answer the purpose of the dealers to pay the carriage for them.'[16]

There was even the Victorian equivalent of the blight in high streets caused today by out-of-town supermarkets. In Ashton-under-Lyne, Stockport and other nearby towns, shopkeepers were complaining that their customers were going into Manchester to shop. The actual construction of the railways also resulted in much protest from the local residents it displaced. Bringing a railway into town was rather like a slum clearance scheme – 'creative destruction'[17] – as it was inevitably routed through the poorer areas; powerful landowners, and even affluent tenants such as James Watt, were able to ensure that railways did not cross their land.

Although the rail service was becoming well used, by the mid-1840s there was still nothing like a countrywide network, and the capacity of the existing railways was severely constrained with, for example, all traffic for the major towns north of London having to run on a single pair of tracks all the way to Rugby. Given the obvious need for more railways and the rapid impact of the first wave of construction, the lull in building new lines was inevitably short-lived. However, the extent of the second wave of expansion was breathtaking and surprising. The expression 'calm before the storm' does not do justice to the events of the middle of the decade when Parliament was inundated with bills and the whole economy of the country was, it seemed, geared towards constructing more and more railways. While there were previous and subsequent periods of booms in railway promotion, the years 1845–7 are rightly known as the period of the 'railway mania' because of their widespread impact and lasting effect.

# FIVE

# RAILWAYS EVERYWHERE

Like all booms, the railway mania started imperceptibly. By the mid-1840s, investing in the railways had become an attractive proposition once again and schemes for new lines began to be drawn up in every region of the country. The financial climate had changed and there was optimism in the air with an upturn in the economic cycle. Interest rates had plummeted, encouraging people to look for a better rate of return on their savings than from government securities, and by the spring of 1844 there was more money available for railway investment than ever before.[1] Moreover, the value of existing railway shares had begun to grow and naturally this encouraged promoters to bring forward new schemes which would appeal to the large pool of potential investors eager to make capital gains.

However, no one quite expected the stampede to form new railway companies that was to ensue. As the supply of finance appeared almost endless, with more and more people eager to jump on the 'get rich quick' bandwagon, unscrupulous fraudsters entered the fray, pushing schemes whose only aim was to deprive investors of their savings. For example, investors were being sought for schemes whose sole purpose was to pay the bills on previous projects drawn up by the same promoters. While such utterly fraudulent schemes were few, there were many more in which investors lost their money because the economics were as shaky as their prospectuses were woolly. There were, quite literally, schemes for new railways everywhere and promoters were knocking on the doors of Parliament on a daily basis to put forward their plans. The rush to promote new railways had begun relatively slowly with 800 miles authorized in 1844, representing a third of the existing railway's mileage. To put this in perspective, barely fifty miles had been authorized during the six lean years from 1838 to 1843.

The real rush started in the autumn of 1844, the deadline for tabling Bills to be considered in the next parliamentary session. Whereas forty-eight Acts had been passed in 1844, 240 bills were presented to Parliament in 1845 (of which precisely half were sanctioned), representing 2,820 miles, a doubling of the existing network. Had all these railways been built, the capital required – about £100m – represented more than one and a half times the country's gross national product of £59m for that year. There is no equivalent in modern times of such a major investment scheme accounting for so much of a country's economic activity, but perhaps the closest comparison would be the allocation of resources to Britain's defence expenditure during the Second World War.

With a further 3,350 miles authorized the following year, the peak of the boom was reached and the number declined over the next two years until the mania was brought to an abrupt halt not only by its own unsustainability but also as a result of a downturn in the economic climate. Overall, the total mileage authorized for the four years of the railway mania from 1844 to 1847 reached 9,500,[2] which would have needed £250m of capital to build. It represents nearly 90 per cent of today's total route mileage on the UK rail network of 11,000 miles. Historians tend to view much of this 'mania' in negative terms, pointing out that over a third of the mileage authorized in those four years was not built. However, the more pertinent fact is that two thirds of these railways were actually completed within a few years and, indeed, several of the failed schemes were revived and built as a result of the subsequent smaller booms of 1852–3 and the early 1860s. Furthermore, the vast majority of the railways constructed in these years survive today as the backbone of the network.

The process of building this network was haphazard and chaotic, although for a brief period it looked as if Parliament would adopt a more strategic and consistent approach to the process of passing or rejecting railway bills than simply considering each one in isolation. The sheer volume of railway business had begun to overwhelm any other parliamentary business and to address this problem, Gladstone's 1844 Act made provision for an advisory board, under the aegis of the Board of Trade, to consider the merits of railway plans before they reached Parliament. The chairman of the five-strong board was Lord Dalhousie, a skilled administrator who, as India's Governor General, would later be responsible for building the sub-continent's railways through a combination of state planning and private enterprise. Still, the board had only an advisory role because Gladstone had been too fearful of alienating the powerful and seemingly ubiquitous railway interests to insist on stronger regulation. Despite that handicap, the board succeeded in setting out some clear strategies, which led to a modicum of rationality in the railway system and Parliament concurred with the vast majority of its decisions.

The board's remit included rejecting schemes whose primary purpose was to block other more legitimate and viable railways as well as those which seemed to offer little benefit to the public. Moreover, the committee was supposed to discourage unnecessary competition, which was a radical departure from past practice as Parliament had generally supported rival railways battling against each other. Indeed, the laissez-faire ethic of encouraging competition in order to reduce the monopolistic power of the railways prevailed throughout the Victorian era and the board's more sensible approach to the issue of competition was a short-lived outbreak of common sense.

The board's attempt to reconcile the question of whether competition or coordination should be its guiding principle inevitably resulted in contradictions and tortuous language in its reports. For example, while the members argued that existing companies which put forward schemes for contiguous additions to their network should not necessarily be favoured, the board pointed out that incumbents would have a better chance of seeing their scheme through to completion than newer, possibly less financially viable, rivals and therefore should be favoured.

Dalhousie's team delivered measured and sensible decisions on groups of schemes, examining, on a geographical basis, about half the Bills presented to Parliament in the 1844–5 session. Then railway interests, angry at the board's rejection of various schemes, succeeded in forcing its abolition in July 1845. It was 'the one and only successful attempt to establish a body whose function it would be to guide the development of the country's railway system on national lines'.[3] Its abolition was regrettably short-sighted because 'the succeeding years brought only uncertainty, waves of promotion being followed by periods of despondency and an absence of vision on the part of the legislature as to the general lines of development of the railway system'.[4]

London was to be the one exception where a laissez-faire approach could not be allowed to prevail since there were vested interests in the City even more powerful than the railway promoters. With proposals for nineteen urban lines and termini being lodged in Parliament,[5] Lord Dalhousie's considerable administrative talents were transferred to chairing the Royal Commission on Metropolis Railway Termini, which reported in 1846 and essentially created a rectangle around the centre of London through which railway lines were to be banned because of the potential damage to existing buildings. The report's findings put paid to the dream of a unique central London station, spouting out lines in all directions in the tradition of a German *Hauptbahnhof*[6], and instead led to the construction of the Metropolitan and District lines of the Underground system along which nearly all London termini are situated.[7]

Elsewhere, the vagaries of the parliamentary bill process prevailed and a huge back-office industry emerged merely to service the legal and administrative requirements of the massive influx of promoters seeking to push their schemes through Parliament. There were not only the obvious beneficiaries such as lawyers, parliamentary agents and surveyors, some of whom were reportedly earning up to 'fifteen guineas per day',[8] but a host of others who serviced the needs of this railway Klondike. For example, there was a shortage of competent printers to produce the highly decorative engraved share certificates, without which no self-regarding promoter would ever attempt to persuade investors to part with their cash. Therefore engravers were commissioned from across the country, and even from France and Germany, to draw up the elaborate certificates that still adorn thousands of studies (and loos!) today.

Another industry that thrived on the back of the boom, irrespective of whether the schemes came to fruition or not, was the press. At the height of the mania, the leading London papers were earning £12,000–£14,000 per week from the advertisements of railway companies.[9] A specialist press devoted to the railways had also sprung up. By the autumn of 1845, there were no fewer than fifteen weekly railway journals, and even a daily, the *Iron Times*.[10] The most prominent were the *Railway Times*, which claimed a circulation of 27,000 copies in 1842, and the *Railway and Commercial Journal* whose editor-owner, John Herapath, was so forthright in his views that it was known simply as *Herapath's Railway Journal*. The breadth of news on the progress of bills, technical developments and descriptions of schemes was impressive even if, at times, the reliability of the information could be uncertain as owners like Herapath were not averse to speculating in shares themselves.

This press burgeoned thanks to the interest of a new type of railway investor. No longer were the majority of those putting their money into the railways attracted by local promoters holding meetings in public houses to explain their schemes in the hope of exploiting residents' self-interest. This rather quaint method was still the principal way in which promoters initiated schemes, but once they had issued their shares, the certificates were traded in an unprecedented way and the stock market was revolutionized by this huge influx of new railway securities as the volume of dealing soared.

The range of investors[11] was also spreading down the social scale in a way that would have delighted Mrs Thatcher, the Conservative Prime Minister who extended share ownership through the privatization programme of the 1980s. Given that the number of people rich enough to invest was comparatively small, there must have been few members of the upper and middle classes who did not speculate on the railways, many of whom were to lose their money. The clergy, for example, traditionally poor and frugal, were particularly keen, with 257 'Rev' and 'Very Rev' names on the share registers. In fact, all the professions were represented, from 'the physician who perilled the savings of a life and the well-being of a family' to the 'chemist who forsook his laboratory for a new form of the philosopher's stone'.[12] At the other end of the scale, there were the big players, including 900 lawyers and 364 bankers who invested more than £2,000 each (as a broad rule of thumb, these figures can be multiplied by 70 to give some notion of today's values, though this is a very inexact science). One banker subscribed £240,000 while the largest investment risked by a solicitor was £154,000. If one wonders why Parliament was so ready to authorize dubious schemes, the fact that no fewer than 157 MPs (nearly a quarter of the 658 members) declared a financial interest in the railways (one of whom invested £291,000) suggests there was just a hint of self-interest in their decisions over the future of various bills. Indeed, one of the larger railway companies boasted of being able to command a hundred votes in the House of Commons. The Lords were much sought after as figureheads to give respectability to businesses, much as they are today, and one fortunate fellow was a director of no fewer than twenty-three railway companies.

Railway shares became far more sought after than the government securities that had been the staple fare of the big brokers and traders. The relationship between shareholder and promoter became more distant and consequently more fraught with risk. The investor had little to go on other than the often sparse information in the prospectus. Yet the momentum of the boom – just like the South Sea Bubble of the early eighteenth century or the dotcom madness of the late twentieth – swept along people who were in too much of a hurry to consider what they were doing. Dealings in railway securities became the lifeblood of both the London stock exchange and the host of smaller exchanges that had emerged in provincial towns, which frequently sold stock at a premium compared to the price in the capital. Investors in Leeds, according to one contemporary account, were particularly prone to having the wool pulled over their eyes: 'In no town were men more easily duped by the falsehoods which it paid to promulgate. In lines known to be worthless, . . . if a rumour were judiciously spread . . . the Stock Exchange was in a ferment and prices rose enormously, to the loss of the holder when the contradiction came.'[13] Shares in one company which sold in London at £21 were traded in Leeds at £25 10s, according to the same account.

This is the point in the story where it becomes impossible to be comprehensive or to mention any but a small minority of the schemes that were under consideration or being built. Just listing a few of those authorized in 1845 shows the way that the rather sparse network was being filled in and, at times, duplicated. Possibly most important, there was at last to be a connection via Berwick between the English and Scottish railway systems, and no fewer than 423 miles of railway north of the border were sanctioned. Wales, too, which had seen little of the earlier railway expansions, was to get 311 miles,[14] including the long Chepstow to Milford Haven line in the south. A route enabling Manchester to be reached without passing through Birmingham – the Trent Valley line – was approved,[15] as was a new line from London (on broad gauge) to Wolverhampton via Oxford – the Oxford, Worcester & Wolverhampton railway. The start of the Berks & Hants line, which would eventually provide a route from London to Exeter avoiding Bristol, was authorized, as was the beginning of the Bristol & Exeter as far as Yeovil. The Southampton & Dorchester was another major scheme encompassing sixty miles, and Weymouth was also to be reached for the first time by railway.

And so it went on, with 1846 seeing the density of the network increasing in many parts of the country and whole swathes of suburban networks beginning to emerge in south London, Birmingham, Liverpool, Glasgow and Edinburgh, among others. The Cornwall railway was approved to go to Penzance, completed in 1852, and reached Falmouth in 1863. Ireland, an integral part of Great Britain at the time, but still with few railways in 1850, had more than 1,300 miles alone authorized in two years.

Building a railway seemed such a simple task then, no more difficult than opening a grocery store or throwing up a row of houses. It was rather like building a narrow road, and while it was important to ensure that gradients were minimized, technically there was not much else to trouble the promoters: stations, apart from those serving major towns, were simple, often little more than a raised wooden platform; signalling was by time interval; and maintenance was minimal, and carried out by poorly paid staff. The average cost of building a railway in the 1840s has been calculated[16] at just £31,000 per mile – say around £2m in today's money.

Take, as a small example, the seven-mile-long Gravesend & Rochester Railway,[17] initiated by the Thames & Medway Canal Company in early 1844, which started operating within a year of the idea first being mooted. After a contractor had put forward the idea of turning the canal towpath into a railway, the company decided to do the work itself and commissioned John Rastrick, who had built various lines including the Stratford & Moreton Railway, to be the engineer. While running the line along the towpath was straightforward, the canal entered a two-mile tunnel at Strood and the proposed solution was to put the line on timber supports across the water, leaving just enough space for navigation. This Heath Robinson-like solution was accepted by the Board of Trade, even though the trains passed so near the wall of the tunnel that grilles had to be placed over the carriage windows to prevent passengers seeking a breath of fresh air from being beheaded.

Work had progressed so fast that the company reckoned it could start running trains as early as September but extra safety requirements required by the Board delayed the opening until February 1845. With three locomotives, the company ran six trains a day in each direction, at a fare of 8d (3.3p) and 1 shilling (5p) for second and first class respectively, including a steamer trip between Rochester and Chatham. But the fares proved too expensive and they were reduced a month later, with the result that passengers flocked to the railway, which then expanded its service from six to twenty trains per day. Even the importance of integrated transport seems to have been recognized as half the trains had horse omnibus connections on to Maidstone.[18]

While such small schemes were being put forward and built around the country during this frenetic period of activity, there were also, at the other end of the scale, massive enterprises that would take many years to complete. One of the largest was the construction of the Woodhead tunnel on the Sheffield, Ashton-under-Lyne & Manchester Railway, giving a second route through the Pennines to rival the Manchester–Leeds route. The tunnel was three miles long, took six years to build, and was one of the worst projects in terms of loss of life – at least thirty-two navvies were killed in accidents during its construction, possibly more, and there were 140 serious injuries.

On the other hand, there was a whole host of schemes that were, quite rightly, rejected because they were put forward on the most spurious grounds and their prospectuses were so blatantly misleading or dishonest that the parliamentarians could not fail to do their duty and throw them out. Adrian Vaughan cites the 'Somersetshire Midland' from Frome to Shepton Mallet, Glastonbury and Highbridge which, according to the prospectus, had 'the peculiar advantage . . . that the greater portion of it will be perfectly level'. Vaughan acidly points out that 'perhaps one third could have been level, but the rest would have been very steep as it climbed on to and through the Mendips'.[19] Worse, a competing company appeared, proposing the Bridgwater, Frome & Central Somerset Railway on a route which was said to possess 'every facility for railway construction', whatever that meant. Neither of these survived the parliamentary process, or were ever built.

This deliberate ignoring of topography was particularly noticeable in the brief fashion for putting forward 'direct' railways, as if simply giving a railway that appellation automatically shortened the route. The concept seemed to be based on the fallacy that it was best to avoid any intervening towns even if they were a good source of potential traffic. In September 1845, for example, investors were invited to put up money for the 'Direct Great Western' which would go from Reading 'as near as possible [in] a straight line to Land's End', ignoring the fact that no one lived at the westernmost point of Britain or particularly wanted to go there. Plans for a 'Harwich, Oxford and Bristol Direct' and a 'Cheltenham, Oxford, Brighton Direct' seemed equally far-fetched and unrealistic as they linked relatively modest towns already served by the railway.

While many fanciful schemes were proposed, there were remarkably few completely unviable railways built during this period. There were certainly some which seemed destined never to attract much traffic, such as the connection from Blisworth on the West Coast line to Peterborough via Northampton, which inevitably succumbed under Beeching. However, the marginal or utterly misconceived railways would mostly come later in the century when the potentially profitable routes had been fully exploited and entrepreneurs were still desperate to wring a few extra pounds out of gullible investors. In fact, most of the schemes built in the period were sensible and one in particular stands out – the Great Northern – providing a second line linking London with the north and finally relieving the bottleneck between Euston and Rugby which, until then, carried all traffic heading north out of London. There had been schemes for a railway running north from

London to the east of the existing line ever since the completion of the Stockton & Darlington, even predating what is now the West Coast route, created by the amalgamation of the Grand Junction and the London & Birmingham.[20] The East Coast was a natural route for a railway to Scotland, effectively following the long-established Great North Road, but all those early plans had come to naught. The plans were revived by Edmund Denison, a Yorkshire MP and QC, who used his legal skills to put the case for the Great Northern in Parliament and who was to dominate the management of the railway in its early years.

The Great Northern was the subject of the biggest battle fought in Parliament over a single railway – and with good reason. It was the longest single line approved by Parliament, comprising 188 miles between London and York, as well as a large loop into Lincolnshire and a few smaller branches. It was obvious that such a key trunk route would be a major part of the nation's infrastructure for generations to come. The Great Northern was also the last of the major companies to be created and therefore was opposed as a latecoming upstart by the existing railways, notably the Midland, which were enjoying a monopoly of traffic.

Even before the start of the railway mania, the larger companies had become significant players who controlled much of the existing railway and were often able to dominate their smaller neighbours. In 1844, a mere eleven companies controlled half the mileage while the rest was split between no fewer than ninety-two other concerns – an average of a mere twelve miles each – and as we will see in the next chapter, the trend towards domination by the bigger ones strengthened. Despite the emergence of many new companies, thereby increasing the overall number, a process of consolidation was inevitable. Since the larger railways were able to raise capital for expansion more easily, they had, quite literally, an established track record,[21] and would build on this dominant position. They not only had the best-situated railways, linking major towns where passenger traffic was always going to be greatest, but their infrastructure was in better condition and their engineering standards higher.

At the outset of this spurt in growth of railway mileage – that would see 4,128 miles added to the network in the eight years following the start of the mania – the biggest was the Great Western with 230 miles, precisely the same length as the two principal railways operating on the West Coast route, the London & Birmingham and the Grand Junction (amalgamated as the London & North Western in 1846). The Midland, created in 1844 by the amalgamation of the three railways – the North Midland, Midland Counties and Birmingham & Derby Junction – which converged at Derby, putting paid to the crazy competition there, was the second largest. Amalgamations had been resisted by Parliament – or how else to explain the existence in 1844 of more than one hundred railways for a mileage of 2,235 – but the logic behind the creation of the Midland, the first significant rationalization of the railway network, was irrefutable. The merger provided the central section of a railway that stretched from London to York using the London & Birmingham until Rugby, and at the northern end from Normanton, the York & North Midland, a railway which enjoyed friendly relations with the Midland since it had the same chairman, George Hudson.

Hudson was the dominant railway figure of the period, the first of the big railway barons who emerged as the railway companies expanded, and, according to many railway historians, the greatest, despite the faults and misdeeds that were to prove his undoing. He was not, like the Stephensons with whom he was associated, an engineer, but an entrepreneur and investor – and ultimately a liar and a crook who had a particular dislike of producing accurate financial figures for the enterprises he controlled. He earned the comment from one contemporary wit that he 'became rich by keeping everything but his accounts',[22] and was helped by the fact that the law placed minimal requirements on companies to produce accounts in a standardized form; effectively the directors were free to spin the shareholders whatever tale was likely to keep them happy.

A farmer's son from Yorkshire, Hudson, benefiting from a family bequest of the considerable amount of £30,000, bought himself political prominence in York where he became the Tory Lord Mayor in 1837. He was generous with the town's money, throwing lavish banquets that earned him many political favours that he would later exploit and at which 'so much gas was burnt that the York Gas Company elected him a director out of sheer gratitude'.[23] Hudson was the driving force behind the promotion and construction of the thirty-two-mile York & North Midland Railway, which was completed in 1839. The following year it became part of the growing trunk route network connecting York with London when its southern neighbour, the North Midland, opened and Hudson took advantage of the slump in railway share prices to gain a controlling interest, becoming its chairman. He gave himself the title of chairman of the various companies he dominated but in practice he wielded dictatorial power as the rest of the directors were usually too starry-eyed to notice that Hudson's methods were frequently dishonest. He treated these businesses as his personal fiefdom and his ability to accumulate so much power so quickly within the railways demonstrated that the money men of the City, rather than local mercantile interests, were beginning to control the industry.

It is unclear whether Hudson's early success with the York & North Midland, where he quickly turned deficits into profits, was based on genuine commercial activity or whether it was merely his particular brand of 'creative accounting', a term that could have been invented for him. However, even if he did start off honestly, his *modus operandi* soon became utterly corrupt. His method was to put forward a range of proposals for new railways and amalgamations with the ultimate intention of creating a controlled monopoly. He was a wheeler-dealer *sine qua non*, who promoted new railways, bought out existing ones at bargain prices and, having become an MP, used his political position to push his interests and destroy those of his rivals. At one point he was reputed to be walking around Parliament seeking support for no fewer than sixteen bills and it was hardly surprising that he soon became known as the 'Railway King'.

All that may have been just about above board and within the norms of the way business and politics were conducted at the time, but his method of attracting investors crossed the threshold into illegality. To show how well his existing companies were performing, dividends were paid out of new capital, a practice that, amazingly, was not unlawful, but was clearly unsustainable – and, worse, Hudson creamed off investors' money for his own use. Indeed, personal aggrandizement went hand in hand with his ambitions for the railway. He manipulated the shares of his various companies, disposed of his own land to the railways at inflated prices, bought railway equipment on the cheap and then sold it at a profit to his own railways, and tried whenever possible not to pay his debts.

Exploiting the power and prestige accorded to him by his position at the Midland, Hudson expanded his influence rapidly. The Midland was a heavily used railway that had a pivotal role in the network and was therefore ripe for expansion and alliances with neighbours in all directions. The Midland's potential became apparent when Hudson's Newcastle & Darlington Railway opened on 18 June 1844, creating a rapid connection between London and the north-east. Even with the necessity of changing engines at Rugby, where the Midland's territory started, the celebratory inaugural train took just nine and a half hours to travel the rather circuitous route to Newcastle from Euston – a mere quarter of the time that a stagecoach covered the journey in good weather. As well as the Midland, Hudson controlled both the York & North Midland (whose generous dividends of 20 per cent per annum shrank to virtually nothing after his demise) and the York, Newcastle & Berwick, which had won the right to link England with Scotland as it would join the Edinburgh & Berwick at the border town. Therefore Hudson used his considerable deal-making talent to good effect by ensuring that he would have control of the railways which eventually linked England and Scotland on the East Coast.

The other major railway to fall under his influence was the Eastern Counties. Impressed by Hudson's burgeoning political power as well as his record of turning around the finances of railways – but ignorant of his financial shenanigans – the directors of several other railways invited him to join them on the board, invariably as chairman since he would accept nothing less. Thus, rather like a successful football manager being approached by a failing club to improve the performance of their team, in October 1845 Hudson was asked to take over as chairman of the Eastern Counties. It was a struggling railway, serving East Anglia, an agricultural area with few sizeable centres of population, and therefore had struggled even to complete its authorized route from London to Yarmouth, let alone pay any reasonable dividends. Although the Eastern Counties had only reached Colchester and therefore needed funds for completion, he immediately impressed the shareholders by tripling their half-yearly dividends from 2 per cent to 6 per cent without bothering to produce the accounts that merited such largesse. Subsequent investigation showed that Hudson had obtained £145,000 by manipulating the accounts, £205,000 had been charged to capital instead of revenue and he had consequently paid out £515,000 in dividends when only £225,000 was available. He kept paying dividends of 4 per cent over the next couple of years but after his resignation early in 1849 barely anything was paid for the subsequent four years. And why had his fellow directors acquiesced to such unsavoury practice? Because, they told the subsequent parliamentary inquiry, whenever they started to object to his decisions, he would threaten to resign!

Hudson had had his own reasons for wanting to control the Eastern Counties. He saw its development as a potential alternative to the putative Great Northern for linking London with the North, and came up with various routes to try to block his rival's progress through Parliament. The Bill for Denison's London–York Direct railway, the precursor of the Great Northern, had fallen in the 1845 parliamentary session, partly because of bickering with a rival scheme called the Direct Northern, but when the two were merged the following year, permission for what was destined to be Britain's premier main line route between London and Scotland was at last obtained. Not surprisingly, the Great Northern had been fiercely opposed, too, by the London & North Western which still retained a monopoly on traffic heading north from London, since the Midland used its rails up to Rugby. The cost was to be £5.6m, the largest sum raised for a railway, and the legal fees, too, had been the most expensive ever: £630,000, or 12.5 per cent of the capital, as a result of the protracted opposition. The route was from King's Cross to York, via Hatfield, Peterborough and Doncaster with a large loop, right into Hudson territory, taking in Boston and Lincoln, rejoining the main line just south of Doncaster. Hudson had tried unsuccessfully to use his position with Eastern Counties to put forward an alternative scheme which would have gone from London (Bishopsgate, which was then its terminus) via Ely and Lincoln to York, but the idea never got off the ground. As O. S. Nock, the doyen of railway writers, puts it: 'Hudson, by protocols straight and devious, flamboyant and insulting rhetoric, strove might and main to black it at every stage in the Parliamentary procedure – and afterwards.'[24] It is no exaggeration to say that these power battles at the height of the railway mania determined the shape of the nation's railways for ever. The Great Northern's route to York, Hudson's home base, was thirty miles shorter than the alternative using the Midland via Rugby, and inevitably the go-ahead for the Great Northern in 1846 spelt Hudson's doom, though he would hang on for another three years.

Like its predecessors, the Great Northern struggled given the huge capital outlay required and the shortage of labour. This was the height of the building boom on the railways with 200,000 men working on their construction around the country. There was a shortage of manpower but work started relatively quickly on the line, which was opened in stages between 1848 and 1852. It was actually Hudson's response to the imminent arrival of the Great Northern that precipitated his downfall because his behaviour exposed the conflict of interest between the various railways he controlled. With the Great Northern eager to save the cost of building its authorized line right into the centre of York, Hudson foolishly agreed to a request from his erstwhile rival for running rights over the tracks of the York & North Midland,[25] which was great business for that railway but a disaster for the Midland with its longer route. The author of the principal history of the period points out the clear anomaly: 'How Hudson could have reconciled his own position as chairman of all three companies when the policy of two [the York & North Midland and the York, Newcastle & Berwick, which also benefited from the shorter route to London] of them was directly opposed to the interests of the third and largest company is a mystery only to be explained by his overweening confidence in his own power to extricate himself from any position in railway affairs, however impossible.'[26]

After a power struggle, Hudson was forced to resign the chairmanship of the Midland and the house of cards began to collapse. Soon after, at a shareholders' meeting of his original railway, the York and North Midland, rather more incisive questions than normal were asked into the precise nature of the company's accounts. Hudson was no great public speaker at the best of times and his bluster for once carried no weight as he tried to explain the anomalies in the accounts that had various noughts added to them randomly and which later showed he had appropriated 11,000 Newcastle & Berwick shares fraudulently. The bubble had burst and with similar questioning at meetings of the Eastern Counties and his other companies, his downfall was amazingly rapid. The establishment of a committee of inquiry by Parliament found that he had 'abused the confidence that was placed in him by wielding the power he obtained to forward his own interest'.[27] It was the Enron scandal of its day: the accounts of the various companies were in such a muddle that it was impossible to unravel them. After the parliamentary inquiry had found against him, he was charged with bribing MPs and embezzling £600,000 from his own companies, and was briefly imprisoned for debt. He fled to Paris where he lived in poverty, only returning to Britain just before his death in 1871.

At his peak in 1849, Hudson controlled 1,450 miles out of the railway's total mileage of 5,000, but if the aim was to create a unified national railway, he failed, since the network he controlled was rather a hotchpotch. Its spine was a route linking Newcastle with Bristol, but with the route through to London and the terminus at St Pancras not completed until much later, it was clearly 'work in progress' when his career was brought to its abrupt halt. Amazingly, he survived the end of the mania and the start of the collapse in share values, but once he had lost the battle to stop the Great Northern cutting through the heart of his territory it became impossible to maintain the pretence that all his various companies were profitable.

Hudson is often denigrated as more of a crook than a railway pioneer, but this is too harsh a verdict on a man who understood the importance of melding the haphazard collection of railways into an integrated whole. He was a visionary who saw the potential of running trains, both goods and passenger, across the country, and understood the need to standardize equipment and modernize operating methods. At the height of his fame, he was the guest of prime ministers and royalty, and his large mansion in Kensington, scene of countless social events, became a regular haunt of the great and good. The fairest summary is given by railway historian Jack Simmons: 'His financial chicanery is indefensible, and that met its proper reward. Along with it went a true vision of the weaknesses of the railways of his time and his understanding of the means to repair them.'[28] Hudson's name still hangs over a railway office in York, a recognition of his contribution to the industry.

With the network now consisting of a dozen large companies and ninety others, it was essential to create a mechanism for collecting and distributing income in order to prevent people having to get off trains to purchase new tickets when their journey took them across a company boundary. Hudson had strongly supported the creation of the Railway Clearing House, an idea put forward by the London & Birmingham, and 'without his co-operation, it would not have been possible'.[29]

The Railway Clearing House was launched at a meeting of representatives of nine major companies held near Euston in January 1842. Until its creation, rival companies caused each other – and their passengers – all kinds of complications. Some would not even accept the carriages of 'foreign' companies while others shunned third-class passengers by only accepting second-class tickets from rival railways on their trains. In the worst cases, through booking was simply not possible. The purpose of establishing the clearing house went beyond merely enabling passengers to buy one ticket to cover their whole journey. The huge team of clerks that quickly assembled to deal with this enormous administrative task also allocated the income from such tickets and ensured that inter-company debts were settled. The clearing house had a role in goods traffic too, with the establishment of a group of number-takers – a breed of early professional trainspotters, as it were – who checked on the numbers and contents of goods wagons travelling beyond their own companies' borders so that the right track charges could be applied.

One by-product of the creation of the Railway Clearing House was the standardization of the ticketing system. Obvious ideas are sometimes, well, just too obvious, once someone comes up with them. Tickets had hitherto been little more than scraps of paper made out by hand. Now an enterprising clerk, Thomas Edmondson, a Quaker, appalled at the ease with which company money was expropriated by dishonest ticket office staff (the information on the paper was not necessarily reconciled in the station accounts), earned his name in railway history by suggesting that tickets be numbered consecutively, thereby facilitating accounting and preventing fraud. He also devised a system of serially numbered and dated card tickets ready to be sold to passengers which initially he produced himself on a simple wooden printing frame. His system was quickly adopted by most British railways and he was rewarded handsomely with a royalty of 10 shillings (50p) per route mile. Edmondson tickets became the norm for railway networks across the world and lasted in Britain for 150 years, until the advent of computer-generated tickets in 1990.[30]

Another side effect of the establishment of the clearing house was faster progress towards the standardization of time. Until the advent of the railways, towns across Britain kept their own time, based on the sunrise, and travellers would have to adjust their watches gradually as their journey took them east or west. Plymouth, for example, was twenty minutes earlier than London but this hardly mattered for a passenger on a stagecoach which had taken twenty-two hours to cover the distance. Even railways operating over relatively short distances as a shuttle service could get away without bothering too much about the discrepancy, but once a network built up with a far more complicated timetable, it was essential that the time be standardized throughout its workings. The Great Western, for whom the problem was most apparent since it was an east–west railway, determined in 1841 that trains should operate on Greenwich Mean Time, except that Reading would be four minutes earlier, Chippenham eight and Bristol and Bath fourteen. That was pretty confusing for passengers and not surprisingly there were various accounts in the newspapers of people left stranded at obscure junctions because they had missed the train. Adherence to the timetable was made even more arbitrary by the fact that drivers on the London & Birmingham were injuncted to pull out of stations three minutes after the scheduled departure.

As early as 1845, Henry Booth, still the secretary of the Liverpool & Manchester, suggested that all trains should run to the time kept at the Royal Greenwich Observatory which had been founded by Charles II in 1675, but his proposal to Parliament was defeated. However, as the network grew and the introduction of the electric telegraph enabled time signals to be transmitted instantaneously, the case for standard-ization proved unanswerable. The Railway Clearing House kept lobbying for standardization and the Great Western, to set an example, unified its time in 1852 and most other railways quickly followed. 'London' or 'railway' time, the usual name for Greenwich Mean Time, then began to be adopted on the growing number of clocks erected by local authorities and in shops as well as by the railways themselves. In effect, the railways created the beginnings of the regimented and time-driven society which is now prevalent throughout the developed world. However, it was not until 1880 that the standard time became enshrined in law with the passage of the clumsily named Statutes (Definition of Time) Act. British railways were to have lasting worldwide influence when in 1884, at an international conference in Washington DC, it was agreed that Greenwich should be the zero meridian.

The railway mania bubble burst because ultimately it was based on little more than optimism feeding on itself. When investors realized that the future was not necessarily paved with gold, collapse was inevitable. There was no single event that precipitated the change in climate, but probably as early as October 1845, when the Bank of England raised interest rates, the cannier investors were beginning to cash in their shares and the price curve first levelled out and then turned relentlessly downwards. The sheer breadth of holdings, however, initially stalled the pace of the downturn. Everyone seemed to own railway shares. A caricature in *Punch* magazine even had Queen Victoria asking her husband if he owned any shares, and in Yorkshire, Emily and Anne Brontë had ignored the warnings of their sister Charlotte and invested their small savings in Hudson's York & North Midland Railway.

Consequently, when things went wrong, the effect was universal among the upper echelons of society. A contemporary chronicler reckoned 'no other panic was ever so fatal to the middle class . . . There was scarcely an important town in England what [sic] beheld some wretched suicide. It reached every hearth, it saddened every heart in the metropolis . . . Daughters delicately nurtured went out to seek their bread. Sons were recalled from academies. Households were separated; homes were desecrated by the emissaries of the law.'[31] While there is no small measure of Victorian hyperbole in this account, it demonstrates quite clearly that the middle classes invested far more in the railways than in goods such as cotton or corn which tended to be traded only by professional investors and speculators.

There may have been a range of newspapers covering the railway industry, but there was nothing like the availability of information in today's computer age. Therefore there was no immediate panic as the price of stock began to go down as a result of the higher interest rates, but the process was steady and irreversible. Against an index value of 100 in 1840, railway shares had risen to 149 at the peak when interest rates rose and then fell back to 95.5 by 1848 and to 70.4 two years later. In other words, people had seen the value of their holdings fall by a third, while the least fortunate, who had put their money into failed schemes, lost everything. As ever, there was no shortage of insider dealers who knew when to get out while the average punters – for that is what they were – suffered disproportionately. The public turned their anger on the lawyers who benefited from schemes whatever their success and who had tried to maintain the bonanza by promoting schemes themselves. To cap it all, the lawyers then profited even more from the complex litigation which arose out of failed schemes since there were no guidelines on how to dissolve a bankrupt railway company and disburse any remaining assets.

Although the collapse was deeply damaging both to the railways and the overall economy, the vagaries of investment in the railway industry cannot be blamed for the economic downturn of the late 1840s. It was not so much the internal contradictions of the railway mania which brought about its end, but rather the deterioration in the rest of the economy. The railways had not been the only beneficiaries of unwise investments. Early in 1847, with the Corn Laws abolished, the price of corn began to rise; then in May, when the speculative bubble burst, it fell by 40 per cent over a few days. Banks who had lent on the basis of the high prices were in trouble and both dealers and their bankers quickly started going bankrupt. Interest rates doubled from 3.5 per cent in January to 7 per cent in May and reached 10 per cent in November. This not only killed off any speculative potential for railway shares but also threw the economy into depression. The collapse of the mania, therefore, was not so much the cause of the downturn but rather one of its consequences, intensified by the changes brought about by the repeal of the Corn Laws.

It is easy to exaggerate the damaging aspects of the mania because they affected so many people, but in the long term the positive consequences outweigh the negative. As we saw in the last chapter, the railway network in 1843 was insufficiently developed and had not yet become a national system that could cater for the burgeoning economy and rising living standards. It needed expansion and while the mania might have resulted in over-rapid growth, there had been many gaps to fill. While clearly some unviable schemes were promoted during that period, that does not diminish the contribution of the mania in creating a vital part of Britain's infrastructure which survives to this day. Indeed, the very fact that virtually the entire network of main line railways, with the notable exception of what became the Great Central, had been authorized by the end of the period tends to suggest that, arbitrary as the process appears in hindsight, it did deliver a largely coherent network of railways. While the promotion of new schemes ground to a halt by 1850, there were still a lot of lines under construction well into the 1850s.

The scale of the railway mania can be illustrated by a simple statistic: by 1847 investment in the railways represented 6.7 per cent of all national income. As a result, the 1840s saw the biggest mileage ever added to the railway network of any decade before or after – an extraordinary 4,600 miles. Just to put that achievement in perspective, consider how in recent years it has taken nearly a decade of construction and twice that long in gestation to build a mere sixty-seven miles of high-speed line between St Pancras and the Channel Tunnel. Moreover, the mania, the rather unfair name given to this fantastic period in British engineering, paved the way for a new hierarchy in the industry that would prevail for the next century, until nationalization in 1948.

# SIX

# THE BIG COMPANIES: GREAT BUT NOT NECESSARILY GOOD

By the early 1850s, with more than 5,000 miles of the railways completed, the large companies were in an even more dominant position, thanks to Hudson's consolidation and other mergers. The overall influence of these large railway companies can be underestimated if mileage alone is taken into account, since they often controlled smaller local concerns, either through unlimited running rights or by setting the charges for access to their tracks. Railways are inherently regional, which meant the operations of these large concerns were mostly self-contained, but that did not prevent considerable fighting over territory in the swathes of country between their main lines, often resulting in unnecessary parallel routes being built to protect their monopoly.

By 1854, two thirds of the lines that were to form British Rail's InterCity network – its main line spine – had been built and the biggest gaps were in the further corners of the United Kingdom: Wales, the Highlands, the Pennines north of Skipton, north Norfolk and Lincolnshire. The suburban network around London was then in embryonic form and few of the commuter lines from the south-east into the capital had been built. Indeed, commuting by rail had not yet become widespread, as evidenced by the fact that the average passenger arriving at Euston had travelled sixty-four miles, the equivalent of more than half the journey from Birmingham. The provincial cities had only their main lines, rather than the host of smaller routes which surround them today, and there were few of the branches whose construction would see the mileage of railway doubled over the next twenty years. There were, too, a few competitive routes, or, to put it another way, duplication, especially on services between London and the Midlands and the north, that would be the focus of much of the bigger companies' attention over forthcoming years.

All the big companies were flexing their muscles and expanding. During the mania and its immediate aftermath, the Great Western, still with its broad gauge, had grown through expansion, notably up to Birmingham and the Black Country. The Midland, with 434 miles, had more mileage, but it was not a coherent network; and the Great Northern, blessed with a relatively easy topography, had quickly emerged as a major player when its line opened in 1849, running between Maiden Lane, its temporary southern terminus just north of King's Cross, and York via a meandering route through Lincolnshire.[1] In Scotland and in the south of England, the position was less clear-cut, with, in each case, four major railways beginning to emerge. The dominant company of that period was the London & North Western Railway, created in 1846 by the inevitable merger of the two companies which made up the first 200 miles of the West Coast main line: the London & Birmingham and the Grand Junction, which included the pioneering Liverpool & Manchester that had been taken over the previous year.

The London & North Western may not have been much bigger than its rivals in terms of mileage, but thanks to the importance of its lines it was 'the prototype of the arrogant, self-sufficient, lordly railway company'[2] whose offices were, suitably, housed in the grandeur of Euston with its elegant double staircase and huge classical hall. The company was the big bruiser of the railways, throwing its weight around to intimidate smaller local neighbours as well as its larger competitors on the routes between London and the north. Charles Dickens sounded almost in awe of the London & North Western when he described the company in his weekly journal *Household Words*[3] as being 'wealthier than any other corporation in the world', a status it retained for a couple of decades. Indeed, its value was greater than the capital of the East India Company and the railway carried more people every year than the whole population of Scotland, netting an income greater than that of the entire canal network.

The London & North Western built up its enormous power thanks to its monopoly of traffic between London and the north which lasted until 1850. Even after the company's fierce battle to prevent the building of the Great Northern had ended in failure and the latter started running from Maiden Lane, the London & North Western still maintained its advantageous position because its lines connected Birmingham and Manchester with London by shorter routes than those of its rivals. It was also helped by the talent of its general manager, Captain Mark Huish, who was both a very able traffic manager (a relatively new skill that was increasingly necessary as the lines were filling up with trains) and a brilliant negotiator in dealings with other railway companies. Brought up in Nottingham, he served ten years with the Bengal Native Army, the precursor to the Indian Army, and then became secretary of the small, twenty-two-mile-long Glasgow Paisley & Greenock Railway, one of the earliest railways to serve the outlying towns and villages of a major city. After four years in the job he was poached by the Grand Junction Railway and he successfully negotiated the merger that created the London & North Western.

Railway companies, despite their size, were still pretty crude affairs and the model of a business firm, as we know it today, with departments headed by directors and a board of management, was only starting to develop. Huish introduced novel forms of accountancy and management systems that were to be widely imitated in the future, both within and beyond the railway industry. He encouraged the use of the rail network at night for mail and goods trains, thus relieving congestion in the day and making better use of the railway's assets. As his biographer Terry Gourvish puts it, 'the experience of Huish and his company marks an important chapter in the development not only of railways but also of business management practice as a whole'.[4] Huish was one of the first of a new generation of managers who were not engineers but were appointed for their administrative skills as railways became far more complex organizations.

Like Hudson, Huish favoured monopolies, seeing competition as an unnecessary diversion from the task of building up the railway business through the steady accumulation of capital resulting from high profitability. Under Huish, therefore, the London & North Western was an aggressive company which sought to take over, bypass or crush its rivals using various tactics, such as below-cost fares, the building of new railways or simply trying to bully them into submission with threats. For example, when two railways combined to run a service between Birmingham and Chester using a shorter and therefore cheaper route than its bigger rival's existing line, Huish wrote a letter to the secretary of one of the railways, the Shrewsbury & Chester, in tones that would have done an Italian godfather proud: 'I need not say if you should be unwise enough to encourage such a proceeding [the operation of the service] it must result in a general fight . . .'[5] When the Shrewsbury & Chester refused to back down, Huish lost his temper, immediately closing that railway's booking office at Chester station, which was jointly owned by the two companies, and ordering the hapless booking clerk to be thrown out along with his tickets. Legal agreements over the onward carriage of traffic from Chester to Merseyside were broken and a price war ensued. However, like many bullies faced by courageous opponents prepared to stand up to them, Huish lost. A three-year court case resulted in defeat for the London & North Western and the two companies made matters worse for Huish by soon merging with the Great Western, creating a rival through route to Liverpool.

For the most part, however, the Goliath was victorious in these squabbles and the London & North Western grew through acquisition in the 1850s, taking over several neighbouring railways after making similar threats. However, while the company's income increased dramatically, nearly doubling during the decade, its profitability was reduced because of growing competition and the fact that it was forced into acquiring or building marginal railways that were loss-making.

Huish's desire to limit competition led him to be the driving force behind the establishment of a cartel of the eight railways operating on the Anglo-Scottish routes. This 'Octuple' arrangement, introduced in April 1851, created a complex fares pooling system that involved companies sharing their revenue and allocating it on the basis of mileage covered, once expenses had been deducted. However, it was short-lived as a result of the desire of some members to maximize their share of the huge business generated by the Great Exhibition which opened the following month in London.

The Great Exhibition marked a turning point in the public's attitude towards the railways, helping them overcome the stigma they had suffered as a result of the mania and its collapse. The brainchild of Queen Victoria's husband, Prince Albert, the Exhibition was conceived to celebrate Britain's technological progress and, especially, its dominant position in the world. This 'somewhat arrogant parading of accomplishments'[6] was the first ever international exhibition and was intended to be a major tourist attraction luring visitors from both home and abroad. Early in the planning process, the organizers realized that the railways would play a key role in transporting the millions of visitors needed to make the exhibition viable. The 13,000 exhibits were housed in a huge glass building, dubbed the Crystal Palace,[7] erected in London's Hyde Park. Over six months it attracted a staggering 6,200,000 people (a third of the population of England and Wales),[8] including 110,000 on the busiest day. The whole nation was gripped by Exhibition fever and entire towns and villages would form 'Exhibition clubs' which organized excursion trains up to the capital – for many, their first-ever train journey. People came from abroad, too, though not as many as had been expected, mostly travelling by train and steamship. The South Eastern had arranged a package deal with its partner on the other side of the Channel, La Compagnie du Chemin de Fer du Nord, but complained that the fares imposed by the French company were too high.

The railway companies, initially slow to appreciate the import of the Exhibition business, soon realized that it could be a money-spinner and started organizing special services to the capital. At first they had tried to stick to the Octuple agreement under which they all charged the same fares, but cheap rates offered by steamship companies between Hull and London forced the Great Northern to cut its prices, sparking off a war with its rivals, the Midland and the London & North Western. Soon they responded by offering return fares to London from Leeds or Sheffield for just 5s (a third of the going rate before the price war) and the Great Northern trumped them by promising a John Lewis type 'Never knowingly undersold' deal of 6d less than any other railway offered. Despite the collapse of the cartel arrangements, the railways profited from the Exhibition and the London & North Western, as the largest railway, carried more visitors than any of its rivals. Huish reported that his railway had taken three quarters of a million people in and out of London during the period of the Exhibition, 90,000 of whom had travelled in 145 excursion trains and the rest on its normal scheduled services.

While this influx of visitors helped boost the profitability of the various railways, there was a more important longer-term effect: the efficiency with which they carried these millions of visitors to London and back greatly improved the public's perception of the companies. Without the railways, the Exhibition would never have attracted the volume of visitors or had such a deep and long-lasting impact. The railways had helped to create this huge popular festival which did much to give Britain its sense of identity following the troubled first half of the century. Indeed, the very term 'Victorian' began to be used around this time.

With the Great Exhibition, excursion trains and the expansion of the network into the nooks and crannies of rural England, a mere quarter of a century after the opening of the Liverpool & Manchester, train travel had become commonplace. In 1854, 92 million journeys were made in England and Wales on a network of around 6,000 miles (which demonstrates nevertheless that the intensity of use was far less than today when over a billion journeys are taken on a system of just under twice the size). By then, virtually every town of any significance in England had been connected to the network, the major exceptions were Luton, Hereford, Yeovil and Weymouth, which would all soon get their stations. The importance of a delay in connection to the network can be shown by the fate of Norwich, which was the ninth biggest city in England at the 1831 census but had fallen to thirteenth ten years later, partly as a result of having no rail connection until 1845. Shrewsbury is a good reverse example, showing how a town that had good railway services could be transformed. Shrewsbury had lost its traditional flannel manufacture to nearby Welshpool and Newtown, but quickly recovered by exploiting its position as a railway centre with the establishment of a major carriage works which, by the 1880s, was producing thirty vehicles per week.

While the railways stood in greater esteem after 1851, that was not enough for the parliamentarians to give them what their leaders, such as Huish, wanted – a monopoly over the areas they controlled or at least the opportunity to rationalize the industry to consolidate their dominant position. Huish's plan was to merge with both the Midland and a smaller but highly profitable railway, the North Staffordshire. The latter demonstrated that companies did not have to be big or connected with London to make a profit during this period: serving the Potteries with 112 miles of route and centred on Stoke, the North Staffordshire linked at various points such as Derby and Crewe with its larger neighbours, the Midland and the London & North Western, ensuring a healthy level of traffic. Huish wanted to gain control of the railway to give him a short cut to Manchester. However the Knotty – so named because the badge of the railway was a Staffordshire knot – managed to resist both his blandishments and his aggression, and even had the cheek to propose an alliance with the Great Western that would siphon off some of Huish's traffic. Thanks to its steadfastness, the Knotty in fact survived as an independent railway until the amalgamation of 1923.

The London & North Western's merger with the Midland would have been an altogether different proposition given the latter's enormous but rather uncoordinated network. The Midland, whose very name was a misnomer since its lines extended well beyond the Midlands, had survived the departure of Hudson but the railway had not profited from the Exhibition like its rivals because it lacked direct access to London. Of the two possible solutions – building its own line through to the capital or merging with a company that already had one – the second seemed the easier option for the directors who were in something of a panic after the poor 1851 results. The London & North Western and the Great Northern were approached in turn, and both were somewhat lukewarm, but the following year Huish warmed to the idea and a Bill for the amalgamation was tabled in Parliament. Here again, the opportunity to create a more rational and integrated railway system was lost. Parliament stalled in its usual way by appointing a committee, chaired by Edward Cardwell, a prominent Liberal who later became Secretary of State for War under Gladstone, to examine the issue.

Despite hearing evidence from many senior figures in the industry who were in favour of the amalgamation, after much prevarication the committee effectively ruled against a merger and the Bill was thrown out by MPs in 1854. So too was a plan to merge the various East Anglian railways which, serving a poor and sparsely populated area, were always impoverished and underinvested. Eventually, however, with the threat of bankruptcy looming, they were finally allowed to create the Great Eastern Railway in 1862.

The thrust of the committee's reports had been rather contradictory, setting out both the advantages and disadvantages of amalgamation, and another merger, the creation of the North Eastern Railway from three separate railways centred around York, was allowed through in the same year. This grouping, the fourth largest in terms of mileage, took in the famous Stockton & Darlington nine years later, and was to become one of the great railways of the second half of the century, benefiting from the prosperity of the booming industrial area it served.

With its merger plans stymied, the Midland therefore had to make its own way to London. The company revived an earlier scheme to build a line from Leicester to Hitchin, which had previously been authorized but had fallen into abeyance, quickly obtaining parliamentary authorization to build the line but construction proved to be a major burden for the company. The contractor was Thomas Brassey, who had recently built nearly all of the Great Northern from King's Cross to York and was the most successful contractor of his generation. By the time of his death in 1870 he had constructed a tenth of the mileage of the entire British rail network (and more than double that mileage abroad),[9] while retaining the trust and regard of all those for whom he worked. As his Victorian biographer commented, 'no one, investigating the history of the work that Brassey undertook, has come forward to suggest that it was shoddy, that he broke his word, that his treatment of employees was harsh or mean',[10] quite a testament for a man who spent his life in such a cut-throat and sometimes shady business. Unlike many of his fellow contractors, Brassey, born of modestly affluent yeoman parents, did not do it for the money but for the genuine ambition to create a railway network. Although on his death he bequeathed greater wealth than any comparable self-made man of the Victorian era (£3.2m, say £225m in today's money), Brassey made no attempt to mix in high society and never stood for Parliament (unlike almost every other contemporary prominent developer and promoter of the railways). He was more than a contractor – typically the builders of railway lines often took part of the financial risk, investing their own money to help bring schemes to fruition – but despite his personal financial outlay, he survived the crash of 1868, unlike his sometime partner, Sir Samuel Peto.

The construction of the line, which began in 1853, posed both physical and financial constraints for the Midland. There were four sets of hills to cross and the original plans had envisaged considerable tunnelling, but this proved expensive and a cheaper route, with more gradients and bends, was chosen. The line was being built at a difficult time politically, with the Crimean War in full swing, which not only deterred investors but also pushed up the cost of materials. The Midland limited itself to spending £1m on the line and managed to stick to that budget, a mere £16,000 per mile, which was half the average cost of lines built in the previous decade.[11]

The line from the north and the Midlands through to Hitchin opened in May 1857, where it connected with the Great Northern's tracks to King's Cross, over which the Midland had running rights. Thus, at last, fourteen years after its creation, the Midland could operate its own trains through to London. Yet that still did not solve all its problems. The Great Northern's tracks were crowded and, quite understandably, its own trains were given preference, despite the generous tolls which the company received from the Midland. The Midland's lucrative coal trains from the rich south Yorkshire coalfields mostly used the old route from the north on the London & North Western's tracks between Rugby and London, but those lines, too, were burdened with a heavy load of both goods and passenger traffic. The answer was obvious but it would take another decade before the directors of what had become a very profitable railway were brave enough to decide to build another line to London terminating at that Gothic palace, St Pancras station.

The decision was prompted by the difficulties endured by the Midland in bringing its trains through to the capital. In 1862, ten of its trains were delayed every day by having to wait for Great Northern traffic and, worst of all, during the popular International Exhibition, the Midland had the ignominy of seeing some of its passenger trains routed into the Great Northern's goods terminal because of lack of capacity at King's Cross. The Midland's line to London opened in 1868, though the hotel in the station was not completed until 1873, and caused considerable upheaval. To run lines into London was becoming increasingly costly and necessitated the demolition of ever greater numbers of homes. Here the destructive force of the railway could be seen at its most powerful. Virtually every town connected to the network experienced a certain amount of demolition, though some, rather than face this prospect, pushed the station to the outer edge of the built-up area, a move which was welcomed by the hackney cab drivers but was met with dismay by passengers. London, however, could not be bypassed in the same way and saw by far the greatest level of upheaval. While the 1846 Royal Commission on Metropolis Railway Termini had decided that the railways should be kept out of the centre of the city, there was still plenty of housing in the way of the projected lines as they cut their way to the stations on the boundary determined by the Commission.

Both the Great Northern and the London & Birmingham had already caused destruction and mayhem in a swathe of north London between Camden Town, Euston and King's Cross but the Midland was to be particularly destructive. The company, with fantastic foresight, designed the line as a four-track railway, greatly worsening its impact. Agar Town, a poor area of rookeries and hovels, was virtually wiped out and the construction of the station at St Pancras alone resulted in 20,000 people losing their homes. Even the dead were not immune as part of the Old St Pancras churchyard had to be destroyed, uncovering thousands of decaying bodies which had to be moved, a task observed by Thomas Hardy, the novelist, who as a young man was employed by the architect to ensure the job was carried out properly.

There was an extra side effect of the creation of these lines across cities. The railways which cut through London and other big cities, especially Manchester[12] but also Birmingham and Leeds, were invariably raised on long viaducts or embankments, or buried in cuttings, that split up neighbourhoods and, indeed, the whole city. The railways might have looked fine atop their elegant arched structures but were greatly resented by the remaining local residents who were forced to live, quite literally, under their shadow and the poor usually ended up on 'the wrong side' of the tracks: 'Each of these new railway lines became itself the source of new divisions and demarcations . . . they became the new dialect lines of social distinction, having each of them a right and wrong side.'[13]

Nor was the destruction as beneficial as the railway companies tried to claim. While they argued that they were carrying out a public service by demolishing the slums, in truth that was promoters' gloss masking a far more complicated situation; for example, at Somers Town, just north of Agar Town, much of the housing destroyed by the Midland was in good condition, laid out on streets rather than alleys.

Moreover, while the destruction of large numbers of working people's homes was celebrated as a way of getting rid of slums, there was little consideration of the consequences for the people made homeless as a result. The implication that the destruction of these areas benefited public health was disingenuous since the companies had no obligation to provide rehousing and while the owners received compensation, their displaced tenants were simply left to their own devices. It was not until 1853 that the railways had to take any account of those thrown out of their homes, and even then they were merely required to draw up a 'demolition statement' setting out the numbers. A few tenants were given trifling amounts of compensation but those who paid rent weekly rather than monthly received nothing. After much pressure by social reformers, a standing order passed in Parliament in 1874 was supposed to ensure that the poorest were rehoused by the railway companies – but this was largely ignored. The landlords would, in any case, frequently enable the railways to evade the obligation by evicting their tenants a few days before the properties were transferred. Later, further legislation placed tighter obligations on the companies but even these were largely circumvented. A conservative estimate of the numbers displaced in London alone is 120,000,[14] but the real figure was undoubtedly higher due to the efforts by landlords and railway companies to get around the law and the lack of information about a very fluid and itinerant section of the population.

Ironically, the railways were eager to provide another form of accommodation – hotels – which were well appointed and frequently luxurious. Although trains were becoming faster, the companies made little effort to reduce journey times in line with this technological progress. Railway travel was so superior to any alternative that the companies did not really need to bother. On occasion they speeded up trains in order to compete with their rivals, such as the Great Western, which briefly ran trains from London to Birmingham fifteen minutes faster than the London & North Western despite the greater mileage, but soon abandoned that strategy as expensive and unreliable. There were still stops for refreshments and 'comfort breaks' since there were no corridors or toilets on the trains, as well as for changing the engine or filling the tender tanks, though, later, lengthy troughs, typically 2,000 feet (600m) long, were placed between the tracks to allow locomotives to pick up water without stopping.

Long journeys remained an ordeal. A trip between London Euston and Edinburgh took over twelve hours by day and seventeen by the night mail. Aberdeen was virtually a full day's journey from London, and none of these trains offered any sort of sleeping accommodation. As early as 1838, the railways had begun to offer a rudimentary aid to people wanting to sleep on the mail trains by providing a cushion supported between the compartment's seats by poles which could be hired from the guard. It does not sound very comfortable but was probably better than sitting upright all night. Proper sleeping cars were not introduced until 1873 when the North British Railway started offering a service between London and Glasgow, but at first passengers had to bring their own bed linen.

Inevitably, given the discomfort of train travel, hotels sprang up at stations and junctions to cater for the exhausted traveller, and later for tourists. Until the law on companies was relaxed so that other enterprises enjoyed the same ability to raise capital from a multitude of shareholders, the railways were the only businesses with the capital resources to invest in such big enterprises and soon most of the larger railways had branched out into providing hotels. The first hotel to be built by a railway had been opened at Euston in 1839, the year after the station's completion. Other hotels serving railway passengers quickly followed at junctions such as Derby, Normanton and Swindon, as the railway companies realized that providing accommodation was an opportunity to boost their income. The South Eastern broke new ground by opening the Pavilion Hotel in Folkestone, catering for travellers using the cross-Channel steamers, and soon similar hotels appeared at many major stations, notably the Great Western Royal Hotel at Paddington – the biggest in the country with 103 bedrooms – and the Great Northern at King's Cross, both opened in 1854. The classic railway hotel is at a terminus, straddling the platforms, and the first of these was the elegant Royal Station Hotel at Hull's Paragon station, opened in 1851, which formed two sides of the concourse in an L-shape.

Hotels became an established part of the larger railway companies' businesses and by the end of the century there were railway hotels in all ten largest English provincial cities except Bristol,[15] and at nearly all the London termini. Four Scottish railway companies built hotels for golfers and several companies created 'country hotels', aimed solely at tourists, the first of which was at Furness Abbey, near Barrow, built by the Furness Railway, principally a mineral line, in 1847. Many major hotels remained in railway ownership until the privatization of British Transport Hotels in the early 1980s.

The queen of these hotels was, of course, the Midland Grand at St Pancras, opened in 1873, designed by Sir George Gilbert Scott to dominate the far more simple yet elegant lines of its neighbour, Lewis Cubitt's King's Cross. St Pancras is the most significant urban structure built by the railways. Both its engine shed, the inelegant name given to the enormous glass and iron shelter over the platforms designed by William Barlow, and the George Gilbert Scott hotel would be notable individually, but together they create a world-class terminus that is now enjoying a twenty-first-century renaissance as it has been transformed into an international station served by the Eurostar services to and from Paris and Brussels. The sheer scale is breathtaking in itself as the station is 150 metres wide and twice that distance long, but the Gothic design, with its exaggerated features such as the clock tower, numerous spires and the large statue of Britannia glaring over at King's Cross make it one of London's greatest landmarks. The sheer contrast between those two stations, the Gothic St Pancras alongside the simple elegance of King's Cross, built less than two decades apart, demonstrates both the energy and wastefulness engendered by the emphasis on competition rather than cooperation, which dominated this key period in the history of the railways. Jack Simmons has explained precisely why the Victorians of this era could never have chosen a state-planned system of railway development: 'The spirit [of the times] was competitive through and through: it was commerce against agriculture, North against South, London against the provinces, the middle classes against the aristocracy – and behind it sits Britain in competition with the rest of the world.'[16] The Midland was to epitomize this by embarking on its own, highly successful path to maximize its profits and embarrass and annoy its rivals by abolishing second class and ensure that all trains could carry third-class passengers.

Memories were short and the urge to make money was built into the Victorian psyche. It was no surprise, therefore, that within a few years of the end of the mania, railway projects aplenty were being promoted. The revival of interest in railway investment was facilitated by a change in attitude by the landowners. The hostility of the early years had, with a few exceptions, disappeared. However, the landowners were still not averse to the idea of extorting as much as possible from the railway companies for the purchase of their land, even though they had begun to realize the advantages of having a railway connection on their doorstep. In the twenty years after the collapse of the mania, the railways would again double in size, from 6,000 to 12,000 route miles, and a combination of competitive drive and over-confidence would ensure that a significant proportion of these new lines consisted of unnecessary or uneconomic branches.

# SEVEN

# THE AGATHA CHRISTIE
# RAILWAY

By 1860, memories of the damage caused by the abrupt end of the mania were fading and interest in the railways began to be revived. The next two decades saw mostly steady economic growth, apart from a brief downturn in the mid-1860s, and the more benign financial climate encouraged a new wave of railway promotion and construction. There was technological progress, too, with the introduction of locomotives that burnt coal rather than the more expensive coke used previously, and the development of steel tyres[1] for trains that were stronger than their iron predecessors. Signalling was becoming more sophisticated and safer, with innovations such as interlocking – ensuring signals were coordinated with the points they controlled – being introduced at busier junctions.

The sharp economic growth of the early 1860s stimulated another brief railway boom and although this was brought to an abrupt halt by a further collapse in 1866, people everywhere were clamouring to be connected to the railway. Previously, there had been the odd offshoot from the main railways as well as a host of short lines that were entirely separate from the main network, but now small towns and even villages were beginning to be connected to the national railway system. The advantages of connection were becoming so apparent that local traders would put their life savings into financially dubious schemes in a desperate bid to boost their business. The large landowners had mostly changed their view from an instinctive opposition born of conservatism and fear of change, to a qualified support, aware that there was much in it for them, not least, in the short term a good price for the strips of land requisitioned by the railway developer. Self-interest, as ever, prevailed, but that was not the only catalyst for the spread of the railways: people wanted to be connected with the changing world of the mid-nineteenth century.

There were two ways to initiate a new branch line – top down or bottom up. Some of the larger companies made great efforts to create a network of branches leading into their main lines. The North Eastern, for example, realized that its local mineral industries would be a major source of income and installed private sidings for factories and even for large farms. In contrast, other companies concentrated on their main line network and were rather uninterested in developing branch lines, which they saw as loss-making irrelevancies; in those cases, the initiative had to come from local people, usually those at the far end of a projected route.

But before local people could get a completed railway, they got the navvies, who were rarely welcomed with open arms. Cecil Torr,[2] writing during the First World War, recalls his grandfather complaining about the disruption caused in 1864 when the line from Newton Abbot to Moretonhampstead was being built by Thomas Brassey. There was fighting all night and 'the villains stole all poor old X's fowls . . . there is not a fowl or egg to be got hereabouts'. The grandfather was not unsympathetic, though, and learnt that one 'fine built tall likely a fellow as you ever saw, and nicknamed the Bulldog' worked Saturday and Monday, and received '5s 6d for the two days, slept in a barn and spent all his earnings at the public house'. But other changes to traditional ways of life must have been equally daunting. David St John Thomas describes the considerable general disturbance: 'the closing of roads, the mess and noise of the steam excavator used even on the Sabbath, the luring away of farm labourers who could earn as much on the railway in three ten-hour days as all week on the land, the absence of pupils from schools, the tearing apart of favourite coppices and fields, the putting up of food prices and the occasional scarcities'.[3]

The construction of the branch lines brought the railway to places that hitherto had been unaffected by the nineteenth century's transport revolution. Take the quaint-sounding Ware, Hadham & Buntingford

Railway, opened in 1863. It ran from a junction with the Broxbourne and Hertford to Buntingford fourteen miles away over pleasant Hertfordshire countryside that was gently hilly but presented no problems to the engineers. As with many such lines, querulous landowners had prevented the optimal route being built which would have connected with the main line at Ware, and further resistance stopped the construction of an extension to link with the Cambridge line, which would have transformed the branch into a useful diversionary loop. The only remaining purpose of the railway was, therefore, to serve the 3,000 people living in Buntingford and the villages along the route, and its initial mainstay was freight, principally agricultural produce, although later it would become a commuter line with through trains into London. Inevitably, given the line was a risky financial proposition from the start, the company that built it quickly became incorporated into its bigger neighbour, the Great Eastern, with the shareholders losing much of their investment. The line, like so many built in this period, was closed following the Beeching Report, with passenger services ceasing in 1964 and freight the following year.

There were, quite literally, hundreds of similar lines spreading around Britain. Even the Isle of Wight, an island just fifteen by ten miles, acquired thirty-two miles of railway by 1875[4] and eventually fifty-five by the end of the century, built by no fewer than eight different companies. There were even branches off branches where a train from the junction with the main line might disgorge its passengers at a remote station, only for them to have to change on to an even more remote service. For example, Yelverton, eight miles from Plymouth on the Launceston line, was the starting point of a branch to Princetown, the highest point of the railway in the West Country, reached by a windy line over a deserted stretch of Dartmoor. It could hardly have been a busy line, serving only a sparsely populated area with just three halts and a station at a hamlet called Dousland (the abandoned trackbed can still be seen from the road). The only regular source of revenue was from prisoners and their escorts heading for the bleak prison on the moor, a traffic that lasted until the closure of the line in the 1960s. It was not only the prisoners that were on the wild side; according to one chronicler, 'the train staff were a rugged group who never came nearer to civilisation than momentarily at Yelverton, one of a number of stations where the locomotive changed ends of its train by running into a siding and allowing the coaches (often a solitary coach) to slide past it by gravity,[5] a technique known as fly shunting.

The arrival of a branch line was an event of great significance to be celebrated with a grand opening, like those that marked the inauguration of the first railways. Everyone was given a holiday and the first train would generally start off from the last station on the line, often with a locomotive hauling the railway company's entire stock of carriages, filled with every local person of any note. At each country station on the line, the train would be welcomed by a crowd of local people thronging the area and at the town where the branch joined the main line, there would be a procession and a huge banquet lunch for the notables while the hoi polloi were entertained with a fair and country dancing, followed by a 'cold collation', with beer for the men and tea for the women and children. In Launceston, the day was so marred by heavy rainfall that wet days are still referred to locally as 'railway weather' and when the South Devon Railway was extended to Torquay and Paignton, 'a riot developed about the sharing out of an immense pudding weighing 1½ tons which had been prepared for the occasion'.[6] At every opening, the local promoters would 'unfailingly [be] praised for the endeavours . . . unfailingly the bishop or vicar hoped that the Sabbath would not be disturbed . . . and unfailingly a director diplomatically replied that only those Sunday trains that Post Office and public absolutely demanded would be run'.[7] Indeed, as mentioned in Chapter 2, running rail services on a Sunday remained an issue of controversy well into the twentieth century (although nowadays it is mostly engineering works that make Sunday a day to avoid taking the trains!).

As the railway spread into the rural interstices of the country, it had the same long-lasting effect as those early lines did on their local communities (see Chapter 4), but the changes affected a far higher proportion of the population. The arrival of the iron road was a life-transforming experience, because for the next two generations the railway line rather than the road would be the gateway to the rest of the world. Most immediately, the price of coal nearly always fell by a third with the opening of a new line as horses and carts were an inefficient form of transport for such a basic commodity. Gradually, the railway would start to bring in everything from agricultural machinery to pots and pans: 'Calves, day old chicks, pigs and other reinforcements for the local livestock normally came by passenger train along with the mails, newspapers, and local soldiers on leave. The pair of rails disappearing over the horizon stood for progress, disaster, the major changes in life: the route to Covent Garden and Ypres, the way one's fiancé paid his first visit to one's parents, one's children returned for deathbed leavetaking . . . etc'.[8]

Commodities not previously available would start being delivered by the train, including mail order goods bought through newspaper advertisements. However, while the railway gave local shops easier access to a wider range of stock, it also offered their potential customers a faster trip to the nearest town's High Street. Farmers found new markets for their produce, often at a better price: in 1881, Derbyshire farmers could obtain a shilling for a gallon of milk compared with 8d to turn it into butter or cheese. While they had to pay for carriage on the train, it was still worthwhile just to avoid the labour-intensive and slow processing of the milk into other dairy products. On the other hand, this new efficient market process could result in local shortages while businesses adapted to the new situation. In the 1860s, as the railways of Devon and Cornwall proliferated, so much milk was exported from the region that it became scarce and disrupted the local dairy business.

As we have seen, fares were required by Parliament to be a penny a mile for at least one train, but this was often scheduled at the least convenient hour to make the service as unattractive as possible, so that even poor people were forced on to the more popular trains, which would charge a penny farthing per mile. Second class would cost perhaps 1½d, and first class 2d to 3d, though the local squires tended to have their own family carriage which they would hitch on to the train. The most common frequency was three to six trains per day, usually mixed passenger and goods. Invariably the trains would stop at all stations and sometimes shunt a few wagons off and on while the passengers were rattled around in the spartan second-hand carriages, which was often all the branch line companies could afford. While we may nostalgically think of those Agatha Christie films with a sole passenger arriving at a tiny station manned by a friendly porter/ticket inspector/signalman/station-master, who then ferries his charge to the local mansion in a horse cart, the reality was that passengers were a minor source of revenue for many of these lines, which were only viable if there were a regular traffic of minerals, especially coal, agricultural produce or manufactured goods. On successful branches, takings from goods exceeded passenger revenue by a factor of three or more, the opposite ratio to that on most main lines where profitability was dependent on passenger revenue.

The spread of the branch line was so universal that by 1880 hardly any town of significance was more than walking distance from a station and by the outbreak of the First World War, there was barely a hamlet that was twenty miles away. There was even the odd private branch and station. The ambitious plan to reach Wick and Thurso in the northern Highlands was a slow enterprise and by 1865 had reached no further than Golspie, two miles short of the aptly-named Dunrobin, seat of the Duke of Sutherland. He was so anxious to have the railway connection that he not only financed the completion of the approved section, but built an additional seventeen miles further to Helmsdale himself. When the line was opened, Dunrobin became a private station for the castle and housed the Duke's own carriage, which was hauled by his own private locomotive. To be fair to the Duke, he did eventually give the line to the Highland Railway in 1884, ten years after the route to Wick and Thurso had been completed. He wrote off the £300,000 cost and, had it not been for his generosity, it is doubtful the line would ever have been built. By any rational economics it was a Victorian folly, but proved to be remarkably useful in the First World War (see Chapter 11) and survives to this day. There were other private stations, many of them not listed in the usual railway directories.[9]

The Duke's efforts were part of a trend in both Scotland and Wales, whose large rural areas began to be criss-crossed with railways during this period. The development of Scotland's rail network was a complex and intricate story involving no fewer than 200 different companies – who, interestingly, built parts of their network south of the border, an invasion that their English counterparts never matched. The first major lines were established in the early 1840s, centred around Glasgow and Edinburgh, which were linked in 1842. In 1848 the system was connected with the English network via Carlisle and Carstairs, and also through Berwick on the East Coast, but until 1855 the Highlands had not been reached by the railway, the nearest being the Elgin–Lossiemouth line which opened in 1852. Aberdeen had been reached in 1850 and plans for a Great North of Scotland Railway, running from Aberdeen to Inverness, had been authorized and completed by 1858, giving a very circuitous route south from the Highland capital, a journey that was later shortened by the construction of the line between Inverness and Perth, which became part of the Highland Railway. The Dingwall & Skye Railway reached Stromeferry, for Skye, in 1870, and, as mentioned above, the two little northern Highland towns, Wick and Thurso, were connected to the railway in 1874. Some of these Highland lines ran through areas that were so remote that passenger numbers were minimal. In that famous scene from John Buchan's classic, *The Thirty-Nine Steps*, the hero, Richard Hannay, running from German agents, finds himself at Galloway station which 'proved to be ideal' for hiding since it was in the middle of the moors with 'a waiting room, an office, the stationmaster's cottage and a tiny yard of gooseberries and sweet-william [but] there seemed to be no road from it anywhere'.[10]

Glasgow was the obvious centre of the Scottish rail network, the equivalent of London north of the border, and found itself with a series of main line stations, no fewer than four by the 1870s, of which two survive. That was a reflection of the highly competitive situation in Scotland where there was even less consolidation than in England. Indeed, until the creation of the Scottish Region of British Railways a century later, Scotland did not have an integrated national railway system at all; instead, five major companies,[11] quite a number for such a small population, competed directly on routes where alternative journeys were possible. The difficulties and extra costs resulting from such a disjointed system were well illustrated in Perth, which had three different companies running into its station, each with its own locomotives and carriage sidings, a crazy waste for a relatively small town, which caused constant operational difficulties. Of the five railways, the most significant was the

North British, whose greatest achievement was providing the impetus for the construction of the spectacular bridge over the Firth of Forth, completed in 1890 and carried out in conjunction with two of the other large Scottish railways (see Chapter 9).

The Welsh story is interesting in that the Principality acquired far more railways than its population could ever support, both because of the failure of Parliament to assess the market properly, and also, more sinisterly, as a result of sheer corruption. The railways came late to most of the Principality and by 1850 Wales still only possessed two main line routes, both along its coastlines. The Chester to Holyhead line, completed in 1848, ran along the main communication route established by Edward I, who in the thirteenth century guarded it with a series of castles in towns such as Flint and Conway. These towns were now linked by the railway, which became the principal route for the Irish Mail, connecting with steamers to Ireland. In the south there was a railway from Gloucester to Swansea and Cardiff but there were no lines in between apart from a short branch from the Shrewsbury & Chester to Oswestry. Then, over the next couple of decades, a plethora of lines sprang up, covering central Wales with an unsustainably dense network of railways. Many of the rural lines were promoted by small local landowners eager to get access to larger markets for their produce while the construction of others was stimulated by rivalry between the Great Western and the North Western, with both companies trying to prevent their rival from making incursions into their territory.

In the more industrialized south Wales, a large network of railways built up in Glamorgan and Monmouthshire to service the coal, iron and steel industries. Incredibly, this became the densest network of lines anywhere in the UK (and possibly the world) outside London. Again, competition rather than consolidation was the prevailing ethos, and by 1900 seven companies ran into Merthyr Tydfil while Swansea boasted six passenger termini. Between 1863 and 1867, Brecon was connected to the rail network via four branch lines but no main line railway linked it to the outside world (the quickest route would have been along the Usk valley where it could have connected with the Newport–Hereford main line at Abergavenny). This strange state of affairs was partly a result of a campaign by a canal company, the Monmouthshire Railway

& Canal Company, to block the rail route along the valley, one of the few instances in railway history where canal interests prevailed.[12] During this period several narrow gauge railways emerged in Wales, notably the Ffestiniog (see Chapter 10).

Ireland was part of Great Britain, under direct rule by London from 1801 until the Irish Free State's establishment in 1922, and its railways exhibited many of the same characteristics as those on the mainland, thanks to the same emphasis on competition rather than coordination. Dublin eventually had six termini, and Londonderry, a small town in the north, four (two of which were narrow gauge). Cooperation between neighbouring railways, which for the most part did not duplicate each other's routes directly, was often minimal even when it would have been advantageous for both parties. Because of the sparseness of the population and their poverty, there was considerable state funding of the railways, albeit much of it hidden through the indirect payment of grants.

The Irish railways were mostly built to an odd gauge – 5ft 3ins – after the early lines tried various sizes ranging from 6ft 2ins to the standard 4ft 8½ins used on the other side of the water. While the first lines were completed in the 1830s, railway construction really took off once the gauge had been agreed in 1843 and the bulk of the main line network was created in the ensuing twenty years, despite the horrors of the great potato famine of 1845–8 which reduced the population by a third through death and emigration. Usage at the best of times was inter-mittent and without government support many of the lines would not have been viable. As David St Thomas puts it wryly, 'Travelling first class might be a solitary and prosperous priest breviary-reading in splendid isolation. In the rest of the train . . . there would be people the railway would only carry once: emigrants and soldiers serving the Empire on their way out of Ireland.'[13]

The best source of business for the Irish railways, other than on the Dublin–Belfast route, were the passengers using the steamer services across the Irish Sea and by the end of the century no fewer than four English railways were vying for that traffic: the London & North Western, the Midland, the Lancashire & Yorkshire and the Great Western all offered competing services on different shipping routes. There was also a network of smaller gauge railways, built in remote rural parts of the country that never had a hope of being viable. St Thomas cites the improbably named Schull & Skibbereen (with an intermediate stop at Ballydehob) in the far south-west, 'a district especially hit by famine and decline'.[14] It was a fifteen-mile narrow gauge line built beside the road at a cost of £57,000, with dividends of 5 per cent supposedly guaranteed in perpetuity by the council, but in fact never paid. There were just two trains per day, taking over an hour for the journey to Skibbereen where there was not even a connection to the main line. With such out-of-the-way branches, the network of lines in Ireland eventually reached its maximum of 3,450 miles in the 1920s, excessive for such a small island with a population of barely half its peak of 8 million and, not surprisingly, less than half the mileage survives today.

As well as widening their network deep into the countryside, the railways were becoming a mass form of transit, extending their reach through all the social classes. They simultaneously created the need to commute – by allowing people to live further from their places of work – and then met that need by providing a service, particularly workmen's trains, to ferry people to and from their jobs. In the early days, accommodation for poorer passengers had mostly been designed to put them off using the railway: the Eastern Counties had run 'truck platforms with eight open seats' while on the Great Western the poorer classes were simply dumped into goods wagons without windows, little different to the trains used by the Nazis to transport Jews to their deaths a century later. The very term 'class' came into circulation at this time; earlier forms of transport, such as the stagecoach and ships, had different terminology to distinguish between their types of passenger, for example, 'inside' and 'cabin' accommodation, or 'outside' and 'deck'. Despite Gladstone's 1844 legislation which had forced all railway companies to provide at least one cheap service each way per day, the trains were largely used by the middle and upper classes, much like aviation before the advent of the charter and low-cost airlines, while the poor were confined to an annual excursion to the seaside and the odd essential trip when they could afford the fares. The Midland, the most aggressively competitive of the big companies, set out to challenge that orthodoxy, seeing the potential of attracting the masses on to the railway by providing plenty of cheap accommodation.

Many express trains had no third-class accommodation as the companies developed them as an exclusive service for the well-to-do, although there were exceptions such as the Great Northern which had introduced it on some of its express London–Bradford trains in 1860. At the time, the Midland had responded by putting third-class carriages on all its trains on the same route, but in general third-class accommodation was very limited on faster trains, which greatly reduced the potential market for train travel. In 1872 the Midland took the radical decision to provide third-class carriages on all its express trains. As the historian of the Midland, Hamilton Ellis, points out, this was 'thought to be shocking by some other companies who considered that an express train was something for which travellers should be made to pay handsomely'.[15]

The change was part of a new philosophy introduced by the very forward-looking James Allport, who joined the Midland in 1849 as general manager in the wake of Hudson's demise. Allport, the son of a small-arms manufacturer, who remained general manager for over thirty years, showed considerable commercial acumen in developing new markets for rail travel but was also something of a social reformer who saw it as his duty to provide for the less well-off. Three years later, in 1875, he shocked his rivals even more by abolishing second class on all the Midland's trains. The second-class carriages were immediately turned into third-class accommodation and he ensured that all seats were upholstered rather than making passengers endure the hard wooden benches of the third-class carriages, which he sent to the scrapyard. Passengers were to be given more leg-room so that they did not play knock-knees on crowded trains and the partitions dividing the carriages into compartments were to be built up to the roof, creating a feeling of greater privacy. Hamilton Ellis reports that the move was met by other companies 'with squeals of dismay and disapproval' as it was seen as 'pampering the working classes'.[16]

Allport, who had a keen service ethic long before that became accepted business practice, was also responsible for improving the facilities at the other end of the social scale by copying the idea of de-luxe carriages from the United States. In 1872 he crossed the Atlantic on a fact-finding tour to observe how the Americans catered for their passengers and decided to introduce the carriages provided by George Pullman's eponymous company. For an extra fee on top of the fare, the Pullman coaches offered hotel standards of comfort, initially in restaurant cars with waiter-served meals, and later provided carriages with sleeping accommodation as well. The carriages and attendants were supplied under contract by the Pullman company but the locomotives and the rest of the train remained the responsibility of the Midland. The idea was well received and other railway companies followed suit, including, amazingly, the Metropolitan Railway, now part of the London Underground system, which ran a Pullman train from the remote Verney Junction in rural Buckinghamshire, offering breakfast in the morning and returning with a dinner service in the evening.

The other method through which poorer people were attracted on to the railway was through the provision of workmen's trains. The first service offering cheap fares for workers travelling to their jobs started running as early as 1847 when the Eastern Counties railway provided early-morning services for dockers. The illustrious Stockton & Darlington innovated, too, with cheap trains linking Middlesbrough with the iron-working village of Eston five years later. In a way it was incumbent on the railways to provide such services since, as we have seen, they demolished swathes of housing in the inner city during their very construction, displacing tens of thousands of people. However, it was not until the 1860s, when employment started to soar, intensifying the demand for labour, that the concept really developed.

The nascent Underground was another early pioneer of cheap trains for workers. The first line between Paddington and Farringdon in the City was opened by the Metropolitan Railway in 1863 and the following year the company realized that there was a huge potential market and started running two early trains on which workers could travel for just 3d[17] rather than the usual 9d return. These cheap trains, which unlike some workmen's trains allowed the return journey to be made on any service, proved immensely popular, and contributed to the Metropolitan's high profitability in its early years. That year, too, the House of Lords decided that all railway bills for new lines into London must include the provision of workmen's trains and similar services were operated, though on a smaller scale, in other major cities, notably Manchester, Birmingham (where some trains carried people out of the city centre in the early morning to big factories like Cadbury's Bourneville plant), Liverpool and Glasgow.

However, the railway which most thoroughly exploited the concept of workmen's trains, and in doing so speeded up the development of a whole swathe of London, was the Great Eastern, which set itself up quite deliberately to become 'the poor man's line'.[18] When it obtained authorization to build Liverpool Street station, a process that started in 1861 but took three years, permission was granted only on condition that it would run workmen's trains from Edmonton and Walthamstow to London at a return fare of just 2d, which enabled poorly paid workers to live in distant suburbs up to eleven miles from the City. The Great Eastern made a virtue out of necessity, providing a comprehensive schedule of early-morning trains that helped it to become a profitable railway, despite its early travails of serving a sparsely populated part of England.

As a consequence, a finger of development stretched out around its stations on both sides of the railway in much the same way that many towns grow as a ribbon along major roads. Vast areas of cheap housing sprang up in these north London suburbs, consisting largely of small jerry-built brick boxes, the Barratt Homes of their day, and 'chopped off at the ends where another street crossed at distances prescribed by by-law'.[19] Tottenham doubled in population between 1871 and the following census ten years later, and again by 1891, reaching nearly 100,000. Similarly, Edmonton tripled in size during that period and Walthamstow also doubled at each succeeding census. Originally most of the workmen's trains charged the same 2d for a return fare, a real bargain for up to twenty-two miles' travel, but later there was a differentiation between times, with earlier trains before 6.30 a.m. remaining at tuppence while the later ones, catering for a more affluent clientele who could be in their offices a bit later, cost 3d, 4d or even 5d return.

The workmen's trains may have helped the great cities to expand and their workforces to live in better conditions, but they were not a panacea. The poorest labourers, a significant proportion of the workforce, who were paid meagre rates and were hired and fired by the day, could not take advantage of these services. Even those who could often struggled to pay the tuppence or so for their daily fare, and many people suffered great inconvenience because the cheap trains were timetabled only to run very early in the morning, which meant that many passengers had to hang around near the termini, possibly in the wet and cold, until their places of work opened.

In other parts of London, too, the railways stimulated the expansion of what was then the world's biggest conurbation. The Great Northern, serving places like Hornsey, Wood Green and Southgate from King's Cross, concentrated on attracting more upmarket passengers, the lower middle classes, to whom it offered cut-price season tickets. In the west and south-west, it was the Metropolitan District, the rival Underground line to the Metropolitan, which spread out into green fields and villages that quickly became suburbs, such as Richmond, Ealing and Putney, all connected by 1880. In north-west London, it was the Metropolitan, whose chairman Edward Watkin had grand visions about turning the railway into the core of a network that linked Manchester and Sheffield to Paris (see Chapter 10). He pushed the Metropolitan Railway far out into the Middlesex and Hertfordshire countryside, stimulating the developments that would eventually become 'Metroland' in the 1920s and 1930s.[20] The Metropolitan was unique in that it had the power to act as a developer itself, building houses through its subsidiary, Metropolitan Railway Country Estates. Unfortunately, other railways were precluded by legislation from carrying out their own development, a restriction that has proved enormously damaging to the country's transport infrastructure. There is an obvious logic in allowing a railway company to fund its investment through the additional land value it creates by providing easy access to town centres, a planning process used in other countries, notably Japan.

There were failures too: the construction of a railway into greenfield sites did not automatically lead to its development, as the Great Eastern discovered when it built a huge loop running through Fairlop and Chigwell, which attracted few passengers and even less development. Railways, therefore, were 'a necessary, though not sufficient, condition for outer suburban growth'.[21]

The other area where the overground railways prompted rapid suburban growth was in the south-east of London. Here the story is dominated by competition and rivalry which prevented an ordered development of the railway system and resulted in a complex and underinvested network that still causes distress to commuters today. Little mention of the railways south of the Thames has been made up until now, so a bit of backtracking is necessary. The early railways from London into Kent were developed by the South Eastern Railway, but the territory it served bore no resemblance to the dense suburbs stretching out from central London in a huge swathe from Greenwich to Bromley and across to Croydon that provides such a lucrative market for the railways today. Instead, as Hamilton Ellis points out, there was no suburban sprawl, and a place such as Orpington, now a huge dormitory commuter town, was simply 'a dainty village noted for its chickens, for the Squire's peacocks and for the brook down one street'.[22] The South Eastern had built its railway somewhat on the cheap, with several tunnels between Tonbridge and Hastings that had not been properly lined by its cheating contractors, which meant that for many years special rolling stock had to be used to negotiate them safely. Moreover, its meandering lines connected several towns by very indirect routes. To reach Canterbury, a mere fifty-one miles from London, required a journey of thirty miles longer from London Bridge station, taking in Croydon, Redhill, Tonbridge and Ashford among others.

Until the mid-1850s, at least the South Eastern had a monopoly of Kent and shared in the lucrative London–Brighton traffic with the London, Brighton and South Coast Railway. However, this monopoly ended when a small company called the East Kent Railway built a line from Strood to Canterbury, and was soon authorized to extend it to Dover and, towards London, to St Mary Cray. This was also the eastern terminus of another new railway, the Mid-Kent, which opened from Lewisham to Beckenham in 1857 and thence to Bromley the following year, with a gap filled by the intriguingly named but small West End & Crystal Palace railway. This illustrates the way that many Victorian railways built up incrementally, earning a bit of revenue on an initial stretch to help fund expansion and consequently becoming more and more attractive to a wider market, at the same time as building alliances by obtaining running powers over neighbouring lines.

The East Kent then revealed its true ambitions, changing its name to the London, Chatham & Dover Railway and, in 1861, it started running services between the capital and those two destinations, deep in the heart of the South Eastern's territory. Moreover, the run to Dover on the 'Chatham', as it quickly became known, was ten miles shorter than the South Eastern's route. So by stealth a rival to the South Eastern had emerged, creating a rivalry that was to be one of the most fiercely fought on the rail network. Its legacy today is that this important commuter area remains served by a slow railway, with sharp gradients and countless flat[23] junctions, which make for difficult operation and insufficient trains at peak times. Even worse, many towns had two stations, which did not connect with each other, serving the rival railways.

The battle between the South Eastern and the Chatham was, for most of its near forty-year duration, something of a personal war between two major rail entrepreneurs. The companies were led respectively by a couple of equally belligerent characters: Edward Watkin, who as well as running the Metropolitan was chairman of the South Eastern for almost thirty years, and James Forbes, who had an equally long stay at the Chatham and, incidentally, also ran the Metropolitan District, which competed with the Metropolitan on the London Underground system. It was as one historian put it, 'a great misfortune to have a couple of such aggressive personalities in charge of the transportation companies of Kent'.[24] They were more intent on doing each other down, by competing on fares and building unnecessary lines which duplicated their rivals', rather than attempting to improve the quality of the service for passengers.

The South Eastern made a handsome profit catering for passengers using the cross-Channel ferry services at Dover, and so the Chatham quickly set about tapping into that market. Both companies reserved their best services for the boat trains which were integrated with their own ferries, fleets that included the most modern steamships. But by comparison with other railways, the coaches were still dire, and their condition must have shocked many visitors to Britain whose initial experience of the world's most powerful nation would have been a slow and uncomfortable train ride: both the Chatham and the South Eastern became 'bywords of poverty stricken inefficiency and dirtiness, which was a pity seeing that one or other of them was the first English railway to be sampled by millions of intelligent foreign visitors'.[25] (Hamilton Ellis does point out, a tad jingoistically, that the service on the French side, provided by the Compagnie du Nord was even worse.)

The Chatham, in particular, was a dreadful railway, bankrupted by its urge to compete with its rival. The company fell into financial difficulties in 1864 and went bust in 1866, though it continued to run thanks to special dispensation from Parliament and Forbes's skill at brinkmanship. Its permanent state of penury meant it had precious few resources for investment and, indeed, right from the beginning it had a motley collection of locomotives, many bought second-hand from abroad or borrowed from other railways. One type, built by a designer called Crampton, had the rather unfortunate habit of damaging the track to the extent that the following fast train was derailed, a couple of times with fatal consequences. The coaches were no better, with the Chatham's rickety four-wheeled carriages clattering around the network until the end of the century, long after most other railways used more comfortable stock with six or more wheels.

The South Eastern, by all accounts, was little better with equally grotty coaches and slow trains. Even today, it takes at least an hour and a half to travel the seventy-seven miles from London to Dover by train, while Peterborough, the same distance away from the capital but on a far better line, can be reached by many fast services in just forty-five minutes.[26] The two railways eventually did the sensible thing and merged in 1899,[27] but the damage was already done and Kent was left with the legacy of an inadequate and badly laid out network.

Given Parliament's policy of only rarely allowing mergers, the continued development of the rail network meant there was competition on many other routes. In 1870, seven out of the ten largest provincial cities in England and Wales were linked to London with trains from at least two different companies. There were ridiculous fights between companies. Occasionally a rival railway's engine was captured and temporarily confiscated; this happened to a Great Northern locomotive when the company first tried to run to Nottingham. And in 1884 at South Kensington on the London

Underground, a Metropolitan District Railway locomotive was blocked in by three Metropolitan engines. Indeed, this could be seen as the second front of the long war between Forbes and Watkin given they both ran the Metropolitan District and the Metropolitan respectively for most of that same period.[28]

There is no doubt that as a result of competition many unnecessary lines were built, creating an over-complex system, and thousands of shareholders lost money on investments that could never realistically have made a decent return. However, competition should not be viewed in an entirely negative light. The speed of trains increased as companies vied to provide the quickest journey and fares in general were kept down on any routes that were duplicated and actually plummeted in the course of some local battles. For example, the Great Northern and the Midland vied for the custom of visitors to the international exhibition of science and industry held in London in 1862, which resulted in daily, and at times even hourly, price cuts. The Leeds to London return fare was just five shillings, less than a farthing (¼d) a mile, and the return from Nottingham to the capital a mere 3s 3d. Standards of service began to improve too, thanks largely to the Midland's innovation, and competition also ensured that many places were connected to the network when otherwise they might have been ignored. The feud between the Chatham and the South Eastern extended to London where the rival railways put up six termini between them, with the largest, Victoria, being shared between the Chatham and the London, Brighton & South Coast Railway with only a dividing wall separating them. As we have seen, every major railway wanted its London terminus and each one needed to be grander than the last; between 1860 and 1875 seven new terminal stations were opened in the capital. The south London railways were also keen on having both a West End terminal (Charing Cross or Victoria) and a City one (Blackfriars or Cannon Street).

It was a silly competition, but it has given us some splendid architecture. John Betjeman was inspired to write a book on London's termini, in which he describes Victoria as 'London's most conspicuous monument to commercial rivalry'.[29] Even today it is clearly two stations half-heartedly melded together but it was even more of a mess when first built and, as Betjeman puts it, 'the pleasantly muddled interior must puzzle foreigners. How easily they might find themselves on a Pullman to Brighton instead of a boat train to Dover.'[30] Victoria, though, is conveniently sited and it was remarkable that the two railways managed to build their terminal on the north side of the river, bringing the railway close to the heart of Belgravia, one of the most affluent parts of London, whereas other stations were confined to either side of the riverfront or north of the Euston and Marylebone roads.

With the exception of St Pancras, these stations mostly served the growing suburban traffic and conveniently they were all sited on the Circle Line, completed in 1884, as envisaged by the 1846 Royal Commission on Metropolis Railway Termini, a rare example of successful long-term planning of the railway network. The railways had a greater influence and effect on London than on any other part of the country, and not just because it benefited from the first ever Underground system as well as the world's most intensive rail network, nor merely because it is the country's largest conurbation. Rather, it is because the capital was transformed completely by the arrival and proliferation of the railways in a far more profound way than other cities, and the importance of the railways, both over and under ground, to London remains far greater than anywhere else, as evidenced by the high proportion of the capital's workers who commute by rail today.

Railways affected the economy of the capital in a host of unpredictable ways, wrecking some industries while stimulating the creation of others. Just as the effect of the railways touched every part of Britain, they influenced every part of life in the capital. Take industry: London was a manufacturing city in the mid-nineteenth century, the largest centre in the country, producing 15 per cent of the nation's output. The railways increasingly came to service that sector, and at some plants vast internal railways were built, such as the seventy miles of track laid in the works of the Gas Light & Coke Company in Beckton, on the easternmost fringes of the docks area, linked to a branch from the Great Eastern.

Yet, on the other hand, many plants moved out of London, not least the numerous locomotive builders, because improved transport for their goods, and indeed for their workers, allowed them to shift production to anywhere that was near a railway; for example, manufacturing engines for the South Eastern moved to Ashford in Kent while the London & South Western works was at Eastleigh in Hampshire. Jobs that were lost in the heavy industries such as locomotive production were more than made up for by a host of smaller manufacturers, many of whom were suppliers to the railway industry, producing anything from signalling equipment to hand-bills for advertising train times. Oddly enough, the early railways that served London were slow to take advantage of the potentially lucrative coal trade, partly as a result of regulations and restrictive practices, and most coal continued to arrive by ship until the early 1850s. From the outset, though, the Great Northern resolved to sell South Yorkshire coal and other railways, notably the London & North Western, began to compete. By 1856 a quarter of London's coal was arriving by train, and a decade later, over half. The price went down too, but not very dramatically, from an average of 18s in the 1850s, to 15s 7d thirty years later. However, the railways allowed a massive expansion in the quantity of coal being brought into the capital – it doubled in that period – and without them the old supply route via the Thames would have clogged up with too much shipping.

As London grew in both size and affluence, the demand for food soared and that, too, began to be transported to the capital by rail, changing the tastes of the population. As Jack Simmons reports, 'in the 1830s, the clerk of Billingsgate Market said that the working classes strongly dislike fish, as expensive and undependable in quality. Mayhew, twenty years later, saw it as a main ingredient of their diet.'[31] London began to lose its agricultural smell: the roads into town were no longer full of animals messing and fouling the streets wherever they went as meat could be slaughtered elsewhere and brought in as carcasses by rail; and the cows that supplied milk gradually disappeared from the backyards and cellars of London (there were as many as 20,000 as late as the mid-1850s) because milk could be brought by train, principally by the aptly named Express County Milk Supply Company, the forerunner of Express Dairies. By 1870 half the milk was coming in by rail, and by the turn of the century virtually all of it. Market gardens sprang up in the Home Counties and flourished wherever there was a railhead. Special train services were run to cater for particular produce such as turkey specials from Norfolk (a local speciality long before the days of Bernard Matthews) and broccoli trains from Cornwall during the season.

The shopping habits of Londoners were also transformed by the development of the railway, and, in particular, the Underground. Larger and larger shops established themselves, offering a huge range of goods, and the owners of these 'department' stores realized the advantages of being sited near a station. When William Whiteley was looking around for a suitable site, he chose Bayswater to build his store as it was near the Underground, as opposed to Islington, which at the time was not. It was no coincidence that Ponting's, Derry & Tom's and Barker's all opened next to High Street Kensington station. Entertainment, too, was best sited next to a station. The London, Brighton & South Coast railway funded the removal of the Crystal Palace, once the Great Exhibition was over, to the eponymous area in south London, while Watkin promoted the construction of a bigger version of the Eiffel Tower next to the Metropolitan at Wembley, which was sadly never completed. His rival, Forbes, leased land belonging to the District Railway on which a big wheel was built at Earls Court in 1896. Every racecourse around London soon acquired a station – often equivalent in size to those serving the major towns – since on race days special services would bring in thousands of spectators as well as the racehorses themselves. The very development of professional football and the creation of a national Football League in 1888, as well as a county cricket championship, owe much to the railways. Without them the players and, crucially, the paying fans would not have been able to travel to watch their teams play.

The railways catered for Londoners' other pleasures, even those of the very rich. Golf courses had proliferated in the suburbs and outer districts and had deliberately been built next to railway stations – or in the case of Sandy Lodge (now Moor Park) on the Metropolitan railway, where the station was specially built to accommodate the golfers. The Great Eastern ran a golfers' special on Sundays to Hunstanton, some 112 miles from London, timed to give the sportsmen an afternoon round. Hunters, too, were catered for, with their horses, hounds and servants if necessary, and special hunters' tickets at cheap rates were offered by several railways including the Great Western and the Metropolitan.

Even the dead benefited from the railway network. London's population doubled in the first half of the nineteenth century and the lack of cemetery space meant that graves were frequently reopened, leaving disinterred bones scattered across churchyards. As burying people within the capital's boundaries become more and more impractical because of overcrowding and the high cost of land, trains carrying bodies for burial outside London became commonplace. The cholera epidemic of 1848–9 gave the spur to this initiative, which led to the creation of a special terminal for the departed, Waterloo Necropolis, next to the main station. When a developer, Sir Richard Broun, came up with the idea of buying a large tract of land at Brookwood, in Surrey, twenty-five miles from the centre of London, to create a massive 2,000-acre cemetery, he obviously needed good transport links with the capital and the railway was the only possible solution. Broun's company, London Necropolis, went into partnership with the London & South Western, whose passengers certainly did not want to travel in carriages used by the dead, and therefore special new rolling stock had to be bought.

The trains not only had to be divided into three classes, both for corpses and the grieving friends and relatives, but also had to serve two different stations at Brookwood, one for Anglicans and the other for non-conformist denominations who are buried on the chillier north side of the cemetery. The logistics of dividing up the dead into six categories must have taxed the company and one just hopes that the first-class deceased appreciated the 'greater degree of decoration' that justified the higher fare paid by their loved ones. The first funeral train pulled out of Waterloo Necropolis in November 1854 and the service quickly built up to a train per day, carrying up to forty-eight bodies in the 'stiffs express', as it was known by railway workers. Rival services emerged, notably from King's Cross to the Great Northern Cemetery at New Southgate, but the Waterloo service remained the most heavily used.

While by the 1860s the railways were on the way to becoming ubiquitous, even for the dead, maintaining profitability was still a struggle for many companies as they expanded too rapidly. The mini-mania stimulated by the greater availability of capital and the renewed interest in railway promotion of the 1860s were bound to suffer a similar fate to that of the predecessor. This time the fall in 1866 was even harder, bringing down many railway contractors, including Sir Samuel Peto, and three major railway companies. The roots of the collapse were in the unregulated banking industry, compounded by the way that contractors had kept many railway companies afloat by funding the lines they built. Overend Gurney was the finance house which had staked most on the new railway bubble of the early 1860s, but the projects it funded were proving more marginal and less profitable, for example, the expensive efforts by the London & Chatham and Peto to build a terminus in the City of London and the construction of obscure railways in distant countries, such as Spain and Canada. Peto and others borrowed against these projects, and when they were unable to pay the bank went down, taking with it the whole financial system. The panic following Overend Gurney's collapse led to creditors besieging other banking houses, prompting a near riot in the austere surroundings of Lombard Street, and the Bank of England had to suspend the Bank Act of 1844 to allow other banks to issue paper money instead of gold to creditors.

Up to that date it was the worst banking collapse in British history, later superseded only by the 1929 crash, and its cause could definitely be laid at the door of the railways. Charles Dickens was unequivocal in his criticism of the railway companies, and of the government which had allowed their unfettered growth, describing the events that led to the financial disaster as caused by 'a muddle of railways, in all directions possible, and impossible, with no general public scheme, no general public supervision, enormous waste of money, no fixable responsibility'.[32] The three main railways which collapsed had all been on a financial knife-edge in any case: the London & Chatham was a poor railway, always in financial difficulties; the Great Eastern was struggling with the financial burden of having built Liverpool Street station; and the London, Brighton & South Coast, once very prosperous, had overstretched itself by opening a series of branch lines to protect its territory from neighbouring rivals.

Although the companies went bust, the railways themselves kept running, under the control of receivers, but the industry's leaders were so concerned about their viability that they petitioned the government for nationalization. The leader of the delegation which knocked on Benjamin Disraeli's door at Number 10 Downing Street in March 1867 was none other than Sir Daniel Gooch, Brunel's great locomotive engineer who had recently been promoted to the chairmanship of the Great Western Railway, which was also in dire straits. What made such an arch-Tory go begging to the government was a real fear that the whole railway system would go under and would have to cease operations. The Great Western itself had only just survived the financial crash, and despite huge takings from the fare box was still struggling to pay loans taken out at the high interest rate of 9 per cent. Gooch was accompanied by two rivals, Edward Watkin of the South Eastern and Samuel Laing of the London, Brighton & South Coast, and they put forward the idea of a £1m loan, backed by the government, to rescue the Great Western, presumably with the notion that the other railways would be bailed out too. In truth this represented nationalization by the back door and Disraeli would have none of it since such an idea ran counter to the Victorian *Zeitgeist*. Disraeli simply replied that it was not the government's duty to interfere with the affairs of a private company in that way.

Despite the concerns of Gooch and his fellow grandees, the railways survived this upheaval and, remarkably, started to expand again quite soon. But the financial collapse of 1866 had done untold damage to their reputation and, worse, this was to be compounded by a series of disasters that put the spotlight on their safety record.

# EIGHT

# DANGER AND
# EXPLOITATION
# ON THE TRACKS

Although the railways were now accessible to a much larger proportion of the population by the 1870s, thanks to the spread of the network and cheaper tickets, there was still an important public relations battle to be won. The railways were accepted and well used, but not loved or even, for the most part, trusted. Some of their nicknames say it all: the Manchester, Sheffield and Lincolnshire was the 'Mucky, Slow & Lazy' while the Oxford, Worcester and Wolverhampton was the 'Old Worse & Worse'.

The big companies were singled out for frequent criticism in the newspapers and consequently their image was very poor. The task facing the railways in winning over the public was a complex one. When they tried to improve the comfort of their passengers, offering such amenities as steam-heated carriages and picnic baskets, and better service by speeding up trains and providing better timetables, their profitability went down. They provided the best train services in the world, faster than those of any other country, and competition, together with the provision of the parliamentary trains, kept the fares down, but the financial crash of 1866 had dented confidence in the railways. Share ownership was more widespread now and many widows and the genteel poor depended on dividends to eke out a respectable living. The financial collapse had ruined many of these middle-class investors and quite understandably they pointed the finger at the railways.

If it had just been financial incompetence and the sense that the rail companies were rapacious Leviathans exploiting their passengers, the railways might have won over the public through the improvements in the service they were making. Their Achilles heel, however, was safety, with the number and seriousness of accidents inevitably increasing as more trains crowded on to the system at ever greater speeds. One of the most famous men of the age, Charles Dickens, was caught up in a rail accident and became a major advocate for improved safety. Surprisingly, up to this point, safety had been less of an issue than might have been expected, given the disastrous start with the death of Huskisson and the widespread fears about this new fast form of transport. Initially, there was virtually no oversight of safety considerations and it was not until two Acts, passed in 1840 and 1842, that a body of inspectors was created (invariably men from the Royal Engineers) with responsibility for both checking new lines and investigating accidents.

The early trains were light and travelled slowly, which meant that accidents tended to be relatively minor. The first serious crash was in 1841 on the Great Western at Sonning, near Reading, when a train ran into a land slip. Many passengers, most of whom were workmen building the Houses of Parliament and returning to the West Country for Christmas, were thrown out of the open wagons and eight people lost their lives. The subsequent story of rail safety was characterized by gradual improvement as lessons were learnt from these accidents; this first one was no exception, resulting in all wagons being enclosed by a roof, a welcome measure for many poor passengers travelling in third class who had to brave the elements.

The potential risk of a major catastrophe on the railways was highlighted by an accident in France the following year when a train at Versailles burst into flames following a collision. Fifty-two people were killed, many of them incinerated as they had been locked into their carriages to prevent them jumping out between stations. Unsurprisingly, the accident mostly put an end to that practice and on this side of the Channel it was nearly half a century before there was a disaster with a higher death toll (at Armagh, described in the next chapter).

Accidents became more frequent, however, not simply because there were more trains, but because the number of services increased at a faster rate than the growth in mileage of the system, and this higher intensity of use of the tracks exposed passengers to greater risk. It is no coincidence that many of the major accidents in railway history have taken place in and around London, by far the busiest part of the network. With more trains using the track, the system of time interval signalling was inevitably put under pressure, leading to more collisions. At Lewisham in June 1857 one train went into the back of another, killing eleven people on a busy Sunday night when both were full of day-trippers. It is a recurring theme that many of the worst rail disasters have taken place when people were travelling on excursions or on other special services like troop trains, partly because they were by definition very full but also because they were not in the usual timetable and railway workers, on occasion, forgot about the unscheduled trains.

A similar rear-end collision four years later, in the Clayton tunnel on the Brighton line, was more significant in prompting the public and politicians to put pressure on the railway companies to improve their safety standards. The tunnel is 1.5 mile long and the dangers of a collision had been recognized by the London, Brighton & South Coast Railway, which had installed a crude type of semaphore system with a signalman at each end. The two could communicate with each other through a telegraph system and indicate when a train was through the tunnel. This was an early form of 'block' working, the system by which the track is divided into sections that can only ever be occupied by one train, thereby preventing collisions. Telegraphs, a way of communicating along electric wires that was a precursor of the telephone, had first been introduced on the railway as early as 1836 with a trial on the Liverpool & Manchester Railway. A telegraph system was installed on the Great Western between Paddington and Slough in 1843 and its usefulness was demonstrated a couple of years later when it enabled a murderer, who had jumped on a Paddington-bound train at Slough, to be apprehended, a full sixty-five years before the more infamous Dr Crippen.[1] Soon the telegraph became symbiotic with the railways, both for their own purposes and as the spine of the Post Office's public system.

However, on that fateful day on the Brighton line, Sunday, 25 August 1861, the telegraph did not help and even added to the confusion. Three trains left Brighton in quick succession, two of them excursions filled with day-trippers heading for London, and the two signalmen became confused about which was which. The signalman at the south end thought he had received a clear signal from his colleague, and sent in a train which smashed into the earlier one, killing twenty-three people, many burnt alive as hot coals from the engine started a fire when the second locomotive toppled over, and injuring 176. By coincidence, within a week another sixteen people were killed and 300 injured in an accident at Kentish Town on what is now the North London line. An excursion service from Kew, ironically organized to raise money for a railway benevolent fund to help compensate staff injured in accidents, collided with a ballast train as result of a mistake by a signalman, sending several carriages tumbling down an embankment.

Despite these disasters, there was great reluctance among railway managers to accept any outside interference in their methods of operation and the Clayton tunnel accident did not bring about the obvious improvements to the signalling system that were clearly necessary. Over the previous two decades, there had been several other accidents caused by the time-interval signalling system and the Board of Trade Inspectorate was constantly urging the railway companies to abandon it. However, the companies drew the rather perverse conclusion from Clayton that introducing a space-interval system – i.e. one where sections of occupied track would be protected by a danger signal – would not only slow up traffic but increase the risk as drivers would become lazy and less alert.[2] Specifically, the managers argued that the signal in the Clayton accident had not worked properly and that the space-interval block had failed to prevent the crash. But this was rather like arguing that because a faulty watch does not show the right time, timepieces as a whole are a bad idea! Nevertheless, the railway companies' view prevailed for several years since the inspectors had only an advisory role and could not enforce changes. Nor, in truth, would they have wanted to. The inspectors valued their independence and they did not want to become an arm of government. This, after all, was still at the height of a laissez-faire attitude and no government wanted to become wholly responsible for enforcing safety on the railway. The rather loose arrangements over safety regulation suited all the parties until the roll call of accidents simply became too great.

Four years later there were two further accidents in quick succession, which led to renewed calls for action on railway safety. Both crashes were caused by the failings of trackmen working on the line. In the first, a train went off the rails on the Great Western at Rednal in Shropshire on 7 June 1865, killing thirteen, and just two days later at Staplehurst in Kent on the South Eastern, another derailment resulted in the loss of ten lives. This second accident added considerably to the pressure on the train companies because Charles Dickens was a passenger and not only ministered to the injured and dying but later became a high-profile campaigner for safety on the railways. Thanks to him, we also know far more than we would otherwise about the accident, which demonstrated the lack of any but the most rudimentary safety devices. Indeed, while the immediate circumstances of the crash may have been somewhat unusual, the accident highlighted the way that one simple mistake could lead to disaster if there was no back-up system – now a characteristic of the safety systems of all public transport. In other words, the railways relied on its workers to get it right every time, or else risk causing a major disaster.

In the case of Staplehurst, the hapless individual whose mistake led to the accident was the foreman of the track gang, one John Benge, whose men had to replace a timber on a small bridge that crossed a muddy stream. Astonishingly, they planned to carry out the work in an eighty-five-minute window of opportunity between scheduled trains. Benge made two mistakes and the events leading up to the disaster reveal the patch-and-mend nature of the railways at that time. First, he failed to check the train timetable properly. There were no normal services scheduled during that period but there was a boat train whose timings varied because it connected with a cross-Channel packet that could dock only at high tide. Its times were shown in the working timetable[3] but Benge misread it, believing the train was due to arrive at 5.20 p.m. rather than 3.15 p.m. Secondly, he failed to instruct his men to place warning detonators on the line or to stand far enough from the bridge to be able to warn a train in time for it to stop. By the time Dickens' train arrived at 50 mph, the timbers had been replaced but not the track, and five of the carriages hurtled off the bridge into the stream.

Dickens, whose carriage fortuitously had not plunged into the ditch, immediately turned himself into a type of human St Bernard's. After ensuring that his mistress and her mother, with whom he was travelling, were all right, he grabbed his brandy flask and began administering it to the injured and dying. When the drink ran out, he returned to his compartment to get his other full bottle of brandy. While Dickens suffered no more than bruises and sprains, he never really fully recovered from the accident and died on its fifth anniversary, aged only fifty-seven. As L. T. C. Rolt puts it in his classic book on accidents, *Red for Danger*, 'we cannot estimate the loss which English literature sustained as a result of John Benge's tragic mistake. Certainly he deprived us of the solution to the *Mystery of Edwin Drood*.'[4]

Disasters were now occurring regularly, notably the awful derailment and consequent fire at Abergele in north Wales in August 1868 on the Irish Mail, which attracted attention not only because the death toll of thirty-three was higher than in any previous accident but also because among the victims were an aristocratic couple, Lord and Lady Farnham. The circumstances, too, were particularly horrific because the passenger train had hit trucks containing paraffin, which burst into flames on impact, and the dead had to be identified by their watches and jewellery.

Very slowly, safety was improving as a result of the hard lessons learnt from such accidents. While that process may appear to be somewhat callous, the development of safety procedures was an entirely new concept and it would have been impossible for an inspectorate to have imposed hard and fast rules from the outset. As ever, the railways were pioneers. Concepts like 'fail-safe'[5] and risk-assessment had simply not been developed, which is why fundamental mistakes were made which, with hindsight, created unnecessary risks. For example, many early signals, notably one controlling the entrance to Reading station in the 1840s, showed only a 'proceed' aspect. The Reading signal was a ball hoisted up on a pole when the line was clear, which meant that the regulations were a double negative: 'If the ball is not visible, the train must not pass it.' This was certainly a recipe for confusion but an understandable mistake to make because the railways had to work out from first principles how to deal with the safety problems posed by transporting unprecedented numbers of people at unprecedented speeds. The series of disasters did prompt some action with the passing of two new regulatory Acts in 1871 and 1873, though they were exhortations rather than regulations, requiring companies, for example, to provide returns on the mileage of their lines that were protected by block, rather than time interval, signalling (as opposed to making the railways fit it as standard). The new legislation also empowered the Board of Trade to set up special courts of inquiry following an accident, but the emphasis remained on self-regulation rather than policing by an external body.

The 1871 Act did, belatedly, recognize that the staff were the group most at risk from the railways' activities. The statistics required by these new Acts reveal the shocking death toll of railway employees: in the five years up to the end of 1878, the railways killed an average of 682 of their workers *every year*, twenty times the number of passenger deaths. Astonishingly, the railways were the third most dangerous profession after mining and the Merchant Navy. Indeed, being a shunter in a busy yard was acknowledged by a parliamentary inquiry to be the most dangerous job in Britain,[6] exacerbated by the onerous working conditions. Adrian Vaughan, an ex-signalman and author, cites the example of shunters at Didcot as late as 1891 who, according to time sheets in his possession, 'routinely worked 14 hours day or night'.[7] Given they worked six shifts weekly, this amounted to eighty-eight hours per week.

The staff were not just a danger to themselves. Long hours, lack of training and inadequate pay were universal and contributed to many of the fatal accidents on the railway. The poor fellow responsible for the 1861 Kentish Town accident described above was a nineteen-year-old partially deaf youth who worked a fifteen-hour day as a relief signalman for just 14 shillings a week. Even an experienced driver working for the Great Western in 1867 was earning just 42 shillings per week. They were the elite and other railwaymen were on far less. The investigation report of a head-on crash at Radstock on the Somerset & Dorset revealed that those involved were equally overworked and under-educated.[8] The telegraph clerk, a boy of eighteen, was on duty from 6.30 a.m. to 9.30 p.m. for 17s 6d per week, and the signalman was a novice who could not read the telegraph instruments. The station-master worked from 5.30 a.m. to 6.30 p.m. and his boy assistant from 8 a.m. to 10.30 p.m.

This was not untypical. The working conditions set by the Liverpool & Manchester, outlined in Chapter 2, became pretty much the norm. As a chronicler of railway workers puts it, 'since a highly successful and profitable railway was the end result, the practices of the Liverpool & Manchester were taken up by most of the early railways in Britain and overseas'.[9] Railway workers were expected to work very long hours for what seemed like meagre wages. At the same time, working for the railways was perceived as an attractive job with wages above those offered in other large industries and well above the pay of an agricultural labourer. Not only did the railways offer long-term stable employment but, for the most part, the work itself was far more pleasant than, say, in a Victorian mine or a factory. Moreover, the low pay was often leavened with perks such as the cheap rental of a railway cottage: the policemen of the London & Birmingham could rent one at Wolverton for a mere 1s 6d but given that their shifts were routinely from 7 a.m. to 10.30 p.m., or 5.30 a.m. to 9.15 p.m., with no meal break, six days per week, they did not need many home comforts apart from a bed. Promotion might take years through the Buggins' Turn system but the prospect was enticing and it was hardly surprising that agricultural and other labourers who were used to a hand-to-mouth existence jumped at the chance of a permanent job on the railways, however long the hours.

From the beginning, the railway companies recruited extensively from the army and navy and created a uniformed service. Soldiers and sailors were accustomed to an even harsher discipline, since flogging was still routine in the forces, and were also used to dressing smartly. Farm labourers were able to take on portering jobs, which required considerable strength in manhandling goods and luggage. White-collar posts would be snapped up by anyone with a modicum of education and, during the 1840s and 1850s when expansion of the railways was at its fastest, there was the opportunity of rapid progress through the ranks for a junior clerk who could perhaps expect to run a small station after a few years. Employment practices were basic with new staff often taken on only after an interview with the board and training was on the job.

The companies almost completely shunned women. According to the 1851 census, there were just fifty-four female workers in the industry, mostly gate-keepers. As Helena Wojtczak puts it eloquently in her history of railwaywomen: 'The railways are imbued with maleness to their very core. Everyone connected with the creation and operation of railways was male: businessmen and financiers, architects and engineers, navvies and bricklayers, managers and operating staff.'[10] That masculinity was also reinforced by the military-style uniforms. Level-crossing keepers were an exception because they could be taken on with no training, frequently on the death of a husband with whom they had shared the task anyway, and they did their job largely hidden from the passengers. There were a few tasks such as ladies' room attendants, which in Victorian society clearly could not be undertaken by men, but there were remarkably few female clerks, in contrast with several European countries where such jobs were routinely filled by women. It was not until the First World War that women en masse were considered for employment on the railways as it then became essential for them to replace the men who had gone to the front (see Chapter 11).

The railway companies' attitude to their workforce was a rather typical Victorian mix of paternalism and autocracy. On the Great Western, for example, staff who kept out of trouble and were good at their work received a bonus every six months. From 1847, a doctor on site was provided, though only the initial consultation for the administration of first aid was free.[11] All Great Western staff were given cheap or free coal and apart from locomotive men who had to find their own white corduroy clothes – the poor womenfolk who had to wash these clothes must have been aghast at such a bizarre choice of colour – all other grades were supplied with a uniform, a practice that was typical of the better-run railways. The porters of the Great Western were decked out in an attractive green and wore an elegant glazed top hat, conferring immediate respectability on men from the most modest of backgrounds. Not surprisingly, these uniforms were a source of great pride for any new recruit and helped to create the sense of belonging that was deliberately fostered. The companies may have been authoritarian and considered that it was a privilege for the men to be 'in service' but the corollary of that was that they inspired fierce loyalty – even when it was not merited. The companies divided and ruled through the increasingly Byzantine grading structure that was based along military lines. There were different grades for every type of task and each job had its own promotion ladder, which was a great inducement for long service. Locomotive men, for example, started as cleaners then became 'passed' cleaners, who were able to fire locomotives, then firemen and 'passed' firemen who were permitted to drive occasionally but were still on relatively low wages. Then, at last, they became drivers but at first were confined to shunting engines around the yard or the occasional short goods run. It was only in their fifties that they would get the freedom of the rails and become one of the elite, driving passenger expresses around the country. In the same way, porters and ticket clerks could aspire, eventually, to become station-masters (and, if they were lucky, then enjoy progression to ever bigger stations) and telegraph boys might eventually qualify as signal inspectors. All this differentiation stimulated jealousy and rivalry between grades, which suited the employers as it ensured that strikes were normally confined to one group of dissatisfied men, making walk-outs across the board difficult to organize and, consequently, rare.

Treatment of their employees varied too, with some companies taking a greater interest in the well-being of their workforce than others – but all were pretty ruthless in making workers redundant in bad times and in failing to pay compensation to those injured at work or to the relatives of those killed. The immediate assumption among the employers was that accidents were the fault of the employees and their cursory reports of incidents make cruel reading, such as these from the Caledonian railway: 'Henry Hughes, platelayer, standing too close to a passing train at the Belmont Station, had his foot so severely crushed that death ensued; John Scott, pointsman, in the act of shifting points, lost his balance and fell under the wheels of a mineral train', and so on. For those who broke the rules, there was little mercy: drivers who went too fast were summarily sacked, as were porters who were rude to passengers, or policemen who fell asleep at work. Yet, shifts of sixteen or even eighteen hours a day, six days per week, were routine and the terms of employment were weighted heavily in favour of the employers, with overtime frequently not recognized but any time off immediately penalized. While a worker wanting to better himself elsewhere would have to give three months' notice, in the absence of any labour laws he could be summarily dismissed if he transgressed or simply became surplus to requirements. The railways expected their 'servants', an expression that was current right into the twentieth century, to do their bidding. The very word suggests that the companies treated their workers rather like the staff of a stately home, and they expected them to be like their children, well behaved, going to church and well turned out: 'The object was to [create] a body of men with instinctive reactions of safety to train operating [a bit of a contradiction given the tiredness engendered by the long hours], willing to work where and when required, for as long as required, whose unquestioning loyalty could be taken for granted, but who could be sacked, fined or suspended for any infractions of the multitude of rules.'[12]

At times, though, the railways exceeded the limits of this unwritten contract and nothing could excuse their steadfast refusal to recognize even the most basic rights of the workers in their quest to maintain the dividends of their shareholders. The railway companies may not have been happy about their staff forming combines, but they were quick to do so themselves, creating in 1854 an effective lobbying organization, the Railway Companies Association,[13] which was influential in preventing unwanted regulation of the railways being passed in Parliament and even, later, in delaying nationalization.

It was hardly surprising that in response to the harshness of their conditions and of the ruthless power of the companies, workers soon tried to organize themselves, first by providing support for each other through welfare schemes and then by creating unions. As soon as the Great Western started running trains in 1838, its workers formed a Provident Society to provide relief for its members who fell sick or suffered an accident, and a rudimentary pension. Although the railway companies notionally supported these societies, they built up their funds largely from contributions from the meagre wages of the workforce. The amounts that these societies were able to pay out were thus often insufficient and several fell into financial difficulties, though in periods of high profits the company would normally bail them out. Rather unfairly, workers in the most dangerous jobs, such as platelayers, were often not allowed to join a scheme because the hazardous nature of their job made the need for pay-outs too likely! The better companies normally did offer a small ex-gratia payment to widows of men who had died but their benevolence could never be relied upon. They also encouraged their staff to indulge in wholesome extra-curricular activity, such as musical bands, sport and even drama. They created Mechanics' Institutes, too, in order to provide a theoretical basis for the skills that workers traditionally acquired on the job and many also offered 'mutual improvement' classes.

It did not go unnoticed among more militant workers that these provident funds relieved the companies of the need to provide such support themselves and thereby boosted their profitability, as the *Pall Mall Gazette* pointed out in 1866: 'The dividends of the shareholders are kept up, and the widows of mangled porters and stokers have a pension from a fund provided by the porters and stokers themselves.'[14] Not surprisingly, the tough working conditions prompted moves to industrial action and the creation of unions and, equally unsurprisingly, these initiatives were resisted strongly by the companies. A refusal to recognize the existence of a union and the mass dismissals of strikers were the knee-jerk reactions of virtually all directors of railway companies, big or small.

The right to organize collectively had been permitted in law since 1824, the year before the opening of the Stockton & Darlington, but that did not mean employers had to recognize any combines formed by the workers. As with so much in this history, the Liverpool & Manchester railway was the trailblazer and, with regard to industrial relations, that meant a draconian approach to labour unrest became the norm. In 1836, a group of engine drivers on the pioneering railway had stopped work, demanding extra pay for firemen. The leader, John Hewitt, was promptly sacked, resulting in a walk-out. Worse, four of the strikers were sentenced to a month's hard labour for breaking their contracts, a punishment that included six hours daily on the treadmill. The directors eventually relented, facilitating the release of the men and taking them back, but 'a stint on the treadmill obviously concentrated the minds of the strikers on their tasks for, in 1842, two of them were awarded £5 [two weeks' wages] for good conduct'.[15]

In the first major attempt at a strike, 178 drivers, firemen and fitters of the Eastern Counties, a constantly struggling railway, handed in their notices to quit in August 1850, demanding that the corrupt locomotive superintendent John Gooch (brother of the illustrious Daniel Gooch of the Great Western) should be sacked. It was they, rather than Gooch and his equally bent chairman, David Waddington MP, who had to go and, to add insult to injury, the men were blacklisted so that they could not find employment elsewhere in the industry. Gooch quickly found 178 replacements from other railways or from the pool of labour that seemed ever available at most times in the nineteenth century.

There were other small local and mostly totally unsuccessful strikes in the first three decades of the railways but the power and obduracy of the employers managed to see off any lasting trade union organization until the creation of the Railway Clerks Association in 1865. While it may seem surprising that the white-collar workers should be the first to organize rather than their blue-collar colleagues for whom the daily toil was far harder, the clerks were viewed as less of a threat by the owners and consequently given an easier passage. It was the locomotive drivers and fireman who had the industrial muscle, though, and it was not long before a strike by 400 men of the London, Brighton & South Coast railway became the first to result in train services being disrupted. They downed tools in March 1867 over their meagre daily pay, which was just 7s 6d for a driver, and 4s 6d for a fireman. The company's attempt to recruit replacements failed and virtually all its services were stopped, including the lucrative race trains for the first spring meeting at Epsom. An accommodation with the management was quickly reached, involving a re-examination of their pay and – crucially – including the guarantee of no victimization for those who had gone on strike. Their fellows on the North Eastern, who were foolhardy enough to attempt to follow the Brighton men's example the following month, were not so lucky, coming up against a far more vicious and tough-minded manage-ment. The men's demands were for a ten-hour day (a sixty-hour week), two hours' overtime to count as a quarter of a day, and time and a half on Sundays. But they were less well organized than the Brighton men and failed to attract all-out support. Blacklegs were quickly recruited, the strike collapsed without having disrupted services and some of the men were prosecuted, though only one successfully. There were threats of strikes on several other railways but following the defeat of the

North Eastern men, these quickly dissipated in the face of a united front from the railway companies; the nascent union to which these men belonged, the Engine Drivers' and Firemen's United Society, collapsed barely a year after its formation.

However, trade unionism clearly could not be held back, given the reforming nature of the times and the growing numbers of workers, but it took the intervention of a sympathetic customer, Michael Thomas Bass, the Liberal MP for Derby, to ease the birth of a union that would encompass the majority of railway workers. Bass was critical of the employment practices of the Midland railway, which carried half a million barrels of his firm's beer annually.[16] Indeed, the undercroft of St Pancras had been built with the beer business from Bass and other Midland brewers in mind: it is supported by 800 columns[17] that are 29ft 4ins apart, the right size to enable barrels to be stored efficiently between them. Bass, therefore, was rather more than a client – his custom, quite literally, underpinned the railway – which meant that the company could not afford to ignore his intervention on behalf of the workers. Bass realized that the long hours experienced by the Midland's workers were probably no worse than many others and helped to organize the first meeting of the Amalgamated Society of Railway Servants in London in 1872. He went on to help fund the nascent union and subsidized its newspaper, the *Railway Service Gazette*.

Attracting members to the new union was at first difficult, given the continued hostility of most employers, and the union concentrated on recruiting the better-paid men, such as guards, drivers and signalmen, rather than porters or platelayers, to stress its moderate credentials. Its strategy was not so much to call its members out on strike but instead it focused on lobbying to reduce hours and improve safety, knowing this struck a chord with the wider public. Improvements came slowly, such as the passing of the Employers' Liability Act in 1880, which meant the employers were no longer free of responsibility for the accidents they caused to their workers. Membership of the union grew in the latter part of the 1880s to reach 26,000 by the end of that decade, though still well under 5 per cent of the industry's workforce. However, the union established the beginnings of a system of collective bargaining when the North Eastern agreed to meet a delegation accompanied by trade union officials during a dispute in 1889. That was to prove the spur to more rapid growth as workers could clearly see the advantages of membership.

The main union for drivers and firemen, the Associated Society of Locomotive Engineers and Firemen (ASLEF), established itself in 1880 through the efforts of a group of locomen on the Great Western and was open only to those on the footplate. This split remains to this day, with the continued existence of ASLEF and the separate Rail, Marine and Transport workers' union (RMT), formed by a series of mergers from the original Amalgamated Society of Railway Servants and later the National Union of Railwaymen, which has a few drivers as members. ASLEF was slow to grow but its endorsement of an ultimately unsuccessful strike by footplatemen on the Midland Railway in 1887 and, crucially, its successful legal support for two men who were accused of manslaughter following a fatal train crash on the Manchester, Sheffield & Lincolnshire Railway in the same year, proved to be strong recruiting agents, enabling the union to build up its membership and industrial muscle.

The length of the working day was the principal issue, from both an industrial and a safety point of view. The more enlightened companies, such as the London & North Western and the Great Western, instructed their men to work a maximum of twelve hours but this was possible only if a relief man were available. The loyalty of workers like signalmen to the railway meant they never simply walked off the job and forced the closure of a line. At the other end of the scale, there were callous employers like the directors of the Cambrian, in Wales, who almost revelled in their harsh treatment of their workers. A parliamentary inquiry in 1891 revealed that for the previous two decades the company had routinely booked men on shifts of thirty-six hours and, on occasion, even forty-seven hours.

As well as this enormous permanent workforce on the railways, which reached 621,000 by the turn of the century, the navvies were still at work building lines. Arguably the greatest main line in Britain, and certainly the most scenic, was one of the last to be built: the Settle & Carlisle line which created an alternative route to Scotland and was an essential part of the Midland's expansion plans. The beauty of the line through the most remote country in England was probably rather lost on those poor navvies who built it. The difficulty of their task was compounded by the mountainous terrain ravaged by blizzards in winter and the absence of any significant town throughout its seventy-three-mile length.

The decision to construct the Settle & Carlisle can be seen as the last throes of the railway companies' competitive urges. Crazy as it seems, there was a case for a third trunk route to Scotland, evidenced in hindsight by the fact that despite an attempt by British Rail to close the line in the 1980s, it still flourishes today as a vital freight and diversionary route, as well as attracting considerable tourist traffic. The Midland was eager to develop its Anglo-Scottish traffic once St Pancras was opened in 1868 but was hamstrung by having to combine its carriages with those of the London & North Western, which made sure its rivals' passengers were punished for not using its own trains. Midland passengers were transferred at a small North Yorkshire station called Ingleton, then hitched to the back of a freight train which meandered over the moors to a freezing platform at Tebay on the main line at the base of the climb to Shap. Here they were routinely dumped to wait for a connection.

Not surprisingly, the Midland sought to build its own route across the North Yorkshire moors and obtained parliamentary authorization in 1865, in alliance with the Lancashire & Yorkshire and, crucially, the North British. This Scottish railway had expanded from its original route on the East Coast between Berwick and Edinburgh to reach Carlisle, south of the border, in 1862; therefore, once the Settle & Carlisle was built, it would provide a route for the Midland's trains to all Scotland's cities.

The Settle & Carlisle, however, nearly didn't happen. The Midland got cold feet when the London & North Western cunningly promised better treatment of its Scottish passengers if the Midland's madcap scheme were to be abandoned. Its chairman, W. P. Price, MP, wondered if the company really wanted to build this difficult railway, which would eventually cost £3.5m (£250m in today's money), half as much again as the original estimate of £2.2m, through country with virtually no inhabitants or local business, just for the sake of its Scottish traffic? Price, urged on by his shareholders, tried to ditch the scheme. But that was not easy, since it required a bill through Parliament and the Midland's two allies objected to its passage as they saw enormous advantages for themselves.

The Midland gritted its teeth and set out on this momentous task. It found a willing surveyor, a gaunt and tall young Tasmanian, Charles Sharland. Just as Stephenson had determined the route of the Liverpool & Manchester by pounding across the moors and fells half a century before, so in a similar way, armed with nothing but a few rudimentary instruments and a couple of assistants, Sharland spent months, including three weeks totally snowbound at an inn, working out where the line should go in this barren countryside. He managed to keep the gradient to 1 in 100, which was impressive given the hilly terrain, but the downside was that more than a quarter of the route would need such an incline, and expensive tunnels and viaducts were needed throughout. From Settle, the railway climbed 700 feet over twelve miles, then reached the mile and a third-long Blea Moor tunnel, which took four years to hew out of the limestone and shale. Hamilton Ellis, the chronicler of the Midland Railway, writing some eighty years later, suggests 'it proved a damp, terrible tunnel. It drove men mad so that they could go underground no more. To this day, though much shorter than many English tunnels, it is a horrible place'[18] where smoke seemed to linger and black icicles formed threateningly from the ceiling. In all there are 3.5 miles of tunnels and dozens of viaducts, the longest of which is Ribblehead, which stretches a quarter of a mile on its twenty-four arches. It is built of the local limestone with the result that, despite reaching 165 feet above the valley floor, it blends seamlessly into the countryside, especially on one of the all too common bleak grey days. The decay of the limestone was the excuse British Rail gave for its attempt to close the line in the 1980s but repairs were made and now the line's future is assured.

Work started in 1869, and it took seven years and the efforts of 6,000 men to complete it. Poor Sharland, whose route was used faithfully, never saw the completion of the scheme. He died soon after his survey at the age of just twenty-six, his health broken by the effort. He was the line's first victim but by no means its last. The total death toll is unknown but over a hundred navvies and members of their families succumbed to smallpox in the summer of 1871 in the parish of Batty Green, which took its odd name from the nearby pothole called Batty Wife's Hole. The Ribblehead viaduct alone claimed one death per week during the five years it took to build. Though it is impossible to prove, the line probably took the highest toll on its workforce of any railway built in Britain, as a result of the harsh conditions and difficult terrain; the evidence is in the various cemeteries and memorials along its route.

The Midland's route to Scotland, via the Settle & Carlisle, may have been more circuitous than those of its East and West Coast rivals', but the company, realizing it was at a disadvantage in terms of the length of the journey, offered a far better service to its passengers than its rivals. Pullman and sleeping cars were provided in carriages that incorporated the innovation of sprung wheel bogies (which gave a far smoother ride than simple wheels on axles). According to Jack Simmons, writing in 1978: 'A Midland Scotch express of 1876 belongs firmly to the modern world; those of its West Coast and East Coast rivals were still, one might say, medieval.'[19] The Settle & Carlisle line was the last to be built by traditional methods, using little more than the sheer brute strength of the navvies and lots of dynamite – barely different from those employed by Stephenson on the Liverpool & Manchester over half a century before. Thereafter there would be increased mechanization and less reliance on the navvies.

There was one other significant line built around that time, the Hull & Barnsley, born of the Corporation of Hull's dissatisfaction with the monopoly of the North Eastern railway. The name was a misnomer since the railway, which was completed in 1885 after five years of construction, never reached Barnsley. It was to prove an expensive mistake right from the outset as it had to cut through two miles of chalk which, together with other construction difficulties and the fact that its near eighty miles of railway merely duplicated other lines, resulted in the company going bankrupt soon after the railway opened. One more main line remained to be built, the Great Central (see Chapter 10) but most of the energy of the railway companies was now being focused on improvements rather than further expansion and expensive lines that duplicated those of their rivals.

# NINE

# SPEEDING TO DANGER

There never was truly a golden age of the railways. There was always something that was not quite right in the world of the iron road, whether it was a spate of accidents or the financial difficulties of the railway companies or complaints about poor service. The railway network was always evolving, always needing to be improved as passengers became more demanding and technologies developed. The railways could, as it were, never stand still and their managers were always faced with a complex set of questions for which there was never a perfect answer. There was a continual requirement to upgrade lines, develop faster locomotives, provide more efficient timetables and improve stations. Traffic on some lines would decline due to external circumstances such as rural depopulation, while on others it would start exceeding what could be easily provided.

However, the last two decades of the nineteenth century and the first of the twentieth were probably as close to a golden age as the railways ever achieved. The network was nearly complete and the trains were getting less 'medieval'. The railway tradition had been to look after the locomotives better than the carriages, with engines being 'groomed and polished like so many *objets d'art* while many carriages were little better than so many dog boxes on wheels'.[1] Now this was changing. Services were more regular and carriages were more comfortable with facilities such as better lighting, toilets and dining cars beginning to appear in the 1880s. The first all-corridor train ran on the Great Western in 1892 and electric lighting started to be used around then too, but did not become universal on new trains until after the First World War.

All these developments came quite slowly. For the first half-century of the railways, passengers had no other form of heating than the occasional portable foot-warmer which was nothing more than a flat metal container full of hot water. After a long gap between stations, there would have been a rush to swap the now cold metal boxes for fresh hot ones. It was only towards the end of the century that heating became widely available, mostly using steam piped through the train. Lighting originally consisted of stinking oil pots that gave a feeble light and it was only in the early 1880s that a better system using gas became widespread, although this obviously presented a safety risk. According to Stanley Hall,[2] electric lighting became available in the 1890s and by the outbreak of the First World War 'there were only 12,000 electric lit carriages in service', fewer than a quarter of the total. Toilets, again, only started appearing in the 1870s, along with the corridors that enabled all passengers to have access and until then train timetables were slowed by the need for convenience stops at those stations where huge facilities had been made available.

Most crucially, though, the railways now had no significant competition from any other mode of transport until motor buses started appearing in substantial numbers towards the end of the Edwardian period. Instead, the railway companies had the spur of competition between each other and on some routes began races which drove them to reduce journey times. The first series of contests started as a curious side issue of the decision by the three East Coast partners (the Great Northern, North Eastern and North British) which provided the through services between London and Scotland to allow second-class passengers on their fastest trains for the first time in November 1887. The West Coast companies (London & North Western and Caledonian) had long allowed second-class customers but their trains took ten hours, a full sixty minutes longer than their East Coast rivals, and consequently they started to lose customers. The chairman of the London & North Western was an austere fellow, Sir Richard Moon, who deprecated fast running because it was expensive, using more coal and requiring extra track maintenance. Moon was described memorably as having an appearance in keeping with his character with 'rocky brows above cold, small, fierce eyes, a strong cranium, a strong nose and a mouth like a steel gin'[3] and was one of the most able managers of his age, 'incorruptible and one of the most terrifying personages in Victorian private business'.[4] Under his rule the London & North Western had been transformed from a loose amalgam of railways to 'a totalitarian corporate state in nineteenth-century capitalism'.[5] Moon dictated that an average speed of 40 mph was quite good enough for his passengers. However, after eight months of watching them desert his trains, he suddenly announced in June 1888 that the Day Scotch Express, the key 10 a.m. departure from Euston, which rivalled the simultaneous East Coast's Special Scotch Express, would have its timing to both Glasgow and Edinburgh slashed by an hour, bringing its average speed up to 43.8 mph.

It took a month for the East Coast to respond but a tit-for-tat battle ensued in August 1888 with each company announcing regular reductions in timings, cutting journey times down to seven and a half hours. In the rush to be the quickest, customers' needs were not always paramount. The lunch stops – at York on the East Coast, Preston on the West – that were essential requirements given that trains were still carriages separated into compartments without dining cars, let alone toilets, were reduced from half an hour to just twenty minutes, with little thought to the damage that might cause to the passengers' digestive systems or their bladders. Peace finally broke out at a conference of the railway companies when it was agreed to put a bit of slack back into the timetable so that journeys would take seven and three quarter hours by the East Coast, and eight hours on the West, with an extra half an hour in the winter.

The race was to resume seven years later with a vengeance, following the completion of the Forth bridge, but within a year it was safety that exercised the minds of railway directors following the worst disaster in the railways' short history. The steady death toll on the railways was accepted rather like today's carnage on the roads. There were perennial protests in the press, accompanied by calls for 'something to be done', but demands usually fell short of expecting a much tighter regulatory regime as that would have been considered as excessive state interference. That said, the new regulations of the early 1870s mentioned in the last chapter were never considered to be the last word on safety on the railways and in 1874 a Royal Commission was held on railway accidents. It proved to be a laborious inquiry lasting three years and while the committee collected a mass of evidence, it led to precious little change and the number of accidents kept rising, making the 1870s the worst ever in railway history for passenger deaths.[6]

If anything illustrated the reluctance by the railway companies to deal with the issue of safety with sufficient urgency, it was the failure to provide trains with proper braking systems. It took the terrible Armagh disaster of 1889, the result of inadequate brakes and sloppy procedures, to bring about change and then only because the government introduced new legislation forcing the railway companies to act. There had been a series of accidents caused by the inadequacy of the trains' braking systems. By the 1870s trains were occasionally reaching the unimaginable speed of 80 mph (although not with Queen Victoria aboard). Yet, remarkably, locomotives were still being built without any direct means of stopping. Drivers were forced to rely on tender handbrakes, putting the engine into reverse, and telling the guards in their vans[7] to apply their brakes, communicating with them by a whistle code.

As public pressure to fit continuous brakes to passenger trains intensified, progress was held up by a lengthy 'battle of the brakes' over which type should be used. The Board of Trade favoured automatic brakes which failed safe (in other words were applied by default when the system malfunctioned). However, not only were these more expensive than conventional systems, but their unreliability and unpredictable failure, which resulted in delays, meant their installation was resisted by many train companies. Sir Edward Watkin, the chairman of the Manchester, Sheffield & Lincolnshire Railway, was at his megalomaniac worst in refusing to countenance automatic brakes and it was only after two serious accidents within three years on his railway, in which forty-nine people died, that Watkin agreed to a change of policy in 1884.

In a continuous braking system, the application of brakes is transmitted through the whole of a train either by vacuum or air pressure, and there were strong proponents of both systems.[8] Most British railways were trying to develop vacuum brakes until George Westinghouse visited Britain in 1871 to demonstrate his highly effective air brake. The response of British railway management to

Westinghouse's invention was, as O. S. Nock records, 'extraordinarily parochial. Not only did they resent the intrusion of any device invented or developed outside the country, but many of them were exceedingly reluctant to use good ideas that had been developed on another railway in this country.'[9] In fact, it was worse than that. It was precisely because the Midland was interested in the Westinghouse brake that the London & North Western refused even to countenance it.

The death toll from accidents either caused or exacerbated by inadequate braking kept mounting but it took the sheer horror and inevitability of the Armagh accident on 12 June 1889 to make the public's demands for change irresistible. The disaster involved a very heavily laden excursion train which was taking 940 people, including 600 children, on a Sunday school excursion from Armagh to Warrenpoint, a journey of just fifteen miles but crucially involving a three-mile climb up a steep gradient of 1 in 75. The train driver, Thomas McGrath, had little experience of the line and he struggled to get the train of fifteen fully loaded carriages, including two brake vans, up the hill. Indeed, he had argued with the station-master at Armagh that the train was overloaded but eventually agreed to accept it and at first his progress up the hill was steady. However, just a couple of hundred yards from the summit, the train stalled and McGrath, together with James Elliot, who was in charge of the excursion, made a fatal mistake. Instead of protecting the back of the train with detonators and waiting for the regular service train to push the stricken excursion carriages up the hill, they decided to lighten the load by splitting off the back ten coaches. As ever with such accidents, other mistakes contributed to the eventual disaster. The guard was asked to chock the train with stones but McGrath started the uncoupling process before this had been done properly because there was a dearth of suitable rocks in the area.

The train was not fitted with an automatic brake. Instead, once the pressure was released on the vacuum brake, the coaches were left with no brakes except for those in the brake van. And, not surprisingly, they proved inadequate for the task of holding the heavy train. The ten coaches started rolling back and despite efforts by Elliot and the guard, Thomas Henry, to put stones under the wheels, nothing could stop the carriages from gathering speed. Meanwhile, the regular service train was chugging up the hill, oblivious of the runaway carriages. One can imagine the panic of the schoolchildren as the train gathered momentum downhill, since, despite previous disasters (such as the one mentioned on page 147 at Versailles), they had been locked in their carriages to prevent unlawful entry. The loose coaches reached a speed of 40 mph before smashing into the regular train, whose driver, on seeing the escaped carriages, managed to all but stop his locomotive, hence reducing the speed of impact. The front wooden carriages were nevertheless smashed to smithereens by the collision and the toll of eighty dead and 250 injured was by far the highest on any British railway up to that point. It would have been greater had it not been for the heroism of the crew of the second train, who managed, despite being injured, to prevent their coaches from rolling down the slope after they, in turn, had become detached by the collision.

It was the most significant accident in British railway history as 'in those shattered coaches of the ill-fated excursion train, the old happy-go-lucky days of railway working came to their ultimate end and the modern phase of railway working as we know it began'.[10] The public response to Armagh was remarkably rapid, especially in the light of the failure to act in the aftermath of other, equally preventable, accidents. There was an outcry following the accident, heightened by the death of so many children. As a result the government found the ability to move far more quickly and forcefully than ever before and rushed through – within weeks of the accident – the Regulation Act.

The Armagh accident had highlighted two fundamental inadequacies of the safety regime on the railway network: the braking system and the continued use of the time-interval method of keeping trains apart rather than any form of signalling. The three pillars of the new safety regime introduced by the Regulation Act of 1889 were, therefore, 'lock, block and brake'. The first refers to interlocking, a crucial aspect of rail safety which ensures that the indications on the signals correspond to the way that the points on the rails are set. Signals were controlled mechanically by levers in signal boxes connected to cables, pulleys and rods, and it was relatively easy to devise methods of interlocking to prevent trains being sent in directions other than those shown by the signals.

'Block' refers to the method of dividing up the track into sections – or blocks – which the signalling system ensures can be occupied by only one train at a time. This innovation was made much easier when track circuits, an electrical device that shows when a train is in a particular section, started to be introduced in 1901. Like many developments on the railways, track circuits took a long time to be implemented throughout the network, and even at nationalization in 1948 many sections of track still did not have this form of protection.

The third element of the legislation required the fitting of continuous automatic brakes, but did not specify what type, and every company seemed to prefer its own version. As mentioned before, there were arguments in favour of both vacuum and air brakes but, as Jack Simmons puts it, 'what was indefensible was the failure to agree, in a small country where so much through working of vehicles took place between one company's lines and another'.[11] It would not be until nationalization after the Second World War that a standard braking system would be adopted and then, oddly, the vacuum method was preferred over air, which was used in most other railways in the world. Since then, the situation has reversed and all trains in the UK now use air brakes (with the exception of a few heritage railways).

While the legislation passed after the Armagh accident may have ensured that the companies took safety seriously, in fairness it really only speeded up improvements which the railways had been putting in place anyway. The rate of accidents tailed off immediately and in 1901, for the first time since the 1840s, and then again in 1908, no passenger was killed in a railway accident during a calendar year.

If Armagh was the accident that had the greatest long-term impact, the one which made the deepest and longest impression on the public was the Tay Bridge disaster a decade before. This not only highlighted the risks of taking short cuts in engineering, but also ensured that the much more ambitious project of crossing the Firth of Forth was carried out successfully. The Tay Bridge was not the first railway bridge to collapse, a dubious honour which went to the three-span structure designed by Robert Stephenson to cross the river Dee in Cheshire that plunged into the river in early 1847, killing five people, but it was by far the most spectacular in railway history.

The scheme to build a bridge across the Tay was attractive to the North British Railway as it would not only provide direct access to Dundee from Fife, rather than having to detour via Perth, but it also allowed the company to compete for traffic against its old rival, the Caledonian. It was an ambitious enterprise. Two miles long, the bridge was then the longest construction in the world and it took several years for the manager of the North British, Thomas Bouch, to convince his employers that the project was worth while. However, with its passengers facing the unpleasant choice of a ferry ride or a sixty-mile detour, the company eventually agreed and the bill to build a bridge costing £300,000 (say, £22m in today's money) was passed in 1870. Bouch designed the bridge and oversaw the work, which started two years later. The single-track bridge, which consisted of a steel box on stone piers, was completed in 1878, having cost the lives of twenty of the 600 men who built it.

In the summer of 1879, Bouch was knighted by Queen Victoria, whose annual journey to Balmoral was shortened by the new bridge, but within months he was to be vilified for having caused the worst-ever disaster resulting from a structural failure on these shores, an unhappy record that remains to this day. The bridge, which had eighty-five spans, rose slightly from the banks to ensure there was space for shipping and it was this high section that was to collapse on the stormy night of 28 December 1879, killing all seventy-five people travelling on the train which plunged into the murky water below. The weather was so foul that when a signalman found that communications with the other side had been lost he attempted to walk across the bridge to check on the train, but was beaten back by the weather. On descending to the shore he realized that the whole centre section, known as the 'high girders', had vanished.

The precise cause was never ascertained although Bouch appeared to have greatly underestimated the structural requirements needed to resist the Force 10 gales that blow regularly in the Firth of Tay area. The train may have derailed, dislodging one of the 'high girders', all thirteen of which collapsed into the Tay, but in a recent assessment of the disaster, researchers concluded that the fault lay principally with Bouch's design.

In a way the Tay Bridge disaster was timely. Bouch had been commissioned to design the even more ambitious Forth crossing which, while only having to cross a mile and a quarter of water, was much grander in scale and conception. Bouch had even laid the foundation stone for a suspension bridge, but not surprisingly work ceased immediately after the Tay disaster while the design was reassessed and the discredited engineer was promptly removed from the project.

The Forth Bridge,[12] which was to become the most famous single structure on Britain's railways – portrayed on everything from £1 coins to biscuit tins and advertisements for ladies' stockings – had long been discussed as a vital connection between Edinburgh and Fife but such a huge enterprise was beyond the means of a single railway company. Therefore, in 1873, four companies which stood to profit from a quicker route through Scotland – the North British, the North Eastern, the Great Northern and the Midland – joined together to form the Forth Bridge Railway Company which, after aborting its first effort following the Tay Bridge disaster, obtained a new Bill in 1881 authorizing the construction of the bridge. It was the Midland, eager to boost traffic on its newly completed Scottish route using the Settle & Carlisle line, that was the most enthusiastic supporter of the project, tossing a cool £1m, a third of the required capital, into the kitty, and work started in 1883.

The elegance of the bridge, using a novel cantilever design with spans far longer than anything previously attempted, is testimony to the engineering skills of its designer, Benjamin Baker. In truth, the bridge was probably overspecified to withstand the winds, but that was understandable given the Tay disaster and does not detract from the sheer beauty of the structure, which is perhaps best illustrated by haunting photographs of the cantilever sections standing separately in the mists of the Firth during construction, looking like the skeletons of three vast ships growing out of the water. The bridge is supported by three huge towers standing on bases sunk into the water. However, the cantilevered design enabled the enormous structure to be self-supporting while being erected, avoiding the expensive and risky need to build temporary columns in the water. The dangers during construction were so obvious that boats were on permanent duty below to pick up men who fell off the structure, but many of the workforce (a

The railways were responsible for the advent of mass tourism as they enabled people to reach their destinations cheaply and quickly. They exploited this burgeoning market with posters advertising the delights of the resorts they served. This 'Summer & Winter Resorts' poster was produced by the London, Chatham & Dover Railway in 1897.

Locomotives of the Highland Railway, which catered largely for tourists in the summer but also played a vital role in the First World War. This picture is from the 1890s.

Midland Railway porters unloading milk at Somers Town dock, just west of St Pancras, in 1890. The churns were transported in ventilated wagons, ensuring fresh milk for Londoners whose diet was greatly improved by the spread of the railways.

Railway servants were expected to work long hours for modest pay, but job security and the uniform ensured a steady supply of labour. Drivers, like this one on the Great Central Railway in 1907, were regarded as a social elite and were extremely proud of their responsible position, as shown by this man's clean oil can and gold watch chain.

Women railway workers replaced many men on the railways in both world wars. Here they are working on gas lamps at the Lancashire & Yorkshire Railway's Horwich works in Greater Manchester in May 1917.

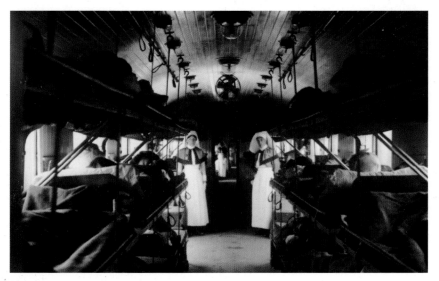

Ambulance trains with extensive medical facilities, including a pharmacy, were widely used in the First World War, carrying a total of 2,680,000 soldiers.

This spectacular accident at Penistone, south Yorkshire in 1916 did not result in any casualties because the subsidence which caused it started relatively slowly.

Strike-breaking staff and volunteers posing on a London, Midland & Scottish locomotive at St Enoch Station, Glasgow during the General Strike of 1926.

total of 4,600 at its peak) took ridiculous risks like jumping from one girder to another while drunk. The eventual death toll of fifty-seven, which included seventeen men who worked in compressed-air chambers to build the support columns, seems relatively low given the constant level of danger.

The Forth Bridge, which cut thirty-one miles out of the journey between Edinburgh and Dundee, was opened by the Prince of Wales, the future Edward VII, an eager supporter of things new; six months later he cut the ribbon on the City & South London railway, the world's first deep-level underground line. At the party following the opening of the Forth Bridge, Edward and his guests celebrated by gorging on a pie containing 300 skylarks, a favoured delicacy of the time.

With the new Tay Bridge – built to higher standards with twin rather than single tracks – also now open, the East and West Coast companies could indulge in a new race – this time from London to Aberdeen – and the competition was conducted with even fiercer rivalry than the one seven years previously. The contest broke out in the summer of 1895, coinciding with the start of the grouse season, which brought the lucrative traffic of the hunting brigade up to Scotland for the Glorious Twelfth, along with the court hangers-on who moved up to Scotland with the Queen for the summer. 'They were the most valuable passenger traffic on the English railways . . . They travelled with perhaps their wives – certainly a female companion – plenty of servants, dogs, guns and luggage. Above all, they paid their lavish way in golden sovereigns and out of their own pockets.'[13] They were known irreverently by railway workers as 'The Grouse Traffic'.

The rival companies had broadly kept to their agreement of timetabling the East Coast trains at fifteen minutes quicker than those on the West Coast until on 1 June 1895 the West Coast companies brought forward by ten minutes the arrival of the overnight 8 p.m. train from Euston. The move was designed to allow extra time for the wealthy passengers with their mounds of luggage to change to the local Deeside train that served their hunting lodges. However, it meant the Euston train reached Aberdeen by 7.40 a.m., just five minutes behind the East Coast service, which then responded by cutting a quarter an hour off its train's scheduled time. A tit-for-tat battle ensued, with the

West Coast cutting more than an hour off its timing, aiming to reach Aberdeen by 6.35 a.m. For seventeen days each group of companies sought to better their rivals' time. The effort which went into the contest was considerable, requiring fresh engines to be prepared far earlier than normal and signalmen to be alerted. The companies were ruthless in their pressure to save time. The West Coast companies effectively abandoned their timetables, rushing passengers on at intermediate stops and departing straightaway, irrespective of the scheduled time – a breach of standard railway practice, which is never to leave early so that punctual passengers are not inconvenienced. At Crewe one evening, in the rush to get the train away, a hapless porter who had made the mistake of helping an old lady on to the train found himself taking an unexpected trip to Glasgow. On the East Coast, the North Eastern and the North British insisted at first on adhering to their timetables but later discarded them in the rush to beat off their rivals.

The race caught the public imagination and every evening at both Euston and King's Cross, as well as at intermediate stops on the route, crowds gathered to cheer the racers on their journey and the newspapers provided information on the previous day's runs in great detail, as if reporting the Derby or the Grand National. Indeed, the press even complained that the races had encouraged gambling on the outcome. The finishing post was not really Aberdeen but Kinnaber Junction, thirty-eight miles south, where the two routes met. Amazingly, the signalman there, who was a Caledonian man and therefore part of the West Coast partnership, allowed through the East Coast train just a minute ahead of its rival, a decision very much in keeping with the spirit of the railway which, despite the intense rivalry between companies, was felt by the workforce to be one family. By the end the timings were incredible. On 20 August, the East Coast train burst through to Aberdeen in just eight hours forty minutes, arriving in the granite city at the unearthly time of 4.40 a.m.

In response, the West Coast cheated. It stripped a train down for racing and did the journey – which had until recently been timetabled at nearly twelve hours – in just eight hours thirty-two minutes, at an average speed of 63 mph. That marked the end of the race as the companies became aware that the massive resources being ploughed into the contest were not only being wasted but were actually becoming counter-productive: fewer people were travelling on these trains, perhaps out of fear of an accident, but also because the ride at such speed was at times very uncomfortable. Moreover, what was the point of arriving at Aberdeen in the small hours to be thrown out of one's sleeper car only to have to wait two hours for breakfast and three hours for the connection? It would take eighty years and the introduction of high-speed trains for the timings achieved in that infamous fortnight to be beaten regularly. Even today, over a century later and with state-of-the-art trains, the fastest day services take just over seven hours, a mere hour and a half less than in those heady days of August 1895.

Superficially, these races appear to have been mere braggadocio on the part of the railway companies, but in the long term they helped to transform Britain's railways. They jolted the companies out of a torpor and helped them to concentrate on improving the service they were providing. It was 'a fine and spectacular advertisement for British railways'[14] which gave Britain the world record for speed.

But there was a negative legacy, too. The races had led to renewed concerns about safety: speed was still a relatively new concept as, for the first half-century of their history, the railways had concentrated more on expansion. There was no doubt that during such races, drivers, excited by being allowed to open up their regulators, adopted a gung-ho spirit that may well have resulted in unnecessary risks being taken, particularly given that they were at the controls of massive machines which did not have speedometers. Certainly, the drivers were taking curves at a far greater speed than that recommended by the permanent way (track) engineers. Although no accidents occurred during the races, a crash a year later in Preston on 15 August at the height of the holiday season revived the concerns of the doomsayers. In fact this derailment of the night train heading for Scotland was caused by the inexperience of the drivers on the London & North Western train. Travelling northbound through Preston involved negotiating a curve with a nominal restriction of 10 mph, but most trains regularly went round it at double that speed. Neither of the enginemen had driven a train that was scheduled to go through the station without stopping, and must have been conscious that keeping good time in the holiday season was important. However, that should not have excused their attempt to speed through the town at 45 mph, which inevitably led to disaster when the leading engine jumped the rails. Although the accident claimed the life of only one of the sixteen passengers on board, according to O. S. Nock 'this was the case of an accident where the outcome was out of all proportion to the casualty list. Few accidents in British railway history have had a more profound effect on both public and railway opinion. [It] resulted in express running times between London and Scotland being slowed down and remaining stagnant for more than 35 years'.[15]

Not all companies were so timid. The Great Western, for example, retained a focus on reducing journey times and races broke out on other lines such as those between London and Manchester. There were even a couple of sections of four-track railway where different companies raced directly against each other, notably from York south to Church Fenton where the tracks of the North Eastern and the Lancashire & Yorkshire ran side by side for eleven miles. Southbound trains belonging to both railways left York at 2.35 p.m. every day and normally the North Eastern, which ran lighter trains, beat off its rival.

While on the Scottish routes a tacit agreement between the companies spelt the end of the races, a decade later further competitiveness arose between two rival railways for passengers arriving at Plymouth from the United States. Plymouth was the best disembarkation point for passengers coming across the Atlantic as they could save a day, by not remaining on the boat all the way to Southampton. The rail companies were eager to serve this market, which included plenty of affluent first-class passengers, and competition to be the fastest service to London arose in the early 1900s between the Great Western and the London & South Western.

Focusing on speed was a relatively new development for the Great Western, which, since a series of amalgamations in the 1860s, had become the railway with the greatest route mileage. Until Daniel Gooch, the great locomotive engineer and latterly chairman of the Great Western, died, still in post, in 1889, the railway had long been a 'majestically slow, stately, superbly well-engineered railway'.[16] Its biggest challenge had been converting its broad gauge lines to the standard ones, a process that had started as far back as 1868. The task was finally completed in a spectacular weekend in May 1892 when all the 213 miles west of Exeter were converted, an almost unimaginable achievement of project management and coordination. To undertake this enormous task, 3,400 men were drafted in from around the country, divided up into gangs of twenty, each of which was allocated about a mile of track to convert. While straight sections of track were relatively easy, on curved sections the rails had to be shortened and every set of points presented particular difficulties.[17] In 1886, the Great Western had also completed one of the great engineering feats of railway history by building the 4.4-mile Severn tunnel, the longest on the British railway network and wettest.[18] It took thirteen years to finish as the site was dogged by flooding which required constant pumping operations (and still does today).

After the death of Gooch, the Great Western began to take an interest in modernizing and speeding up its services. In March 1892 the railway launched what Adrian Vaughan has called the first 'modern express train in Britain'[19] on its Paddington–Birkenhead route, offering the kind of comforts that were soon to be taken for granted. The train accommodated first-, second- and third-class passengers in carriages that were heated by steam through radiators under the seats and had corridors with connecting gangways that would enable restaurant cars (which Great Western introduced four years later) to be added. The clerestory roofs allowed for extra height and light and the coaches were panelled with walnut and satinwood that would not have been out of place in a gentleman's club. There was an electrical bell-push to 'summon' the guard and a novel form of emergency cord. Although emergency cords for passengers' use had been fitted on some services as early as the 1850s, the Great Western's new trains adopted a much more sophisticated system that allowed passengers to alert the driver who would stop the train as soon as practicable.

Even after the Preston accident, the caution being exercised by the West and East Coast railways found no echo at the Great Western. Quite the contrary. With the broad gauge gone, the Great Western managers seemed eager to show that they could live up to the railway's nickname – 'God's Wonderful Railway' – rather than the name that was being used in the popular press, 'Great Way Round'. Locomotive design was improving rapidly, and trains became heavier. The *City of Truro*, one of the Great Western's new types of locomotive designed by the greatest traction engineer of his time, George Churchward, became the first to achieve the magical three figures when it was allegedly timed at just over 102 mph on a mail train down to Plymouth one evening in May 1904.[20]

The railways serving the country south of London were very different. Here there was, as *The Times* called it, a 'crawl to the south'[21] rather than a race to the north. The slowness of travel to the Kent Channel ports has already been mentioned in Chapter 7 but the Brighton line was also famous – or rather infamous – for delays and tediously long journeys. The town was served by two railways, the South Eastern and the London, Brighton & South Coast, but a shared section of track between Coulsdon and Redhill gave them the opportunity to blame each other for delays. Delays on the Brighton line had turned into a national joke, becoming the butt of music-hall routines and regular comments in *The Times*: 'Very bad they both are, this at least the most severe critic must admit, difficult as he would find it . . . to say with certainty which of the two has the better right to call itself absolutely the worst line in the country.'[22] Spurred on by this constant criticism, a new six-mile section of line opened in 1900, bypassing Redhill and leading to much better service patterns. The joke was over, and even the old South Eastern and London & Chatham, which had merged, were now offering a better service, blending their rival lines into a homogenous network that catered for the burgeoning London commuter network. Travel did remain slow, however, on many branch lines, where it seemed in keeping with the cadence of life. David St John Thomas, who wrote much on rural routes, reckoned that the slowest service was from Bournemouth to Bath through the Mendips on the Somerset & Dorset joint main line, which took over four hours to cover just seventy-one miles, gruesomely slow progress.

The London & South Western always had a better reputation than its southern neighbours, offering efficient and frequent services from its 'untidy and confused collection of platforms, passages, stairways, cab yards and offices'[23] at Waterloo to Southampton and Bournemouth that did much to stimulate growth in those towns. The company may have lacked the charisma of the East and West Coast companies but it was a good solid railway serving a variety of useful markets ranging from soldiers stationed at Aldershot to holidaymakers heading for the Isle of Wight, and it had expanded by buying Southampton Docks and running ferry services to France and the Channel Islands. However, the staff of the London & South Western won no prizes for politeness, according to its passengers; railway historian Hamilton Ellis reckoned that South Western was one of the lines 'which had a bad reputation for uncivil behaviour by officials' but then again, while the Great Western's men were more pleasant, 'a traveller could spend much time waiting at Great Western stations'.[24]

It was the Great Western's ambition to do away with its fusty image and establish itself as Britain's premier railway that led it into a fully fledged battle with the London & South Western. While the Great Western went through Bristol and Newton Abbot, the London & South Western's competing route to Plymouth was over the West Country moorland, running on the same tracks as the Great Western for just a couple of miles outside Exeter and then on a more southerly route through Salisbury.

The London & South Western, which had traditionally carried most of the Atlantic passengers from Plymouth, as well, of course, as all those from Southampton, could not resist entering the fray when the Great Western, which already transported the mail, threw down a challenge by improving its times to London. O. S. Nock, that illustrious chronicler of accidents and much else on the railway, is in no doubt that the race for the lucrative Atlantic passengers led to corners being cut: 'In the heat of the competition . . . considerations of safety gradually seemed to recede and there is no doubt that in the running of some of the rival trains . . . serious risks were taken on the curves.'[25] The accident, on the curve beyond Salisbury, bore uncanny similarities to the one at Preston: disaster struck at a station which was being run through at speed by a driver accustomed to stopping there. Like the Scottish sleepers, these special boat trains were exceptional and not run to a normal schedule. Once it was known that a liner was to arrive at Plymouth, a train was despatched as soon as possible, whatever the time of day, and it was a point of honour to run these trains at fast speeds. Special sleeping cars were laid on if the journey was to be overnight.

To shorten journey times, the London & South Western ran non-stop from Plymouth, apart from an engine change at Templecombe, about halfway through the trip, which meant running fast through Salisbury where there was a sharp curve with a speed restriction of 30 mph. A special boat service had left Plymouth just before midnight on 30 June 1906 but had been running behind schedule after the Templecombe engine change. By the time it reached Salisbury, however, the train had picked up speed and – disastrously – attempted to go through the town at 70 mph, more than twice the permitted level. The engine toppled over, hit a milk train on the adjacent track and the carriages were wrecked so comprehensively that twenty-four out of the forty-three passengers on board were killed. More care was taken with the boat trains thereafter but it was not until 1910 that a formal agreement was reached between the two railways, ending their battle.

As with the Preston accident, the Salisbury disaster had a powerful effect on public opinion and 'any speeding on the railways was for a time looked upon with the gravest apprehension'[26] irrespective of whether the conditions were risky or perfect for fast running. The public's fears were exacerbated by a further totally unexplained crash at Grantham just three months later, when another night sleeper, due to stop at the station, ran through at 45 mph and was derailed at points that had been set for a goods train to go to Nottingham. Here, too, the effect was disastrous with a fire compounding the damage, but as both the driver and the apprentice acting as fireman were killed, the real reason why the train missed the stop was never ascertained.

Nevertheless, despite these concerns about safety, the railways were at the height of their pomp in the Edwardian period, still unchallenged by the motor car or even buses: at the outbreak of the First World War, there were only 39,000 motor buses and taxis in the whole of Great Britain, and just 64,000 lorries. The railway companies may have fooled themselves that these new-fangled vehicles would go the way of the steam road carriages mentioned in the Introduction. They were wrong but nevertheless they continued to enjoy a period of monopoly and dominance for a few more years.

# TEN

# THE ONLY WAY TO
# GET THERE

All the significant lines on the railway, and indeed most of the insignificant ones, had been completed by the start of the twentieth century. The last major new line to be built was the Great Central, opened in 1899 and often portrayed as a late-Victorian folly.

The Great Central was the brainchild of Sir Edward Watkin, who pops up in this story in various guises, not only a genuine entrepreneur but also the best-known railway director who was rarely out of the newspapers because of his penchant for courting controversy. Watkin, like George Hudson, was a flawed character, described as a 'megalomaniac and a gambler' by Jack Simmons[1] but a contemporary writer, John Pendleton, suggests rather more kindly that Watkin was 'one of the busiest and most versatile of men'.[2] He not only wrote a biography of a renowned Manchester alderman but was busy discovering coalfields, buying Snowdon, attempting, unsuccessfully, to build a rival to the Eiffel Tower at Wembley (see Chapter 7; it reached 155 feet, the first platform, before being abandoned) and planning the construction of a Channel Tunnel.

It was this latter enterprise that prompted the building of the Great Central. Watkin wanted a line that ran from Manchester to Paris and he already controlled three companies that would have provided much of the route. As well as the South Eastern, which linked the Channel ports with London, and the Metropolitan, which extended from the City far north into Buckinghamshire, he was chairman of the Manchester, Sheffield & Lincolnshire, a railway which as its name implied went nowhere near London. Watkin even had interests in a French railway that would have provided the trains on the other side of the Channel. First, though, he had to get his main line railway to London. Although it is difficult to discern his precise intentions, as he seemed to change his mind frequently, the very fact that he drove the Metropolitan Railway fifty miles out of London, far beyond the sensible boundaries of a suburban railway, suggests he always intended to link up his various railway interests. To do so he proposed a scheme to build a ninety-three-mile line from Annesley in Nottinghamshire through Nottingham, Leicester and Rugby, criss-crossing the Midland Railway, to a junction with the Metropolitan north of Aylesbury.

There was opposition not only from the other railway companies whose traffic was threatened but, more worryingly for Watkin, from one of the most powerful interest groups of the time, the Marylebone Cricket Club. The fuss arose because the route would take the railway under a small part of Lord's, then as now the headquarters of the MCC. In those days cricket was not the poor relation of football, hitting the headlines only during an Ashes series, but was the major sport of its day, boasting a huge following as well as the most famous sportsman of the time, W. G. Grace, who, one newspaper suggested, should approach poor Watkin to dissuade him from desecrating the ground. No matter that the project only involved building a 'cut and cover' tunnel under the east corner of the ground, well away from the playing field where the hallowed turf would be left untouched, nor that the work would be carried out in the close season, leaving the spectators none the wiser. All the old aristocratic antipathy towards the railway was revived and 'the menace to Lord's was looked upon almost as a national calamity'.[3] Watkin was pitted against the Establishment in all its bluster and, following a lengthy series of parliamentary hearings in 1891, he lost.

Perhaps feeling a trifle guilty, the cricket supporters began to relent, possibly realizing that they could not stand in the way of progress (though it would take another century before women were allowed into their pavilion). The Great Northern, one of the main petitioners against the initial bill, also softened its stance, having thrashed out a deal with Watkin over competition between the railways. Watkin, too, promised that an orphanage for children of the clergy that was in the way of the proposed route would be moved at the railway's expense to Bushey in Hertfordshire, and he abandoned his ambitions for a grand station merging with the existing Metropolitan one at Baker Street, settling instead for a self-contained terminus at Marylebone. All this paved the way for success two years after the initial rejection.

Watkin was a man of many paradoxes who, for example, inspired the fiercest loyalty among his staff despite refusing to recognize the unions which represented them. Getting approval for the Great Central scheme was always going to be more difficult than in the days of Stephenson: late Victorian England was a very different place after half a century of development that had created large cities and brought a measure of affluence to millions of people, many of whom had houses in the way of any proposed railway. Watkin's success at the second attempt shows that he had a more emollient side, prepared to compromise and cajole rather than simply shout and bully.

As ever, the poor were largely left to their own devices as they lacked the lobbying power of the cricketers. The fact that the railway forced some 25,000 working people in that corner of north-west London from their homes hardly raised a stir; even though, under legislation passed in 1885, there was now a rehousing obligation on the railways, the chaotic nature of life in the slums and the absence of any checks on the activities of the railway company suggest that many people were simply evicted and left to find their own alternative accommodation.

In 1894, shortly after pushing the scheme through Parliament, Watkin suffered a stroke and was forced to retire, but he was able to watch as his railway to London, Britain's last main line, was built. In engineering terms, the railway was a beauty, with relatively gentle gradients and just one level crossing in its whole length. By now mechanical methods were being used to build railways and fewer navvies were required; while the cost of £6.2m (around £550m today) may have all but bankrupted the company, it seems pretty modest for such a grand enterprise. There was a huge new station at Nottingham, a lengthy viaduct over Leicester – which also resulted in the displacement of many poor people – and a near two-mile tunnel at Catesby in Northamptonshire. But the railway was perhaps too beautiful for its own profitability as its route covered large underpopulated swathes of the Midlands. The Manchester,

Sheffield & Lincolnshire became subsumed into the Great Central – and the 'Money Sunk and Lost' became the 'Gone Completely'. As a result shareholders never received any dividends for their investment. All the major towns through which the new line passed were already served by rival railways, the biggest exception being the Leicestershire market town of Lutterworth, but its 1,800 souls given easy access to the railway for the first time were hardly going to line the pockets of the Great Central's shareholders.

It was no wonder that the railway never flourished, though its managers tried their hardest by creating a luxury service. The Great Central even attempted to outdo the Midland in terms of offering better facilities for its passengers. Its mission statement was 'Rapid travel in luxury' and its advertising promised all-corridor trains with a buffet car for use by both first- and third-class passengers. In addition to its main route linking London with Sheffield and Manchester, it liaised with several other railways to enable through carriages to be taken to destinations as widely spread as Huddersfield and Newcastle, and Bournemouth and Plymouth, always on a corridor train. The Great Central also improved journeys between London and Stratford-upon-Avon and over large areas of Lincolnshire, including Grimsby, which was the 'quick route to Denmark' via a ferry to Esbjerg. But its lavish trains attracted insufficient custom from rivals like the Midland and the Great Northern and were rarely anywhere near full. Even so, it is difficult to characterize such a great railway as simply a mistake. If it had not been closed by Beeching in the 1960s it would fulfil a vital role as a diversionary and freight route even today.

Perhaps the Great Central was just ahead of its time, rather like Watkin's Channel Tunnel, which, as with his rival to the *Tour d'Eiffel*, was never to be – at least for another century. Jack Simmons dismisses Watkin's idea of a railway between Paris and Sheffield as 'visionary and foolish, a flashy advertising slogan, no more',[4] but Watkin did start building the tunnel, raising money through the evocatively named Submarine Railway Company. This time he came up against opposition from the military who seemed to think it would be possible for the French to invade Britain through the tunnel. While that was clearly a notion born more of paranoia than military logic, it ensured that the project never got beyond the mile-long test bore that Watkins managed to build. Moreover, the figures for such a grand project, financed solely by private enterprise dependent on shareholders, were never likely to stack up, as demonstrated by the travails of today's Eurotunnel.

In one of those neat historical niceties, no main lines were actually built in the twentieth century: the Great Central was completed in 1899, and the two sections of the Channel Tunnel Rail Link, while originally scheduled to be finished in the 1990s, did not open until 2003 and 2007.[5] All the London termini were built in the reign of Victoria, with Marylebone, the last, and undoubtedly the most modest, as it was designed by builders rather than an architect. The poet John Betjeman, a railway buff and early campaigner for the preservation of its heritage, accurately likened the look of Marylebone to 'a branch public library in a Manchester suburb',[6] in sharp contrast with that trio of great termini – Euston, St Pancras and King's Cross – just a couple of miles east.

By the turn of the century, then, the railway network in Great Britain was essentially complete, with 18,665 miles of track. Right up to the First World War, however, the railway continued to grow, with the mileage reaching 19,979 in 1910, an increase of over 1,300 miles since the start of the century, but this was largely a process of infilling, connecting the odd town left off the system and shortening routes with cut-offs. Much of the growth was in London as its suburban network continued spreading right up to the First World War, by which time the capital and its surrounding suburbs had no fewer than 550 stations. The railways, including the London Underground system, which had virtually established its present-day form in the centre of the city by 1907,[7] were an indispensable part of the capital's infrastructure.

But still the railway faced competition in urban areas – initially not from the motor bus and lorry, which came later, but from the tramway which, being electrically powered, proved a more comfortable and flexible form of transport than rickety old steam trains shuttling between urban stations. The first trams were horse-drawn along simple tracks in the road, an idea which spread quickly to many towns and cities after the success of the inaugural line opened in Birkenhead in 1860. However, their potential was limited, not least because of the high cost of the horses, ten or so being required for each tramcar since the poor beasts needed considerable rest between journeys. Steam trams flourished briefly in several cities but electricity was clearly the optimum form of propulsion and throughout the 1890s tram systems popped up around the country, many owned and operated by local municipalities.

In the 1900s, the tram spread even more quickly and by the outbreak of the First World War all major cities and many smaller towns possessed networks. And they were well used. Even by 1907, more people travelled around by tram in Greater London than by train and the tramways made it hard for the rail companies to eke any profits out of the extensive urban networks which they had built up in many provincial cities. Commuting by rail had, nevertheless, become a habit for many and four out of five workers in central London used the train. By 1906, 410,000 passengers arrived daily into the centre of London by train, perhaps two thirds of them early enough to be considered as commuters going to work. The working classes on the likes of the Great Eastern were outnumbered by more affluent commuters, many of whom came from further away as they were able to afford not only the fares but the price of an attractive suburban home. They were the City merchants, bankers and stockbrokers, who had first-class season tickets to Epping or Chislehurst, where they could live in a villa with perhaps twenty acres, a dozen servants and, still, a carriage with horses rather than a motor car. These affluent settlements were still largely villages centred around the station, rather than forming part of an endless ribbon of development as they do today. In between the rich and the humble users of the working men's trains, there were the middle classes, professional people who came in from the outer ring of Victorian suburbs such as Clapham, Swiss Cottage or Newington Green.

With such well-heeled passengers, who would also use the railways for long-distance travel on business, the major train companies were doing their utmost to improve their services to meet the needs of this more prosperous, and consequently more demanding, market. They were spurred on by rivalry with each other, but despite their dominance their profitability waned as they struggled to pay for the improvements to their service.

The London & North Western, for example, which for most of its thirty-year period under the chairmanship of Sir Richard Moon (who had replaced Mark Huish in 1861) had been the biggest joint stock company in the world, was now prepared to spend considerable sums to offer passengers what today would be known as a 'more pleasant journey experience'. Moon had been a brilliant manager, developing the basic managerial concepts such as 'executive responsibility' first set out by Huish, but his very ethos – of providing the best possible service at minimum cost – meant that the company's facilities were rather parsimonious. As we have seen, he was quite happy for his trains to trundle around the country at 40 mph and, until the Armagh disaster, had not even appreciated the necessity of having proper brakes. The London & North Western was a wonderful railway, efficient and punctual thanks to a great attention to detail – goods and passenger lines were separated wherever possible and there was investment in the basics, such as junction layouts – but it was desperately old-fashioned.

While Moon's policies had, for a long time, given the company a solid financial basis and its shareholders healthy dividends, the company realized that in the twentieth century things had to change on its 2,000-mile network. Euston, in particular, required a new layout to cater for an increasing number of trains and this came at the cost of demolishing acres of private housing and offices. The quadrupled track to Bletchley was extended through to Rugby and there was a range of other improvements around the network, including the remodelling of Crewe, where trains branched off for Manchester or Holyhead. All this came with fleets of new locomotives, modern corridor rolling stock and even a couple of new packet steamers for the Holyhead–Dublin service.

Other companies followed suit. Express trains painted and maintained in elegant liveries hurtled through the countryside, overtaking lengthy coal trains that often ran on entirely separate rails, as lines had been quadrupled to cater for slow and fast services. Carriages on express routes were comfortably upholstered and there was now widespread provision of dining facilities in which passengers sat in splendour to be attended at linen-covered tables by smartly dressed and attentive waiters. For the most part it was understated luxury, but there were occasional flourishes such as the stained glass in the clerestory roof lights on the Great Central's Marylebone–Sheffield expresses.

Although there was no attempt to reinstate the rather risky races, there were moves to reduce overall journey times. With corridor trains that had dining and toilet facilities now being widely used, there was a fashion among train companies to run lengthy non-stop services, the longest being the Great Western service between London and Plymouth, a distance of 225 miles. The Great Western, again, was the leading force behind this rush to speed, running several rapid services down to Bristol and beyond. In 1914, the fastest ran the 118 miles from Paddington to Bristol Temple Meads in precisely two hours, an average of 59 mph.[8] By the outbreak of the Great War, the fastest scheduled service was a late-evening train from Darlington to York, which took just forty-three minutes to travel forty-four miles, and consequently was a tad faster at 61.5 mph.[9] There were several others around the network – from Scotland to the south-east – which averaged over 55 mph, a result of the energy which the train companies had devoted to improving their timings.

As we have seen, most major cities were connected to London by more than one route and competition was undoubtedly a spur to improved service. From December 1908, the London & North Western, in conjunction with the North London with which it had a close relationship, ran a service from Broad Street (the now demolished station next to Liverpool Street) non-stop to Birmingham in just two and a quarter hours. While the Great Western offered a train from Paddington that was fifteen minutes faster, the same time as the normal Euston service run by the London & North Western, the latter had the disincentive of an extra Underground or taxi ride for the busy City businessman who was just a short walk away from Broad Street station. Moreover, the 'City to City' trains, as the Broad Street services were called, offered an unprecedented extra facility: a travelling typist, ensuring not a moment of the journey was wasted.

Luxury and speed were now being sold even on the previously laggardly south coast routes too. The London, Brighton & South Coast Railway advertised its Brighton *Southern Belle* service with seven smart Pullman cars (four 'parlour', one 'buffet and smoking', and two 'smoking'), 'exquisitely upholstered, lighted by electricity, comfortably warmed and ventilated and fitted with all the latest improvements'. The journey would take an hour (little more than today's usual timing, including two stops, of fifty-one minutes) and the company also offered 'Pullman Drawing Room Cars' for its services between the capital and Eastbourne (including an all-Pullman train on Sundays), as well as a variety of routes to the Continent on its numerous ships. There was even a service operated jointly with the London & North Western on the cheerfully named *Sunny South Special* between Liverpool and Hastings, leaving both termini at 11 a.m. daily, and several others that connected south coast resorts with their huge potential market in the north.

Travelling on the railway for the holidays on these trains was still a source of awe and wonder for many people, particularly children. Philip Unwin[10] describes starting a journey at Surbiton to board the 'West of England Express', which was really nothing more than a semi-fast corridor train to Exeter and Plymouth that was 'pick-up only'.[11] There was a porter who would 'transport the mountain of luggage, each with its tie-on label' to the station. He was a 'tough individual who led a slightly shadowy existence in a corner of the station yard – half porter and half carter; he had no uniform but wore a brass armlet fixed so tight to his sleeve that it seemed almost to be screwed to his arm . . . [and had] that smell of stale sweat almost inevitable for those who did hard physical work in days before their houses had bathrooms'. There was a fantastic array of baggage – trunks, suitcases, and 'Gladstone bags full of bathing dresses and beach clothes' – which was quite normal even though the Unwin family was by no means rich. The ticket collector was in his best uniform 'of double-breasted frock and braided peaked cap' and the station-master himself would venture out on the platform to 'see these important trains away and make sure that a large party like ours found its ENGAGED carriage safely'. The compartment would be 'ceremoniously unlocked by the stationmaster and the family piled in, each child clutching a small piece of hand luggage while their father took a careful look down the platform to make sure that the pre-tipped porter was stowing all the luggage in the guard's van'.

For most rail companies, profit was most likely to be earned through these long-distance services and with the main lines now all built, the emphasis was on speeding up services by cutting out diversions created by the Victorians in their need for economy. Cut-offs, the precursor of bypasses, were being developed on various parts of the network to reduce journey times. On the Great Western, for example, once the Severn tunnel opened in 1886 Bristol became a bottleneck for services to Cardiff and Swansea and the alternative via Gloucester was certainly the 'Great Way Round'. The Great Western, therefore, built a forty-mile route through what is now called Bristol Parkway, which opened in 1901, shaving half an hour off the journey between the English and Welsh capitals and on a route twenty-five miles shorter than the Gloucester one. The local aristocrat, the Duke of Beaufort, showed that *noblesse oblige* survived into the twentieth century by extracting his ha'p'orth for allowing the line to cross his estate; he insisted that he had the right to stop any train at Badminton, his own ducal station, a concession that survived until its closure in 1968. Another Great Western shortcut was the continuation of the Berks & Hants line via Castle Cary, providing a much more direct route to the West Country, also avoiding Bristol, this time to the south.

Cooperation between companies resulted in other new routes and the operation of joint lines to reduce distances on longer journeys. In 1906, the Great Central, which under the management of Sam Fay quickly established itself as a deal-maker in its desperate attempts to generate traffic on its somewhat superfluous railway, joined with the Great Western to build a nineteen-mile line between Northolt in Middlesex and High Wycombe. This new line reduced the distance for the Great Western's trains to Birmingham to two miles fewer than the London & North Western's West Coast route, while providing the Great Central with a new market to tap in outer suburbia.

In the north, a second bridge was built over the Tyne at Newcastle to relieve congestion on the old Stephenson one which had only three tracks. In nearby Sunderland, another massive new bridge, 330 feet in a single span, a combined railway and road bridge on two decks, opened in 1910, a cooperative effort between the local council and the North Eastern railway. South of London, even the merger of the London, Chatham & Dover and the South Eastern bore fruit with a link between the two through the Bickley loop and, later, a junction from

Chislehurst to the Chatham main line that greatly improved services in those areas.

For the suburbs, though, electrification was the key, but the nascent technology was slow to be adopted. Apart from tramways, the earliest electrified railway in Britain was the world's first deep tube line, the City and South London Railway, which opened in 1890. Unable to use steam engines, given the depth and small diameter of the tunnels, it had originally been designed to be run with cables but that proved impractical. The Liverpool Overhead railway of 1893 was next and another deep tube line, the Waterloo & City, opened in 1898. However, it was not until the early years of the new century that the growth of electrified lines gathered pace with the conversion of the District and Metropolitan lines on the London Underground and of several heavily used suburban lines on the Lancashire & Yorkshire, and the North Eastern, which used different and incompatible systems.[12] The London, Brighton & South Coast realized that electrification for commuter services offered far more flexibility with quicker turn-around times as well as cleaner trains for its affluent travellers, and opened its south London line, a loop between Victoria and London Bridge via Brixton and Peckham, in late 1909. The Brighton Railway chose overhead electrification but its neighbours, the London & South Western and the South Eastern, both plumped for the cheaper third rail, which then was universally used on what became the Southern Railway after the war. Despite the war, the Brighton Railway had converted all its suburban lines by 1925, at which time several other suburban railways, such as the North London Railway's line between Broad Street and Richmond, and the London & North Western's London to Watford service, had followed suit.

While none of this work was on the scale of the great railway construction of the previous century, it demonstrated that the railway in the Edwardian years was still dynamic, expanding and improving all the time. There was a sense of pride among the big companies – and just a hint of smugness which perhaps prevented them doing enough in the face of the competition from motor vehicles. Their profits were being squeezed by the need to make improvements but nevertheless their businesses were steady and mature, mostly able to compensate their shareholders adequately, if not richly. Even real financial basket cases, such as the Hull & Barnsley, were profitable in the early years of the twentieth century.

Competition was fierce and for the first time companies began to sell themselves through publicity and public relations. Until the last decade of the nineteenth century, the railways had done little to sell their wares, relying instead on their monopoly position. There was, of course, much free advertising space at stations: bills were posted and checked by 'bill inspectors', whose job consisted solely of touring around the company's network to ensure that the bills had been properly fixed. Companies advertised extensively in newspapers, listing timetables and fares for regular services as well as announcing excursions and cheap trips, and in the 1870s the Great Western, something of a pioneer in this respect, issued comprehensive summer timetables for 'Tourist Arrangements', catering for those seeking to enjoy 'picnic or pleasure parties'.[13] However, it was only in the 1890s that pictorial posters and illustrated guides for holiday accommodation became more widespread and the Great Western, serving the country's biggest tourist area, began producing summer timetables listing a few 'principal places of attraction'.

By the turn of the century, the companies began more actively to rid themselves of the monopolist image that was still the dominant perception of the public. Sam Fay at the Great Central even set up a publicity department with its own manager in 1902 in recognition of its need to market itself. Trainspotting would have to wait another generation before becoming the number one pastime of schoolboys, but already the rail companies were beginning to exploit the affection of the public for trains and, particularly, for steam engines. The London & North Western produced millions of postcards, sold through vending machines, invariably showing trains passing through picturesque stretches of track.

The Great Western, which continued to be the most innovative of the companies in respect of publicity, printed over 100,000 copies of *Holiday Haunts*, a guide to suggested destinations reached easily by rail. More weighty travel books were produced by the company too. The first was a quite lavish 152-page book, *The Cornish Riviera*, published in 1904, costing just 3d, and it set a standard which the company maintained until nationalization, far outstripping the imitations produced by its rivals. During this period, too, the greatest master of publicity, Frank Pick, was beginning his work at the London Underground, forging an image for that institution which is still evocative today. The famous roundel was a very early example of a logo and the remarkable series of posters advertising the Underground became renowned, transcending the barrier between advertising and art. The Great Eastern produced strange maps which suggested that the straightest way between London and York was via its station at Liverpool Street, rather than the Great Northern's more direct route from King's Cross. The London & South Western also pretended its links between London and Paris were the shortest, compared with those of the Chatham & South Eastern Railway that could genuinely boast the lowest mileage for the journey.

Freight services were also improving and benefited from much-needed modernization. Passenger trains had had priority on the tracks and the increase in their number resulted in freight trains, particularly those loaded with coal, simply getting lost in the system as they waited for the go-ahead to proceed on their journey. The Midland, in particular, carried numerous coal trains that were invariably held up for days in sidings and yards. The fault was the system of regulation – whereby each train was handed on from one signal box to another – and freight trains were often left in sidings, watching passenger services whizz by, for hours on end. The solution to that problem was another recent invention, the telephone. Every morning the local controller would phone all his district managers to find out about any delays and they in turn would contact signalmen up and down the line. Signalmen were then required to phone their controllers, alerting them precisely when each train left their section. This simple communication system ensured that when bottlenecks occurred, they were quickly discovered and extra resources devoted to unblocking them. It might sound basic but the system developed by the Midland in 1907 proved so successful that it was adopted by all railways following the grouping of 1923.

Some freight, however, did take priority – and with good reason. The Great Central exploited its Lincolnshire lines to create a massive one hundred acres of docks around Grimsby and Immingham, and the railway's fast fish services were widely acclaimed. Presumably, fear of the smell would have ensured that the cargo reached its destination promptly overnight.

The concentration on improving existing services meant that, for the most part, the urge to build long parallel lines to pinch traffic off rival railways had died out. The Great Central's lack of dividends clearly made this an example not to follow but that did not stop the companies running daft loss-making services to annoy their rivals. The Great Western, for example, operated trains down from Paddington to Southampton via Reading and Newbury, a journey few passengers would have chosen over the London & South Western direct service from Waterloo.

Despite the fact that the country was overrun with railways, in the early years of the twentieth century there were still dozens of little branch lines being built to connect any town that had been left off the system by reason of geography or topography. In order to overcome the lack of viability of such branch lines, the government, eager to foster the spread of the network into rural areas which had been affected by the depression of the 1880s, encouraged the construction of a simpler type of railway (built to a lower standard than the conventional ones) by passing the Light Railways Act in 1896. This enabled the construction of cheaper railways, able to carry axle-loads of only eight tons, far less than standard lines, at a maximum speed of just 25 mph, as a way of overcoming the high costs of conventional branch lines. The Act was an early attempt at rural regeneration as it allowed government grants to be paid for the construction of these lines, a rare form of subsidy for what the state always considered to be a private industry that should stand on its own feet.

While such light railways were commonplace in France, and particularly in Belgium, which boasted 2,400 miles of minor lines, a huge number for such a small country, earlier attempts to build them in Britain had foundered for lack of funding and the costs of obtaining parliamentary approval. On the Continent, there was a tradition of more powerful and financially independent local authorities which were willing to finance such important transport links. Before the Act of 1896, a handful of low-cost lines had been built in Britain during the 1870s and 1880s, the most notable being the narrow-gauge Ffestiniog

Railway in north Wales (see Chapter 7). It was used for slate-carrying and demonstrated the huge savings that could be made by building lines on a smaller scale and to lower standards. The line still survives as a tourist attraction today but it had few imitators in Britain at the time because building even a modest railway still required jumping the hurdles and costs of the parliamentary procedure and, occasionally, overcoming the resistance of local Luddite landowners.

Yet the 1896 Act, which attempted to boost the construction of these lines, largely failed. Agricultural decline accelerated in the 1880s, by which time most of the country was already well served by the railways. Moreover, the large companies rather turned their noses up at building rickety little lines for single-carriage trains to chunter up and down at 25 mph. While applications to authorize light railways poured in, few were actually built and even then the companies tended to revert to type by constructing them to conventional high standards.

Light railways had a strange and persistent advocate, one Colonel Holman Fred Stephens, who did the most to promote these toytown railways – still known today as Colonel Stephens's railways. Stephens was an enigmatic character about whose personal life little is known apart from the fact that he never married. He was tall, with a neat moustache, and always with a bowler hat and cane, and his whole life was devoted to creating seemingly impossible railways on the cheap, 'the more rural the surroundings, the greater the challenge'.[14] Is there a railway with a better name than one of Stephens's early efforts, the Hundred of Manhood & Selsey Tramway, a seven-mile line from Chichester to Selsey in West Sussex, built for just £19,000 and so called, apparently, to avoid conforming to the normal standards of branch line railways? Stephens's lifetime work was making use of the Light Railways Act to construct or adapt a couple of dozen railways around the country, most of them, remarkably, standard gauge. He managed or funded several himself, ensuring everything was done on the cheap, creating a railway that Heath Robinson would have appreciated: 'all [were] truly lines of character on which no new piece of equipment was ever purchased if anything secondhand would do'.[15] They ranged from the clay-carrying North Devon & Cornwall Junction Light Railway, which became a branch of the Southern Railway, to the Snailbeach

District Railway in Shropshire, built to half the standard gauge, which he rescued and made profitable for a while. Few survive, the most notable being a branch stretching out to Gunnislake, near Plymouth, originally built to a smaller gauge, and the Kent & East Sussex, which is a heritage line. Stephens was in the habit of turning up unannounced at his railways, ordering a special train and handing cigars around if everything was functioning well – but brickbats and coruscating memos if not.

It was not only the railway companies that turned their noses up at the notion of these ramshackle railways. The public had become accustomed to receiving a decent service and was reluctant to use them. In *The Country Railway*, David St John Thomas is critical of this attitude, which bumped up the costs of what might have been viable railways if they had been built without the usual bells and whistles: 'Britain wasted every opportunity to develop basic, integrated country transport services at economic prices.'[16] He cites the Kelvedon & Tollesbury Light Railway, known locally in Essex as the 'Crab and Winkle', opened in 1904 and costing £50,000, as an example that should have been more widely followed. It joined the main line just forty miles away from London's Liverpool Street: 'The contrast between London's busiest terminus and a slow mixed train wandering over the Essex marshes a mere hour and a half later was as keen as anything experienced by air travellers even in the jet age.'[17] So what, he argues, if there were no signals because 'the solitary engine had not acquired the art of running into itself' and why should passengers 'be amazed when the fireman climbed down to open the gates at a crossing over the main road'. It was a railway that served its district well, carrying up to 1,000 people per day as well as huge amounts of jam from the nearby Tiptree factory, and was one of the successes of the 1896 Act. The jam kept the railway going for over half a century, but it closed to passengers in 1951, long before the Beeching cuts, and to freight a decade later.

With so many marginal lines built since the 1860s, it is hardly surprising that there were some early closures. By 1914, about 200 miles had permanently closed for passengers, including half a dozen railways of ten miles or more that did not even see out the nineteenth century. Most had been built principally to carry freight and some continued to do so after closing for passengers. Overall they represented a tiny proportion of the total mileage. But that does not mean all the surviving railways were solvent – quite the opposite. Many were bankrupt almost as soon as they opened. The Bishop's Castle Railway Company on the Welsh border, for example, was insolvent as early as 1866, five years after it opened, but 'its trains toddled to and fro between Bishop's Castle and Craven Arms'[18] until its closure in 1935.

The reason for the small number of closures was simple. In the rush to build railways, no legislative provision had been made to allow for their closure, so there was no legal way to close a railway. Indeed, Parliament felt that as landowners had been forced, sometimes very reluctantly, to release their land with the expectation of creating a useful and permanent service, it was incumbent upon the railway to keep lines open. A parliamentary procedure was required, even for the abandonment of a scheme authorized by an Act but not actually built.

While assessing the profitability of building and running a branch line would appear to be a simple matter of subtracting the cost of maintenance and operation from the income from ticket sales and carriage of freight, the issue is far more complex in reality. As we will see in the debate over the Beeching cuts (in Chapter 14), the kernel of the problem was to determine what proportion of that revenue would be permanently lost, as many people using a branch line travel on it at the start or end of a far longer journey. As regards maintenance too, determining the precise cost of keeping a small section of track in good fettle is more art than science given how difficult it is to identify the costs attributed, for example, to a gang of trackworkers who spend only part of their time on the branch. Since most branch lines soon became incorporated into a large company's portfolio, such minutiae were of little concern. Was it worth antagonizing a local community, or possibly breaking the law, to save a few bob when it was impossible to know how much revenue the branch contributed to the main line network? Clearly, with so few closures occurring before the First World War, the companies' implicit answer until then was a resounding 'no'.

The Light Railways Act had also come too late for another reason, as demonstrated by the failure to build a long-proposed extension of the eight-mile-long Helston branch in west Cornwall. The Great Western had expressed strong support for the idea put forward by local people to extend the little Helston line – itself only completed in 1887 – to serve several villages in the Lizard, but negotiations dragged on for several years. Eventually the Great Western lost interest and in August 1902 began to operate a service with a petrol-driven motor bus instead, the first such service ever offered by a railway in Britain. The bus had arrived, stymying any further growth of the railway in rural areas, where its flexibility and the fact that, unlike the railway, it did not pay its track costs, would ensure it was cheaper than building little-used lines. However, initially buses were confined to feeding the railway by serving the nearest station, rather than competing over longer routes, since neither the roads nor the buses were good enough to cover substantial distances.

The railways, though, missed a trick here. They were in a strong position to extend their monopoly from the track to the road by creating bus networks specifically tailored to serve their interests by linking with train services. While several railway companies did begin to run quite extensive bus networks, they were slow to exploit their advantage or to invest quickly enough to establish a monopoly. Mostly, railway companies did not want to demean themselves by operating road vehicles, but it was a mistake for which 'they paid heavily in the twenties and thirties'.[19]

There was also the aeroplane, but it had only just been invented and the notion that it would ever challenge the train seemed far-fetched. War, too, seemed for much of the Edwardian period a distant prospect, and little did the railway companies realize that the coming conflict, more than anything else, would change the structure of the industry for ever. However, there was one threat which the railways did face before the war: their own workforces – 'the enemy within' as Mrs Thatcher would later call them – who, as living standards rose, became more militant and ready to challenge the hegemony of the railway owners.

As we saw in Chapter 8, labour on the railways had been slowly becoming more organized but attempts at industrial action were met forcefully by the railway companies which remained reluctant to recognize any workers' rights. The worst labour conflict of the nineteenth century on the railways had been in Scotland in 1890. The

North British Railway had traditionally overworked its men, with twenty-five-hour shifts not uncommon at holiday times. Its 'express' trains were slow, taking up to three and a half hours for the under-fifty-mile journey between Edinburgh and Glasgow, and the company struggled even to keep to this undemanding schedule because of overcrowding on the tracks and lack of both platform capacity and passing loops. The opening of the Forth Bridge had merely made congestion worse and the men were angry that they were paid only for the scheduled time of the train, with no extra for overtime caused by delays, which meant they frequently worked ninety hours in a week while being paid for just sixty.

The other large Scottish railways, the Caledonian and the Glasgow & South Western, were little better and the exasperated men from all three companies went on strike on 22 December 1890, timed to cause maximum disruption in the holiday season. The union, the Amalgamated Society of Railway Servants for Scotland, had organized effectively for several months behind the scenes and 9,000 drivers, firemen and guards walked out, stopping both passenger and freight trains. Many English people hoping to return home for Christmas were stranded because there had been no forewarning of the industrial action, and many factories ground to a halt as the coal trains, the lifeblood of the economy, stopped running. Apart from the Clyde and a few lochs, there was no alternative form of transport since the horse and cart had mostly been put out of business by the intense network of railways in Scotland. Food began to rot in the warehouses, which, stuffed with carcasses and vegetables in those days before cold storage was widespread, could be smelt for miles around.

The railway workers' demands were hardly revolutionary – a ten-hour day and recognition of overtime – and consequently the strike attracted widespread public sympathy at first, but as shortages became more acute, criticism of their action mounted. The men became more desperate, putting boulders on the line to stop a 'scab' express that they heard was running between Perth and Inverness. Early in the New Year, the Caledonian, needing to accommodate blacklegs who had come from England, evicted railway families from tenements at Motherwell, sparking a riot that led to the local station being wrecked. After a fortnight the strike began to weaken, with the return of the Glasgow & South Western men, but many others held out for a further four weeks, costing the companies an estimated £300,000 in lost revenue. The strikers gained little, except to show the potential of solidarity and to confirm their ability to disrupt not just the railway but the economy as a whole. However, their action did attract the attention of Parliament, which held its first-ever debate into railway workers' long hours.

As the Scottish strike showed, the underlying issues were really the profitability and modernization of the railways. The railway companies did not want to take on more staff, which they would have to do if the men's hours were limited. Most railways had a policy of one crew per locomotive and therefore any delays simply resulted in unpaid overtime for the driver and fireman. If hours were limited, the railway companies would have to carry out costly improvements, such as adding passing loops or doubling sections of track in order to improve punctuality.

But it was a losing battle. The unions were strengthened as a result of the Scottish workers' action and membership of the Amalgamated Society of Railway Servants (ASRS), which had been just a few thousand in the 1880s, leapt to 86,000 in 1897, when the long-standing General Secretary, Edward Harford, was pensioned off. Indeed, not only that, but the railway – or rather its unions – can lay claim to the birth of the Labour Party. The ASRS had long realized the importance of political, rather than industrial, action and had sponsored the resolution at the Trades Union Congress conference in 1899 that was to lead to the creation of the Labour Representation Committee, the precursor of the Labour Party.

The railway workers' union, too, was involved in a landmark strike on the Taff Vale railway that would help establish the legal footing of the trades unions, even though initially it was a terrible defeat for the workers. The Taff Vale railway was one of several based in the Welsh coalfields that became highly successful and profitable by transporting coal from the valleys to the docks. The intensity of traffic on these railways is shown by the neat statistic that the Taff Vale carried nearly as much coal on its 124 miles of track as the Great Western did on its 3,000 miles. The union had negotiated a sixty-hour week following a brief strike in 1890 but then the company employed a general manager,

Ammon Beasley, who would have no truck with organized labour. It was a highly prosperous railway, paying double-figure dividends every year, partly thanks to sweating the labour of men who were overworked and underpaid. After years of bullying by Beasley, the workers finally went on strike for ten days in August 1900, demanding union recognition. They quickly found themselves in the courts and the strike was called off, resulting in a kind of score-draw, with the company agreeing not to victimize the strikers and accepting the establishment of an independent conciliation board. However, the legal issues rumbled on and in a devastating decision that ensured Taff Vale's prominent place in the annals of union history, a High Court judge ruled that the union was liable for any losses by the company resulting from the strike. The decision was eventually upheld by the House of Lords and the ASRS had to pay the company £42,000 in damages and costs. More importantly, the judgment made any industrial action all but impossible.

Beasley was rewarded with £2,000, a pair of candelabra and a brooch for his wife, but while the battle was won, the war was soon lost. The injustice of the case stimulated not only a rapid increase in trade union membership but contributed to the massive defeat of the Conservatives in the 1906 General Election. For the first time, Labour established a strong presence with twenty-nine MPs, confirming the party as a new political force. Parliament that year passed the Trade Disputes Act, which gave British trade unions immunity from legal proceedings in respect of damages committed in pursuance of legal action – effectively the right to withdraw labour.

It was not long before the unions sought to use their new industrial muscle. The ASRS immediately demanded an eight-hour day for drivers and a ten-hour day for the rest and a wage increase. The Railway Companies Association – as mentioned previously, they, of course, had been allowed to form a 'combine' long before the trade unions – refused even to discuss the claim. In consequence, the ASRS, along with the General Railway Workers Union which represented unskilled grades, balloted its members and called what could be seen as the first general rail strike for November 1907.

The companies' obduracy in the face of this increased militancy was partly traditional: they had always resisted dealing with organizations purporting to represent their workforce on the basis that trade unionism was not compatible with the military-style discipline required to run a railway and was therefore akin to mutiny. But, their resistance was also born of necessity. The companies, while still the largest businesses in the land, with more capital employed than any other industry,[20] were being squeezed by having to pay for better services as well as by the intense competition between one another. The railways were also paying the price for being the first in the world, mostly having been built at least fifty years previously. Equipment desperately needed renewing and this investment had to be paid for out of current profits.

On the workers' side, their wages were being squeezed by the grim economic situation. Almost for the first time since the creation of the railways, the economy was barely growing, while prices were rising. The railway workers were one of the groups most affected by this phenomenon – now known as 'stagflation' – because the companies were not at liberty to increase fares in response to rising costs. Following pressure from traders and merchants, a series of Acts had been passed in the 1880s and 1890s to control the charges for carrying freight because the railways were essentially monopoly providers. Many fares, too, remained controlled and therefore the railway companies were unable to respond to their workers' demands by increasing wages paid for out of selling their product at a higher price. Conflict in this situation, given that the unions now had legal protection, was inevitable.

The 1907 strike was warded off by David Lloyd George, then the President of the Board of Trade in the Liberal government, who managed to bang heads together, forcing the employers to agree to the formation of a conciliation scheme, even though, stuck in their nineteenth-century time-warp, they still refused to recognize the unions. The unprecedented intervention of the government into this industrial dispute highlighted the vital role of the railways in the economy. It is difficult to exaggerate the extent to which the economy was dependent on the continued running of the railways, given its dominance as the main mode of transport but also as one of the country's half dozen biggest industries, employing 643,000 by the outbreak of the war.[21]

In 1911, however, the government was unable to stop the railway workers from downing tools. The conciliation boards had seemed to work against the interests of the unions and their members, who called them 'confiscation boards'. Thanks to the machinations of the board, the average weekly wage had stagnated at around 25s 9d between 1906 and 1910. Walk-outs in other industries were becoming commonplace and the railwaymen were becoming increasingly frustrated as their fellow workers in jobs outside the rail industry seemed to manage to increase their wages while they could not. In 1910 the economic situation had improved, with rail company dividends increasing, and yet still the railway workers did not get any extra money. It set the scene for a classic battle of capital v. labour. Matters came to a head the following summer when there was a walk-out of men on the Lancashire & Yorkshire Railway, the worst paid in the area, and unofficial action quickly spread with 50,000 railway workers going on strike. The executives of the four rail unions[22] met on 15 August and sent an ultimatum to the railway companies, demanding recognition or talks, with the threat that their members would go on strike within twenty-four hours.

An immediate reaction came not from the railway companies but the government, terrified of the economic consequences of a national rail strike. The Prime Minister, Herbert Asquith, tried to see off the men, meeting them personally the following day and offering a Royal Commission – but the prospect of another 'talking shop' after the failure of the conciliation boards was never going to satisfy the unions in their militant mood. Telegrams were sent out calling for a national strike and on 18 August the railways ground to a halt.

The railway companies had also met the government, declaring that they would rather face a strike than negotiate with the unions, the only major group of employers to remain so obdurate in the face of changing times. Winston Churchill, at the time temporarily ensconced with the Liberals as Home Secretary, was convinced that the strike was part of a revolutionary plot by syndicalists, who believed social change could be brought about by united industrial action, and he instantly mobilized 58,000 troops to provide support for the rail companies. In Llanelli, there was a riot after strikers stopped a train and two innocent bystanders were shot dead after the order was given to fire. This tragic event, which only reinforced the solidarity of the strikers, ensured the action came to a swift end.

That very day, the unions and the companies were brought together in the same room – a historic first – by the new President of the Board of Trade, Sidney Buxton. He cajoled the companies into conceding a small pay rise in return for relaxing the price controls on the industry contained in the 1894 Railway and Canal Traffic Act, and a Royal Commission was established to examine the failings of the conciliation boards. The companies had also promised that there would be no victimization, but several broke that commitment, notably the Great Western which marked the service records of prominent strikers with a 'D' for disloyal and kept records showing who had made speeches during the action. The railways, and the country, returned to normal after just five days, but the railway companies seemed not to have learnt that their disdain for their workforce could not survive in the modern world. When the Royal Commission report appeared in October, parts of it were unacceptable to the unions and it took a further threat of strike and an unprecedented resolution in the House of Commons calling for a meeting of employers and unions to persuade the companies to come back to the negotiating table. A deal was eventually thrashed out with modest wage increases and reduced hours, and the creation of a Byzantine structure of grades which would ultimately be to the disadvantage of many workers as it would entrench the system of playing off one grade against the other.

Three of the unions – the Amalgamated Society of Railway Servants, the General Railway Workers' Union and the United Pointsmen and Signalmen – realizing there was strength in unity, merged after lengthy negotiations in 1913, creating the National Union of Railwaymen (NUR). However, the Associated Society of Locomotive Engineers and Firemen (ASLEF), the locomotive drivers, remained aloof.

The old industrial order had been upset by these events and the change was to prove irreversible. The railways, too, were talking of amalgamation and consolidation rather than competition, which had for the most part dried up: one company emerged as dominant on nearly every route, with revenues being pooled through the Railway Clearing House. The London & South Western, for example, gave up competing on the Plymouth route in 1910 and revenues were pooled with its former rival, the Great Western.

The Railways Act of 1912 allowed the companies to offset higher wages through increased charges, but they were hard pressed to pay decent dividends. The railway in the Edwardian years had been at its most dominant, its apogee at the heart of the nation's transport system, and yet the companies still struggled to make sufficient profits in the face of an increasingly demanding public, competition from one another and the demands for better conditions from their workforces. The war, when the railway companies would reach the peak of their usefulness in meeting the nation's transport needs, would also be their undoing, unfairly treated by government and, despite their brilliant performance, still not sufficiently recognized by the public.

# ELEVEN

# FIGHTING TOGETHER – RELUCTANTLY

The strategic importance of the railways in wartime had been realized as early as 1855 in the Crimean War when the army shipped out 900 navvies to build the Balaklava Railway, which ultimately played a key role in the fall of Sebastopol by providing a supply line that was far more efficient than the roads. Plans to create a circular railway around London to enable armoured trains with artillery to protect the capital were even mooted in response to invasion fears and later the railways also played a significant part during the Boer War in South Africa at the turn of the century. It was inevitable, therefore, that in the event of a major war the government would want to control the railways. Provision for such a takeover had been made as early as 1871 through the Regulation of the Forces Act and, as the situation in Europe deteriorated, in 1912 the government formed the Railway Executive Committee, consisting of nine (later eleven) managers of the biggest railway companies, to run the railways in the event of war.

As soon as war against Germany was declared on 4 August 1914, the government exercised this power and the Railway Executive Committee took immediate charge of the railways.[1] The committee was immediately confronted with a huge military task: the despatch through Southampton Docks to the European mainland of the thousands of troops making up the British Expeditionary Force. The difficulties of this massive undertaking – which was supposed to be kept secret from the public – were exacerbated because the war had rather inconveniently been declared on the Tuesday of a Bank Holiday week when Territorial Army reservists were being sent to train at their annual camps and enormous numbers of holidaymakers were also cluttering up the railway system. Eight trainloads of reservists had already arrived that weekend at Wareham in Dorset and a further ten were about to be sent there when the order came for the operation to be reversed so that troops could be sent to France.

Fortunately, as part of the government's preparations for the long-anticipated war, emergency timetables for major troop movements had already been drawn up and the operation passed off remarkably smoothly. The British Expeditionary Force timetable was an amazingly detailed document, envisaging that special trains would arrive at Southampton every twelve minutes, for sixteen hours per day. Any train not keeping to its allotted arrival time would lose its place, but in the event all were on schedule. Remarkably, by the end of August, 670 trains had carried 118,000 men, along with 37,650 horses, 314 large guns, 1,800 bicycles, as well as thousands of tons of baggage[2] to Southampton for boarding ships to the Continent, and all these trains had arrived on time or early.[3] Apart from the cancellation of a few special holiday trains, this huge movement of men and matériel was undertaken without disruption to the normal traffic.

This first military task for the railways was achieved with such remarkable efficiency that it transformed the status of the railways overnight. No longer were they Aunt Sallys but national heroes. The commander of the Expeditionary Force, Sir John French, praised the railways for having performed the task without any delays, saying 'each unit arrived at its destination [in France] on schedule'.[4] Lord Kitchener, the Secretary of State for War, and the man on the famous 'Your country needs you' posters, went further by telling the House of Lords that the railway companies had more than justified the confidence placed in them by the government and that all grades had worked with 'untiring energy and patience'.[5] Indeed, the unions, for their part, had instantly declared peace. The new National Union of Railwaymen had been planning a further round of action, threatening the companies with a strike in December 1914, but as soon as war was declared the leaders agreed to an industrial truce that was to last throughout the war, with the exception of a few local disputes and, in 1917, a major stand-off which nearly led to a national strike.

Similar large troop movements continued throughout the conflict and the London & South Western, which served Southampton, bore the brunt of this part of the war effort. The South Western had already long been the pre-eminent 'military line', serving no fewer than '176 barracks or camps'[6] including Aldershot and Salisbury Plain as well as the naval bases at Portsmouth and Plymouth. Moreover, since 1892 the railway had owned Southampton Docks, which remained the main transit point for forces and matériel throughout the war, with seven million soldiers passing through them. The South Western alone carried 20 million soldiers in the four-year period, an average of 13,000 per day, and 'no single railway company, large or small, made a greater contribution to winning the war than the London & South Western'.[7]

The pressure on Southampton was intense. Here the duplication created by competition between the railways bore fruit as it gave Southampton an exceptional position in the British railway network. In addition to the busy London line, the port could be reached by five separate routes, giving access to south Wales, the north and the Midlands and avoiding the congested railways around the capital. Two of those lines, from Salisbury and Basingstoke, were double-tracked while the other three were single lines but nevertheless they were used intensively during the war and stretched the resources of the company to the limit. Moreover, the South Western had to cope throughout this period without its two principal directors, since its general manager, Herbert Walker, and his assistant, Gilbert S. Szlumper, were respectively the chairman and secretary of the Railway Executive Committee. Walker was one of the great railway managers of the period and, as we see in the next chapter, was instrumental in melding the Southern Railway into a coherent network.

The railway credited with playing the second most important role in the war could not have been more different in every respect from the South Western. The Highland Railway was at the opposite end of the country and served an area with the lowest, as opposed to the highest, density of population in the UK. Two of the three main navy bases were located in northern Scotland at Cromarty Firth and Scapa Flow in

Orkney, and the sleepy railway was virtually the sole conduit for all the supplies needed by the fleet. The Highland stretched from its two northernmost points, Wick and Thurso, twenty miles from John O'Groats, down to Stanley Junction, just north of Perth, where it joined the Caledonian. The line ran over the tough mountain range of the Grampians, where the tracks climbed up from Perth, 1,484 feet above sea level on the Druimachdar Pass, where trains could be snowed up for days in winter, eventually descending to sea level again at Inverness. Given the sparse population served by the railway, three quarters of the 273-mile line from Perth to Thurso – virtually the same distance as London to Newcastle – was a single-track line with few passing points or sidings. 'No railway could have been less well adapted to the performance of this vital military function.'[8]

The tiny tortuous line, which even today takes three hours and forty minutes from Inverness to Wick or Thurso, twice the time in which the distance can be driven[9] – and which, as we saw in Chapter 7, had only been built on the whim of a laird, became a vital supply line for the war effort. Normally it was busy only during the tourist and hunting season but now it needed to become a key transport artery. From February 1917 there was even a daily train to and from Euston, largely for military personnel, which took twenty-one and a half hours[10] to cover the 717 miles, earning it the nickname of 'misery special'. A huge ammunition dump for the fleet was created at Inverness where the line was extended to the harbour, and Invergordon, a little village on Cromarty Firth, also served by the Highland Railway, became a massive encampment for 7,000 men as well as an engineering and repair base for the navy. Thurso, a small port at the end of the line, was the staging post for Scapa Flow.

Essentially, all the supplies for the ships had to be carried on the railway as well as, later in the war, the thousands of mines that constituted the Northern Barrage, stretching from the Orkneys to the coast of Norway, designed to protect British shores from attack. The outbreak of the war came at a bad time of the year for the Highland as normally its services would have been winding down in the autumn, its heavily used engines in need of an overhaul after the busy tourist season; instead the little railway faced four continuous years of intensive working. Not surprisingly, a third of its locomotives had broken down within a few months and the overstretched railway suffered from a shortage of locomotive power throughout the war. The Highland's locomotive fleet of 150 had to be boosted by the loan of twenty others through the Railway Executive.

Fortunately, coal, which was still the principal fuel for most fighting ships, did not have to be carried on the Highland Railway. Before the war, it had been shipped direct from south Wales but the threat of U-boats made this impossible. Instead, it was taken by rail on lengthy trains called 'Jellicoe Specials' from south Wales to Grangemouth in the Firth of Forth, from where it was shipped north which created considerable extra traffic for the railway south of the border. There were, on average, nine of these large slow trains every day throughout the war, sometimes as many as a hundred per week, all additional to the normal routine of the already heavily used south Wales railways and, as we see below, one of them played a minor role in the run-up to the terrible Quintinshill railway disaster of 1915.

Other railways, too, supplied the military. The South Eastern & Chatham served the Channel ports of Folkestone and Dover which, despite being closed to civilian traffic, were still overstretched. To accommodate the military traffic, a secret new port had to be built at Richborough, near Sandwich, which quickly grew into a large military railway with sixty miles of sidings and branches that could handle 30,000 tons weekly, all of which had to be brought in on the South Eastern & Chatham. A train ferry berth was built at Richborough[11] to accommodate three new ships which were capable of gobbling up whole trains: each had four tracks on their lower decks that could carry a total of fifty-four fully loaded wagons. Quantities of railway equipment were sent over to France in that way, including 675 locomotives, 30,000 wagons and 30 ambulance trains to be used on the network of lines that had been built hastily to serve the Front.

Ambulance trains were heavily used in the UK, too. The sick and wounded dominated the traffic in the ferries and ships back across the Channel and initially they were all taken to Dover. Soon, however, the Kent port, far smaller than it is today, was unable to cope and reception centres were opened at several other ports, stretching from Plymouth to

Thurso, and the casualties were taken to large military hospitals by train. These ambulance trains, many converted from existing coaches, were well fitted out and modern, with special carriages for doctors, nurses and even a pharmacy, and they could accommodate up to 500 patients, 200 in beds in the special ward carriages and 300 walking wounded. The sheer scale of the conflict and the role of the railways is demonstrated graphically by the simple statistic that 2,680,000 sick and wounded soldiers[12] were carried on the railways during the war.

Even some of those impoverished railways that had been poorly engineered and were loss-making suddenly came into their own, becoming vital arteries for the war effort. One was the ailing Stratford-on-Avon & Midland Junction, formed by the amalgamation of four railways in 1908 and well described by its nickname, the 'Slow, Moulding and Jolting'. It had been built largely to carry ironstone but had fallen into decline as a result of cheap imports, then flourished again as the war cut off the shipping trade: 'a heavy traffic in iron ore, iron and steel ran over this serpentine byway to and from south Wales and the Midlands'[13] on track that was completely unsuitable for such dense traffic.

Surprisingly, the London Underground also played a significant part in the war. The system offered a route through London on what were called the City-widened lines, a link built soon after the first line opened in the 1860s to allow trains to reach the rail network south of the Thames. This was one of only four rail connections across the capital and was the most direct. Consequently it was used intensively by troop and other special military services with an average of sixteen military trains every day throughout the conflict, in addition to the normal Underground services. At the peak, during one fortnight in the build-up to the offensive early in 1915, there were an overwhelming 210 trains on those tracks daily, one every seven minutes around the clock.

Every railway in the land was called up in some measure to the service of the war effort, but it did not all run smoothly. Adrian Vaughan documents the fact that fifty-four loaded railway wagons stood immobile from August 1914 until the end of June 1916 at Harwich's Parkeston Quay.[14] There was much pilfering and delay because of overcrowding and the scarcity of basic items like ropes and tarpaulins to cover wagons. Trains became mobile warehouses as sidings and yards were full and factories needed to get stock out of the door. There were shortages of wagons and even the crucial Jellicoe Specials were frequently held up by overheating of the axles on their Victorian wagons. The railway had to carry whatever the military threw at it and that included very dangerous loads. The most hazardous was nitro-glycerine, made at a plant near Pembrey in Carmarthenshire which employed 5,000 people, who themselves had to travel there principally by rail. The highly volatile explosive had to be taken by rail to factories in Kent and Surrey in hermetically sealed vans. With typical gallows' humour, the railway's official telegraphic code for these trains was 'Ignite', though fortunately 'none of them ever did'.[15]

Across the Channel in France, the railways also had a role to play. A network of narrow-gauge railways built and maintained by the substantial railway divisions of the British, American and French armies was the principal method of supplying the frontline. No other war would be fought over such trench-bound territories, whose location moved so little over such a long period, making them very suitable for supply by rail. In 1917, there was again fulsome praise from the military after the summer offensive at Passchendaele. Sir William Robertson, the Chief of the General Staff, praised the railways for carrying 200,000 tons of ammunition and 50,000 of stone for roadbuilding: 'All these things meant a tremendous amount of railway work . . . I would like to acknowledge the most valuable services rendered to the Army by the railway managers and the railway employees who have gone out to do that work for us in France.'[16]

The railways coped with all these difficulties and new responsibilities, despite suffering from a further difficulty – the loss of thousands of key staff to the military. Rather foolishly, the government made no attempt to prevent railway workers from enlisting and, consequently, like their fellows in other industries, they flocked to sign up. It was, for example, rather unfortunate for the Highland Railway that the barracks of the Cameron Highlanders was just beside the railway at Inverness and that the regiment was given the task of raising an extra battalion soon after the onset of war. The railway lost vital staff such as signalmen and drivers, and crucially fitters from the works, which became severely undermanned and therefore took far longer to bring locomotives back into service. The patriotism which took those men to the war was, with hindsight, somewhat misplaced as they would have been more useful in their existing occupations. The government of 1939 avoided falling into the same trap and, at the outset of the Second World War, decreed that the railways would be a 'reserved' occupation, requiring special permission for any workers to sign up (see Chapter 13). And it was not only the unskilled and blue-collar workers who were temporarily lost to the railway. In addition to top managers like Herbert Walker, 2,000 railway officers were 'loaned' to government to fulfil various important managerial roles. Albert Stanley, later Lord Ashfield, who ran the London Electric Railway Company, the precursor to London Underground, was even made President of the Board of Trade, and Sam Fay of the Great Central was given responsibility for running the War Department's own railways.

It was hardly surprising that railway workers were a source of recruitment. At the outbreak of war, there were 625,559 railway workers, reflecting the fact that the industry was necessarily very labour-intensive in those pre-electronic days. Wages, as we have seen, were low, providing little inducement to investment in labour-saving devices. Porters were required to carry luggage and handle goods at even the smallest station, which of course were all staffed with booking office clerks, ticket collectors and a station-master, though sometimes these tasks were rolled into one. There were countless signal boxes which had to be near the points and junctions they controlled because the tracks were connected directly to the boxes by a system of rods and wires.[17] There had to be two men on each footplate – a driver and a fireman – and a guard as brakeman for every freight as well as passenger train. While some of these tasks could be dispensed with, the railway could not function safely without the great majority of these workers. The burden of overwork often fell on the footplatemen, with shifts lasting twenty or more hours becoming commonplace as a result of delays caused by overcrowding on the network. A driver or fireman might end up in charge of a heavily delayed train and not return home for days, sleeping in whatever nook and cranny he could find and scrounging food from the free buffets provided for servicemen –

although, cruelly, they were often turned away: 'there was no patriotic glow to be got out of feeding sooty railwaymen who were hauling the ammunition and ambulance trains'.[18]

The hordes of men enlisting left huge numbers of vacancies: by the end of the war 30 per cent of the pre-war workforce, a total of 184,000 railwaymen, had gone to war. These vacancies could not be filled until an alternative source of labour was tapped – those women who were being thrown out of their old jobs in great numbers as factories producing non-essential goods were shut down and the well-to-do laid off their servants. The women were eager to find new work and by April 1915, 47,000 had registered for war duties. The solution may have seemed obvious, but even though the suffragettes had begun their campaign for the vote, women's choices were still very circumscribed, with only unmarried girls expected to work and then in a very restricted range of jobs.[19] For women to take on these male roles was therefore seen as controversial, with potential long-term repercussions. Moreover, it was an issue on which unions were unwilling to challenge the railway managers who were reluctant to take this radical step. Despite the unions' supposedly progressive nature, they were deeply resistant to women replacing the enlisted men, even temporarily. In fairness, the unions' fears that women would be taken on at lower wages were well founded, as this had happened in other industries, but their objections went deeper than this. In her book, *Railwaywomen*, Helena Wojtczak argues that many railwaymen were shocked at the idea of women replacing them, not just because of their view of women's role in society but because of genuine doubts about the ability of the 'weaker sex' to undertake the work: 'The dominant beliefs about women's correct sphere in life were coupled with the conviction that women were, as individuals, incapable of performing such work.'[20]

However, women were beginning to replace their menfolk in other industries and after the Railway Executive Committee had created a sub-committee, which after much deliberation eventually recommended the employment of women in some male grades, the bar on women was lifted in the spring of 1915 and they were initially allowed to take up jobs like carriage-cleaners and clerks. Men were subject to conscription from January 1916, and increasing numbers of women had to be taken on then, which meant that they made inroads into even more traditionally male roles, notably in the uniformed grades such as porters and ticket collectors. The brave women pioneers who took on these jobs must have found it tough as they had to expose themselves daily to curiosity from the passengers, and even the press.

In the end, women carried out a very wide variety of tasks on the railway (there had been a smattering of signal workers and crossing keepers even before the war). The unions were at first reluctant to allow women to be paid the same wages but realized that they would undermine their own industrial strength if there were a significant differential. The railway company managements, meanwhile, sensing that they could cut women's wages even in peacetime, were quite eager to let them take on new tasks such as shunting and track maintenance, a move resisted by the unions. Consequently, women were never allowed near that male redoubt, the footplate, as a result of the unmovable opposition of ASLEF, which even tried, unsuccessfully, to prevent women from being engine cleaners.[21] Women were also discriminated against by not receiving automatic annual rises, being banned from overtime, and initially not being paid the war bonus of two to three shillings weekly which was introduced in early 1915 to compensate for the high rate of inflation. Eventually, though, women did receive part of that bonus, which had to be increased several times during the war. On the London Underground women were permitted to serve as guards and they became so vital to its continued functioning that when the Watford extension of the Bakerloo line opened in 1917, all the staff except drivers were women. Women became commonplace throughout the railway, no more so than on the ticket barrier where three quarters of collectors were female, carrying out a job which the press had warned was unsuitable because they would not be able to handle obstreperous passengers.

And there were many such passengers, as rail users had more than their normal cause for complaint on the overstretched railways. At first the companies largely maintained their normal schedule, apart from certain sections of line, such as the routes to the Kent ports, which were restricted to military use. A few branch lines were closed and some little-used stations shut. Routes were rationalized, so that there was only one way to travel between major cities: while before the war a passenger travelling between London and Edinburgh had three choices of route, now they could go only from King's Cross and on the London to Glasgow route, in the morning they could go only from St Pancras on the Midland but after midday they would have to take the West Coast from Euston. On some routes where alternatives were still available, passengers could use tickets interchangeably, an unprecedented concession. For example, the holder of a ticket between London and Birmingham could travel by whichever route was more convenient, rather than, as normal, being confined to the Great Western or the London & North Western.

Rail travel became less pleasant as not only were the trains overcrowded but facilities like restaurant cars disappeared from many services and nearly all were withdrawn by the spring of 1916.[22] Sleeping car services mostly survived on the basis that government officials travelling on business needed a good night's sleep, although there was much public feeling that these services catered largely for the rich. Passengers were asked to limit their luggage – few people travelled in those days without at least a large trunk or several suitcases – but these injunctions were frequently ignored and had to be enforced by regulation in December 1916, restricting people to 100 lbs (45 kg, still a lot by today's standards and three times Ryanair's baggage allowance!). Shortage of rolling stock meant that old non-corridor trains were reintroduced on several long-distance routes, which meant much crossing of legs for passengers used to trains with toilet facilities.

At holiday times travel was particularly arduous because so many people were desperate to get away from the towns. The railway companies and government officials attempted to put people off from travelling with advertising campaigns saying that 'joy riders' should stay at home. However, many people were earning higher than normal wages with little to spend it on due to wartime shortages and were understandably eager to obtain some respite from the war. Passengers often turned up in their droves at Christmas or Whitsun, forcing the railway companies, rather reluctantly, to lay on extra trains. Surprisingly, though, the railways were happy to provide lucrative excursion trains to the coast on lesser-used lines. In fact, the government cancelled the 1916 Whitsun Bank Holiday, but even that did not deter a large number of passengers from travelling during that week. Not only did they ignore the requests to stay at home, they did not always adhere to necessary wartime precautions and happily raised the blackout window blinds during air raids, forcing the government to insist that the rail companies turned out all the lights when the sirens started. Initially, trains were ordered to halt once the alarm had been sounded but this caused such widespread chaos across the network that they were soon instructed to proceed at a reduced speed, partly in case of damage to the track but mainly to reduce the need to fire the boiler as the flames could be seen from the air.

The railways in the First World War suffered little from bombing, although Zeppelin airships did attack London in the early months, sending people scurrying into the Underground for safety, but in nothing like the numbers that were to seek shelter there during the Second World War. The airship attacks ended after a few months, but from early 1917 there were concentrated attacks by aircraft and in the worst attack on the railways, twenty people, including eight railway workers, were killed by a bomb at St Pancras on 17 February 1918. Unusually, the North Eastern was put out of action for a few days when a German cruiser bombarded Hartlepool and neighbouring towns in December 1914. Oddly, the greatest damage to railway equipment took place at sea with the loss of several railway-run steamships on their vital shuttle services across the Channel. Overall, there were few attacks on the rail network, and the total death toll of railway staff killed while on duty was twenty-four during the whole war.

The worst incident on the mainland did, however, occur on the railways but it was unconnected with enemy action. The terrible Quintinshill accident, which involved three trains near Gretna on the Caledonian Railway on 22 May 1915, remains by far the worst catastrophe in British railway history and the death toll remains one of the highest in the Western world. The direct cause was sloppy working practices by the signalmen, but the story reveals the pressure that railway workers throughout the country experienced from the greatly increased traffic. The Caledonian main line approaching Carlisle from the north was, according to O. S. Nock, 'one of the busiest stretches of double line railway in the Kingdom'[23] during the war. On the morning of 22 May, the small signal box at Quintinshill near Gretna Junction, ten miles north of Carlisle, which controlled the sidings that were used to allow fast services to overtake local and freight trains, was particularly busy. The two overnight sleeping car expresses from London were late, as often happened, and in order to keep time a northbound local train had been sent ahead with the intention that it would be shunted into the sidings at Quintinshill to allow the express through. But both the sidings were full, one with the empties of a Jellicoe Special returning from Grangemouth, and therefore the local train was directed across to wait on the southbound main line instead. There was nothing unusual in that manoeuvre itself, provided the signalmen remained alert to the danger. They did not. The time was just after 6 a.m., which was supposed to be the point at which the signalmen changed shifts, but the two men, George Meakin and James Tinsley, had a private arrangement whereby the latter would often ride on the footplate of the local and the shift change would take place half an hour or so later. In order to cover their tracks, Meakin would put any details of trains after 6 a.m. on to a piece of paper for Tinsley to copy later into a logbook. Such informal arrangements were strictly against regulations but may well have been quite commonplace in such rural outposts. This time they were to prove fateful. On changing shifts, Tinsley, too busy copying up the register, forgot that the local had been shunted on to the southbound-running line and gave the 'line clear' signal to a troop train carrying 485 soldiers of the Royal Scots, who had just finished their training in Stirlingshire and were en route to Gallipoli in Turkey. Also against regulations, the fireman of the local and two brakemen from the goods trains were all chattering away in the box about the war, along with Meakin who was reading the paper Tinsley had brought. This hubbub distracted Tinsley so much that he did not realize he had just given the 'line clear' signal to the troop train, even though the local, *on which he had just travelled*, was standing in full view below his box.

The troop train had no chance, coming down the slight gradient at 70 mph, and smashed into the local service head-on with such force that all the carriages were telescoped into just seventy yards, a third of its original length. Worse, old wooden and gas-lit rolling stock from the Great Central was being used, and several cylinders, stored underneath the train and unfortunately recently replenished, exploded, setting the carriages and the poor soldiers alight. And finally, to compound the horror, a minute later the delayed second express heading north which could not be stopped by the panicking signalmen ploughed into the wreckage. The hapless signalmen were sentenced to prison for manslaughter, Tinsley getting three years and Meakin eighteen months. Wartime censorship meant there was little press converage of the disaster and the official death toll of 227 may well be an underestimate as the regimental records of the troops were lost in the conflagration. Even so, that figure is twice that of the second worst disaster in Britain, the collision of three trains at Harrow in October 1952 when 112 were killed (see Chapter 14).

Although normal passenger services had been cut back slightly over the first three years of the war, the shortage of skilled railway staff and rolling stock eventually forced the government early in 1917 to implement more stringent measures in an effort to reduce demand for rail travel. Fare levels, unchanged since 1914, were raised by 50 per cent[24] and most concessionary tickets scrapped, while 400 minor stations and many branch lines were closed (although many stations were kept open for freight), some suffering the ignominy of having their rails lifted and transported to France. Holiday trains were no longer run and passenger services throughout the network were cut back through the introduction of new timetables, with far slower timings, designed to save fuel. Even these draconian measures did not have the required effect, cutting usage by only 7 per cent, far less than the government had hoped. Despite all these restrictions and regulations, in some parts of the country the old competitive urges survived. The Great Central, with little war traffic, maintained its pre-war standards, taking traffic from the Midland, whose onerous war use meant it provided a far inferior service than before 1914.

Given the railways' contribution during the war, it was fitting that the armistice should be signed in a railway dining car on 11 November 1918. Ironically, one of the reasons for the ability of the railways to keep the supply lines open, even at times of great demand, was the fact that many routes had duplicate lines run by different companies: 'The main factor in [the railways'] wartime success was the main defect of their pre-war situation. The wasteful peacetime competition, ensured that there was plenty of spare capacity to cope with traffic surges.'[25] In other words, the competition that had been stimulated by the Victorians' fear of monopoly had, at last, found a purpose. Again, ironically, it was the war that killed off most competition by leading to the creation of four large amalgamated railways out of the plethora of pre-war companies; the process by which it got there was a tortuous one that would leave the railways feeling unloved and, more importantly, cheated out of millions of pounds.

The aftermath of the war was always going to be a time of trouble and strife for the railways. Not only had they been managed under a completely different system, which raised questions about their future structure, but they had been heavily used and simultaneously starved of investment. The financial situation of the railways had also deteriorated substantially because the government was unwilling to pay what the companies felt to be fair compensation. First, however, there was the fraught industrial relations issue which had been bubbling under the surface for several years and only kept in check by patriotic need.

In truth, a strike during the war had been only narrowly averted. In 1916, the railway unions had been agitating to increase the war bonus, which was their members' sole protection against rampant inflation. A few local unofficial strikes broke out and the National Union of Railwaymen struggled to keep control of its members, who were angered at the loss in real wages and were threatening an unofficial national strike. There were several meetings with the Prime Minister, Herbert Asquith, and his successor, Lloyd George, who took over at the end of 1916, and finally, in the spring of 1917, the war bonus[26] was increased by five shillings. These bonuses were paid at the same set rate to all railworkers, which had the effect of flattening differentials. The footplatemen, who traditionally were far better paid than other workers, and their union, ASLEF, had pressed their long-standing claim for an eight-hour day, which met with a pledge from Albert Stanley, the President of the Board of Trade, that this measure would be implemented after the war.

The end of hostilities, therefore, was bound to release this pent-up pressure from the unions. The demand for an eight-hour day was quickly met, becoming standard for all railwaymen in February 1919. The locomotive crews, too, were bought off with a generous wage settlement – incorporating their war bonus now worth thirty-three shillings per week –which stipulated 120 miles was considered to be a day's work. However, the government made the mistake of trying to drive down wages for the rest of the workforce, who were already less well paid and belonged to the industrially weaker NUR, by scrapping their war bonus and decreeing that wages should be returned to 1913 rates – whereas prices had increased by 150 per cent in the meantime. It was tantamount to an invitation to strike and even the union's remarkably moderate leader Jimmy Thomas was forced into action.

A strike was called for 27 September 1919, and since it was supported by the footplatemen in ASLEF, despite their generous rise, the stoppage was near total. Thomas was ill-prepared, having been convinced he could negotiate a deal, and it was only thanks to the support of the Co-operative Wholesale Society, which enabled strikers to receive emergency payments, that the strikers did not starve. Support, however, was very solid and even the press, hostile at first, came round to the view that the men's claims were reasonable. Interestingly, for the first time ever in a strike, there was a battle in the newspapers with both sides vying for advertising space to put forward their case. Ministers' claims that Thomas was the head of an 'anarchist conspiracy' were scarcely credible given that the leader of the NUR was far to the Right of most of his members and after a week Lloyd George, who had been re-elected in the 'khaki election' of December 1918, caved in, allowing the workers to continue receiving their war bonus and their existing level of wages. Why he ever thought he could get away with such shabby treatment of the railway workers remains unclear but historians are agreed that it was his obstinacy which caused the strike.

The 100,000 women who had come into the industry during the war fared less well. At the peak they comprised a sixth of the labour force compared with just 2 per cent in 1914 – but the men wanted them out, even though many were reluctant to leave. Only around a third of those working in male grades resigned within a few weeks of the armistice but as there was no equal rights legislation in force (apart from a 1919 Act which prevented married women from being disqualified from certain jobs merely on the basis of the marital status), many women were peremptorily sacked to make way for the returning men. Helena Wojtczak sums up the bitterness of many of these women: 'women's heroism and sacrifice, however, were to be rewarded with a return to ill-paid, menial, women's work, or by a place in the dole queue'.[27] The 35,000 women in male grades at the end of the war dwindled to just 200 within five years and over successive years a few thousand were employed as clerks because, foolishly, union leaders had allowed these female grades to be paid less.

Cruelly, women were largely written out of most railway histories, their role being either ignored completely or portrayed as marginal or, worse, denigrated. In the standard reference book on railways in the Great War, Edwin Pratt[28] complained women had been late or absent from work far more often than men, but completely ignored the fact that, unlike the men they worked alongside, they had to cope with childcare, domestic chores and shopping as well as their jobs. He also argued that women did not seek training for higher branches of railway work when they were specifically dissuaded from doing so since their status was temporary.

For their part, the railway companies had their own grievances about the way they had been treated after their gargantuan efforts during the war, but in their case the argument was with the government. Under the 1871 Regulation of the Forces Act, which allowed the government to control the network in wartime, the railways were supposed to be handed back in the same physical and financial state as pertained before the takeover. This was supposed to happen as soon as hostilities ended but the government, realizing that things would never be the same, prevaricated as the politicians debated the future structure of the railways. There were two issues to sort out: the level of compensation, if any, to be paid in relation to the wear and tear and lack of investment caused by the war, and the future structure of the railways given that a return to the pre-war situation with nearly 200 companies was not feasible. The railways had not only provided four years of free services to the government, but there had been many hidden costs too; there had been very little maintenance and renewal of the railways, nor had there been much replacement of equipment as the workshops had been transformed into munitions factories.

The compensation issue came to a head over the case of the Scottish railway, the North British, in what has been described as 'the biggest row that had ever been between railway company and government'.[29] At first there was no great urgency to resolve the problem as the railways were still profitable. However, as war traffic came to an end, an economic depression, which always affect the railway industry disproportionately, set in. Since the government had not allowed fares and charges to rise in line with inflation, and yet had agreed to an eight-hour day for the workforce and a wage bill that had risen from £47m pre-war to £160m, the railways' financial situation was precarious. From annual net receipts before the war of £46m, the railways were now losing a similar amount and the government had to double fares and freight charges in July 1920 in order to make up that deficit in the short term. Not only were the fare increases highly unpopular but they reduced traffic at a time when passenger numbers were falling anyway because of the depression.

Since August 1915 the government had made payments to the railways in recognition of deferred maintenance and renewal of equipment, but after hostilities ceased the government seemed reluctant to pay up. The bigger companies had fared better, and some, like the Great Western and the London & North Western, had managed to set aside these payments into a depreciation fund. On the other hand, the South Eastern & Chatham was in such a bad state that its chairman would positively have welcomed a permanent nationalization under the terms of Gladstone's 1844 Act that promised shareholders compensation equal to twenty-five years of profits. The North British, which was in a sadly decrepit state, had been forced to spend all its compensation on day-to-day expenses with the shareholders getting no return. At the end of the war, the railway claimed £616,194 but was offered only £186,194. The matter went to court and the Treasury eventually coughed up all but £1m of the much larger sum of £10.7m which the North British by then claimed it was owed.

However, the issue of compensation generally was not settled by the case and the government's new creation, the Ministry of Transport, asked for independent advice from its auditors. Public opinion on the question was split. While it was widely recognized that the railways had performed well in the war, there was a lingering distaste for anything that might smack of 'profiteering' in wartime, a feeling which greatly muted potential support for the railways' position. The government argued that the companies had been protected against the post-war depression and therefore were not entitled to as much compensation as they claimed. For their part, the railways claimed they had provided countless free services for the military, both passenger and freight, which the auditors estimated to have cost £112m. Taking into account other unpaid compensation, the government's own auditors decided that the companies had a reasonable claim for £150m (including compensation), but in the event the railways received just £60m when they were restructured in 1923.

That restructuring was the subject of equally fierce debate and controversy. Under state control, the British railway network had been unified as never before and in many ways operated far more efficiently than before the war, carrying more traffic with fewer workers and less rolling stock. The pooling of wagons meant they no longer needed to be returned empty to their place of origin, locomotives were transferred to lines short of motive power and the duplication of services on parallel routes was reduced. Michael Bonavia summed it up well: 'The lesson, that substantial economies could be obtained by getting away from traditional independence and operating the railways more or less as a single system, was learnt both by railway managers and outside observers.'[30]

This inevitably led to a debate about the structure of the railway industry in peacetime. Various suggestions ranged from complete nationalization – supported of course by the unions but also less predictably by Winston Churchill, still then a Liberal minister – to a return to the pre-war status quo. Both were unlikely, although nationalization was definitely considered for a while, but working out a viable compromise between the two extremes was never going to be easy. The fact that grouping was inevitable showed how quickly the mood had changed. The idea of amalgamations had, as we have seen, long been resisted by parliamentarians, but now there were virtually no voices in favour of retaining the higgledy-piggledy structure of 178 independent companies. Rationalization, rather than nationalization, was the flavour of the times, but ever since the first railways began to cover the land there have been widely differing views on how best to administer them. Mergers involving some of the larger companies had been discussed even before the war but any solution was likely to antagonize some of the big players and vested interests.

A key figure was the Conservative politician, Sir Eric Geddes, the first ever Minister of Transport, whose background as a railway manager was not evident in the decisions he made on the future of the industry. His rise through railway management had been meteoric; he was a dynamic man whose 'breast was encrusted with medals when he was in full regalia'[31] after carrying out a variety of roles during the war. After the post-war election, he had been given the important job of reorganizing the railways, despite an apparent vested interest since he was still nominally a director of the North Eastern Railway.

The government issued its proposals for the future of the railways in July 1920: initially the idea was that there should be seven groupings with Scotland and London having their own networks. Ireland, where Home Rule had just been established, though still wracked by civil war, was left alone. In what was an amazingly radical suggestion at the time, inspired by the need to respond to growing revolutionary movements in Europe, the Ministry suggested there should be worker directors on the board of the new railways. This met with objections predictably from the Railway Companies' Association but also more surprisingly from the unions: although Jimmy Thomas, the NUR leader, had at first supported the plan, his members mostly favoured nothing less than nationalization with a 50 per cent representation on the board – workers' control by any other name. As a result, rather strangely, the two sides of the industrial divide united to persuade the government to drop the plan for worker directors. Instead, the trade unions were given the right to represent workers at disciplinary hearings and the National Wages Board was established as an arbitrator of wage levels.

As for the structure, seven was eventually whittled down to four groupings, which became, after much wrangling over names, the Great Western, London & North Eastern, London, Midland & Scottish and

Southern. London, therefore, was split between all four companies and Scotland divided up between two since the London & North Eastern had the eastern side of the country (and, oddly, the West Highland line to Fort William and Mallaig). The failure to proceed with London Lines, as it was tentatively called – a kind of precursor to British Rail's Network SouthEast of the 1980s – was a missed opportunity to set up an integrated transport system for the capital that later could have been merged with London Transport to establish a truly regional system. Scotland, too, would have fared better with its own railway, but, as mentioned previously, that had to wait until the Scottish Region was formed by British Rail.

The Great Western was the only one of the four which easily slipped into its new structure, simply by taking on twenty-six minor, mostly Welsh, railways as subsidiaries ranging from the substantial South Wales coal and dock railways to all twelve miles of the Lampeter, Aberayron & New Quay Light railway. Its name, too, was an obvious choice, and in effect it was the only company to survive largely unchanged into the amalgamation era because it was so dominated by one company. For the other three, there was much wrangling over territory, management and, most of all, names. The Railways Act 1921, however, had an in-built Damoclean sword which forced the directors of even the fiercest rivals to the negotiating table; the alternative was allowing the structure to be determined by the bureaucrats of a new body called the Amalgamation Board.

Fortunately, the Board's services were never called upon, apart from having to rubberstamp agreements thrashed out between the companies. How these crusty old railway directors, used to ruling their fiefdoms, must have choked at having to co-operate with their local enemies to avoid the indignity of a forced merger. The Act set the deadline for amalgamation in July 1923, but several railways merged voluntarily long before that date. There was no easy principle by which the territories could be established, although of the three the Southern was the most straightforward, taking in the London & South Western, the London, Brighton & South Coast and the combined South Eastern & Chatham railways. Even so, getting the railways to merge together by government fiat was a painful process. As the biographer of Sir

Herbert Walker, the first chairman of the Southern, put it: 'Innate rivalries do not slacken because a government passes an act of Parliament.'[32] The South Western was dominant and the South Eastern and Brighton men had to fight hard for their corners with disputes over everything from electrification methods to, crucially, assessment of the relative financial value of each business so that the new shares could be apportioned fairly.

There were similar battles in the other two companies. The London & North Western had moved quickly, absorbing the Lancashire & Yorkshire, but merging with its old rival, the Midland, proved more difficult and two Scottish railways, the Caledonian and its old enemy the Glasgow & South Western, also had to be reconciled. The Scots were more willing to hand over their railways to an English-dominated concern than merge with one another, which may explain why the country did not get its own railway at this stage. The name, too, was a long source of debate with the London, Midland & Northern being put forward initially, but since it ignored the sensibilities of people north of the border, London, Midland & Scottish was chosen for what proved to be the largest of the Big Four. Again, as well as the larger railways, twenty-seven 'constituent companies' (subsidiaries) had to be incorporated, including tiny railways like the charmingly named Garstang & Knott End in Lancashire, an eleven-mile line near Preston, built in 1863 to take farmers' produce to market.

There was much controversy over the name of the fourth grouping, which took in seven large railways including the North Eastern, the Great Northern and the Great Eastern, all of which suggested that North and East should be in the title. In addition there were twenty-six smaller subsidiaries, including tiny railways such as the nine miles of the Gifford & Garvald railway company of East Lothian, which carried strawberries, pit props and malt whisky.

Because the mergers had taken place voluntarily, albeit under pressure of the Act, they were largely completed by the beginning of 1923, six months ahead of the official deadline. Eric Geddes, meanwhile, a man who had cut his teeth on the railways and steered through the legislation, left them to their own devices, perhaps sensing that the future of transport lay elsewhere. He went off first to a directorship in the motor industry, with Dunlop, and then into aviation, becoming chairman of Imperial Airways, the precursor to British Airways.

The only significant railways to be left outside the system were the Metropolitan and the London Electric Railway, which in 1933 became part of the London Underground, and a few joint lines that had been operated by more than one company. The forty other railways were insignificant, averaging just nine miles each. The amalgamation brought to an end the haphazard system created by the Victorians, which had survived because of successive governments' reluctance to allow consolidation, out of fear of monopoly and encouragement of competition. With hindsight, it is easy to be harsh on this sprawling, cumbersome structure. After all, the system delivered a remarkably good service to virtually every community in the land, all built with private capital and no recourse to the taxpayer. But the old system, based on competition rather than coordination, would never have survived the competition with the road network that the railways were about to face.

The failure of the government to compensate the railways fully for their war effort meant the four companies started out with one hand behind their backs. To some extent the 1921 grouping was 'a disguised nationalization'[33] because the railway companies – artificial constructs formed by legislation – were forced to charge fares set by the government. They had to start rebuilding their railways, and could do so only slowly thanks to the lack of cash, rather than devoting all their energies to preparing the railways for the threat they faced from lorries and cars. That legacy of underinvestment was to hold them back for the next two decades until they faced a second world war that was to prove even more damaging.

# TWELVE

# COMPROMISE —
# THE BIG FOUR

So then there were four. The era of the 'Big Four' companies that was to last precisely a quarter of a century is often portrayed as a golden age thanks to the exploits of the record-breaking expresses on the East and West Coast Main Lines. In truth, that reputation owes more to the skill and originality of the advertising departments of the Big Four than to the experience of train travel for most passengers. The vast majority of services were far more mundane than these posters suggested. From the outset, the amalgamated companies suffered from a number of handicaps including the shabby treatment of the railways at the hands of government in the aftermath of the war and the growing threat of competition from motor vehicles. Just before the mergers, the rail companies had fought unsuccessfully to be allowed to become road hauliers, but the nascent road transport industry successfully lobbied against the idea, arguing that the railways would kill off private initiative and keep costs high. As a result, the government barred them in the interests of competition, allowing them to offer road services only to feed freight into their rail heads. Worse, in the run-up to the war, the government had introduced subsidies for the purchase of petrol-powered lorries in return for allowing them to be called up in wartime: before that, there had been virtually no long-distance transport of goods by road. Moreover, thousands of former soldiers, who had learnt to drive in the services, were able to turn themselves into one-man freight haulage businesses by buying cheap ex-army vehicles with their demob money and greatly undercutting the railways. The post-war era saw the rapid development of a new road haulage industry based on small and highly competitive firms, largely consisting of very flexible owner-drivers helped by the low cost of petrol. Indeed, road users were lightly taxed and unlike the railways paid little towards the cost of the construction of their infrastructure. Within a few years, road transport had wiped out many local freight services on the railways, though rail still retained an advantage for longer distance traffic.

For their part, the railways suffered the additional disadvantage of being common carriers, a remnant of the Victorian rules that obliged them to transport everything from small packets and perishable fruit to whole farms and circuses. Road hauliers were not bound by such regulations and could not only pick and choose whatever load they reckoned might be profitable but also set their own prices. It was not until the 1930s that the railways began to be aware of the extent of the threat they faced and started to lobby against the unfair terms of competition set by the government. Amalgamation was undoubtedly a sensible idea given the wastefulness of the old system, but the railways were still burdened with a network that was clearly too large for such a small country. Surprisingly, the division into four groups, which was designed to bring about coordination rather than competition, still left several main traffic arteries with two routes served by rival companies. For example, from London, there were alternative routes to cities such as Birmingham, Manchester, Sheffield, Exeter, Edinburgh and even far-off Aberdeen, while conversely there was only one company covering Bristol, Cardiff, Liverpool and Newcastle. In some cases this continued duplication appeared quite deliberate. The Great Eastern and the London, Tilbury & Southend both offered pretty similar timetables to Southend from Liverpool Street and Fenchurch Street stations respectively but while the former was incorporated into the London & North Eastern, the latter, bought by the Midland in 1912, became a virtually self-contained fiefdom within the London, Midland & Scottish. In other words, many of the nineteenth-century rivalries were perpetuated rather than ended by the regrouping and would continue for the quarter of a century that this system survived.

To compound the difficulties for the companies to establish themselves, passenger numbers were in decline and, as we shall see below, would fall by 8 per cent in the inter-war period. While this was not catastrophic, such a decline was a disincentive for investors and a sign that the heyday of the railways was finally over. On the whole, the service provided by the railways in terms of timing, punctuality and passenger comfort was not much to boast about except on certain key routes. The Big Four tended to concentrate on a few show trains, whose shorter timetabled journey and comfort were widely publicized, but which were in sharp contrast to the rest of the services. This was not unlike the situation in France today where there is a great difference between the much-lauded high-speed lines and the often decrepit and infrequent provincial services. This was particularly true on the Great Western where a few fast through trains offered the fastest timings in the world while the rest provided the lackadaisical 'take it or leave it' service typical of monopolies. The exception was the Southern which, throughout the inter-war period, concentrated on improving a large proportion of its services through electrification.

The railways were thus hamstrung by their past and by the onerous government regulation. Moreover, the two northern companies faced tremendous difficulties in assimilating their disparate empires, while the Great Western was parsimonious to a fault. Only the Southern showed the kind of enterprise needed to retain, and indeed increase, passenger numbers. The apparent hostility to the railways by the government was, in part, left over from the distrust felt towards them in the days when they were monopolists needing to be controlled and also a failure to recognize the extent of the revolution created by the advent of the internal combustion engine. The amalgamations had been designed to give the railways receipts from freight equivalent to 1913 levels, but that was never achieved, which weakened their financial situation and, in any case, constituted unnecessary state interference. Freight was crucial to the profitability of the companies but the amount being carried began to decline as the economy became less reliant on the heavy industries of the north, such as coal and steel. A lengthy coal strike in 1921 had, too, dented the railways' profits and was a portent of the further decline in freight revenue that was to come.

There was more to this bias against the railways than fear of the old monopolies. The railways may not have been nationalized but they were perceived as a quasi arm of the state. They were a mature industry, with little scope for expansion and frequently seen as old-fashioned. Unlike the motor industry, they were perceived as neither innovative nor entrepreneurial. Cars and roads were exciting, young, aggressive and 'became the flagship of those opposed to state intervention'.[1] They supported an individualized method of transport in contrast to the railways which were public and inherently more socialistic.

The Big Four, then, were born at a difficult time when the industry faced an increased need for investment and renewal just as traffic was beginning to decline. They each had different characteristics and different styles. The largest was the London, Midland & Scottish with a network of close to 7,000 miles, nearly two thirds of today's total, stretching from Southend to north-west Scotland and taking in parts of Wales as well as most of the west side of England north of London. It employed 275,000 people, owned 10,000 steam locomotives,[2] 20,000 passenger carriages and 207,000 freight wagons – and 9,000 horses (astonishingly, 7,000 were bequeathed to British Railways a quarter of a century later). Given the rivalry between two of its main constituents, the London & North Western and the Midland, with their long-standing differences in policy, it was hardly surprising that it took some time for the railway to be melded into anything like a coherent unit. It was not until the arrival of Sir (later Lord) Joshua Stamp as president[3] three years after amalgamation that there was any attempt to create a unified business. Stamp, who soon became chairman, was an economist rather than a railwayman and his focus was very much on the bottom line: his 'economics were those of the tax inspector'.[4] He ran the company in an autocratic way that gradually blended together its component parts into an effective, yet largely unexciting, railway.

Early on, Stamp wondered why the LMS[5] expresses out of Euston required 'double-heading' (two locomotives) while those operated by the Great Western and the London & North Eastern were invariably headed by just a single engine. The answer was that various attempts before the war to design a locomotive that could have done the job alone had failed for a variety of reasons. Stamp then commissioned his locomotive engineer, Sir Henry Fowler, to produce a new class of locomotives, the Royal Scots, which eventually did the trick, though they took some time and several modifications to attain the right level of performance.

The LMS excelled at the backroom tasks, like repairing locomotives and building carriages, but was not so good at what is known today as the 'customer-facing' role. Stamp was parsimonious to a fault, which meant that there was an effective moratorium on many types of expenditure, big and small. The letter paper was famously thin and staff were encouraged to use both sides of every sheet; on a larger scale, only one major station – Leeds – was fully refurbished during the twenty-five-year existence of the company. Stations tended to be cleaned infrequently, and most lacked a lick of paint, giving the railway a run-down feel. Carriages, too, were dirty, and in terms of services the LMS was the worst of the Big Four at speeding up its timetables back to pre-war levels. Alone of the four companies, the LMS had no planned modernization programme, although on paper its officers delighted in producing grandiose schemes that they knew would never meet with the parsimonious Stamp's approval. The company was also 'surprisingly unprogressive'[6] and showed scant interest in electrification or in modernizing its freight wagon fleet.

The LNER, the second largest of the Big Four, was another mishmash, incorporating the three railways that made up the East Coast Main Line (Great Northern, North Eastern and North British), and also bringing together the disparate three lines that went into London and which, ironically, had been refused permission to amalgamate five years before the war: the Great Northern, the southern end of that East Coast line, was principally a main line railway that did not serve its London suburbs well; the Great Eastern, with its monopoly of East Anglia and covering that swathe of suburbs in north-east London which it had helped create; and the relatively new Great Central, a railway without a clear purpose. The LNER's inaugural chairman was William Whitelaw, who had gained prominence in Scotland as chairman of the North British railway and was the grandfather of the politician of the same name under Mrs Thatcher. Whitelaw's policy was far more liberal than that of the LMS, encouraging the various railways to retain their own identity in a loose federation. The overall ethos was to retain existing policies rather than go for standardization, providing they were not detrimental to the overall interests of the company (in sharp contrast to the autocratic rule from the centre of the LMS). The LNER, with its strong network in the northern heartlands, was essentially a freight railway. In 1924, 61 per cent of its receipts came from freight, compared with 58 per cent and 56 per cent respectively on the LMS and Great Western; the Southern, with its strong commuter base, earned barely a quarter of its revenue from carrying goods.

Given the decline in freight, particularly from the heavy industries of the north, the LNER always struggled financially, and was much the weakest of the four. Out of necessity, then, the LNER was more entrepreneurial than the LMS, making much play of its fast trains such as the *Flying Scotsman* and creating popular specials such as the 'Garden Cities and Cambridge Buffet Expresses', known rather more prosaically by Cambridge students as 'Beer Trains'. They linked King's Cross with the two garden cities, Letchworth and Welwyn, as well as Cambridge, affording plenty of drinking opportunities for the undergraduates at a time when pub opening hours were short and fixed. Even the hotels on these two big railways differed in character and style. According to Michael Bonavia, with a few exceptions, the LNER hotel 'tended to be less pretentious but to offer more solid bourgeois comfort and perhaps a friendlier atmosphere'.[7]

Given that the Great Western consisted of the eponymous pre-war company with a few, largely Welsh, additions, it had little difficulty in maintaining its image and its traditions. The Great Western also had the advantage of having by far the best engines, designed by George Churchward, the engineer who had built the 100 mph *City of Truro*. His 'Star' and 'Saint' classes, introduced before the war, were years ahead of any of their rivals and the 'Star' derivatives, the 'Kings' and 'Castles' built by his successors in the mid-1920s, were made to far higher standards of workmanship than their equivalents on other railways and survived until the end of the steam era. Consequently, the Great Western recovered its pre-war timetable much more rapidly than the others and by 1925 was running faster and more frequent expresses than in 1914. The company not only had a highly stable workforce and a paternally minded management – which had both advantages (good welfare funds) and disadvantages (relatively low wages) for the workforce – but between amalgamation and nationalization there were only two general managers, Sir Felix Pole for the first six years and then Sir James Milne. All of this was good for profits too, and the company paid healthy dividends of 7–8 per cent throughout most of the 1920s and not all the profits were disbursed to shareholders. The Great Western invested heavily in station refurbishment and was the pioneer in terms of safety, having developed an automatic warning system that alerted drivers to a red signal ahead. The initial version, Automatic Train Control, first introduced on some important signals in 1906, used a system of magnets to alert the footplate crew with a siren and, from 1912, to apply the brakes automatically as well, unless the driver cancelled it. The Great Western was the only one of the four railways to fit this safety device, which, although not installed throughout its network, must have saved countless lives. Yet amazingly, its successor, the Automatic Warning System and its more sophisticated offshoot, the Train Protection and Warning System (TPWS), were not made mandatory on the British rail network until after the Southall accident of 1997.

The Southern was a completely different animal from the other three because of its dependence on the suburban commuter traffic – its lifeblood. It was blessed, too, by having the most illustrious and competent railwayman of the age at its head, Sir Herbert Walker, who set about melding its three main constituents into one railway and, crucially, speeding up the electrification programme which proved to be by far the cheapest and most efficient form of traction for a railway that ran high-frequency services on short routes. Walker was a tall imposing figure, with the type of powerful presence that ensured colleagues would leap to their feet as soon as he entered the room, but he lacked the common touch of some of his peers who were able to talk to managers and footplatemen alike. Nevertheless, he was the outstanding figure of the railways during the inter-war period.

The task of blending the three sections of the Southern into a coherent railway was made easier by the fact that they had blunted their competitive instincts and had moved more towards cooperation during the run-up to the war. The Southern rejoiced in having a shiny new station, too, the vast Waterloo, which had taken twenty-two years to build, replacing the ramshackle mess that had built up over the years. It was opened finally by the King and Queen in March 1922, boasting twenty-one platforms, its own telephone exchange and no fewer than 240 synchronized clocks.

While the three Southern railways knew each other well, their operating methods and styles were different, and old jealousies and rivalries persisted; for example, it took a year to open up passageways between the Brighton and South Eastern sides of Victoria station, and half a decade for similar improvements to be made at London Bridge. At first, the three general managers were supposed to run the new unified outfit jointly, but that was clearly unworkable. Walker, by far the most gifted as well as the youngest, assumed control as general manager in 1924, and over the next thirteen years was responsible for steering through the electrification programme.

Like today, the railways of the Southern were always in the spotlight, rarely in the limelight. The suburban services were used by the great and good, the bowler-hatted commuters from the leafy villages of Surrey and Kent, and the prosperous suburbs of outer London, and they knew how to make a fuss when things went wrong. While there had been carping coverage of the Southern's predecessors in the press, a particularly vehement campaign was launched in the latter part of 1924 as a result of a series of obscure timetable changes designed to reduce wasteful competition between London and Portsmouth. Places that suffered a reduced frequency in service, such as Chichester and Arundel, might have had few inhabitants, but they included a duke and a bishop, both of whom protested loudly. The outcry increased in intensity during the winter, and every little breakdown – a hot axle box here, a signal failure there – seemed to find itself highlighted in the newspapers. As Hamilton Ellis put it eloquently, 'hitherto patient season-ticket holders began to bay at the winter moon of their discontent'.[8]

There were indeed grounds for genuine complaint. Many of the old Brighton & South Coast and South Eastern carriages were shabby and decrepit, and the little tank engines used on these services were constantly breaking down as any available money was channelled away from routine maintenance of near-redundant stock towards the electrification programme. There was, too, the equivalent of the famous 'wrong kind of snow' incident that was to plague the railways for much of the 1990s: a train full of returning Orpington commuters was mistakenly routed on a different line and the furious passengers could only be brought back home after a long detour through Tonbridge. The subsequent cartoon in *Punch*, the *Private Eye* of its day, captioned 'the train that took the wrong turning', brought universal derision on the railway.

Walker responded in a novel way by employing a public relations officer to combat the newspaper campaign. The fellow who was appointed to this groundbreaking role, John Blumenfeld Elliott, the son of the illustrious Edwardian journalist, R. D. Blumenfeld, later claimed to have invented the very name of the job, PRO, and set about countering the newspaper stories by writing articles in space bought in the newspapers. The very fact that the Southern's reputation was so bad at the outset meant things could not get much worse and Elliott exploited this. An advertisement headed 'The truth about the Southern' was the first counterblast and reminded readers of the important role of the railway in transporting troops to and from the recent war, and how this overuse had contributed to the wear and tear of the fabric of the railways. That article was followed by a series of factual, well-written accounts of what the Southern was doing in terms of improving the track, electrifying lines and increasing services. Amazingly, Elliott's counter-attack, backed strongly by Walker, had the desired effect and the Southern's reputation was turned around, helped by the rapid progress of the electrification scheme.

There is no doubt that the electrification programme was the most notable achievement of the railways during this period, resulting in the creation of the biggest electrified suburban railway in the world, stretching far beyond the suburbs of London. First, however, the debate over what system was to be adopted had to be resolved. The London, Brighton & South Coast had begun to electrify its suburban lines using an overhead system[9] while the London & South Western had been persuaded by Walker to adopt a third-rail system for its early electrification projects covering its Shepperton and Hampton Court lines. There were pros and cons for both methods: the overhead system offered extra power, useful for a long route such as the line to Brighton, and its electrical sub-stations could be spaced more widely apart.

Crucially, too, there was no risk of electrocuting unfortunate maintenance workers who stumbled on the track or of the conductor rail icing up, breaking the contact, a frequent occurrence on the third-rail system in icy wet weather. On the other hand, installing gantries for the catenary (the overhead wire) was expensive and necessitated moving some signals as their visibility was obscured.[10] Moreover, parts of the South Eastern had been built so economically that the tunnels and road bridges did not have sufficient headroom to accommodate overhead wiring. The third-rail system therefore had the advantage that it could be applied throughout the Southern Railway and, since it was also cheaper and simpler to fit, Walker adopted it. Despite its problems, the system survives today to the bemusement of many commuters who have travelled on the Continent where overhead electrification is the norm.

Cleverly, as a further way of reducing the overall cost, Walker devised a rolling programme so that there was a continuous flow of work for the team installing the system. Thus, for example, Waterloo to Guildford and Dorking, and Victoria to Orpington and Crystal Palace were electrified in 1925 and the following year several lines of the South Eastern such as North Kent, Bexleyheath and Dartford ensued. By 1930 Gravesend and Windsor were reached and three years later, the first major main line, London to Brighton, got its third rail, replacing the old overhead system that had been installed on the suburban section of the route.

Walker was now extending electrification far beyond the London commuter lines, reckoning that the increase in traffic and the savings in costs justified the policy. Before Walker retired, routes from London to Eastbourne and Hastings and both lines to Portsmouth were electrified. The policy proved to be an undoubted success, contributing greatly to the profitability of the Southern railway and, indeed, stimulating the development of many suburbs and outlying villages where a fast and frequent train service ensured that commuting into the capital was bearable. Moreover, electrification allowed for much faster acceleration and braking, which meant that capacity on the railway could be greatly increased and trains could call at more stops within the same timetable. Walker exploited the advantages of electrification by providing more frequent services and it paid off. There was a 'sparks effect' on every route that was electrified, with passenger numbers increasing, ensuring that the company's board was happy to see the programme continue. Walker 'made suburbs of Chatham, Brighton, Portsmouth and Alton, with two or three trains up to London every hour of the day'.[11]

In another far-sighted measure, Walker's policy was to standardize running times outside peak hours on the clockface principle, with long-distance trains leaving London on the hour, and others departing at regular intervals at the same minutes past the hour during the day. In 1934, according to Walker, the electric services ran two and a half times more frequently than the steam trains they had displaced and annual takings on these lines were £6.2m compared with £4.4m with little increase in overall operating costs.[12] In fact, Walker probably made a mistake by choosing the third-rail technology for the longer-distance routes, but had he not done so the railway would have faced the extra costs and inflexibility of having two (or possibly more) different systems. As it is, virtually all later electrification schemes on Britain's railways used overhead catenary but that was partly because technological developments reduced the cost.

Walker's judgement was not always right, but his mistakes were generally forced on him by the constant need for penny-pinching due to the lack of resources. The condition of the coaches in which passengers travelled was a case in point. As an economy measure, many of the electrified carriages were simply old pre-war stock converted by fixing them on to bogies with electric motors, which was far from ideal. Walker favoured the old compartment stock without corridors for the suburban journeys because this speeded up boarding, even though the carriages were uncomfortable for standing passengers forced to squeeze between the two sets of knees of those lucky enough to have grabbed the seats. Special compartments were provided for women who could not face such close contact with the opposite sex and, later, trains which were open-plan but still had doors at every bay for quick entry and exit were introduced.

If only the other companies had been so adventurous in electrifying their lines, Britain would have a very different railway today.[13] However, they showed little interest, not only out of penury, but also because they reckoned that steam traction technology could become far more efficient and cheaper. The government, anxious to create jobs, looked at funding a national scheme in 1931 but missed the chance, finding that it would cost £261m and earn, at best, a 7 per cent return – which in fact for the railways would have been more than adequate. This was the kind of short-sighted calculation that has always dogged investment in the railways: successive governments failed to recognize that spending on the railways had far more value to society than the narrow economic returns obtained from the fare box. The Southern had proved this by stimulating growth and development in a swathe of south-east England, but it was the only one of the four railways to generate sufficient resources[14] from its own profits to enable it to undertake such an ambitious programme.

Elsewhere on the network, there was little impact on passengers in the immediate aftermath of amalgamation or, indeed, for some years afterwards. In those days before plastic decals which can be used to change the logo on a set of carriages overnight, there was little apparent difference with the old names and company liveries surviving several years. The services out of St Pancras remained far more pleasant than their counterparts leaving Euston just down the road, as they had been before, thanks to the Midland's long-established tradition of catering for passenger comforts. The liveries were standardized over time, with the Derby red of the Midland being applied to all the LMS trains, the LNER retaining the handsome green engines and teak carriages of the Great Northern and the Great Western keeping its customary chocolate brown and cream. The Southern adopted an olive green livery, chosen as it blended in well with the countryside but replaced just before the outbreak of the Second World War, by the brighter (malachite) green which survived into British Railways days. Michael Bonavia fantasizes how, even after amalgamation, a blindfolded rail enthusiast would still be able to tell each of the London termini by the various odours: 'At Paddington, there was the smell of warm oil and steam, a faint odour of straw and also of spilt milk' which contrasted strongly with Euston where 'the smell of spilt milk was stronger and mixed with that of fish traffic' and King's Cross where 'the acrid smell of South Yorkshire coal would afflict the nose'.[15]

There were a few new services. The longest train journey in Britain could be made on a through carriage from Aberdeen to Penzance, using the lines of three out of the four companies and taking in a variety of secondary towns such as York, Leicester, Swindon and Plymouth. It must have been a tortuous experience, however, as the average speed was barely 30 mph, which meant twenty-two hours on a train with no sleeping accommodation. While few people would have actually travelled the whole distance, it was good publicity for the railway and provided a useful service for the intermediate towns, allowing connections that did not require going through London and the genesis of today's highly successful CrossCountry services, initially developed by British Rail. While the pre-amalgamation companies had many trains which ran over another's tracks, this now became easier as there were only four organizations involved.

Industrial problems were never far below the surface given the rough deal the railway workers had been given in the immediate post-war period. These were, of course, revolutionary times, with events in Russia casting a shadow over domestic politics and raising fears that any industrial unrest would trigger a wider political change. There were two major rail strikes in the 1920s but the first one, in January 1924 – over cuts in drivers' wages – was confined solely to ASLEF, the drivers' union, with the NUR staying at work. Drivers' pay had steadily been reduced since 1920 as the railway companies sought to improve their profitability following the agreements made during the period of government control for an eight-hour day and the consolidation of the war bonus that had put them under financial pressure. The drivers, even without the help of the NUR, were able to bring the network to a halt for ten days, but won only the small concession of having further reductions of their wages phased in rather than introduced all at once. In fact, as it turned out, this was the high point of profitability for the Big Four as they would never recover from the depression later in the decade.

The second walk-out by railway workers, as part of the May 1926 General Strike, was a much more serious matter, as it was part of a concerted attempt by some workers to bring down the Tory government of Stanley Baldwin, although the unions distanced themselves from this revolutionary intent. Not only did Baldwin survive, but the strike had the unintended side-effect of showing that the railways were not quite as indispensable as they had been at the time of the first walk-out fifteen years previously. The strike was triggered by the action of the miners, who downed tools because of threatened wage reductions: when the mine owners locked them out, the Trades Union Congress called out workers in the key industries of the railways, docks,[16] print and steel.

The government, however, was well prepared and was quick to call on middle-class volunteers who were willing to drive buses and even trains. The transport system was largely paralysed on the first day, 3 May, but a few trains ran with fatal consequences. Four people on the LNER were killed in separate collisions at Edinburgh and Bishop's Stortford, caused by using the old time interval system, which had been temporarily restored because so many signalmen had walked out. In another incident, an East Coast express was derailed when part of the track was uprooted after a volunteer gang had been chased away by strikers. With the moderate leaders of the TUC desperately trying to avoid the strike turning into a revolution, and the government standing firm, defeat was inevitable and after ten days the General Strike was called off. The miners held out, unsuccessfully, for several months, which caused difficulties for the railway both because of the scarcity and poor quality of the coal but also due to the loss of a key source of revenue. The road haulage industry proved to be the real beneficiary since its efforts had kept the country running to a great extent and as a result some traffic was lost to the roads for ever: 'from the companies' point of view, the strike had had a bad psychological effect showing people that with their railway services stopped down [sic] to a not very constant trickle, they still could survive'.[17] The slight decline in this period from 1.3 billion journeys in 1923 to 1.2 billion in 1937, an 8 per cent drop,[18] showed that they were starting to lose market share to the roads.

For the most part, though, throughout the inter-war period, the railways remained the backbone of the passenger transport system. The fares were still relatively good value, and were largely based on mileage: the standard third-class single was fixed at 1½d (0.625p) per mile while first-class passengers had to pay 2½d (or just over 1p). These fares, fixed by government, remained the same throughout the 1920s and there were many concessions available such as excursions and tourist tickets. As traffic began to tail off, the railways reduced the price of return fares and extended their validity, making their use more flexible. Long-distance excursion specials, which were much cheaper than the normal services, were highly popular, enabling thousands to go not only to the seaside but also to major sporting events. For example, one of the best deals was the 25 shilling (£1.25) return trip on the LNER from London to Edinburgh to see the rugby internationals. It made for an exhausting weekend, however, with two nights sleeping on the train which was timed to leave London after a day's work at 10 p.m. from King's Cross, arriving in the Scottish capital at 6.30 a.m., and returning on the Saturday evening to reach London in time for the fans to attend their local church services. At the other end of the market, the LNER sold seven-day tours of Scotland for £20, travelling all the way around the Highlands and other Scottish tourist sights in a first-class sleeper.

Contemporary photographs of railway stations show that everyone dressed smartly when they took the train. Commuters on their way to work would all wear a hat and gloves, all the year round, however hot and crowded the trains were, and even on the day excursions every man donned a tie and there is hardly an open collar in sight. Women, while not quite putting on their Sunday best, would make every effort to look respectable in their smartest coat with hat and gloves. And meals on board were not a snatched sandwich at a buffet bar, but full service affairs with all the trimmings: a 'lavish profusion of agreeable stewards, waiters and attendants [provided] an unhurried, leisurely serving of lunch from Euston with a minimum three hours journey ahead preceded with the offer of a drink directly you sat down'.[19] A typical menu in the 1920s offered on the ex-Midland trains out of St Pancras was green pea soup, boiled turbot and potatoes, roast mutton and potatoes, cauliflower and carrots, cabinet pudding (layers of bread soaked in liqueur with dried fruit and custard!) and cheese and biscuits, all for 3s 6d with coffee 4d extra. In the 1930s, the LNER restaurant cars were furnished in Louis XIV style with freestanding armchairs (banned by health and safety regulations today) and concealed lighting, while the kitchen next door was furnished with electric fridges and cookers. The LNER had inherited a tradition of fine wines from the Great Eastern, which it maintained, and provided even more luxurious accommo-dation in its Pullman cars. Even for passengers on the shorter trips on the Southern, there would be a freshly made pot of tea and toast for the thirty-mile dash from Waterloo down to Guildford and on services such as the *Brighton Belle* and the *Bournemouth Belle*. There was, too, the *Golden Arrow*, which from 1929 ran between London and Paris in just six and a half hours including a steamer crossing, and which, on both sides of the Channel, consisted of all Pullman coaches with a meal being served to every passenger.[20]

Philip Unwin recalls a journey he made in 1932 as a newly married man, from Euston to Rugby on the start of his honeymoon in the Lake District, where he was served tea and toast: 'I never forgot the pretty tea set decorated with pink roses and the charming steward,'[21] but his bride must have wondered what she had let herself in for when he rather ungallantly 'ran up to the front of the train to inspect the engine'. On his return trip to London, he was less fortunate, missing the connection with the Irish Mail and ending up on a relief train with tea served in 'plain white cups from a trolley on the station platform', but he adds 'at least they had saucers and were not made of plastic'. Relief trains were commonplace and so were Saturday-only services mostly to and from seaside destinations, aimed at catering for the ever-increasing numbers of people able to afford a trip to the coast. Travelling by rail did have its downsides since smoking was allowed everywhere *except* where banned. Fewer than half the compartments were non-smoking and on some trains only a third, as companies felt that smokers were in the majority.

There was little improvement to the wartime timetable in the early days of the Big Four and it took many years for services to resume their pre-war speeds. In 1924, a detailed analysis by Cecil J. Allen[22] showed that trains were taking nearly a quarter as much time again as pre-war and even by 1929 both the LNER and LMS were considerably slower. The best time from London to Manchester, for example, was still four hours and to Leeds three hours and fifty-two minutes, compared with three hours forty minutes for both pre-war. The Great Western did improve its timings but that was achieved chiefly by concentrating on its prestigious trains, rather than its expresses as a whole, and really only the Southern made all-round improvements to its services, thanks largely to electrification.

By the end of the 1920s the railways were no longer a monopoly for passengers and motor bus services were emerging around the country.

The railway companies realized that they would have to fight to retain traffic and compete by making the journey more pleasant for the passengers. Steam heating became universal on locomotive-hauled trains and lighting was improved too. The trains no longer remained dark in tunnels – which had been a scary experience for some travellers – as the guard could switch lights on and off centrally and shoulder lights for reading began to appear on expresses. However, the changeover from gas to electricity was by no means universal and almost 3,700 gas-lit carriages, 10 per cent of the total, were bequeathed to British Railways in 1948. Amazingly, even on the mainly electric Southern, much platform light remained gas-generated until after the Second World War. Sleeping cars for third-class passengers, who previously had to make do with a rug and pillow, were provided on overnight routes. Geoffrey Freeman Allen (Cecil J. Allen's son) notes that open-plan seating was introduced in this period because 'they were thought to appeal to third class passengers by resembling the interior of road motor coaches'[23] and, of course, they had the added advantage of carrying more people.

Despite these improvements, 'progress in the level of passenger services was steady rather than spectacular'[24] in the inter-war years. It took until 1937 for services overall to be faster than 1914 and that acceleration only came about when the companies realized they would have to improve the timings to attract passengers. The Great Western and other companies to a lesser extent had begun to produce PR material before the First World War but now they adopted sophisticated modern marketing techniques, highlighting the efficiency and modernity of their crack expresses.

First, though, the companies had to start providing trains they could boast about. The LNER began to make much play of its punctuality, issuing its guards with large pocket watches, and giant clocks began to proliferate at its stations. The GWR boasted of having the fastest train in the world, the rather lightly loaded *Cheltenham Flyer*, which covered the stretch from Swindon to London (yet with no equivalent fast service in the other direction) at a thundering 71 mph.[25] Initially, the focus for improvement was on providing long non-stop runs. LNER soon started running a non-stop service from King's Cross to Newcastle, a distance of 268 miles, but quickly realized that offering a similar service to Edinburgh would be a promotional boon.

LNER's most famous train was the *Flying Scotsman*, the name given to trains leaving both London King's Cross and Edinburgh Waverley at 10 a.m. every day since its introduction in June 1862. The timings had not improved since the post-race truce (see Chapter 9) but now Nigel Gresley, the company's illustrious chief mechanical engineer, thought up a great wheeze to ensure the train could run non-stop between the two capitals and spearhead the whole company's drive to improve its image. The problem for such a long run was that the crews, particularly the fireman, could not be expected to operate the train for over eight hours without a break. Gresley, one of the greatest ever locomotive engineers, hit upon the idea of incorporating a narrow corridor, just five feet high and eighteen inches wide, into the tender carrying the water and coal, which the crews could squeeze through to and from the locomotive. They could then rest 'on the cushions' as the railway workers say, while the relief crew took over. Gresley built the first corridor tender in great secrecy and it was introduced in May 1928.

In 1932, the LMS and LNER finally tore up the thirty-year-old agreement of a minimum of eight and a quarter hours between London and Edinburgh when it became clear that railway services would have to be speeded up in order to keep ahead of the road competition. The trains not only had to go faster, but they had to look good, and the idea of streamlining became popular. While it might seem a relatively simple matter to streamline an engine, the covering had to be carefully sited to prevent smoke blowing down into the driver's face, and Gresley had spent considerable time perfecting the design. In 1932 the LMS appointed William Stanier as chief mechanical engineer but his efforts to streamline the locomotives were less successful as they caused smoke problems for the drivers. Even the Great Western tried, briefly, to streamline their 'Kings' and 'Castle' series but it ruined the appearance of these beautiful compact locomotives.

Stanier and Gresley, though fierce rivals to produce the best steam locomotive, were also friends, with offices barely a mile apart and they met frequently to discuss developments. The high-speed trials themselves attracted a lot of publicity as one of Gresley's Pacific[26] A3 engines reached 108 mph, beating the *City of Truro*'s disputed 100 mph claim on the Great Western thirty years previously (see Chapter 9). The test runs proved successful, and in 1935 the LNER started a service using streamlined engines on the London and Newcastle called 'Silver Jubilee' in honour of King George's quarter of a century on the throne. They ran at a maximum speed of 90 mph, far faster than any other British train, which gave a timing of just 240 minutes for the 270-mile run, a whole hour less than the previous best journey time.

The success of the Silver Jubilee prompted demands for a faster service to Edinburgh and also incited Stanier and the LMS to respond, despite the steeper gradients and greater number of curves on the West Coast line. The LMS, which had previously been intent on improving all its services rather than concentrating on one express, now retaliated by introducing the *Coronation Scot*, using Stanier's streamlined 'Princess Coronation' Pacific engines, which connected London with Glasgow in just six and a half hours, a rather conservative schedule given that a test run had achieved five and three-quarter hours.[27] But it was the LNER that caught the headlines. The company introduced the *Coronation* train from London to Edinburgh which took six hours, and on a covert run under cover of a brake test in July 1938 one of Gresley's A4 Pacifics, the famous *Mallard*, achieved the remarkable speed of 126 mph, a record for steam engines that was never to be broken. The regular *Flying Scotsman* service between London and Edinburgh was reduced to seven and a half hours in July 1932 and then precisely seven in 1938.

But it was not only speed that was used to attract customers. Services were improved with passengers being given free newspapers and magazines, and even offered, for a shilling, the loan of a headphone on which, thanks to a cable socket at the back of their seats, they could listen to the latest news and a selection of gramophone records, hosted by the world's first mobile DJ. Another time-honoured way of marketing the railway was to apply names to superior services, a practice that had started in the mid-nineteenth century but was now exploited to the full on all kinds of obscure routes. While some, like the *Flying Scotsman* or *Golden Arrow*, were universally recognized, it would take a fully qualified trainspotter to know what stations the

*Orcadian*, the *Palatine*, the *Granville Express*, the *Further North Express* or the *Comet* might have served. There was also a secret way of getting a fast train without taking one of those crack expresses, and that was to jump on one of the newspaper specials that left London in the small hours and, of necessity, made good time. The Taunton night train from Paddington took precisely two and a half hours to cover 143 miles while Philip Unwin recalled travelling on the 1.25 a.m. from Waterloo which reached Exeter, with only two intermediate stops, at 5 a.m.; and a bit further down the line 'an obliging porter at Okehampton would fill my mug with boiling water so I could shave in comfort while the train waited there'.[28]

The promotion of these expresses was the highpoint of the publicity campaigns run by the Big Four. According to a history of *Mallard*'s achievement, 'LNER express drivers became almost as famous as today's football stars'.[29] Indeed, after the war, drivers of the A4 Pacifics had a little slot on the cabside in which they put their own nameplates and enthusiasts eagerly sought their autographs. The company produced all kinds of paraphernalia, ranging from paperweights and small models to special versions of Snakes and Ladders and dozens of different sets of playing cards.

Posters were the mainstay of the publicity campaign, as they could make use of the acres of free wall space available at stations and the costs could often be shared with the local resorts they were promoting. Cecil Dandridge, the man responsible for LNER's marketing, produced a series of forty posters promoting seaside towns and Scottish tourist attractions reached easily by the East Coast line, and even commissioned a designer, the illustrious Eric Gill, to produce a typeface to blend in with the elegant illustrations on the posters.[30] The LMS responded by commissioning a famous series of vivid posters in a characteristic 1930s style from the artist Norman Wilkinson, featuring lochs, ships and locomotives. Indeed, this period saw the production of a wonderful array of posters, showing streamlined engines speeding through the bucolic splendour of Britain, far away from the nasty industrial regions which the railways had helped to create. Many of these posters still adorn many living room walls today, creating a rather more romantic image of the railways than perhaps they merited.

Until the battle between the LNER and the LMS, the Great Western had long been the most innovative in terms of promoting its services and developed the slogan 'Go Great Western', which was used extensively in books and leaflets,[31] even on jigsaws and inkwells. Now the Great Western got in on the act by making much play of its hundredth anniversary in 1935, a unique event since no other railway company before or since was able to boast such continuity. Oddly, the main publication to celebrate this anniversary was a jokey booklet entitled *Railway Ribaldry*, produced by Heath Robinson, the man whose name is synonymous with impractical and eccentric inventions. The Great Western was responsible, too, for 'Quicker by Rail', the most famous line of advertising copy at the time, which was first used in 1934 and soon adopted by all the companies. Although death rates on the roads were far higher than today and car transport posed a much greater risk to travellers than the railways, railwaymen were too superstitious to use another suggested slogan, 'It's safer and quicker by rail'.

These publicity campaigns were an important part of the railway companies' belated response to the threat from the roads. The railways felt that they had been treated unfairly by government in comparison with road transport, and were particularly angered that the long-standing rules which controlled the prices they could charge for freight had not been changed, allowing road hauliers to cherry-pick the best loads. In 1930 a Royal Commission granted them a few concessions, such as forcing road transport to be licensed, which did slow down their growth but did little to redress the fundamental imbalance between the two industries. The railway companies also finally rid themselves of the Railway Passenger Duty, first imposed in 1832: at the time of its abolition in 1929, courtesy of the then Chancellor of the Exchequer, Winston Churchill, the duty was levied on all passenger fares above 1d per mile. But the decision to abolish it was out of concern about rising unemployment rather than any largesse towards the railways. In 1935, the government also provided some direct support to the industry, providing loans for investment in locomotives, station improvement and modernization which they could not afford to undertake themselves.

There were other changes too. Under legislation in 1928, the railways were given the right to run their own bus services, which spurred some into linking up with existing bus companies to form integrated[32] transport organizations. However, coordination between bus and train was the exception, with bus times rarely shown in the timetable. Strangely, the railways invested heavily in the two main bus groups – British Electric Traction and Tilling – leading to the development of services that took traffic away from rail. In 1933, the railway also bought a controlling interest in the famous Pickfords haulage and removal firm, as well as another big haulier, Carter Paterson. And the railways even obtained a toehold in the aviation business, forming the Railway Air Service, based at London Croydon airport, which flew to Scotland, Northern Ireland and several provincial towns.

But greater government involvement could also be a poisoned chalice. The Big Four effectively became government tools of wider macroeconomic policy since they were a huge source of employment and found themselves at the mercy of government whims, which were not necessarily in the railways' interest. They were encouraged to undertake inappropriate investment because of the government's desire to protect jobs when a carefully drawn-up programme of culling the most uneconomic branch lines and several of the duplicated longer routes might have given them a more stable financial basis. Not only did the government provide little financial support, it refused to endorse moves by the companies to reduce capacity. It was certainly not a commercial decision that left the LMS, at the outbreak of war, with three major rolling stock manufacturing and repair facilities with a combined workforce of 100,000: the government would not sanction closures of such major plant at a time of fragile economic recovery.

During the inter-war period, only 1,240 miles of railway were closed, just 6 per cent of the total, which Jack Simmons reckoned was 'not nearly drastic enough',[33] especially as part of the rationale behind the amalgamation of 1923 was to improve efficiency and reduce duplication. In fairness to the railways, as mentioned before, the precise economics of a branch line were little known and as a result of the reluctance to close lines, the rural railway, that spider's web of branches built in the nineteenth century, largely survived, uneconomic though they were. Because of the railways' obligations as a common carrier, very slow goods trains ran on many of these lines, picking up a parcel here, delivering a ton of coal there and averaging 5 mph or possibly on a good day 10 mph.

As a result, the Big Four struggled financially, especially in the 1930s following the depression. They were not completely unprofitable and most started off by paying reasonable dividends to their shareholders, with the Great Western giving 8 per cent in 1924 and the LMS 7 per cent. The Great Western maintained payments of 3 per cent throughout the period, though only by dipping heavily into reserves and raising eyebrows at the Stock Exchange, while the LMS, with far greater expenses despite the efforts of Stamp, eventually paid nothing at all during the bad years following the depression. The LNER and the Southern, which both had more complicated share structures, also struggled to pay adequate dividends. Compared with the other railways, both the LNER and the Southern were keener on investing in the railway than paying their shareholders.

A clearer relationship between the state and the railways was needed; the one part of the country where there was anything akin to a coherent transport policy was London. The London Passenger Transport Board, known universally as London Transport, was created in 1933 and brought together all modes of transport in London except, unfortunately, suburban rail services, which were excluded at the last moment under pressure from the Big Four. However, London Transport was an example of how to coordinate rail and bus transport with strong direction from the government on the type and frequency of services that should be provided. Creating this massive combine, which was disliked by the Big Four, allowed public transport in the capital to compete much better with its true rival, the motor car.[34]

By the late 1930s, however, the financial position of the Big Four was becoming untenable. On average, between 1935 and 1939, the Great Western gave the highest dividends (2.75 per cent), with the LMS on 2.7 per cent, while the Southern's shareholders received just 0.65 per cent and the LNER paid nothing. By the outbreak of the Second World War, only Great Western was paying a dividend. Jack Simmons is unequivocal about where the blame lies for the parlous state of the Big Four's finances: 'Whereas in the 1830s and 1840s, *laissez-faire* was the orthodox policy expected of governments, in the 1930s that policy was clearly outmoded. In fact, the Government refused to intervene not from any devotion to the principle of *laissez-faire* but from timidity.'[35]

The companies realized that they needed to do more to protect their interests and in 1938 launched 'the square deal' campaign, seeking to be allowed to fix their own freight rates and fares, just as their rivals could. They argued that the railways faced bankruptcy if they were not given the same commercial freedom. Whereas before the First World War there had been fewer than 100,000 vehicles on British roads, there were now 1.8 million cars and nearly half a million lorries. The road haulage industry, with all the wit of a Jeremy Clarkson, countered with the slogan 'Give the railways a square wheel'.

# THIRTEEN

# AND THEN THERE
# WAS ONE

The railways were even more used and abused in the Second World War than they had been in the First. This time the Big Four, together with London Transport, were taken under government control on 1 September 1939, two days before the outbreak of the war, and again they were run on behalf of the government by a Railway Executive Committee consisting of experienced railway managers.

Private cars, buses and lorries were now commonplace and many people had become accustomed to travelling by road. Now, almost overnight, the railways regained their position as a virtual monopoly. Petrol rationing was imposed to ensure that the meagre amounts of oil getting through the German blockades were reserved for military purposes, and it was left to the railways to cope with the influx of people and freight which had previously gone by road. Trains, of course, were run on home-produced coal but the number of passenger services was curtailed in anticipation of widespread bombing, putting added pressure on those that remained. Rationing through travel permits was briefly considered but reckoned to be impractical and instead the government settled for publicity posters featuring the famous slogan 'Is your journey really necessary?' and the rather more prosaic and indeed confusing message 'Give your seat to a shell'.[1]

This time, the railway lines and stations were one of the principal targets for enemy attack, and it was not a matter of a few airships or small aircraft dodging the barrage balloons as in the First World War. The Luftwaffe was out to destroy Britain's infrastructure and the railways were effectively on the front line. Fortunately, the attacks did not start until the spring of 1940, by which time the railways had been able to make some preparations. Rather wisely, the Railway Executive installed itself in a disused Tube station, Down Street in Mayfair on the Piccadilly Line, a bunker which became the nerve-centre of the railways throughout the war, and the control offices which were vital in keeping the system running from central London were dispersed to less likely targets such as Woking, Gerrards Cross and Shenfield. This, too, was a canny decision since the main line stations where they had been housed previously were all later hit by bombs.

Coincidentally, as in 1914, the declaration of war stopped the unions from calling a strike. There had been industrial peace since the General Strike in 1926 but as traffic had been improving – though not shareholder dividends – the unions felt that it was time to put in a strong wage claim. Just as the storm clouds of war were gathering, ASLEF, ever more militant, announced that a strike would start on 26 August, but its leaders were talked out of it by Ernest Brown, the Minister of Labour, who intimated that the railways might be needed to take the children to safety. He was to be proved right within days but the unions nevertheless pursued their claim which was referred to a national tribunal. When it reported in October, the Commission gave some concessions to the workers by raising minimum wages to £2 7s in rural areas and £2 10s in London, although wage packets were already much fatter thanks to overtime, and in any case drivers received more than double that minimum. As the war inevitably brought inflation in its wake, the railway workers were again paid a war supplement which started at 4 shillings for men and 3 shillings for women, and rose throughout the war. There was a big wage differential between the sexes, with average wages in mid-1943 of £3 4s for women and £5 5s for men – because they did more overtime and were given all the supervisory posts – but for both sexes these were good wages compared with other industries.[2]

The government did not repeat its mistake of allowing railwaymen to sign up indiscriminately. Railway employment was made a 'reserved' occupation, which meant that requests to join the forces were considered individually. Nevertheless 60,000 railway workers joined the forces in the course of the war, 3,500 of whom lost their lives, and a further 45,000 were released for other vital occupations. Interestingly, these totals include 4,000 women who, of course, were not allowed to go to the Front but did serve in various military capacities. As in the First World War, the administrative skills of railway managers were in great demand and large numbers were seconded to various government departments.

Women were recruited in large numbers to fill the gaps and this time there was no need for debate, although they still faced much of the same prejudice as in 1914. At the outbreak of the war, there had been only 25,000 women in the railway industry and this soared to over 105,000, representing just under a sixth of the total workforce of 650,000 by 1943. They performed a wide range of jobs, including guard and signal work, as well as portering and carriage-cleaning, but again there was a total ban on women working on the footplate. Supervisory and managerial jobs were also closed to them, and girls were not allowed to take up apprenticeships. There was a repeat of the discussion among the unions about whether women should receive equal pay: this time, in order to avoid concerns that employing them would lower wages, women performing jobs defined as male grades were generally paid 4s per week less for the first three months, and then the male rate. After the war, as before, most were forced out of their jobs but this time a higher proportion remained.

The railways had been something of a closed shop until now. Reg Robertson, who was a fireman in the war, explains how the railway had been a 'family affair': '[Normally] to stand any chance of a job, you had to come from a family that already had the breadwinner working for the company.'[3] Applicants related to a railway worker might get in while total outsiders had their applications rejected. But times had changed, and in late 1940, Robertson answered an advertisement in the *Brentwood Gazette* for engine cleaners, the first rung on the ladder to becoming a fireman and then a driver.

As in 1914, the railways were called into immediate action and successfully carried out an enormous logistical task within days of the start of the conflict. This time it was the evacuation of children and others considered vulnerable from the cities in order to protect them from the bombing that was thought to be imminent. Within a couple of weeks, 1.3 million people had been moved into the countryside on 3,800 special trains, half from London and the rest from major cities such as Liverpool, Newcastle and Glasgow. The meticulous planning, which included reducing congestion at London's main line termini by starting trains from suburban stations such as Watford and Wimbledon, paid off and there were remarkably few mishaps. Many of the children drifted back during the phoney war of the next nine months and a similar, though smaller, evacuation exercise had to be carried out again when the bombs actually started falling.

Troop trains were soon running, with the first part of the British Expeditionary Force being dispatched from the port of Glasgow, having travelled there on twenty-two special trains. Soon after, Southampton received over ten times that number of military traffic en route to France. Some of these trains were far longer than normal, with up to twenty-five coaches, and while that allowed many more passengers to be carried, these sluggish behemoths compounded congestion on the network.

Another crisis soon ensued. The retreat from Dunkirk required hundreds of trains to evacuate servicemen, some of them badly injured, away from the Channel ports. Fortunately, the trains carrying the escaping men, who had been strafed and machine-gunned as they had tried to get off the French beaches, were not attacked by the Germans as they left the British Channel ports, even though they would have been an easy target. Overall, nearly 300,000 Dunkirk survivors, many injured, were transported in just ten busy days straddling May and June 1940 in 620 special trains. Again, as in the First World War, the railways had passed their initial test with commendable efficiency. The GWR, ever with an eye to publicity, even produced a booklet, *Dunkirk and the Great Western*, publicizing its role in the rescue using both its trains and ships. In fact, it had been a remarkable cooperative effort from all the railways, which had supplied a total of 186 trains,[4] each ten coaches long and hauled by whatever locomotives were available.

For the public, however, travelling by train during the war was a grim and, at times, expensive experience. The Brighton trains which had previously been among the slowest expresses in the country, averaging just 52 mph, suddenly became the fastest as speeds were reduced on most services around the network. All the lights were turned off in the crowded coaches so that enemy aircraft could not spot the trains, and until hooded lamps and efficient blinds could be installed passengers had to endure night travelling with just the barest glow of a faint blue lamp. Initially excursion and cheap day tickets were scrapped, though the latter were reinstated but only for off-peak times. Other fares remained the same throughout the war and the biggest problems were overcrowding and delays. Conditions on the LNER's East Coast line were particularly unpleasant due to the reduction in services and the fact that it attracted the most attacks, being the nearest railway to the German airfields: the trains were of 'caravan length and often quite incredibly crowded with corridors jammed with men and women sleeping propped up in gangways and lavatories'.[5] The sheer volume of people weighed down the carriages on to their springs, giving a bumpy and uncomfortable ride.

The number of services was cut back on most lines, sometimes dramatically. On the Great Western, for example, there were just fourteen daily trains from London to Bristol, compared with twenty pre-war, and services between London and Glasgow on the LMS were halved from twelve to six daily. Of the remaining services, many did not run – by 1942 it was common for 200 trains per day to be cancelled, leaving thousands of people milling about at stations to be crammed into the next service. Moreover, people had to endure the awful conditions on the trains for far longer than before the war as the scheduled journey times went up by 50 per cent or more. Plymouth, with all trains now being routed via Bristol rather than the direct way, using the Berks & Hants line, took six and a half hours to reach from London, compared with a best time before the war of four hours, and Glasgow was a massive ten hours from the capital, a third longer.

Worse, even these extended scheduled times often bore little relationship to reality. Delays were inevitable as the extra services on the network, often carrying troops who were given priority, caused hold-ups on congested lines. There were plenty of other reasons why trains were late which were largely out of the railways' control. Materials and people to repair the track were in short supply, countless temporary speed restrictions which, in effect, became permanent were imposed because of the poor condition of the track, and the overlong trains were not only slow but often required two stops at shorter stations to give passengers a chance to get on and off, causing yet more delay. Even reductions in the number of train services could, paradoxically, cause difficulties. On the Southern, the regular passage of trains ensured that the third rail did not ice up, and longer intervals meant a greater risk of breakdowns in freezing weather. All these changes to the timetable and disruptions had a very widespread knock-on effect, and there is much truth in the old railway adage that a timetable change in York can cause delay to a branch line service in Cornwall.

Most of the pleasures of railway travel soon became a distant memory. First class was abolished in 1941 to allow better use of available space and restaurant cars went the same way three years later. There was also the ever-present risk of being bombed or strafed by the Germans and the railway authorities had to work out how best to cope with an attack. At first, in the spring of 1940 when the Blitz began, they made the same mistake as in the First World War and issued an instruction that as soon as a warning of approaching enemy aircraft was announced, trains were to stop at the next station to allow any worried passengers to get off and then proceed at a mere 15 mph. Goods trains were supposed to slow down to a snail's pace of 10 mph. However, these rules caused the network to grind to a halt far too often, given that attacks were almost continuous in the south and on the east coast, and consequently the rules had to be relaxed if the railways were to function at all. Instead, trains were generally allowed to proceed at 30 mph but even at this speed severe dislocation and delay was caused to passengers. Both passengers and railway workers faced a variety of new hazards from the blackout conditions: platform edges were painted white but nevertheless many people fell on to the track and the death rate among the workforce soared because of the risks of working in the dark.

The overall burden on the railways was far greater than in the First World War and again various outposts of the network became frantically busy. This time it was not Scotland but Norfolk where the construction of 150 bomber airfields required vast quantities of material to be transported, often ending up at tiny country stations which might previously only have handled a couple of coal wagons each week. Moreover, once these airfields were built, the RAF relied on the railways to transport the personnel using them, and the fuel for the planes, which put further stress on these little-used lines.

The military traffic reached a peak in 1944 when the railways ran an average of 500 special trains for the government every day, many of them part of the preparations for the invasion of France. The complexities of such an exercise are impossible to exaggerate. Trains cannot just be put on the tracks randomly and allowed to follow whatever the signals and points instruct. Each additional train required a route plan – a train path – to weave the train into the existing pattern of traffic, taking into account the weight of the train, the power of the locomotives, and military requirements such as stops to feed the troops en route. Even goods trains had to be scheduled in a way that ensured the availability of crews with the right route knowledge,[6] which was even more essential since the blackout conditions of the war made driving much harder. Normally such timetables would have been drawn up at leisure several months in advance using graph paper, by a timetabler who would need to know every nook and cranny of the route[7] but with so many extra trains changes had to be made daily to accommodate them. The most extreme pressure was in the run-up to D-Day and its immediate aftermath, when the railways near the coastal towns were working at well beyond their maximum expected capacity, and it was only the skills of the railway managers, the signalmen and the drivers which ensured their smooth running.

On the freight side, the key issue was to reduce the wasteful carriage of thousands of empty wagons back to their home depots. To this end, the entire fleet of 655,000 railway-owned wagons, together with the 585,000 in private hands, was used as a single resource, controlled by the unimaginatively named but vital 'Inter-Company Freight Rolling Stock Control' at Amersham. It set up a novel system, making every station in the country file daily returns on its need for wagons and the equally vital sheets and ropes to cover them. Thanks to coordination and these backroom administrative tasks, the amount of freight carried on the railway rose by nearly 50 per cent by 1943 without any extra wagons being introduced. Special services had to be accommodated on the network, too, such as ambulance trains that had to travel particularly slowly and, most bizarrely, armoured trains which were built to help repel an invasion with a heavily protected locomotive at the front and gun platforms at both ends. They patrolled the south coast for the early years of the war but in the event served little purpose as fears of an invasion receded, and gradually they were left in the sidings.

To compound their difficulties, large swathes of the railways were frequently under attack and suffered substantial damage. Once the Blitz had started in earnest in the summer of 1940, the railway began to suffer massive damage and over the space of the next five years there were 9,200 'incidents', 247 of which put the line concerned out of action for a week or more. London and the Southern railway took the brunt of the attacks but the East Coast line and the Midlands suffered too. There were two bad phases: the bombing raids of the Blitz in 1940–1 and the flying bomb rocket attacks towards the end of the war in 1944–5. In the first series of attacks, the Luftwaffe made a concerted attempt to destroy communication links and some of the frequent hits on the City and St Paul's were actually aimed at the nearby Snow Hill to Blackfriars line, which, as in the First World War, was a vital route through London and was one of the most bombed sections of track in Britain. A particularly devastating attack on the rail network was the destruction of a bridge in Southwark Street, just south of the Thames, in April 1941, which cut off access to the Snow Hill line for a couple of months until a temporary structure could be erected; it took a year and a half to install a permanent new bridge. Marshalling yards, the dockyard railways and the London main line stations, just by their sheer size, proved to be easier and frequently hit targets. In Doncaster, a decoy goods yard was even built in order to protect the real one on the other side of the tracks. On the worst night of the Blitz in May 1941, seven London termini were damaged by bombs and only Marylebone of the capital's major stations was left unscathed. At Waterloo, the most badly damaged, it took a month to restore services fully. Of course it was not only London. Late in 1940, three arches of the brick viaduct carrying trains into Liverpool on the LMS were bombed and a second attack destroyed much of the repair work, while Middlesbrough station was completely destroyed in a raid in August 1942.

Despite the damage sustained by the railway, the Germans never even came close to paralysing the network. The duplication of lines helped, as it had done in the First World War, but the main reason was that the Germans found it virtually impossible to direct bombs on to a thin line of tracks without a guidance device. The Allies were to find this out in the latter stages of the war when attacks on the French rail network to prevent the Germans bringing in reinforcements proved ineffective. Instead, they had to call on the French railway workers sympathetic to the Resistance to sabotage the system. However, where the Luftwaffe's targeted attacks had mostly failed, the random aim of the V1 and V2 bombs later in the war caused more havoc on the railways. The first V2 happened to strike the railway at Bethnal Green and several others caused devastation to railway property including one which hit the track in front of a Kent Coast express that promptly fell into the hole killing several passengers.

Once the bombs hit, the unsung heroes of the civil engineering department came to the fore, men who had stayed at home, not always by choice, but nevertheless risked their lives like their contemporaries fighting in Europe. They did not wait until the 'All Clear' was given, but as soon as they were alerted that the railway was damaged they went out immediately to start effecting repairs, working at great risk not only from continued enemy attacks but also from trains running on nearby tracks. Other railway workers, running isolated signal boxes or setting out to work during air raids, were equally heroic.

The most famous tale of heroism on the railways during the war was the action of the driver and fireman of a long munitions train of fifty-one wagons, carrying tons of bombs and detonators, in the small market town of Soham in Cambridgeshire on 2 June 1944, just four days before D-Day. As the train was going through the town, the driver, Ben Gimbert, noticed flames coming up from under a wagon. Instead of just abandoning the train where an explosion would have flattened the whole town, he got his fireman Jim Nightall to uncouple the rear part of the train and then carried on with the burning wagon to try to reach the open countryside. However, he had got only a short way out of the station when the remaining wagons on the train, loaded with forty-four 500-pound bombs, blew up, causing the biggest explosion on British soil during the war. Amazingly Gimbert survived, despite being thrown 200 yards by the explosion, but both Nightall and the signalman, Frank Bridges, were killed and though every window in the town was shattered, its inhabitants were saved by the actions of the railwaymen. Gimbert and Nightall (posthumously) were awarded the George Cross, the highest award for bravery available to a civilian. There were countless other heroic deeds by railway workers, many of which went unrecognized. Helena Wojtczak[8] uncovered the tale of a stewardess on a Great Western liner, Elizabeth Mary Owen, who saved several lives after her ship, the *St Patrick*, was sunk on the way to Rosslare in Ireland. She repeatedly dived into cabins to bring out passengers and was awarded the George Medal. Sadly, her efforts were totally ignored in the company's official account in its *Great Western Magazine*.

The outdoor suburban sections of the London Underground were frequently damaged by bombs too, while its deep-level Tube lines became a refuge for hundreds of thousands of people. Originally the authorities had tried to dissuade Londoners from using the Underground to hide from the bombs, but soon bowed to public pressure. Up to 200,000 people a night took shelter in the system at the height of the Blitz, while the trains kept running normally during the day and evening. The numbers in the shelters fell sharply when the worst of the Blitz subsided in 1941 but people returned en masse during the attacks of 1944. Although there were a handful of incidents when bombs did, through terrible bad luck, penetrate deep into the system, the shelters undoubtedly lived up to their reputation as the 'best shelters of them all'. The deadliest incident was not a result of enemy action but involved a panic at Bethnal Green station in March 1943, started by the noise of anti-aircraft guns. The long, poorly lit stairs had no handrail and a woman with a baby fell over, triggering an horrific stampede that left 173 people, including sixty-two children, crushed to death.

Whereas in the early days of the war, passengers had accepted the injunction not to travel unless they had to, as the conflict wore on the trains filled up again as people were desperate to get away from the troubled cities whenever they had a chance of a break. Huge numbers of service men and women on leave, as well as newly arrived Americans desperate to see the London sights and experience the night life, crowded on to the system. By the latter stages of the war, when the V1 and V2 flying bombs were raining down on London, the war-weary population flocked to the railways and ignored the injunctions. By the end of the war, railway usage had reached record levels. There were about a million passengers per week more than in 1938, with the annual total for 1944 reaching 1.3bn journeys.[9] Of the Big Four, only the Southern, which had lost much commuter traffic, showed a decrease, while numbers on the Great Western had risen by over 50 per cent.

O. S. Nock had no doubts about the achievement of the railways in this grim time: 'In plain terms, the cumulative effort of the British railways over the years 1940–1945 represents the greatest achievement in railway transportation in the history of the world.'[10] Yet, the public, ever critical of the railways, did not fully appreciate this success. Many of the more affluent classes, who had been forced out of their cars to travel by railway for the first time, were not impressed by their uncomfortable and slow journeys on overcrowded trains, and that climate of criticism helped to ensure that public protests against Labour's plans to nationalize the railways after the war were muted.

In a near repeat of events after the First World War, the railways were dealt a rough hand by the government over the financial arrangements resulting from their wartime nationalization. The government, a coalition of all three main parties, had initially promised to allow them to have first call on any profit up to £40m and a share of subsequent profits up to a total £56m. But a couple of years into the conflict the railways were being allowed to retain only £43.5m of their profits annually, divided in set percentages between the Big Four and London Transport,[11] an arrangement which proved lucrative for the government. While before the war the five railway businesses (including London Underground) had an annual income of £200m, and made profits of £40m, by 1944 they were netting £93m on double the turnover. There seemed to be no rationale for the government to retain just over half the £350m in profits generated by the railways during the war, although in compensation it created a trust fund for investment in the railways and most of the money, about £150m (£3,750m today), was handed over to the British Transport Commission (which ran British Railways after nationalization).

Immediately after the end of the war, the General Election of 1945 brought to power a Labour government committed to nationalization, not just of the railways but also other key industries such as coal and steel. In a November parliamentary announcement, Herbert Morrison, the Deputy Prime Minister and the creator of London Transport, confirmed the manifesto promise of nationalization. The policy was not as controversial as might have been expected. The struggles of the Big Four in the run-up to the war and the efficient running of the system as a unified network since 1939 had ensured that there was no question of returning to the old system. Moreover, support for nationalization was again not confined to left-wing circles. Large public corporations like the BBC, the Central Electricity Board and London Transport had been created between the wars by the Tories. As Terry Gourvish, the official historian of British Railways, put it, 'an increasing body of opinion in all parties certainly favoured a greater measure of governmental control in the interests of both industry and the consumer'.[12]

The railways were on their knees and ripe for nationalization: the war had drained them far beyond the experience of the First World War and the industry had already been in a financially strained situation in 1938, with only the Great Western paying a dividend that year. Intensive use had also taken its toll: by the end of the war, the railways were carrying 50 per cent more freight and passenger mileage had increased by two thirds with the same amount of equipment; to make matters worse, routine permanent-way maintenance had been slashed, creating an estimated backlog of 2,500 track miles,[13] about two years' work in normal circumstances. Bridges, tunnels and buildings had also been allowed to decay, while many locomotives were at the end of their useful lives. Over 8,000 locomotives, 40 per cent of the total, were over thirty-five years old as was a fifth of the 56,000 coaches. Moreover, apart from resuming work on a couple of long-planned electrification schemes, no improvements to the network were carried out. Previous commitments made during the war to a major modernization of the system were quietly dropped and not revived until the mid-1950s.

Yet, despite the desperate need to improve the state of the railways, the money available in the government's trust fund remained largely unspent because the rail companies showed little interest in improving the railway or even bringing it up to standard. The top brass were distracted by their decision to resist nationalization in every way possible rather than work with the government, but even when they did make concerted attempts to restore the railway's physical condition, their efforts were hampered by the lack of raw materials and skilled labour, both of which were in short supply following the war. Even more 'temporary' speed restrictions had to be imposed because of the condition of the track and travelling on the run-down railways, therefore, was not an attractive proposition as the companies failed even to keep to their slacker timetables. Carriages were tatty and many stations had not seen a lick of paint since long before the war. Petrol rationing eased, enabling the more affluent to take to the roads, while the rest, their income squeezed as the austerity of the post-war period began, could not even afford rail travel. Consequently, passenger numbers fell by a third in the first couple of years after the war[14] and inevitably the companies' finances suffered. This downward spiral was to last for the rest of the decade, turning their profits into heavy losses.

Even safety was compromised by the poor state of the track and the lack of investment. Safety had improved in the pre-war days of the Big Four. In the 1920s and 1930s, only an average of thirteen people per year were killed in train accidents, far fewer than in any period since the mid-nineteenth century, but the war inevitably led to a sharp rise in fatalities. There was no equivalent to the terrible Quintinshill accident of 1915 but there were a lot of minor accidents and collisions, and the death rate among workers also increased dramatically, hardly surprising given the risks to the gangs on the track in darkness. (The roads, incidentally, were far more perilous and the death toll reached its highest ever – 9,000 annually – three times today's figure, principally as a result of drivers not being allowed to use headlights on roads where streetlamps had been switched off.) After the war, the accident rate on the railways increased sharply and there was a spate of disasters in 1946–7 culminating in two crashes in the space of three days in October 1947, at South Croydon and Goswick in Northumberland, which killed a total of sixty people. That year, in his annual report, the Chief Inspecting Officer of the Railways blamed the poor safety record of the railways on the backlog of track maintenance and the failure to replace old semaphore signalling with the safer colour lights – which had become all the more necessary given the frequency of pea-souper fogs, caused by widespread burning of domestic coal. Even when trains were not crashing, they were breaking down with ever greater frequency. The performance of the railways was particularly bad in the summer of 1947 when the poor quality of locomotive coal caused by the fuel crisis of the previous winter, the coldest on record, was responsible for many engine failures and delays. Hugh Dalton, the Chancellor of the Exchequer, echoed the feelings of many when he told Parliament in December 1946: 'This railway system of ours is a very poor bag of physical assets. The permanent way is badly worn. The rolling stock is in a state of great dilapidation. The railways are a disgrace to the country.'[15]

That did not stop the railway companies receiving over-generous compensation terms, a result of timid government and powerful lobbying from the companies and their City friends. The hostility of the train companies to nationalization meant they concentrated more on maximizing compensation for their shareholders than on ensuring their networks were in a reasonable state when they were handed over to the British Transport Commission. Their profits may have been falling, but they made sure their shareholders received some last-minute rewards. Despite the capping of the total profits at £43.5m, the shareholders, with the exception of those unfortunate enough to hold LNER stock, had done well out of the war thanks to the increased traffic. Dividends during the war were well above pre-war levels, and in 1946–7 the payments on all four were increased substantially: the Great Western paid out over 6 per cent, the LMS nearly 4 per cent and the Southern 3.5 per cent, with the LNER, as ever lagging behind, with just 0.4 per cent, having paid nothing in the war. These rises were a deliberate strategy by the companies to boost shareholder income in the run-up to nationalization in the knowledge that the government's compensation would have to be based on these figures.

The shareholders were given £900m (a remarkable £22.5bn in today's money) in government stock which guaranteed 3 per cent annually. The government had initially suggested a lower sum but pressure from the companies, helped by sympathetic press coverage, notably in *The*

*Economist*, weakened ministers' resolve and the railways were saddled with a valuation that is now widely recognized to have been far too high. This was a political fudge, not based on any transport imperatives or financial rationale but on 'political and administrative expediency'.[16] The government used the Stock Exchange prices of the first week in November 1946 when the shares were doing well, and then used the interest rate from the spring of 1947, just after it had risen from 2.5 per cent to 3 per cent. In any case, the Stock Exchange price was an artificial one, based on the temporary high level of traffic in the war and further boosted because investors knew the government was about to take over the industry. The valuation of the railways failed to take into account the likely future performance of the industry in the face of increased road competition and the burden of the backlog of investment. In other words, the shareholders got a good deal in both respects, as the stock was overvalued and the interest rate paid on it was high, guaranteeing them a handsome income for ninety years even though the railways were a mature industry, likely to stagnate, at best, or even decline. British Railways was burdened with annual interest payments of £27m (£675m today) to reward these stockholders,[17] a handicap that was to hamper its ability to invest in the railways.

The other issue to sort out before the handover was the future structure of the railways, and here again mistakes were made from the outset. Instead of giving the railways autonomy, they were placed under the control of the mammoth British Transport Commission which oversaw the ports, lorry haulage and the waterways – and had the difficult financial remit of breaking even as a whole organization. While the railways had their own executive, there was a lack of clarity about whether the Commission, housed in the London Transport headquarters at 55 Broadway over St James's Park station, or the Railway Executive, sited at 222 Marylebone Road, opposite Marylebone station, was in charge. The tension between the two was ever present and was deeply damaging for the industry. The railway needed to be an independent financial entity so that its investment needs could be properly identified, rather than being buried in the Commission. Moreover, the Railway Executive was weakened by the refusal of many former managers of the Big Four to sit on it because of their opposition to nationalization. The Executive's directors were 'essentially a body of experienced railwaymen of the old school', in other words, lacking the innovation and dynamism which was so needed at this crucial time. It is hardly surprising then that the Executive barely changed the existing structure of the railways, creating six regions out of the four companies by hiving off the Scottish lines from the two northern railways and splitting the LNER into two at Doncaster. These regions were again to become fiefdoms for the managers who ran them. For the public there was very little difference in the railway network when British Railways[18] was created on 1 January 1948. As a measure of the continued importance of railways in the nation's transport system, at the time of nationalization there were 20,000 private shunting locomotives used in company sidings, the same number of engines that would be transferred to British Railways from the Big Four.

It was around this time that trainspotters – or gricers as they have become known – began to appear at the end of platforms, with their uniform of flimsy anoraks, pencils in one hand and the Ian Allan *ABC of British Railway Locomotives* in the other. Trainspotting is a strangely British phenomenon, which for a couple of generations was to become the principal hobby of boys (there were few girls) of all classes.[19] The legendary Allan was a clerk on the Southern railway when he first produced a list of all the rolling stock for his own benefit, and published it after the war. There had been railway enthusiasts before then and special trains had even been run by the Great Western between the wars to visit the workshops at Swindon, but Allan's rapidly burgeoning publishing empire turned the hobby of a few into an activity for the masses with its own language and odd mores. Most trainspotters were attracted by an interest in steam engines and it seemed that their days were numbered as diesels had begun to appear on the network. However, as we see in the next chapter, the railway industry clung on to steam technology for far too long and the trainspotters had a field day as British Railways continued to build locomotives right up to the mid-1960s.

The railway companies were keen to advertise their facilities for travellers wishing to venture further a field. This poster produced for the Southern Railway in 1926 promoted rail services that linked with Atlantic Ocean crossings by the White Star, the world's largest liner at the time.

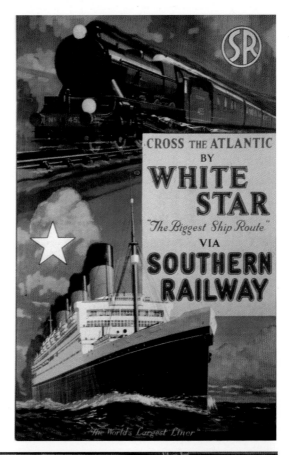

CROSS THE ATLANTIC
BY
WHITE STAR
"The Biggest Ship Route"
VIA
SOUTHERN RAILWAY

"The World's Largest Liner"

This painting by Leonard Campbell Taylor of the interior of a London, Midland & Scottish dining car in the 1920s shows the lavish dining facilities available – at no great cost.

Railway poster art flourished between the wars. This 1932 London & North Eastern Railway advertisement made an oblique reference to a similar Southern Railway poster, emphasising the LNER's more exciting services.

The electrification scheme of the Southern Railway attracted vast numbers of extra passengers onto the railways.

The streamlined A4 Pacific locomotives were the elite fleet of the LNER, one of which, No 4468 *Mallard*, broke the world speed record for a steam engine in 1938.

Mail was carried by the railway from its earliest days and from the 1860s special mobile sorting offices like this one were introduced. This scene of postal workers dates from 1935.

The railways were a labour-intensive industry, as evidenced by the large number of men in this repair gang replacing a rail in 1940.

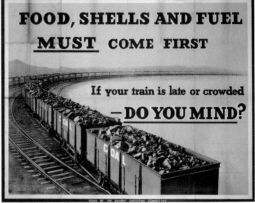

The mass evacuation of children from British cities presented an enormous logistical problem in the early days of the Second World War. The railways rose to the occasion, however, and the scheme was carried out with remarkable success.

During the Second World War the government produced posters emphasising the primacy of the war effort for the railways. It even tried, unsuccessfully, to dissuade people from using the system.

Widespread fears that the Germans would use gas in the Second World War led to the wearing of gas masks by breakdown crews. The task for this gang on the Southern Railway in September 1943 was to re-rail a carriage while remaining in their protective clothing.

Kent miners in the 1950s waiting for a train to take them to work.

Holidaymakers queuing outside Waterloo station in July 1946 to take trains to the seaside.

British Railways' coat of arms from the 1950s. Various versions were used in subsequent years.

The railways were slow to adapt to diesel technology, which would have saved considerable sums and made the economics of many branch lines more viable.

Privatisation in the mid-1990s led to a proliferation of liveries and logos and the most radical shake up of the industry in its history. This included the separation of the operating companies from Railtrack (later Network Rail) which was responsible for the infrastructure.

The development of the InterCity brand and its popular services was one of the great successes of British Railways, reviving the market for long distance train travel in the face of competition from the motorways.

A sensitive approach to maintaining the heritage while modernising the railway pays dividends, as illustrated by this refurbishment of Norwich station.

A test run of a Eurostar train into St Pancras, the train shed of which was totally refurbished for the 2007 completion of Britain's first High Speed Line linking the station with the Channel Tunnel.

# FOURTEEN

# AN UNDESERVED
# REPUTATION[1]

Just as the Big Four companies had started out with one hand tied behind their backs, so British Railways (BR) on its creation on 1 January 1948 had to cope with several handicaps from the outset. As just one of several transport organizations buried within the structure of the unwieldy British Transport Commission (BTC), it struggled to establish a separate identity. The attempt to nationalize virtually every mode of transport, apart from local lorry deliveries, was over-ambitious; although, at first glance, it might have had the appearance of a sensible integrated transport policy, in practice it was not thought through at a local level, where each mode was kept separate. The BTC was not one unified organization but a series of empires that were deeply hostile to each other and there were frequent rows between the Railway Executive and its supposed masters at the BTC.

Melding such a diverse, unwieldly system of railways – replete with old rivalries and a variety of long-established practices – into one organization was never going to be easy. But doing it at a time of austerity and shortages in post-war Britain compounded the difficulties. No one quite knew how many staff there were, with estimates ranging between 632,000 and 649,000, and the extent of the undertaking was vast: 20,000 steam locomotives, 1.2 million freight wagons, 56,000 coaches (of which 631 were restaurant cars), 54 hotels and 7,000 horses, some of which remained working in the yards until 1964.[2] Moreover, British Railways lost the central control that had been enjoyed during the war when it was split into regions which continued to act independently, without common standards or working practices, and with fierce rivalries little different from the competition between the old companies.

Above all, there was the legacy of underinvestment, combined with the overuse of assets. BR's historian Terry Gourvish concludes: 'The postponement of essential maintenance and renewals, coupled with the more intensive use of the network and the effects of war damage, proved to be a most unfortunate legacy for postwar managements.'[3] To compound these problems, the railways lacked a champion. There was no equivalent of Aneurin Bevan, the Health Minister who was the father of the National Health Service, to nurse the railways into public ownership. Alfred Barnes, Attlee's Transport Minister, has rightly been consigned to obscurity by history despite being the longest serving custodian of that job. The new structure of the industry was devised by civil servants and committees – a lethal combination, especially as there was negligible input from railway managers. The railways were off the government's radar, despite their continued importance in providing one in five of all passenger journeys.

Despite these difficulties, nationalization did not start off too badly. In 1948, performance improved considerably with fewer delays and cancellations and an increased number of trains in the timetable, partly because the winter was far milder than in 1947, one of the worst on record. Famous trains such as the Pullman *Queen of Scots* between King's Cross and Glasgow via Leeds were restored and BR quickly revived the policy of naming particular services in order to attract passengers back, even though journey times were far longer than pre-war timetables. The *Bon Accord*, the *St Mungo* and the *Granite City* all linked Glasgow and Aberdeen while the *Capitals Limited*, later renamed *The Elizabethan* in honour of the young Queen, was a non-stop summer train between King's Cross and Edinburgh. There were thirty-eight named trains which were 'intended to cast a touch of glamour over rather uninspiring performances'.[4] Only Brighton trains from London took the same time as before the war – sixty minutes; other trains from the capital were far slower, with York taking seventy-five minutes longer and Glasgow nearly two hours more.

Travelling by train in this post-war austerity period was only marginally more pleasant than during the conflict because there were fewer people on the trains and travellers were not at risk of being killed by a bomb. Little work had been done on the coaches and the stations were sorely neglected. Phil Kelly, a lifelong rail enthusiast, recalls: 'When we went to the seaside in the early 1950s, Wigan Wallgate and Southport Chapel Street stations appeared not to have been painted since the 1920s. There was soot everywhere and you never saw a clean station, though I can't remember seeing any litter – and even that may just be nostalgia.'[5] At the top end of the market, in contrast, standards had been maintained. Tony Telford, a lecturer in railway studies, has a more favourable recollection of his holiday journeys in the same period, which started with a ride on the Yorkshire Pullman from Hull Paragon station: 'We always took morning coffee and lunch. The bowler-hatted station-master would appear just before departure which was a real event. I remember the "schlump" rather than the clatter of the door being shut, the quietness of the Pullman Car disturbed only by the chinking of crockery and cutlery as we got under way, the masses of people on stations watching the train go through, and the eyes of the Senior Conductor piercing anyone who had the temerity to say they were not taking lunch!'[6]

One curiosity was the introduction in 1949 of two double-deck trains for Southern Region services to Dartford. The idea has recently attracted the attention of transport ministers keen to find ways to relieve overcrowding but it was not a satisfactory solution. The clearance in tunnels and under bridges is smaller on British tracks than on the Continent and the trains proved too cramped for comfort, despite an ingenious attempt to make more space by putting the upper-level seats below floor level to create a bit of extra headroom. Moreover, the double-decked carriages caused extra delays at crowded stations as passengers – used to trains with doors for every compartment – struggled to get on and off them. Needless to say, the experiment was not extended and the trains were withdrawn in 1971.

British Railways recognized early on that there was a need for a massive modernization programme. Rail managers looked enviously to Europe where renewal was taking place on a large scale with the help of American Marshall Plan money in countries like Holland and France, whose railways had been bombed into oblivion during the final days of the war. In Britain there were no signs of a similar programme being introduced by the government. It was not only the shortage of materials and skilled labour, but also the want of ambition in those early days of a nationalized industry. BR was struggling so hard to regain pre-war standards of performance and service that there was little attempt to think about the future role of the railways.

Safety continued to be a major concern: in 1952 and 1957 there were two very serious accidents which killed over 200 people between them, both caused by drivers going through signals set at danger. The disaster at Harrow and Wealdstone station, at 8.15 a.m. on 8 October 1952, was the second worst accident ever on Britain's railways after Quintinshill, with a death toll of 112, and Lewisham, five years later, was the third worst, with 90 dead. At Harrow, the driver of an overnight sleeping car train from Perth struck a local train heading south at 60 mph and then a minute later, a northbound express ploughed at full speed into the wreckage, greatly increasing the scale of the disaster. It was never discovered why the Perth train driver, a regular on the route, missed the signal on a clear autumn morning (although he was running late and normally that service would have had an unencumbered run into Euston rather than being slowed by the rush-hour traffic).

At Lewisham in December 1957, fog, that perennial danger on the railways, contributed to the failure of the driver of a streamlined Pacific locomotive hauling a Cannon Street to Ramsgate express to see two successive yellow signals.[7] By the time he saw the red, it was too late and his train crashed into the rear of an electric one. The heavy locomotive wrought tremendous damage, bringing down a girder bridge carrying the Nunhead–Lewisham loop line, which collapsed on to the wrecked train. It was fortunate that the driver of a train approaching the bridge spotted its absence just in time to stop his train on the edge of the abyss.

The inspectors in both accidents pointed out that the disasters could have been prevented by the installation of the Automatic Warning System (mentioned in Chapter 12). After Harrow, British Railways began a programme to install it throughout the network, although oddly the disaster did not seem to increase the urgency of its implementation, and it was not made mandatory until very recently.[8]

There were policy mistakes, too, which damaged BR in those early days. The Railway Executive made a fundamental error in failing to recognize that the steam era was drawing to a close, partly because its members felt that the continuous availability of coal was assured, whereas the steady supply of oil was, at the time, doubtful and had to be paid for in expensive dollars.[9] Instead of examining alternative power sources – diesel and electric – BR ran a series of tests called the Locomotive Exchanges, during which the regions were told to accept 'foreign' locomotives on to their tracks and to pit them against their own to see if any could be used as the models for the rest of the network. The trials, which attracted considerable interest and publicity, were asking the wrong question and inevitably found that no existing design was suitable. Politically, of course, it would have been difficult for BR to have adopted an LMS or Great Western design for universal use on the whole railway since that would have infuriated the other regions. Instead a series of twelve different types of BR locomotives was commissioned, which might have helped create a corporate image but was a waste of scarce resources. David Henshaw, the author of a study on the Beeching cuts, put it wittily: 'The British Transport Commission had inherited 400 odd [in fact it was 448] classes of steam locomotives and dealt with the problem by producing another 12 standard classes,'[10] all of which would be scrapped within a couple of decades.

Precisely 999 of these new BR locomotives were built in the next decade and a half, culminating in *Evening Star*, the last British-built steam engine (apart from a few for export), completed at Swindon in 1960. Astonishingly, that did not stop the various regions from continuing to produce their own established types of steam locomotives simultaneously during the next decade, with a total of 1,500 being completed by 1957. The Western Region, for example, added nearly 300 shunters to its stock in the first five years of nationalization when diesels, which were more expensive to build but cheaper to run, could do the job much better. Nor did such profligacy prevent the Western from boasting, in 1966, that it was the first of the regions to stop using steam traction.

Continuing with such an extensive steam-engine building programme for so long after the war was clearly an expensive mistake, since an earlier move towards diesel and electricity would have saved millions. Yet the lessons suggested by the massive increase of traffic on the Southern after electrification did not percolate through to the rest of the industry, despite the opening of another successful electrification scheme in 1949: the completion of the project to electrify the busy lines between Liverpool Street and Shenfield that had been started by the LNER before the war led to an immediate 50 per cent increase in traffic.

There was a marked reluctance among senior BR managers to embark on further electrification schemes. The only other scheme was the Manchester to Sheffield route under the southern part of the Pennines through the three-mile-long Woodhead tunnel, one of the longest on the network. The idea was to use electricity to run both freight and passenger trains; indeed, the line's principal purpose was to haul coal from the south Yorkshire mines to the huge Fiddlers Ferry power station near Warrington. Like the Shenfield electrification, this project had been started and then shelved at the outbreak of the war, but was revived even though it required the huge expense of building a new double-track Woodhead tunnel because the two old single bores were a century old and in a poor state of repair. The scheme was finally completed in 1954 but proved to be something of a white elephant as the trains ran on a different electrification system from that subsequently used for the West Coast Main Line. When Fiddlers Ferry changed over from coal to oil in the 1970s, the line became redundant and closed in 1981.

These electrification schemes were definitely the exception, and BR was similarly slow to make use of diesel technology. The failure to convert many local and branch services to diesel was a missed opportunity given that the resulting cost economies could have made these lines far more resistant to the Beeching axe wielded in the 1960s. This was not for lack of available technology. As far back as 1921, one of Colonel Stephens's railways, the Weston Clevedon and Portishead, had introduced a petrol-engined railcar on its fourteen-mile length and in Ireland the first diesel railcars in the British Isles started running on the small County Donegal Railways in 1926. Despite the unfortunate tendency of early models to lose their front wheels – luckily without causing injury to any passengers – they proved a great success. They seated forty people each and cost only a third to run compared with conventional steam-hauled trains.[11] They were fast, reliable and flexible as they saved on the laborious business of shunting the engine round at each terminus. In the 1930s the Great Western had begun to introduce carriages with underfloor diesel engines on a few branch lines and the Southern had experimented with diesel shunters, but there had been no appetite in any of the Big Four companies for a wholesale introduction of diesel railcars (or 'multiple units' as they were now called), despite the huge savings that could be made. Even in the 1950s, when similar trains were being introduced all around the world, British Railways remained reluctant to follow suit and 'there was really little excuse for the excruciatingly slow progress made in Britain where modern rail traction was concerned'.[12]

British Railways did make better progress in improving its fleet of freight wagons, but the cost was high. Of the 550,000 wagons it had bought from private owners at nationalization, the British Transport Commission soon realized there were 85,000 coal wagons which were surplus to requirements and needed to be scrapped immediately, an expensive mistake.

While BR dithered over alternative power sources, it was quick to sort out the vital question of a livery for the organization and a series of high-profile 'beauty contests' were held. The first, in January 1948, was at Kensington Olympia, where various locomotives bearing the contrasting greens of the Great Western, the LNER and the Southern, as well as the black of LNWR and a blue Southern Region colour for electric units, were paraded to hordes of rail enthusiasts. Various colours ranging from blue for the largest express passenger locomotives to unlined black for goods and shunting locomotives were chosen. The Southern Region kept malachite green for its trains while the few electric multiple units in other regions were painted in a lighter green. British Railways' heraldic insignia featuring a lion and a wheel was also selected after much discussion – Gerard Fiennes fittingly called it an 'emasculated lion [riding] rather uncomfortably on a wheel'[13] – but, as Michael Bonavia points out, 'the shortage of staff for cleaning locomotives and of washing machines for coaching stock made the whole exercise pretty unrealistic',[14] and in any case the blue for expresses was phased out within a couple of years because it showed the dirt too easily!

With the proposed motorway building programme stalled due to lack of funds, BR's senior managers had the opportunity to consider seriously the role of the railway in the age of the motor car. Instead, this period was wasted in building steam engines, trying to sort out the administrative complexities of a massive new organization, continual feuds between the British Transport Commission and the Railway Executive, and in trivial tasks such as selecting liveries and insignia. All of this meant the railways were not in a fit state to compete against the car by the late 1950s when the motorway building programme was in full swing.

The changeable political climate and unstable structure of the railways did not help. Attlee's Labour government was thrown out when he lost the second election held in the early 1950s, and its Tory successor, led by the ageing Winston Churchill, was quick to reorganize the British Transport Commission which they saw as a socialist construct. Privatization of the railways was not on the agenda but the 1953 Transport Act denationalized road haulage, resulting in the sale of 24,000 lorries to small, mostly one-man, companies which were far more adept at handling loads for short and medium distances efficiently. The Railway Executive was abolished and instead area railway boards were placed directly under the aegis of the BTC. This was the first of 'several defective solutions'[15] to change the organizational structure of the industry during its fifty-year history of state ownership – all devised by outsiders with little understanding of the industry. Crucially, British Railways was still not allowed to stand on its own but remained subsumed within the monolithic British Transport Commission until the latter's abolition a decade later.

Surprisingly, though, the Tories were to give the railways one last chance to prove their worth with an ambitious and comprehensive modernization programme set out in a document published in January 1955. By then the railways were deeply in the red, as rising costs, road competition and perennial strikes resulted in losses of £22m (about

£400m in today's money) that year. The Modernization Plan was prompted by the belated realization that there had been no adequate investment in the railways for fifteen years. Indeed, there had been a net disinvestment of £440m since before the war (£8bn in 2007 prices)[16] – in other words, the assets of the railways had deteriorated far faster than they were being renewed. The modernization programme was aimed at addressing that backlog but also at creating a railway that could cope with the competition from the roads. The plan was breathtaking in its scale and involved the complete reorganization and refurbishment of the industry. It envisaged spending £1.24bn (£22bn today) by 1970 to replace steam with diesel, to create 1,500 miles of newly electrified line and replace old wooden and brick stations with concrete and glass palaces. The plan, drawn up by the British Transport Commission, was accepted by both ministers and Parliament with little debate, despite the cost.

While the investment was desperately needed, the plan was ill conceived and unrealistic, evidenced in its opening words: 'The Modernisation Plan will win traffic back from the roads. Freight traffic will also return and grow.' The Plan used a scattergun approach, attempting to improve all aspects of the railway without sufficient thought about where investment would have the greatest effect. The focus was on hardware – shiny new locomotives and vast new marshalling yards. And because British Railways was now run by powerful regional managers, who were all vying for the largest slice of the cake for their patch, there was never any coherent programme to focus the investment where it was most needed. Local managers came up with crazy schemes such as electrifying vast swathes of line in the Eastern Region that served remote communities in the Lincolnshire fens (which soon fell to the Beeching axe). The London Midland Region tried to bid for the ridiculous number of 660 electric locomotives for the West Coast Main Line when 100 later sufficed. Such proposals were rejected but other daft schemes went ahead, notably the £1.6m (£30m today) Bletchley flyover on the West Coast line which was never used and survives today as a monument to incompetent planning. The flyover was part of a very sensible scheme to use the Oxford–Cambridge line as an east–west route avoiding London, but not only was that plan never implemented, sadly much of the route was closed in the 1960s.

The biggest folly was the construction of a series of thirty huge marshalling yards. Freight, which was still packed into small wagons that often went missing for weeks, was the service most at risk from road competition since lorries offered a more flexible and cheaper service, especially as they could use the motorways and new bypasses spreading fast around the country. The yards were supposed to make freight more economic by reducing the need for smaller sidings but the market for rail freight was already receding. Although BR was finally relieved of its common carrier obligation to charge set rates for freight in 1957, the decision came too late to prevent many basic products like grain, fish, horses, cattle and even some of the newspaper trade from transferring to road haulage. The £85m (£1.6bn today) spent on these yards, at a time of declining freight carriage, was testimony to the unreality of the Plan. The delay in building many of these yards only compounded the waste. Perth, opened finally in 1962, initially handled 1,200 wagons per day, but within six years all that traffic had disappeared and the yard closed. Yet, while those yards were springing up around Britain, opportunities to save millions in running costs were being shunned. For example, in 1968 there were still 7,000 freight guards even though few trains had a brake van and their role was not immediately obvious. Similarly, thousands of firemen were still on BR's books a decade after the last steam engine had been retired. Under the Modernization Plan, 300,000 new freight wagons were ordered in an attempt to ensure that all BR's huge but underused fleet was power-braked but the cost of the scheme caused it to be abandoned halfway through which meant that expected savings from using this modern equipment could not be realized.

The mistake in delaying the conversion of steam power to diesel and electricity was then compounded by implementing the changeover too quickly and in a haphazard way that greatly increased costs. The Modernization Plan envisaged the ridiculous number of 174 pilot diesel locomotives to be tested before large orders were placed. But in fact there was a panic to get the work done quickly and orders were placed for hundreds of locomotives before proper testing could be carried out.

No fewer than twenty-six different classes of diesel locomotives were ordered, many before a prototype was built, when five would have been sufficient. As a result, British Railways soon had hundreds of unserviceable locomotives, whose frequent breakdowns attracted much unfavourable press coverage. The introduction of the diesel multiple units was a similar mess. More than 5,000 cars were called for in the Modernization Plan and BR which right up to the 1980s built virtually all its own locomotives and coaches, realized its workshops could not cope with such huge demand and commissioned seven private manufacturers to build some at Swindon and Derby. The result was a hopeless mix of engines, transmissions and braking systems that greatly increased maintenance costs. Passengers, too, were inconvenienced because there were at least five different types of coupling and therefore many of these units could not be joined together. Many units, not necessarily the worst but those that happened to have been built in fewest numbers, were soon scrapped as the Beeching cuts (see below) began to bite.

The Modernization Plan had called for a large programme of electrification of the West Coast Main Line to Manchester, Liverpool and Birmingham, the East Coast up to Leeds, and possibly York and a variety of commuter lines in London and major cities. But the programme stalled, partly as a result of technical incidents such as transformer explosions in both Glasgow and north-east London, and partly due to political changes which resulted in the shelving of both East and West Coast schemes, even though work had started on the latter. This stuttering start was to set the pattern for future BR electrification – wild optimism and enthusiasm followed by rising costs, loss of government confidence and a halt to any coherent programme. Electrification teams were hired and dismissed over the years, knowledge was lost and costs escalated – contrasting starkly with the experience in France and West Germany where the electrification of the main lines and the commuter routes was achieved through five- or ten-year rolling programmes. Even today, there is no plan to electrify one of Britain's major routes, the lines out of Paddington to the West Country.

By 1959, it was clear that the Plan was not sufficiently focused on the railway's strengths, such as rapid connections between major cities and

London commuting and as a result, it inevitably failed to turn around railway finances. While British Railways managers were concentrating on creating huge marshalling yards and doing little to improve services for passengers, the upwardly mobile British public were taking to the roads. By 1960, one in nine families owned a car and most of the other eight were saving to buy one. As both freight and passenger traffic went down, losses increased from £15.6m in 1956 (a slight improvement on the previous year) to £42m four years later[17] and questions on the viability of the railways began to be asked in Parliament.

A comprehensive report on British Railways' finances, published by the House of Commons Select Committee on Nationalized Industries in July 1960, suggested that most of those £42m losses had been incurred on passenger services, particularly on branches and lightly used services. The Committee was highly critical of the Modernization Plan, whose cost had risen to £1.5bn, arguing that the return on the investment was likely to be far lower than expected. The notion of investing out of the crisis was quickly being replaced by the idea that salvation lay in reducing the size of the network and cutting back on services.

In fact, this process had started before the war, albeit very slowly. From the peak mileage of over 20,000 in the early 1920s, just 1,240 miles of railway were closed to passengers[18] during the era of the Big Four, mostly small branches with no hope of ever paying for themselves, such as the Devil's Dyke, a steep railway that ran up to the top of the Downs from Brighton, which was closed in 1938. Another early casualty with an equally intriguing name was the Invergarry & Fort Augustus branch, completed in 1903, one of the last railways to be built in Scotland. Eventually, it would have reached Inverness as part of a Great Glen trunk route, but, having been built at great expense to main line standards, it carried an average of just six people per day in 1933, its final year of operation.

At nationalization British Railways still had 19,414 route miles, and the British Transport Commission began to accelerate the rate of closure. It formed a Branch Line Committee which scoured the country looking for the least used lines. There were some easy pickings, with plenty of contenders for the least remunerative line in the country. The winner was probably the Llangynog-Llanrhaeadr-ym-Mochnant branch line in

Wales, which netted just £252 annually – 15 shillings per day, but understandable given the village it served had a population of under 300 – but it was a wonder that it survived until 1952. The committee also selected a few slightly larger fish and while the pre-war closures had been uncontroversial, now a protest movement was beginning to stir and some proposals started to attract national press publicity. The biggest fuss was over the Princetown branch from Yelverton (see Chapter 7) which served Dartmoor prison. The opponents of the closure, who included the governor of the prison and Sir Henry Slesser, the former Solicitor General in Ramsay MacDonald's Labour government who had retired locally, argued that the road was often closed by snow in winter and that the line had considerable tourism potential as it wound around some of England's most beautiful rugged countryside. Their protests were to no avail and the line was shut in 1956.

Despite opposition, spearheaded by the Railway Development Association whose principal luminary was the poet John Betjeman, the BTC closed 200 branches with a mileage of 1,500 miles by the time of its abolition in 1962. The pace slowed somewhat towards the end of the 1950s as diesel multiple units began, at last, to be introduced, greatly improving the economics of marginal lines and raising doubts about the closure policy in the minds of railway managers. The BTC's closures were confined to branches and still left nearly 17,500 miles of railway, served by no fewer than 6,800 stations and 600 marshalling yards.

But the reprieve for many lines was to be short-lived as doubts about the viability of the railway network in the Select Committee report found a ready audience in government circles. The Transport Minister appointed in Harold Macmillan's Conservative government after the 1959 election victory was Ernest Marples. Transport Ministers tend to be either pro-roads or pro-rail, and he was definitely in the first camp, not least because he had made his fortune by starting a firm, Marples, Ridgeway & Partners, which specialized in road-building and had been one of the contractors on the M1.[19] A hyperactive politician, he was responsible, *inter alia*, for introducing parking meters, seatbelts and yellow lines, and in an earlier post, subscriber trunk dialling, the ability to make calls across Britain without going through the operator.

Marples appointed another committee to examine railway finances and it advised him to freeze railway investment, stop work on the West Coast Main Line and to examine the viability of the network. It suited Marples to portray the railways as a moribund business when in fact their finances were not so dire, especially when taking into account the unfair competitive environment in which they were forced to operate. Indeed, in 1959, passenger takings had increased by £2m and operating costs had been substantially reduced and, contrary to the view of the Select Committee on Nationalized Industries, it was the performance of freight, notably coal, that was responsible for most of the losses. Undeterred by such considerations, Marples appointed Richard Beeching to head a revamped British Railways Board, released from the clutches of the now-abolished British Transport Commission, marking the end of Attlee's experiment with transport integration. British Railways was given a far greater measure of commercial freedom and its debts were written off – but there was a heavy price to pay for this largesse: the railways were now expected to be run as a profit-making business, with no consideration of any social obligations, and therefore a sharp reduction in the size of the network was inevitable.

It is a sad reflection of the state of the railways during this post-war period that someone who spent his time closing lines and cutting services – rather than building them – should be the most famous railwayman of his generation. Beeching, aged forty-seven, was a scientist who was seconded to BR from his job as technical director of ICI, the huge chemicals conglomerate, at the phenomenal salary of £24,000 (equivalent to £500,000 today). He had a rather unprepossessing appearance – balding, with a round face – and would sit behind his desk smoking expensive cigars. Yet he was happy to chat in a friendly and informal way with his colleagues, a very different approach to his predecessors, who were obsessed with formality and hierarchy, as demonstrated by the fact that BR's headquarters had five different canteens and messes for the various grades. His rather ponderous manner and gravelly voice were misleading. According to Anthony Sampson, Beeching could be mistaken for 'one of those large phlegmatic men who tell long stories over a pint of beer in a country pub'.[20] In fact, he was no pub bore, possessing an extremely sharp mind, an ability to cut to the quick and the self-confidence to shake up British Railways with little regard for its traditions and institutions.

Beeching's report, *The Reshaping of British Railways*, was published in 1963, and was elegantly and persuasively written; it triggered the biggest changes in the railway network since its creation. Its aim, as with the Modernization Plan, was to make the railways commercially viable, but he argued the remedy was not to invest in the whole system but to close large swathes of the network that were considered inherently unprofitable. Investment would then be limited to those areas where it might make the best return, principally the intercity passenger market and trainload freigh.

Beeching found that the railway was a very unbalanced network, with many assets being greatly underused. A quarter of fare income came from just thirty-four stations (0.5 per cent of the total), while at the other end of the scale, half the rest produced just 2 per cent of the income and generated just 4 per cent of the parcels business. Only 5,500 out of 18,500 main line coaches were in use all year round, and coal trucks, on average, stood idle for two days out of three. Half of BR's 17,830 route miles carried only 4 per cent of the traffic. And so on. It was a picture of a railway with a few highly profitable lines but around half that did not even cover their operating costs, let alone their maintenance and renewal.

Beeching set out a fifteen-point plan to bring the railways into profit by 1970. Most stopping services would be discontinued, a third of the 7,000 stations would be closed as would 5,000 miles of track. It would not be just branches – duplicate trunk lines would also face the axe. Thousands of coaches would be scrapped, so that holiday traffic would be deliberately damped down. Bus services, which were far cheaper to operate, would replace many branch line services. There were to be improvements, too, with the modernization of coal and other heavy mineral traffic, but loss-making freight services would also be slashed, using higher tariffs to force these goods on to the roads.

David Henshaw, a critic of Beeching, suggests that looking at the railways in this way was dishonest: 'Had the Government paused for a moment in 1960, weighed up the relative worth of various forms of transport . . . the vast majority of minor roads would have been deemed uneconomic. The density of road traffic was spread just as unevenly as rail traffic.'[21] As he concludes, 'it was because railways were deemed to be a secondary, duplicate means of transport'[22] that they were considered ripe for closure because by 1962 only 10 per cent of journeys were by train. There is no doubt that the railways at this stage suffered from the perennial bias against them. The government was paying for investment in roads, notably the motorways, so there was a good case that there should be equivalent support for railway infrastructure. However, expenditure on roads has always been deemed to be investment, while rail spending has been classified as subsidy.

It was not all Beeching's fault. His terms of reference had been too narrow: he was only supposed to find a way of returning the industry to profitability as soon as possible rather than consider the overall social and wider economic value of the railway or examine the economics of other methods of transport. There was no attempt, for example, to produce a cost-benefit analysis taking into account the extra deaths from traffic accidents as a result of pushing people on to the roads. Such techniques had not yet been developed but in any case logic was not part of the Beeching process. These caveats were quickly forgotten in the orgy of closures that ensued. The Beeching report had been commissioned in order to demonstrate that minor railway lines were fundamentally uneconomic and it was hardly surprising that this was its conclusion. He was searching for that Holy Grail, the myth of the profitable railway.

Of course many of these branches and lines were not viable and were ripe to be axed, but the closure programme went too far, with little regard for the future needs of the railway once the roads filled up.[23] Most of the mistakes were made after Harold Wilson became Prime Minister following Labour's narrow victory in the October 1964 election. Whereas in opposition, the Labour party, backed by the unions, had strongly opposed the shutting of lines, in government it performed a complete U-turn, and increased the rate of closures. After much prevarication, Wilson finally announced in March 1965 that he did not have the power to stop any of the thirty-eight line closures put forward by Beeching, twenty-five of which had already been made. Far from being reviewed, the closure programme was speeded up by the new Transport Minister, Tom Fraser, with the closure of 1,071 miles in 1965, eighty more than in the previous year under Marples. Moreover, Wilson announced extra closures such as the Oxford–Cambridge line, which even Beeching had not suggested. The biggest casualty was the Great Central, which provided an alternative route from London to the Midlands and the north-west, and while it duplicated other lines, it would have been very useful for freight and as a diversionary route. Other mistakes included shutting the alternative route between Exeter and Plymouth, which avoided Dawlish where flooding over the sea wall causes perennial problems; the Somerset & Dorset, which provided an important connection in an area with a rapidly increasing population; and, as mentioned above, Oxford–Cambridge which not only provided an east–west route avoiding the capital but served the new town of Milton Keynes which was scheduled for rapid expansion. One particularly damaging cut was to deprive the sizeable Lincolnshire port town of Boston, once a main line station, of its direct London link – which means it can now only be reached circuitously via Sleaford and Grantham – just to save sixteen miles of track.[24] Another nonsense was to cut the direct link from London to Stratford-upon-Avon, one of Britain's biggest tourist attractions, and turn it into an outpost of the West Midlands suburban system. Henshaw recognizes that the completely uneconomic branch lines had to go but reckons that a third of the lines closed by Beeching, around 1,200 miles of passenger railways, 'should never even have been *contemplated* for closure'.[25]

As if to reinforce the inconsistency of Labour's policy, some Beeching targets were reprieved for reasons of political expediency, such as Glasgow–Stranraer and the central Wales line which serves very isolated communities with marginal constituencies. The East Suffolk branch was saved by Gerard Fiennes, a lifelong railwayman who would later make his name by writing a book called *I tried to run a railway*,[26] which earned him the sack from British Railways. He sketched out the concept of a basic railway, using diesel multiple units and minimal repairs to maintain passenger numbers while slashing costs, that made the line viable and it was retained. Had similar calculations been made on many other lines by equally enterprising managers, today's railway mileage would be considerably longer. The anomalies left by the ill-thought scheme were legion. While relatively busy lines, with the kind of effort demonstrated by Fiennes, could have been made viable, isolated communities in rural areas like mid-Wales, the Scottish Highlands, Cumbria and Norfolk were left with stations that are seldom used by more than a handful of passengers per day.

Beeching's fundamental mistake was to underestimate the contribution of branches to the economics of the railways and he was wrong to assume that people who travelled by rail would happily shift to buses. *The Oxford Companion to British Railway History* sums up the Beeching era thus: 'Unfortunately, he was expected to produce quick solutions to problems that were deep-seated and not susceptible to purely intellectual analysis.'[27] Beeching himself viewed it differently: 'I suppose I'll always be looked upon as the axe man, but it was surgery, not mad chopping.'[28]

Overall, the closure programme was a haphazard process based on flawed logic and the assumptions by Beeching about the lack of profitability of many lines were proved wrong. Even in cool economic terms, Beeching's closures were never going to turn around the finances of the railways. He calculated they would save around £30m annually, at a time when the railways were losing nearly three times that much. In February 1965 Beeching produced a second report[29] which suggested even further cuts, reducing the railway to 3,000 miles of main line which would be intensively developed and 4,500 miles of other routes that would be maintained to a minimal level. He had overstepped the mark and Wilson sent him back to ICI a year before the end of his contract.

Viewed in the context of the long-term history of the railways, Beeching merely accelerated a process of closures that had already started. Nevertheless, the figures for the 1960s are startling. By the end of the decade there were just 3,002 stations, compared with over 7,000 in 1961, and nearly 6,000 miles had been closed, leaving just 12,098. As with the conversion of steam to diesel, the process had been too slow for many years, but then proceeded too fast to retain any coherence and to fulfil strategic aims. Contrary to Beeching's protestations, it *was* slash and burn, with marginal closures justified by dubious figures drawn up by British Railways staff intent on fulfilling narrow short-term financial targets. His figures for revenue were skewed because the data was collected in April – outside the holiday season when many marginal lines made huge profits.

With hindsight, much of the responsibility for the contradictory policies of the 1950s and 1960s can be laid at the door of successive governments, which set the railways an impossible task. On the one hand they were expected to act commercially and be profitable, but on the other they were not allowed to raise fares in line with inflation, as this was politically sensitive, and they were required to remain as a common carrier and to transport at a fixed price whatever was dumped on them, whether it was a small parcel or a whole farm (farm removals by rail still occurred in the 1950s). There was, too, the feeling within government that cheap fuel for motoring was a permanent fixture and therefore the demand for travel by railway would inevitably fall over time.

It was not until the late 1960s that the social obligations of the railway were finally acknowledged in Barbara Castle's 1968 Transport Act, which relieved the railways of the impossible target set by Marples of breaking even or making a profit. She recognized, for the first time, that the railways needed financial support from the government, creating a distinction between commercial services which should pay for themselves and 'social' ones which needed subsidy. She wiped out the accumulated debt of £153m and encouraged BR's managerial and business flair to blossom in the 'commercial railway' – the trunk inter-city routes mostly radiating from London. She created the Passenger Transport Executives in six conurbations which received large grants from the Ministry of Transport to pay for both new railway infra-structure and to run the services. They have subsequently been very successful in reviving the suburban networks of provincial cities and boosting usage. The pace of closures slowed dramatically with only 900 miles being shut in the four years following the passage of the 1968 Act, and thereafter there was only a trickle, which stopped completely in 1977.

British Rail[30] did, however, try one last major closure in the 1980s, the spectacular Carlisle to Settle railway built at such a high cost, both financial and human, by the Midland (see Chapter 8). BR claimed, with little justification, that the Ribblehead viaduct was crumbling and would cost too much to repair. The opponents of closures, emboldened by the aftermath of Beeching and now far better armed with statistics and legal experience, were able to ensure the line's survival – which is fortunate since it is now not only a very useful diversionary route when either the West or East Coast line is closed but has also become an important freight artery as well as carrying considerable tourist traffic. Indeed, it is so important to the network of the twenty-first century that in 2004 Network Rail embarked on a five-year improvement programme costing £60m.

The Carlisle to Settle controversy was, however, an exception. A new atmosphere was developing inside British Rail, now that the threat of closures and redundancies had receded. Growth and development were no longer dirty words. Over 300 stations were reopened between 1970 and the end of the century, a tacit admission that Beeching had gone too far. In 1963, work resumed on the West Coast Main Line electrification which was to be the flagship of British Rail and the concept of InterCity was developed.

However, the first major innovation for passengers on long-distance routes was the 90 mph Blue Pullmans, decked out in a soothing sea-blue colour and powered by huge diesel engines at each end, a novel idea, introduced in 1960, that allowed for rapid turnaround times. The trains ran on both London Midland and Western Region lines, providing limited stop services to places such as Manchester and Birmingham.[31] The five train sets were luxurious and the service was an example of railway customer care at its best: for the first time on a British train, full air conditioning and armchair seats with padded foam were offered, but unfortunately the bogies were poorly designed which meant that sometimes the ride was too bumpy for comfort. The service, which was initially only for first-class passengers but was later extended to second class, proved popular, but the trains themselves were prone to breakdown and only lasted until 1973. However, the Blue Pullmans demonstrated that the concept of fast journeys in modern coaches was the way forward for the railways and the technology of having a power car – a locomotive – at each end was adopted in the High Speed Train, the InterCity 125. British Railways managers were beginning to realize that the role of the railway in the age of the motor car was no longer to act as a common carrier, trying to cater for every possible journey, but instead to focus on passenger flows where the railways had a real advantage, for example as an alternative to motorway travel for business people.

It was on the East Coast that, in the short term, speeds increased the most. With electrification shelved (and eventually carried out at the end of the 1980s), the BR manager in charge of the line, the innovative Gerard Fiennes, persuaded BR to build twenty-two high-powered diesels capable of cruising at 100 mph, the huge Deltics. Timings between London and Edinburgh were cut from seven to six hours, and Leeds was just three hours away, the best journey times since before the war – and that was on every train, whereas in the 1930s these speeds were achieved only on the daily prestige service.

Similarly, diesels were introduced on services from Paddington to Bristol, St Pancras to Nottingham and Liverpool Street to Norwich. Carriages, too, were improved. Coaches had been standardized since 1951 with the introduction of the Mark 1, which was better than its predecessors, but it was not until the arrival of the Mark 2 that there was a major improvement. It could provide a comfortable ride at 100 mph thanks to more sophisticated bogies and the interior was far superior to anything that had been offered before.

However, the standards of passenger comfort varied enormously from line to line and creating the InterCity concept was an attempt to provide a consistent level of service across the network. Modern marketing and branding techniques began to be used by the increasingly adventurous and commercially minded British Railways. The iconic twin track logo, which survived privatization, was introduced in 1965 to demonstrate the modern face of the railway, and the InterCity brand for fast services between major cities was launched in April of the following year when the West Coast electrified services began running. Instead of naming individual expresses, the whole service was branded as InterCity.[32] The new timetable on the West Coast was a vast improvement on any service previously offered on the line. Trains departed at the same time every hour and many journeys were timed at an average of 80 mph, which required sustained running at 100 mph for long stretches. Stations such as Euston, Stafford and Macclesfield were completely rebuilt to give the railways a new modern image that unfortunately has not aged well (Euston's baroque great hall was demolished and replaced with a glass and concrete monstrosity that had no seats for waiting passengers). A massive publicity campaign, including TV advertising, was launched, the first of several over the next twenty years that would establish InterCity as one of the top five brands recognized by the British public. Passenger numbers soared, with a two-thirds increase from the previous year, a phenomenon that became known as the 'sparks effect', and the frequency of services had to be increased to meet demand.

In the early 1970s, therefore, British Rail turned the corner. The success of the West Coast electrification and the development of InterCity marked a renewed confidence in British Rail. Under the leadership of the forward-looking former Transport Minister, Richard Marsh, growing and improving the railway, rather than continuing to run it down, was now seen as the objective. British Rail managers started to fight back, reckoning that the financial discipline to which they had been asked to conform was becoming an end in itself, rather than part of a policy to improve a vital service.

But the government was ever contemptuous of the railway managers; there was 'a firm belief in Whitehall that railway managers were inbred, inward-looking and resistant to change'.[33] In fact, when outsiders from other industries, like Batchelors Peas or Palmolive, joined the railways, they invariably discovered that running the railways was a far more difficult proposition than selling consumer goods to shoppers. British Rail was frequently at loggerheads with Edward Heath's Tory government, which was in power for the first four years of the 1970s. BR had learnt the lesson of Beeching and produced a strategy document in 1973 which stated there was absolutely no 'financially viable' network size. Moreover, the oil crisis of that year reminded the politicians of the railways' existence and their ability to carry large numbers of people using far less fuel than road vehicles.

When the Labour government was re-elected by a tiny majority in the February 1974 election, it had to rescue the industry with another Transport Act passed that same year. Prime Minister Harold Wilson allocated £2.1bn to BR, including £1,500m for the next five years to subsidize loss-making services through a newly created mechanism, the Public Service Obligation. However, there was still no solution to the conundrum that railway managers had faced ever since nationalization between their commercial and social remits. Moreover, passenger numbers declined as fares doubled between March 1974 and May 1975, an increase which was well above even the very high rates of inflation raging at the time. Nor was there any attempt to answer the fundamental question of what the railways were for.

Despite this, thanks to a forward-looking group of railway managers, there was a radical improvement on InterCity services with the introduction of the High Speed Train. This was a similar concept to the Blue Pullmans but with a more robust design, which is why these trains have survived into the twenty-first century. In fact, the High Speed Train was not supposed to spearhead the improved services; that was to have been the Advanced Passenger Train, a tilting train that was ahead of its time but became a sad casualty of the loss of nerve by both the industry and the government in the face of a barrage of negative media coverage. The idea was to reduce journey times by enabling the train to go around curves faster using a tilting mechanism; it would also reach speeds of 155 mph on straight sections. Development by British Railways engineers started in the mid-1960s and a prototype was put in public service in 1981. However, the train received a bad press, with claims that people were made sick by the tilt. The trains also proved unreliable, with frequent failure of the tilt mechanism, and the project was soon abandoned, even though engineers claimed that the problems could have been overcome. Indeed, tilting trains became commonplace in Europe and were eventually reintroduced with Italian technology by Virgin Trains in 2003 for their Pendolinos on the West Coast Main Line. The High Speed Train was, therefore, somewhat of a fallback option, but it was to prove a lasting success. Development of a diesel train with a 125 mph capability, which could run on existing lines without tilting, started in August 1970 but then was held up for a year because of a boycott by the unions because the trains were being designed to be controlled by a single driver.

Nationalization had not brought the hoped-for industrial relations peace. Quite the opposite. Railway workers were no longer prepared to accept the trade-off between stable employment and relatively poor pay which the railways, especially outside the big cities, had offered. They were losing out compared with other industries where higher productivity benefited both workers and shareholders. The rail workforce felt they deserved better pay, even though the industry was declining, but British Railways was not allowed to put up fares without government permission, which meant they fell in real terms during the 1950s and 1960s. Not surprisingly, therefore, there were continual battles over productivity. The workforce was reduced dramatically, from over 600,000 in 1950 to 275,500 in 1979, which meant that the unions were rigidly opposed to more cuts, though the introduction of redundancy payments in 1959 had been an incentive for railway workers to leave the industry. Every aspect of railway work required fewer employees thanks to improved technology. Diesel and electric locomotives were easier to maintain and clean; signal boxes were being closed and centralized; the track was being replaced with longer stretches of continuous welded rail which was easier to look after, resulting in the replacement of the local gangs who maintained the track with fewer men in charge of longer sections. Strikes were not uncommon but rarer than myth would have it and they were all partial since there was no national rail stoppage until the 1980s. There had been a particularly damaging seventeen-day stoppage in 1955 by the drivers' union, ASLEF, but although it made a sharp dent in the finances of the British Transport Commission, the action did not entirely paralyse the network. While there was massive inconvenience to long-distance travellers and London commuters, life in the country went on as normal, which showed the railway workers that their industrial muscle had been greatly weakened by the advent of the motor car.

The boycott was the other weapon in the unions' armoury and was successfully deployed to ban work on the High Speed Train until BR agreed that double manning should be retained for 125 mph running, though the practice was eventually phased out with the agreement of the unions in the 1980s. The prototype of the High Speed Train, developed by BR engineers at Derby, outperformed its specifications with a record-beating speed of 143 mph on a test run in June 1973. The HST represented a significant technological breakthrough as it gave a stable ride at 125 mph thanks to the precision of the engineering and the use of disc brakes, which were much more efficient, therefore allowing the train to run at full speed without the need for a new signalling system.[34] (Older readers may remember the strong smell of brake lining which permeated through the air conditioning of trains as they slowed down, until the problem was finally dealt with in the 1990s.)

The trains were introduced on the Western Region in October 1976 and on the East Coast line two years later, reducing journey times at a stroke since previously the top speed on the network had been 100 mph. Improvements to the track were also made to allow the new trains to run at high speeds for longer, further reducing journey times. Bristol could be reached from London in just seventy minutes and, on the East Coast, Newcastle was now under three hours from the capital, a saving of forty minutes. The 'journey experience', as the marketing people call it, was much improved too with comfortable seats with tables for most travellers, full air conditioning, and restaurant cars on every train, serving the famous Great English Breakfast in the mornings. InterCity was blessed too with a series of brilliant advertising campaigns devised by the Tories' agency, Saatchi & Saatchi, notably the famous Jimmy Saville series 'We're getting there'.

The HST saved the concept of express train travel and enabled the railways to remain competitive with the car on the now completed motorway network. InterCity was a people's train service, with no supplement for its use, and it was so successful that yield management techniques to maximize revenue (through charging higher fares at times of peak demand), now familiar in the aviation industry, had to be developed by British Railways to choke off-peak-time demand (through cheap fares aimed at leisure customers travelling off-peak and high fares at times of the day when business people wanted to travel). A new breed of long-distance commuter emerged as it was now possible to travel daily from places as far from London as Bristol, Doncaster and even York.

For a while, the InterCity High Speed Train service was a world leader. By 1979, when the timetable had been adjusted to take account of the new trains, BR's fastest time between two stations – Reading and Swindon – was 106 mph, beaten only by the Japanese bullet trains running on their own dedicated tracks, which managed a mere 4 mph more. Sadly that position would soon be eroded as countries across Europe, and later Asia, introduced similar high-speed services on dedicated tracks. Nevertheless, the InterCity name and concept spawned a number of imitators around the world, from Cameroon and New Zealand to Spain and Austria. Indeed, in 1989 the Deutsche Bundesbahn in West Germany christened their new 300 km/h high-speed trains, InterCityExpress or ICE.

Peter Parker, another outsider, who took over as head of the British Railways Board from Richard Marsh in 1976, was quick to exploit the improved image of the railway resulting from the introduction of HST. He managed to get several electrification schemes under way, including the Bedford–St Pancras (BedPan, as it was known) line, where the work was completed in 1982 (though causing major ructions with the unions, again over single manning). This was also the year of the ASLEF dispute over 'flexible rostering', a term that briefly attracted national attention and which essentially meant the right of BR to roster workers for shifts other than the standard eight hours.

Overall, however, the 1980s were a far better time for the railways than the previous decade, despite the government's continued stop-start policy which prevented the industry planning its long-term future. On the one hand, Mrs Thatcher's Tory government set up a commission in 1982 to investigate the future of the railways, headed by a former civil servant, Sir David Serpell, whose recommendations made the Beeching cuts look remarkably modest; on the other, the government gave the go-ahead for the modernization and electrification of the East Coast line, the biggest project on the railways since the West Coast scheme in the 1960s.

The trigger for the establishment of the Serpell Commission was the financial crisis suffered by the railways soon after Mrs Thatcher's election in 1979. Part of the report was sensible, suggesting, for example, that BR should divest itself of its workshops, which still accounted for half of spending (no other railway, other than that in India, still built its own trains). However, the second part of the report lacked any political nous and caused an almighty furore that ensured it was quickly consigned to the dustbin. Serpell produced six options for a pruned-down British railway for the twenty-first century, ranging from the culling of just a couple of hundred miles to the infamous option A which proposed reducing the 10,370 route miles to just 1,630, comprising only the West Coast Main Line, the East Coast as far as Newcastle, and the routes from the capital to Norwich and Bristol, and a few key commuter lines. Implementing this scheme would have left whole swathes of Britain such as north and mid-Wales, the West Country and much of Scotland without a railway. By highlighting the worst option and mounting an aggressive counter-attack, the British Railways Board soon ensured that Serpell's ideas were never further considered.

Despite Mrs Thatcher's antipathy for the railways – which she rarely used herself[35] – the government changed tack and, rather than imposing these cuts, it supported a series of development programmes including modest investment in rural lines and, crucially, the much-delayed electrification of nearly 400 miles of the East Coast Main Line at a cost of £300m.[36] The work began in 1985 and was completed in late 1990. New trains were introduced – the InterCity 225 stock which, as its name implies, was supposed to run at 225 kph (140 mph) but in fact has always been limited to 125 mph by the condition of the track and signalling. Again, there was a massive increase in passenger numbers, even though the electrification had been done on the cheap[37] and on the windy East Coast the catenary (overhead wires) were brought down all too frequently, causing major delays.

Very gradually, things were getting better: in spite of the 1982 strikes, the industrial relations situation improved during most of the second half of BR's existence as the number of employees continued to shrink and Mrs Thatcher's anti-union legislation weakened the industrial muscle of the workforce. Whereas strikes and disputes had been a constant subject of discussion by the British Railways Board in the 1960s and 1970s, now the absence of strife meant they were rarely considered. Relations with government also improved markedly. Sir Bob Reid,[38] who replaced Peter Parker, had a fruitful relationship with the Transport Secretary, Nicholas Ridley, one of Mrs Thatcher's pet ideologues, and at last there was a dialogue about what the government wanted from the railway. Investment was seen as a way of reducing costs in the longer term, for example, replacing conventional signalling on remote lines in the Highlands with electronic radio signalling that was far cheaper to maintain and replacing worn-out diesel multiple units and locomotive-hauled trains on regional routes with modern air-conditioned stock.

In 1983, Reid broke up the old regional baronies of the railway that had still held considerable sway,[39] and instead created three passenger business sectors: InterCity, London & South East (renamed Network SouthEast in 1986) and Provincial (later Regional) railways. Freight was separated into two companies, one dealing with train loads, the other with smaller consignments. Under pressure from the government, the various subsidiary businesses such as hotels and ferries were sold off. InterCity was given the task of breaking even, which was achieved with a bit of fiddling over allocation of costs and by ensuring that certain profitable routes, such as London–Norwich and, oddly, the Gatwick Express, the only InterCity route completely south of the Thames, were included. From making a loss of £100m in 1984, InterCity became Europe's only profitable railway, making substantial profits in the boom years of the late 1980s, even after paying its allotted share of the infrastructure costs.

Network SouthEast, the London suburban network melded together by a forward-looking career railwayman Chris Green, also managed to break even at the height of the boom, thanks to a coherent marketing strategy and the development of a series of travelcards that allowed people to make multiple journeys for a one-off payment. It was a remarkable achievement for a commuter railway and Green also pioneered the concept of total route modernization, using scarce investment resources to improve all aspects of a particular line, from the signalling and the track to the rolling stock and the station paint. The first line to receive this treatment, Chiltern, which had been threatened with closure, was a great success, attracting massive numbers of new passengers but the demise of BR stopped this programme.

The railways were no longer in retreat. All three new business sectors enjoyed significant increases and passenger traffic went up by a quarter between 1982 and 1989. Britain's railways were the most efficient in Europe and the least subsidized (though the downside was that fares were high compared with those on the Continent). In the best year, 1987/8, the subsidy to the railway was just £495m, which, as we see in the next chapter, is far lower than anything achieved under privatization.

But the improved quality of the services could not protect British Rail against the recession that followed the 1980s boom. Railways are always highly dependent on the performance of the overall economy and with the sudden end of the rather artificial growth spurt created by Chancellor Nigel Lawson, passenger numbers slumped. The number of London commuters, a key market, fell by 100,000 to 350,000 in a three-year period and the level of subsidy increased sharply, partly due to the fact that property sales, which had been used to fund investment, dried up.

The railways also suffered another major disaster at that time – the type of accident that happens once in a decade or two. Most of the major accidents on the railway occur around London because of the capital's high concentration of busy lines. This time the scene was near Clapham Junction, the busiest station on the network, where, early on the morning of 12 December 1988, a train from Basingstoke that had stopped at a signal was rammed from behind by another from Poole and the wreckage hit a third one, fortunately empty, on the opposite track. Thirty-five people were killed in the accident, which had been caused by a signal showing green instead of red, the result of faulty wiring in an electrical box following poor maintenance by a signalling engineer. Sir Bob Reid immediately admitted that British Rail was at fault for failing to supervise the work properly and the subsequent inquiry led to greatly tighter safety standards: the hours of safety-critical staff were restricted and signal-testing procedures following maintenance were strengthened.

Overall, though, the safety record got better throughout BR's period of tenure. Each successive decade brought fewer passenger deaths than its predecessor. Safety for staff had improved remarkably too. In 1949, 209 railway employees were killed at work, compared with just thirty-six by 1977 and now the number most years is below ten. This could be attributed to a mixture of modern technology, greater productivity requiring fewer workers[40] and a far more rigorous health and safety policy.

Organizationally, British Rail reached its apogee with the 'Organization for Quality' reform, completed in 1992, which involved devolving all the railway's functions to the sectors and dividing them into profit centres. The BR Board still set the overall objectives, but the powerful devolved sectors would be responsible for all aspects of their railways. This business-oriented structure proved to be highly efficient but also, ironically, paved the way for privatization. The mounting losses at BR, caused by the recession rather than anything under its control, gave the ideologues in the Treasury and the Conservative Party the opening they needed to press home their case for the privatization of the railways, which was then included in the Tory manifesto for the 1992 election.

During the privatization process, British Rail came in for a lot of criticism in order to justify the break-up and sale of the railways. In fact, its record was at worst patchy, but often, particularly in its final fifteen years, excellent. Even the frequently told story about its awful curly-edged sandwiches is not true, as British Rail actually developed the concept of shrink-wrapped sandwiches and towards the end of its existence commissioned celebrity chefs like Delia Smith and Clement Freud to improve its menus.

Even the most famous excuse supposedly given by British Rail for late-running trains is untrue: no one working for British Rail ever said that it was down to 'the wrong type of snow'. In fact, after a bout of bad weather had caused delays in February 1991, Terry Worrall, at the time BR's Director of Operations, gave an interview on BBC's *Today* programme, saying, 'It is not the volume of snow that has caused us problems but the type of snow, which is very dry and powdery.'[41] Worrall had a point as this particularly cold snow delayed trains throughout Europe, but it was an *Evening Standard* sub-editor who used the canny headline, 'The wrong type of snow', which has been trotted out in almost every subsequent article on the ills of the railways.

One of the perennial problems for the railway is that the ministry dealing with transport has invariably been dominated by those more interested in building roads than in supporting the railway. BR became a 'political shuttlecock'[42] as Tory governments generally favoured a withdrawal of the state from the industry while Labour sought greater involvement. Overall British Rail was a success despite these difficulties and the constant changes of policy its leaders had to endure. As Terry

Gourvish, the official historian put it, 'Once a rather unwieldy, monolithic structure, British Rail provided comparatively safe, improving services, began to revolutionize marketing and showed greater attention to customer care.'[43] He cites successes such as the InterCity brand and the Network SouthEast livery, the Travellers Fare concept which greatly improved catering, and developments in collaboration with the private sector, such as Liverpool Street station. One memorable illustration that the BR managers were prepared to make hard commercial decisions was that at the start of the privatization process, BR had just 121,000 employees, fewer than a fifth of the total at nationalization.

The lack of a long tradition of public ownership of the railways in Britain contributed to the fraught nature of the relationship between government and the industry, whereas in other countries, where public ownership of the railways was long established, the relationship was more relaxed. Thus it was no coincidence that Britain would become the pioneer of rail privatization under John Major's government.

# FIFTEEN

# THE FUTURE IS RAIL

It now seems as if the railways have turned full circle. They are back in the private sector after fifty years of state ownership and they have strange entrepreneurial-sounding names, some with a traditional bent such as South West Trains or GNER (Great North Eastern Railway), others – such as C2C and 'One' – showing all the signs of having been dreamt up by drunken marketing staff in a brainstorming exercise. In fact, the railways have a completely different structure from that of any other time in their history: British Rail was broken up and fragmented into over a hundred organizations linked through a series of contracts and financial arrangements that are far too complicated to outline here.[1] Moreover, far from solving the thorny issue of the relationship between the state and the railways, privatization has made it even more complex and, even more strangely, the requirement for government subsidy has been far greater than ever before.

The new names for the various lines are the products of a privatization that has been widely accepted as being 'botched' – even by its supporters – but which strangely has been retained by a Labour Party which in opposition was against every detail. It was a tragedy that just as British Rail had entered something of a golden age, with a structure that was robust and commercially minded, the organization had to be broken up on the basis of false assumptions – that BR was inefficient and cost too much – and broken promises – that the railways would cost less in subsidy and be free from government interference. Just at this point, the rail network suffered the most violent upheaval of its history, greater than the amalgamation of 1923 and the nationalization a quarter of a century later. Politicians, as usual, were motivated by ideology rather than a desire to improve the system and the result was years of chaos, including the worst ever disruption to the network in peacetime and a system that has proved both dysfunctional and expensive. An organization that had taken nearly half a century to start functioning properly was shattered on a whim in a process that cost hundreds of millions in consultancy and legal fees, and would eventually cost the taxpayer billions.

Yet the privatization of 1996–7 very nearly didn't happen. The Conservatives put the idea into their manifesto for the 1992 election but no one expected them to win it. The notion of selling off the railways had been kicking around Tory circles for some years but had been firmly rejected by Mrs Thatcher whose political antennae were too well attuned to take on such a controversial issue. She realized that the question of what to do about the subsidy and the strength of likely opposition, given the fondness of a significant section of the public for the railways, made it a far more difficult industry to privatize than others. However, she changed her mind just before her downfall, allowing rail privatization to be announced by her Transport Secretary, Cecil Parkinson, at the October 1990 party conference.

With Mrs Thatcher gone, the pace hotted up, driven by the Privatization Unit of the Treasury, led by Steve Robson, which had run out of things to privatize. Robson was an ideologue with a strong dislike of the public sector and he found that the new Prime Minister, John Major, was far more enthusiastic about privatization than his predecessor. However, Major's Transport Secretary, Malcolm Rifkind, was unclear about what model should be chosen and dithered, which meant that the eventual plan was cobbled together in great haste. While Rifkind himself was undecided, Major favoured a regional model, recreating a version of the Big Four which, having been born in 1943, he was not quite old enough to remember. A working group of ministers and civil servants was set up and here the crucial mistake that was to be so damaging to the railways was made: the Treasury rejected Major's idea and insisted that the track and infrastructure should be separated from the operations, splitting the crucial 'wheel–rail' interface and, crucially, allowing on-rail competition.

At the time of the election, there was still precious little detail about how the privatization would be carried out, although the manifesto did mention the separate management of the tracks and operations. Transport matters rarely pop up in election debates and rail privatization was no exception – despite the radical and unprecedented nature of what was being proposed, the issue did not feature in the hustings for the election held in April 1992. When the Tories woke up the day after to find John Major still in Downing Street with just enough of a majority to survive a full term, they realized that privatizing the railways within a single term of office would be a momentous task.

The manifesto was, in fact, misleading. It had intimated that British Rail would still exist, whereas the proposed new structure represented a complete abolition of the organization.[2] A White Paper, *New Opportunities for the Railways*, was hastily drawn up by the new Transport Secretary, John MacGregor. Published in July 1992, it was a sparse document of just twenty-one pages which set out for the first time the way that services were to be franchised to private operators: they were to be given a contract to run the train services on a particular set of lines, usually with a specified frequency and timings for the first and last train. They would either pay a premium or receive a subsidy, depending on the profitability of the line, and keep all the fare revenue, which was supposed to incentivize them to increase passenger numbers and keep their customers happy. They would own no assets, as trains would be leased from rolling stock companies, and they would pay a charge for track usage to the infrastructure provider (initially Railtrack and now Network Rail). The White Paper was desperately short on detail and important aspects, such as the number of franchises, their size and their length. Moreover, it suggested that the infrastructure company – which would become Railtrack – would not be privatized until the next term of Parliament, a decision that was later reversed, and there was even the suggestion that some lines might be privatized as integrated operations with their infrastructure.

The whole Byzantine system was a massive experiment – untried elsewhere before or since – foisted on a reasonably well-functioning industry for ideological reasons. Not surprisingly, the proposals were greeted with unanimous opposition and there was widespread scepticism about their workability from practically anyone who had experience of railway operations. The opposition was wide-ranging, taking in large sections of the media, including traditionally Tory newspapers like the *Daily Telegraph*, as well as rail user groups, the trade unions and, of course, the Labour opposition. One of the most vociferous critics was Robert Adley, a Tory MP who was chairman of the Commons Transport Select Committee and author of several railway books. He dubbed the process 'a poll tax on wheels' and had begun to muster opposition on the Conservative benches when he died suddenly of a heart attack in the summer of 1993. His death removed the last chance to moderate this ill-thought-out legislation as he was the one Tory backbench MP who had the knowledge and support to have pushed through changes to the Railways Bill which became law that autumn. Although there was some opposition in the House of Lords, the main opponent, Lord Peyton, who had been Transport Minister in the Heath government, was bought off with an amendment that allowed BR to bid for franchises. However, it was conditional on the permission of the franchising director, Roger Salmon, and when it came to the sales process, he banned BR bids, thus neutering the amendment.

There was an obvious contradiction at the heart of the new structure: the fundamental conflict between franchising out a whole area and allowing open-access operators. The Treasury had insisted on splitting the infrastructure and the operations precisely to ensure that new entrants to the rail market could compete with incumbents. They liked the idea of on-rail competition between different private sector operators, which might go faster or offer better meals. One minister, Roger Freeman, was even foolish enough to mention that privatized companies might offer 'cheap and cheerful' services for secretaries while their bosses could take separate trains.[3] However, if companies were expected to take on franchises, with all the risk of possible falls in fare revenue, then they could hardly be expected to accept the idea that some upstart 'open access' operator might cherry-pick their most valuable services by, for example, running a train five minutes earlier. In other words, the whole structure of the privatized industry was based on a theoretical idea that was unworkable in practice. Worse, the civil servants who had to flesh out the details of the plan knew it was a nonsense, as Patrick Brown, at the time the Permanent Secretary at

Transport, admitted a decade later: 'I don't think any of us in the Department for Transport thought that open access, as described, could have any part in the privatization. But you couldn't say so.'[4] In the event, open access operators were effectively banned from most of the network as ministers realized that bidders would charge more for franchises that faced such competition and although one successful operator, Hull Trains,[5] did eventually emerge, it runs just ten trains per day, a tiny fraction of the 19,000 daily total.

The government, though, was not listening, driven by the imperative to get the scheme completed within the lifetime of the Parliament. British Rail managers were deliberately excluded from the consultation process after one meeting with MacGregor at which the heads of the profit centres unanimously warned that the scheme was unworkable, a message the government did not want to hear. Paradoxically, they were also asked to bid for franchises, as the government favoured management buy-out schemes, but eventually they would win only three of the twenty-five franchises.

The government decided that franchises were to be for terms of seven to fifteen years, which meant that the rolling stock would have to be leased, since trains generally have a life of twenty-five to thirty-five years, and franchisees could not be expected to buy them. Consequently, three rolling stock companies were formed which took over all of British Rail's 11,260 coaches[6] and these were the first part of the organization to be sold in early 1996. There was a paucity of bidders, because the City was wary of an unproven market, and they went for £1.8bn, which was far less than their value since, within two years, all three had been resold for a total of £2.65bn. The National Audit Office later found that the taxpayer had lost out to the tune of around £700m in the sale.

Railtrack had been separated off from BR in 1994 and was privatized by a public flotation in the spring of 1996 with shares being sold to the public at £3.90. They eventually rose to a stunning £17.68 two years later, but then the boom collapsed after the October 2000 Hatfield crash and finally the shares were bought back by the government at just £2.62. The other important part of BR to go under the hammer were the thirteen infrastructure units, responsible for renewal and maintenance,[7] which had been separated off from Railtrack, a disastrous decision as it meant the company had no engineering expertise. They were divided into regional maintenance and renewal companies, and were sold for a total of £169m, but the purpose was not so much to bring in money as to turn Railtrack into a kind of shell company whose main function was running contracts. It was to prove a terrible mistake.

Meanwhile the franchise process was under way. It had taken a long time for the Office of Passenger Rail Franchising, created to run the franchise system, to prepare the contracts for privatization and there was a belated legal challenge from a pressure group, Save Our Railways, which delayed the process. However, after these delays the franchises were let out remarkably quickly in eighteen months, with the process being completed in time for the whole industry to be in the private sector by the May 1997 election. At first there was very little interest in the contracts but a bus company, Stagecoach, saved the day by bidding for the early franchises and winning one of them, South West Trains, in a very generous deal that was to give the firm handsome profits for many years. There were problems with the other two in the first batch, which resulted in the preferred bidders not obtaining the contracts but to a large extent the sales process went off smoothly. It was clear that the government was not expecting much growth or development of the railway but, instead, was attempting to manage a declining industry as cheaply as possible. Towards the end of the franchise process, many more bidders came forward, attracted by the early generous deals, and put in offers that proved to be far too optimistic. They obtained franchises predicated on rapid increases in revenue or, more usually, sharp cuts in costs which were not deliverable. BR had been far more efficient than the private companies had reckoned and consequently several new operators soon found themselves in financial difficulties.

The biggest failure was on the West Coast Main Line where Virgin had bid very optimistically on the basis of a fully refurbished line with a new untried radio signalling system that promised to increase capacity dramatically – all of which was supposed to be delivered by Railtrack with private sector investment. In the event, Railtrack had been far too optimistic about the technology and its failure to bring about the West Coast improvement contributed in no small part to the collapse of the company. The government had to bail out the Virgin franchise and it became a management contract, which means that it paid Virgin a fixed fee (with a small profit margin built in) to run the trains, irrespective of passenger numbers and without any risk to the private company.

Virtually every aspect of the sales process attracted controversy and the opposition was relentless, which forced the government into several concessions. There were rows over fares, the number of stations selling tickets and network benefits. On fares, the government was forced to accept that season tickets and savers would be regulated, initially at 1 per cent below the level of general inflation,[8] and a proposal by the Rail Regulator that tickets should be sold only at 400 key stations was quickly thrown out. The government also promised that network benefits such as the inter-availability of tickets and railcards, like those for young people and senior citizens, would be retained under the new system.

Labour ultimately ducked out of full-scale opposition to the privatization. There was a moment when, in the preparation of its statement for the Railtrack sale prospectus, it could have committed itself to reversing the process. Tony Blair, the new Labour leader, had indeed promised a 'publicly accountable, publicly owned' railway at the 1995 party conference, but when pressed he never explained what that meant. Labour allowed the moment to pass and, indeed, helped to ensure that all the franchises were let by the time of the 1997 election by encouraging the Passenger Transport Executives not to block deals over their local franchises. Worse, its posturing cost the taxpayer money. When Clare Short, the Shadow Transport Secretary in 1995, expressed Labour's opposition to sale of the rolling stock companies, the City lost interest and consequently the price was lower than expected.

Labour's antipathy to the rail companies continued in government, but without any suggestion that renationalization was being considered. John Prescott, who took on the transport role after the 1997 election victory, was openly hostile to the train operators, but it was made clear to him by Tony Blair that the new structure would be retained virtually intact. After a couple of years of inactivity, Prescott managed to create a Strategic Rail Authority, which had the task of managing the franchises and setting long-term strategic goals for the industry, something it largely failed to do in its short existence.

At first, privatization worked quite smoothly and the performance of train services even improved, mainly because the staff continued to work as if they were still serving one organization. There were some beneficial changes: the creation of a National Rail Enquiry Service, replacing the haphazard system of regional centres and stations, was a massive improvement and some of the new operators provided far better information systems on platforms. Fleets of modern trains were introduced on several lines, notably the Pendolinos and Voyagers on Virgin's two franchises, although much of this investment would have been made even if BR had not been abolished. There was some expansion of services, notably on the Midland main line between London and Leicester, but on the whole it was business as usual.

However, difficulties soon emerged as a result of the contradictions inherent in the policy and fundamental flaws in the structure. In particular, there were two successive and partly interlinked problem areas: safety and cost. During the first few years of privatization, there was a series of accidents that undermined confidence in the safety of the railways: Southall (1997, seven dead), Ladbroke Grove (1999, thirty-one dead), Hatfield (2000, four dead) and Potters Bar (2002, seven dead). The first two were caused by trains going through signals at danger, the others by poor track maintenance. The new post-privatization structure of the industry was responsible in some measure for all of these accidents[9] and, crucially, the public's confidence in the railways was dented, even though, statistically, this was one of its safest periods.[10] The most damaging of these accidents was Hatfield, ironically, as it was the one which resulted in the fewest deaths. Caused by a broken rail which had not been maintained properly, it led to a panic among Railtrack executives who, thanks to the fragmented privatized structure, did not have the engineering expertise to assess how many other sections of track might be in a similarly dangerous condition. With only the advice of consultants to call upon, they agreed to the imposition of hundreds of speed limits around the country,[11] many of just 20 mph, which effectively brought the railways to a standstill in what the chairman of the Strategic Rail Authority, Sir Alastair Morton, called a 'collective nervous breakdown'.[12] Travelling on the railway suddenly became a nightmare, with nationwide disruption on a scale not seen since the Second World War. On several lines, such as the East Coast and West Coast, barely a quarter of trains were running on time and the media was full of horrendous tales of passengers being delayed for hours. The damage was long-lasting as it proved hard to remove the speed restrictions because of health and safety rules, and in performance terms it took the railways five years to recover.

The long-term consequences of Hatfield were enormous. The accident bankrupted Railtrack because of the penalties it suffered under the performance regime for having imposed the speed restrictions and the cost of the often unnecessary repairs that it undertook. Railtrack's shares started plummeting and despite making a staggering loss of £534m in the 1999/2000 financial year, the directors still made a dividend payment to shareholders. This daft move was the last straw for Railtrack as the company was forced into administration by the Transport Secretary Stephen Byers. Billions of pounds were spent across the network in order to prevent another Hatfield and the cost of the work soared as safety procedures were tightened up. Another half a billion pounds was spent on fitting the Train Protection & Warning System, that automatically prevents all but the fastest trains from going through red lights and significantly slows down the others. This ensured there would be no repeat of Ladbroke-Grove type disasters, caused by trains going through red lights, known as Signals Passed at Danger (SPADs).

As fears about safety on the railways receded, another problem emerged: the massive cost of the railway to taxpayers, particularly when compared with British Rail. The biggest irony, and indeed failure, of privatization was that far from reducing the cost of the railway to taxpayers, it soared to unprecedented heights. Privatization also brought with it a lack of transparency about the financial affairs of the railway, making comparisons difficult, but a reasonable estimate of the cost to taxpayers since the creation of Network Rail stands at around £5bn annually.[13]

The reasons for this increase are not at all clear,[14] although there are some obvious pointers. There is, as supporters of privatization argue, more work being carried out than before but it is also very clear that much of it does not represent value for money. The hopes that operation by franchises would lead to a reduction in subsidies were soon dashed. Several companies got into financial difficulties and came begging, Oliver Twist-like, for more, which they were duly given (until Connex, the French company running the South Eastern services, was finally given the boot in November 2003 at the second time of asking). The idea that the total amount allocated for franchise payments, which had been doubled at privatization from £1bn to £2bn in order to attract bidders, would go back to the BR level within five years therefore proved fanciful.

The rolling stock companies (roscos) were another source of increased cost. As we have seen they were privatized too cheaply, but then bought at more realistic prices, making it necessary for the roscos to keep leasing prices, particularly of old trains, relatively high. The roscos are not regulated but have an effective monopoly since there is very little spare rolling stock in the system and, in any case, it is often difficult to move stock between lines.[15] The high profitability of the roscos finally angered ministers so much that in 2006 they launched an inquiry in an attempt to cut the cost by £100m (about 10 per cent).[16]

However, it was the demise of Railtrack and the post-Hatfield traumas that did most to push up costs. With safety fears paramount and the depletion of engineering skills within Railtrack, both the cost and amount of work being carried out soared. There was a total lack of financial discipline. After a year of administration in which costs rocketed, Railtrack was replaced by Network Rail, a company of limited guarantee (in other words, it has no shareholders and profits are recycled through investment). In reality, this was a renationalization since it is a quasi-public sector company which can borrow money on the basis that the loans are government-backed. Yet it pays high salaries and bonuses to its top managers comparable with those in the private sector even though it does not take entrepreneurial-type risks. Network Rail sensibly took back the maintenance in-house, putting the private companies out of work, although they received considerable compensation and their workforces mostly joined the new company. Although this saved some money, costs still remained high and as a result subsidy has been far higher than under BR for several years.

A veteran BR manager, Ivor Warburton, who used to be in charge of the West Coast Main Line, explains best how the new system fails to keep down costs by telling the story of a culvert which had some risk of collapsing during the days of BR. At the annual budget meeting, Warburton asked his local engineer whether the culvert would hold up another year. The response was equivocal, but Warburton, needing to save money and work to the budget, decided not to replace it. In fact the culvert did collapse that year, causing some delays, but Warburton remains convinced he made the right decision: 'The single negotiation with government over the budget feeds through the whole organisation and someone makes a rational judgement that has a risk associated with it, with a possible operating inconvenience that has to be contained within the overall target.'[17]

That story encapsulates why the railways are so expensive to run today. Under the current system, no one would be able to make such a reasoned risk assessment. Instead, repairs and renewal which could possibly wait a year or more are carried out because the industry has become so risk averse and no one is taking decisions in the context of a tight annual budget. The railways need to be under the control of a single organization with its own budget and a decision-making process that balances all aspects of the railway, from the ballast and rails to the catering and rolling stock, when allocating funds and resources. With the fragmentation of the industry into over one hundred companies, each of which needs to make a profit and has complex contractual and legal relationships with the other companies, the ability to control expenditure has been lost. Decisions, often incompatible, are made by the various stakeholders, none of which has the overall interests of the railway in mind. The most obvious case of lack of coordination was the debacle over the Southern power supply when train operators found that there was not enough power to run the new trains they had ordered through the leasing companies. Nobody, it seems, had bothered to check whether the trains could run on the existing power supply and they had to sit in sidings awaiting the upgrade which eventually cost Network Rail and therefore taxpayers £700m.

Another pertinent example is the fact that train companies are paid millions of pounds annually in compensation because Network Rail closes a line for track repairs or for other improvements. In other words, the operators receive money for not running trains whilst at the same time allowing their supplier, Network Rail, to provide them with a better service. The great railway barons of the nineteenth century would never have tolerated exercising so little control; they were genuine risk-taking capitalists. Under the present system, in contrast, a game of 'pretend capitalism' is played, with the taxpayer always in the background to pick up the tab. Moreover, there has been a huge increase in staffing costs since all these companies have chief executives and finance directors on very high salaries, as well as other executives such as communication and human resource directors, in addition to the widespread use of lawyers and consultants.

Alistair Darling, the Transport Secretary between 2001 and 2005, realized that the railway was not efficient and launched a rail review in 2003 to look at the structure of the industry. It reported the following year but ducked the fundamental issue about reintegrating the railway, arguing that it was too complicated in an age of many rail companies as they would have to run over each other's tracks. In the past, of course, such arrangements were commonplace.

The Railways Act 2005 that resulted from the rail review abolished the Strategic Rail Authority after just five years of existence, dividing its functions between Network Rail and the Department of Transport. It also transferred the Railway Inspectorate from the Health & Safety Executive, which was thought to be imposing unnecessarily stringent safety requirements, to the Office of Rail Regulation, with the idea that there would be a better trade-off between improved safety and increased costs. Because the fundamental issue of reintegration was not addressed the high cost of the railways remains the industry's greatest threat, since it presents a barrier to improvements and keeps alive the fear that an economic crisis could precipitate a sharp round of cuts to railway services.

Strangely, while the railways remained ostensibly privatized, the running of the new system actually resulted in more interference and involvement of civil servants than at any time in the industry's history, as they were required to, for example, specify timetables, think about future strategy and rolling stock needs, such as a replacement for the

High Speed Train, and let the franchises out. Even the Tories who devised the system have admitted they made mistakes[18] but oddly Labour has soldiered on and has made few changes of substance. The one success has been the vast numbers of extra passengers, a 40 per cent rise in a decade, but that has been largely a result of external factors such as the booming economy and congestion on the roads. The publicly-run London Underground has also seen a 25 per cent rise in the same period. Needless to say, this continued growth is putting a strain on the railway and, as punctuality finally returned to pre-Hatfield levels in 2006, overcrowding has become the most pressing problem facing the industry. Unfortunately, the harsh truth of railway economics – the golden rule as it were – is that any extra investment in the network has to be funded largely from the taxpayer as it rarely earns a sufficient return to pay for itself.

Privatization did somewhat better for freight. The Treasury insisted on breaking up BR's principal freight companies into three regional divisions – a daft idea since most journeys involved long distances – and all three were bought in 1996 by the same US railroad company anyway, Wisconsin Central, headed by Ed Burkhardt, a renowned railwayman with a good track record in buying up and improving small, financially stricken railways. The sale included not just locomotives and wagons but also vast tracts of railway land with the potential for significant development rights. The new company, called English Welsh and Scottish (EWS), invested substantially by buying 300 new locomotives to replace the failure-prone fleet inherited from BR. Privatization changed the rules of the game, getting rid of BR's old restrictive practices, which effectively prevented new operators entering the market. Railtrack was obliged to accept requests for track access from freight companies on the same basis as passenger operators, which encouraged new hauliers to enter the market. Therefore, several new smaller operators appeared, but the decline in the amount of freight carried was halted – mainly because coal is being transported for longer distances, a result of the government's energy policy. Drax Power Station, at Selby in North Yorkshire, for example, receives its coal from the port of Hunterston in Scotland and not from the local coalfield. But there are still severe constraints and bottlenecks, not least because of the extra passenger trains crowding on to the tracks. The Beeching era and the mind-set it engendered reduced capacity so much that it is very difficult – if not impossible – to carve out many more paths for freight trains.

As virtually every page of this book demonstrates, the railways transformed Britain. They made possible journeys that a generation before would have seemed completely implausible. They boosted all kinds of trade, stimulated economic development, brought in their wake a whole host of social and political changes, and played a vital part when the country went to war. Yet we have taken the railways for granted and failed to realize what a very special invention they were.

There is a neat arithmetical pattern in the timeline of the railways. The purely private and fragmented system survived for nearly a hundred years from its creation until 1923, while the Big Four, created by amalgamation, lasted precisely a quarter of a century, and British Rail almost reached its golden jubilee. In the decade since the demise of British Rail, the railways have undergone more upheaval than at any time in their history and there is further change ahead. The railways, it seems, can never be allowed to stand still and arguments about their structure, with constant tinkering at the margins, continue to occur in between major politically inspired reorganizations.

At root there is the fraught relationship between railways and government – and it was rather inauspicious that at the opening of the first railway, a government minister was killed. Government cannot stop meddling with the railways because they are such an important part of the infrastructure and decisions cannot be left entirely to the private sector because the system always requires subsidy. Therefore privatization was always going to be partial and tightly regulated since the government was not going to let go of the reins entirely. The notion, enshrined in the Tories' initial privatization plan, that the private sector would be allowed complete freedom, was always going to be fanciful; now, with the collapse of Railtrack and the abolition of the SRA, the railways are in a strange limbo between the private and public sectors. But government interference has by no means always been negative and, indeed, it could be argued that there should have been more in the mid-nineteenth century when the railways were killing far too many of their passengers.

But it has been inconsistent and, most important, the railways have often been poorly treated, especially in relation to the roads which seem to be funded without any of the hand-wringing and parsimony that accompanies any investment in the railways.

While this relationship remains fraught as the privatized structure is still bedding down, rather more happily the railways are booming. The consistent economic growth, together with the crowded roads and growing environmental awareness, means that the railways are carrying more people than at almost any time in their history. The doubts about whether the railways have a role in the twenty-first century have long been buried, but the shape of that future remains shrouded in uncertainty. The railways were a quintessential nineteenth-century invention, reliant on heavy engineering and private capital. They seem ill-suited to the individualism of the twenty-first century where collective travelling on public transport was perceived as being for those who cannot afford better, as Mrs Thatcher suggested. In spite of this, the railways are not just enjoying a renaissance with the old network being revitalized with investment in both track and new rolling stock, but there is now a serious debate about expansion and new lines.

Across the world the railways are expanding, with metro and tram systems popping up in even quite modestly sized towns and cities, and high speed networks, first seen in France and Japan, now being built in countries as diverse as Spain and Italy, Taiwan and South Korea. Yet, here in Britain, we have just sixty-two miles of high speed line – the £5bn Channel Tunnel Rail Link between London St Pancras and the Channel Tunnel, which opened finally in the autumn of 2007 – and no firm plans to build any more. Moreover, in recent years, dozens of tram schemes that would have brought untold benefits to many provincial towns and cities have been scrapped, often after millions had been spent on preparatory work. Outside the densely populated areas of the Far East, railways are rarely able to pay their own running costs, let alone the investment needed to build them. They require subsidy for construction and often to keep running. They sit unhappily in the private sector because of this need for government support. But that does not mean they are a waste of money. They generate economic growth, enable people to travel comfortably, and cause much less environmental damage than the alternatives. Those benefits cannot be captured by the fare box but they help make societies viable. It is sad that this seems to have been understood in so many parts of the world but not in the land of Stephenson, Hudson, Watkin, Gresley, Sir Bob Reid (the first of the two BR chairmen of that name) and so many other heroes of this history. The railways may be flourishing, but in Britain their development is still constrained by a refusal to recognize their value.

The opening of the Channel Tunnel Rail Link, which reduced journey times from London to Paris and Brussels to two hours fifteen minutes and two hours respectively, may prove crucial as a catalyst to inspire the government to support further high speed lines, especially as part of the line is being used to deliver spectators to the 2012 Olympics. The building of High Speed One, as the Link is now called, was an engineering success, with few problems despite the large proportion of the line that had to be placed in tunnels as a result of environmental protests. But at the same time it was a financial disaster, predicated as it was initially on being entirely privately funded through the profits from the Eurostar service. The project had to be rescued with a bit of financial wizardry in 1998 which turned it into a public sector project backed by government bonds. Despite these difficulties, it could open the way for further lines to be built to the north, but the Treasury-commissioned review of Britain's future transport infrastructure needs by Rod Eddington, the former head of British Airways, published in December 2006, was sceptical of the idea and the opportunity to build such lines may have been lost given the lack of space and the high cost.

The dilemma for the politicians, then, is that on the one hand, the railways eat up lots of taxpayers' money which could be spent on what they consider as more useful alternatives such as hospitals, schools and prisons; on the other, they provide a lot of benefits that cannot be captured through the fare box, ranging from relative environmental friendliness to economic regeneration. They have powerful supporters because, unlike buses, they are used by the affluent as well as the poor. Brian Souter, the boss of Stagecoach, once suggested that while dissatisfied bus passengers would throw bricks through the garage window, rail passengers would write to their MP.

But it is unclear whether the government will support the improvements that are necessary to cope with the ever-increasing numbers of passengers. There is, for example, no programme of electrification, even though Britain has a far lower percentage of electrified lines than other European countries. And while minor enhancements such as restoring sections of double track and improving junctions are being undertaken, there is no clear plan to deal with the overcrowding that is now making rail travel intolerable for many passengers. Progress has been painfully slow on initiatives such as double-decker trains and extended platforms to cope with demand. Plans for major schemes such as Crossrail, which involves building a tunnel under London between Liverpool Street and Paddington in order to relieve the overcrowded Underground system, have been repeatedly stalled through lack of money and, more importantly, political direction.

Despite the reluctance of governments to commit more resources, the railways are no longer seen as a dying industry: the days of Beeching and Serpell are long gone. The new focus on the environmental damage caused by road and air transport strengthens the case for investment.[19] Indeed, there are powerful economic, social and environmental reasons for its continued expansion. A report into ways of reducing carbon emissions by the respected Tyndall Centre for Climate Change suggests that railways have a key role: 'Trains are the cleanest form of mass transport, producing on average only a quarter of the carbon dioxide that cars emit for the same distance and just over 10 per cent compared to domestic aviation. Investments in train infrastructure, such as longer platforms for longer trains, could make an important contribution to meeting emissions targets as could investing in infrastructure for double-decker trains.'[20]

It is very difficult to predict future rail demand but further growth is inevitable. Fares are being allowed to rise, which may choke off some demand but the number of rail travellers is highly dependent on the state of the economy. A host of policies are being discussed which could dramatically increase passenger numbers – a shift away from funding roads, road pricing, restricting airport development and higher taxation of both flying and motoring on environmental grounds among them.

It is therefore possible to have confidence that rail travel will survive into the twenty-second century. All kinds of technological developments are in the pipeline. Maglev trains, a kind of monorail propelled by powerful magnetic forces that lift the train a few centimetres above the tracks, have been in development for many years and have been successfully tested at speeds of over 400 mph. There have been suggestions for a network of Maglev trains linking the major British cities, but the advantage over conventional trains in terms of speed is more than negated by the disadvantages, such as the unproven nature of the technology, the impossibility of connecting them with the existing rail network, and doubts about safety, heightened by an accident on a test track in Germany in September 2006 which killed twenty-three people. In any case, conventional high-speed trains are getting quicker, with speeds of 320 kph (200 mph) on the new TGV Est in France, and even 350 kph (220 mph) being mooted, which, given the difficulty of building Maglev stations in city centres, will weigh in favour of the conventional technology.

Trains controlled by radio waves, obviating the need for drivers to see outside signals, are already in use on high-speed lines and metro systems, and the European Commission aims to make these the norm, though the sheer expense and the difficulties of synchronizing systems around the Continent may prove to be an insuperable barrier. Trains propelled by engines powered by fuel cells which burn hydrogen are also being discussed, but are not a realistic proposition for a couple of decades. While trains are indeed more environmentally friendly than any other form of transport, their record in that respect has deteriorated in recent years as rolling stock has become heavier and consequently less fuel-efficient due to safety and disability legislation, as well as the routine fitting of air conditioning. In order to retain its environmental advantage, rail transport must improve its fuel efficiency. In particular, the electrification programme needs to be revived, as electricity can be generated from non-carbon sources such as nuclear, wind and hydro, which reduces the carbon footprint. Technological developments on the track, too, may be significant in improving performance. It is quite remarkable that the same basic method of constructing railways – using rails laid on sleepers resting on ballast – that was used on the Liverpool to Manchester railway, opened in 1830, was also used on High Speed One, completed in 2007.

For passengers, train journeys could be made much easier by provision of better information and easier methods of paying fares. Tickets sold through the internet or the mobile phone will make queues at booking offices a thing of the past and already it is possible to track the progress of individual trains on the internet or via a mobile phone.

Even though the people who saw the first train on its journey from Liverpool to Manchester in 1830 would be able to recognize today's railways as direct descendants of Stephenson's construction, the industry has come a long way in its near two centuries of existence. Most importantly, it has survived and flourished despite the competition from roads and air transport. Rail will continue to provide the best and safest[21] form of transport throughout the twenty-first century. Trains are here to stay, a remarkable testimony to the prescience of Stephenson and all the subsequent pioneers.

# NOTES

## Introduction: Why Railways?

1  A. F. Garnett, *Steel Wheels*, Cannwood Press, 2005, p. 6.
2  The Newcomen engine was not like later steam engines as it was driven by air pressure operating against a vacuum created by spraying water into low pressure steam. The first mention of a steam engine was made by an Alexandrian, Hero, writing in the first century after Christ.
3  Garnett, *Steel Wheels*, p. 15.
4  Frank Ferneyhough, *Liverpool & Manchester Railway, 1830–1980*, Robert Hale, 1980, p. 12.
5  It can still be seen in the Conservatoire National des Arts et Métiers in Paris.
6  As with several elements of this brief early history, there are differing accounts and some suggest that this engine never ran on rails.
7  It is surprising how many people are unaware that train drivers do not actually steer their vehicles but are at the mercy of signalmen setting the correct route at every junction and points.
8  The clever devices in the middle of the back axles of cars which enable them to corner easily by ensuring the inside wheel travels just a bit more slowly than the outside one, which has to cover greater distance.
9  Francis T. Evans, 'Roads, Railways, and Canals: Technical Choices in 19th century Britain', *Technology and Culture*, Vol. 22, 1981.
10  There is some evidence that there were earlier ones on private land which, therefore, did not require an Act of Parliament.
11  Few passengers on the Croydon Tramlink will be aware that part of its track is the original route of the world's oldest public railway.
12  Historians are rather hesitant on this point, suggesting there may have been other now-forgotten services.
13  The railway had various other names and was originally called the Oystermouth Railway and it originally only ran to Oystermouth. In one of the acts of vandalism on the railway heritage, of which there are several other examples in this book, the track was ripped up in 1960 with scant regard for its role in history.

14  Quoted in various places including
    <http://www.welshwales.co.uk/mumbles_railway_swansea.htm>

15  Richard Ayton and William Daniell, *A voyage round Great Britain undertaken in the year 1813*, Longmans, 1814.

16  His book, *Observations on a General Iron Railway*, first published in 1820 by Baldwin, Cradock and Joy, went through four more editions by 1825.

17  B. G. Wilson and J. R. Day, *Unusual Railways*, Frederick Muller, 1957, p. 163.

18  The original main line actually ran from Stockton to Phoenix Pit, Wilton Park City.

19  For those who have wondered why trains no longer go 'tagadada, tagadada' as they used to, the reason is that most main line routes, and indeed many others, such as sections of the London Underground, have continuous welded rails with none of the gaps between rails which caused that evocative noise. Stephenson's early lines, though, had far too many such gaps!

20  Quoted in Garnett, *Steel Wheels*, p. 26.

21  *The Oxford Companion to British Railway History*, Oxford University Press, 1997, p. 477.

22  It was by no means the first railway bridge. That was the Causey Arch in County Durham, built to carry the Dunston railroad. It was completed in 1726 and survives to this day.

23  Quoted in Frank Ferneyhough, *The History of Railways in Britain*, Osprey Publishing, 1975, p. 62.

24  18 November 1824.

25  1 October 1825.

26  Adrian Vaughan, *Railwaymen, Politics and Money*, John Murray, 1997, p. 24.

27  Ibid., p. 26.

28  There is some discussion about whether these were loops, that allowed trains to continue forward once they had passed each other, or, as some accounts suggest, sidings which required shunting in and out to allow the train on the main line to progress.

29  Ferneyhough, *The History of Railways in Britain*, p. 61.

30  Jack Simmons and Gordon Biddle (eds), *The Oxford Companion to British Railway History*, Oxford, 1997, p. 478.

## ONE: The First Railway

1  Harold Perkin, *The Age of the Railway*, David & Charles, 1970, p. 180.

2  Asa Briggs, *Victorian Cities*, Pelican Books, 1968, p. 96.

3  Simon Garfield, *The Last Journey of William Huskisson*, Faber & Faber, 2004, p. 16.

4  Frank Ferneyhough, *Liverpool & Manchester Railway, 1830–1980*, Robert Hale, 1980, p. 13.

5   Garfield, *The Last Journey of William Huskisson*, p. 16.

6   Ibid.

7   Remarkably cheap, given that a new railway would cost anything between £30m and £350m per mile in the UK today.

8   Marjorie Whitelaw in Bryan Morgan (ed.), *The Railway-Lover's Companion*, Eyre & Spottiswoode, 1963, p. 66.

9   F. D. Klingender, *Art and the Industrial Revolution*, Paladin, 1972, p. 123.

10  Ferneyhough, *Liverpool & Manchester Railway, 1830–1980*, p. 22.

11  Ibid.

12  Quoted in Ferneyhough, *Liverpool & Manchester Railway*, p. 24.

13  *The Times*, 2 May 1825.

14  Adrian Vaughan, *Railwaymen, Politics and Money*, John Murray, 1997, p. 58.

15  Terry Coleman, *The Railway Navvies*, Pimlico, 2000, p. 25.

16  Ibid., p. 28.

17  As opposed to the 'four foot', which is the distance between the two rails on the same track, an inaccurate shorthand since it is 4ft 8½ins. The space between the tracks nowadays is normally 6ft 6ins.

18  In fact, the railway was still forced to open itself up to other carriers in 1831 but there were few takers given the complexity of trying to operate on a line largely used by the owners' trains. A similar difficulty still pertains today for freight operators seeking to use state-controlled railways in Europe.

19  Some references suggest this was a tramway with iron plates on which any road wagon could be pulled, rather than a proper railway that could be used only by specially designed vehicles.

20  Fortunately, the company was in financial difficulties which delayed construction and by the time the first section opened in 1835, locomotives were seen as the only viable option.

21  Apart from a brief three-year period in the 1870s, with just one train per day in each direction.

22  One of the inclines, the 1 in 14 Hopton, was operated after 1887 by steam locomotives, the steepest gradient on which conventional steam engines ever ran in the UK.

22  Nevertheless, *Sans Pareil* was fixed and proved to be a workable freight locomotive that spent many productive years on the Leigh & Bolton Railway.

24  The key feature was that the hot gases from the fire were passed through a large number of small tubes which vastly increased the evaporative surface.

25  There is no record of why Stephenson chose that name. It was then merely a description of a firework, occasionally used as a weapon of war, rather than a vehicle used for space travel.

26  There are also many replicas dotted around the world, including one at the National Rail Museum in York.

27  6 October 1829.

28 Quoted in Ferneyhough, *Liverpool & Manchester Railway*, p. 59.
29 Quoted in ibid., p. 64.
30 *The Times*, 17 September 1830.
31 Michael Freeman, *Railways and the Victorian Imagination*, Yale University Press, 1999, p. 31.
32 The Corn Laws, first introduced in 1815 and finally abolished in 1846, kept wheat prices artificially high, protecting landowners from foreign competition and making food more expensive.
33 Indeed, Britain is one of the few countries with a fenced railway, in contrast to, say, the United States where huge freight trains often rumble along main streets or even people's backyards.
34 In the introduction to Ferneyhough, *Liverpool & Manchester Railway*, p. xii.

## TWO: Getting the Railway Habit

1 Frank Ferneyhough, *Liverpool & Manchester Railway, 1830–1980*, Robert Hale, 1980, p. 105. Much of this information was still required for train journeys in India until relatively recently.
2 Ibid., p. 102.
3 It was not so much those opening the doors who were killed but people already on the platform, standing too near the trains.
4 Many passengers perished in this way at an accident in Versailles in France in May 1842 (see p. 147).
5 Quoted in many places. See, for example, Simon Garfield, *The Last Journey of William Huskisson*, Faber, 2002, p. 20.
6 Nicholas Faith, *The World the Railways Made*, Bodley Head, 1990, p. 15.
7 The three mainland Japanese railways are profitable, though they had huge debt write-offs at privatization in the 1980s, and US freight companies do very well thanks to the sheer distance involved in crossing the country. Freight in India and Russia is profitable too, but otherwise, while individual services may make a profit, the need for cross-subsidy means that throughout the world the vast majority of railway networks are loss-making.
8 Quoted in Ferneyhough, *Liverpool & Manchester Railway*, p. 93.
9 As the Bodmin & Wadebridge had been built to standard gauge, it was not directly connected to the rest of the network until 1892 when the Great Western's broad gauge was finally abandoned (as explained in Chapter 9).
10 *The Quarterly Review*, 1833, quoted in Frank Ferneyhough, *The History of Railways in Britain*, Osprey Publishing, 1975, p. 73.
11 Many of the arches are now being converted into upmarket restaurants and fashionable nightclubs.

### THREE: Joining Up Britain

1  There were specific reasons for this: Belgium was a new country, having just broken away from Holland, and the government was keen to establish its national identity through the creation of a railway network.

2  It claims to be the oldest surviving railway station, though sections of the Manchester terminus of the Liverpool & Manchester remain, incorporated as part of the Manchester Industrial Museum.

3  Quoted in Frank Ferneyhough, *History of the Railways*, Osprey Publishing, 1975, p. 71.

4  Overall, there were one hundred underbridges, fifty overbridges, five viaducts, two tunnels and two aqueducts.

5  Only for a few years, as in 1844 the improvement in locomotive technology allowed engines to climb the incline to Camden Town.

6  In *A Practical Treatise on Railways*, A &C Black, 1839.

7  Francis Coghlan, *The Iron Road Book*, 1838, reprinted by E. & W. Books, 1970, p. 32.

8  Both were tragically demolished, despite a huge protest, by British Railways in 1962 in the modernist mood of the times, and replaced by the current banal glass and concrete block which, hopefully, is soon to be redeveloped in turn.

9  Adrian Vaughan, *Railwaymen, Politics and Money*, John Murray, 1997, p. 180.

10  Michael Robbins, *The Railway Age*, Penguin, 1965, p. 67.

11  Quoted in Chris de Winter Hebron, *50 famous railwaymen*, Silver Link Publishing, 2005, p. 23.

12  The actual gauge was a quarter of an inch greater than 7ft, to allow the flanges to run unimpeded on the rails.

13  Rodney Weaver in *The Oxford Companion to British Railway History*, Oxford University Press, 1997, p. 25.

14  Early railways were limited to just 1 in 200, a very gentle slope.

### FOUR: Changing Britain

1  Known in the industry as 'recovery time', and which explains why trains often arrive at the terminus early. There is also a 'working timetable' that contains the real expected timings and includes all freight and other movements, and is quite different from the published timetable.

2  As we see in Chapters 11 and 13, the government took over the railways in both world wars, but under subsequent legislation.

3  Jack Simmons, *The Railways of Britain*, Macmillan, 1968, p. 11.

4  *The Oxford Companion to British Railway History* is slightly sceptical about this tale, suggesting that it was probably 'not a single train, but in a series run in succession'.

5   F. S. Williams, *Our Iron Roads: their history, construction and social influences*, Bemrose, 1852, p. 285.

6   Jack Simmons and Gordon Biddle (eds), *The Oxford Companion to Railway History*, Oxford University Press, 1997, p. 427.

7   Ibid.

8   Interestingly, the line was a long branch but in British Rail timetable maps it was always depicted as a main line, presumably out of deference.

9   Fears had been raised by the terrible accident and fire near Versailles in May 1842.

10  Reported in the *Morning Post*, quoted in W. M. Acworth, 'The railways in 1843', in Bryan Morgan (ed.), *Railway-Lover's Companion*, Eyre and Spottiswoode, 1963, p. 86.

11  Quoted in Acworth, 'The railways in 1843', in Morgan (ed.), *Railway-Lover's Companion*, p. 93.

12  *The Times*, 12 January 1850.

13  Quoted in Acworth, 'The railways in 1843', in Morgan (ed.), *Railway-Lover's Companion*, p. 91.

14  Quoted in Geoffrey Body, *The Railway Age: life and lines in the great age of railways*, Silver Link Publishing, 1982, p. 21.

15  Quoted in Acworth, 'The railways in 1843', in Morgan (ed.), *Railway-Lover's Companion*, p. 90.

16  Quoted in ibid.

17  David Harvey, *Consciousness and the Urban Experience*, Basil Blackwell, 1985, p. 28.

## FIVE: Railways Everywhere

1   Michael Freeman, *Railways and the Victorian Imagination*, Yale University Press, 1999, p. 98.

2   Figures for authorized mileage vary somewhat between sources because sometimes previously approved schemes were incorporated into new ones and the precise relationship between the two is not always clear.

3   Henry Grote Lewin, *The Railway Mania and its Aftermath*, 1936, reprinted by David & Charles, 1968, p. 18.

4   Ibid.

5   Christian Wolmar, *The Subterranean Railway: how the London Underground was built and how it changed the city forever*, Atlantic Books, 2004, p. 20.

6   Berlin and Paris ended up with similar arrangements of separate radial lines ending just outside the city centre, although Berlin opened its Hauptbahnhof, a genuine central railway station, in 2006.

7   The invisible line around central London was to be breached only by the London, Chatham and Dover railway, which broke into the City of London boundary to build stations at Ludgate Hill, Holborn Viaduct and Blackfriars.

8 Freeman, *Railways and the Victorian Imagination*, p. 98.
9 Jack Simmons, *The Victorian Railway*, Thames and Hudson, 1991, p. 254.
10 Freeman, *Railways and the Victorian Imagination*, p. 100.
11 Cited from a House of Commons report in John Francis, 'The mania and the crash', 1851, in Bryan Morgan (ed.) *The Railway-Lover's Companion*, Eyre and Spottiswoode, 1963, pp. 96–7.
12 Ibid., p. 96.
13 Ibid., pp. 95–6.
14 Although part of this mileage consists of the English portion of through routes from England.
15 Interestingly, the Trent Valley remains such an important line that work to expand it from two tracks to four began in 2004.
16 Terry Gourvish, *Mark Huish and the London & North Western Railway*, Leicester University Press, 1972, p. 23.
17 Details are contained in Lewin, *The Railway Mania and its Aftermath*, p. 86.
18 The tunnel which had been hewn through the chalk for the canal in 1824 caused trouble to the railway until 2004 when it was closed for a year to be relined at a cost of £35m.
19 Adrian Vaughan, *Railwaymen, Politics and Money*, John Murray, 1997, p. 116.
20 There is confusion in British railway terminology in that the West Coast route goes nowhere near the sea until one gets a view of Morecambe Bay near Carnforth, over 230 miles from London, and on the East Coast, from the Great Northern railway, the coast is first visible well north of Newcastle. However, we are stuck with this nomenclature and therefore it is used throughout this book.
21 Oddly enough, track record is not a railway expression but probably originated with horse racing.
22 Vaughan, *Railwaymen, Politics and Money*, p. 106.
23 Ibid.
24 O. S. Nock, *150 Years of mainline Railways*, David & Charles, 1980, p. 39.
25 This, rather confusingly, was a separate railway to the North Midland, one of the three railways which merged to create the Midland.
26 Lewin, *The Railway Mania and its Aftermath*, p. 357.
27 Quoted in Frank Ferneyhough, *The History of Railways in Britain*, Osprey Publishing, 1975, p. 88.
28 Jack Simmons, *The Railways of Britain*, Macmillan, 3rd edn, 1986.
29 Vaughan, *Railwaymen, Politics and Money*, p. 107.
30 They only began to be phased out once new ticket machines like the Omniprinter started to be used in 1959 and National Cash Register systems became commonplace in the 1960s.
31 Francis, 'The mania and the crash', in Morgan (ed.) *The Railway-Lover's Companion*, p. 99.

## SIX: The Big Companies: Great But Not Necessarily Good

1   The more direct route, used by the East Coast Line trains today, was fully opened in 1852.
2   Nicholas Faith, *The World the Railways Made*, Bodley Head, 1990, p. 22.
3   *Household Words*, Vol. 8, 1853/4, p. 412.
4   Terry Gourvish, *Mark Huish and the London & North Western Railway*, Leicester University Press, 1972.
5   E. T. McDermott, *History of the Great Western Railway*, Vol. 1, Ian Allen (reprint), 1982, p. 183.
6   See www.victorianstation.com/palace.html
7   The structure was later moved to Crystal Palace, which gave the park, the surrounding area and the football club their name, but burnt down in 1936.
8   About the same number who visited the far less successful Millennium Dome in 2000.
9   There is a list of the railways he built (which stretches to six densely typeset pages) in his biography, *The Life and Labours of Mr. Brassey, 1805–1870*, by Sir Arthur Helps (Bell and Daldy, 1872, reprinted by Tempus Books in 2006).
10  Introduction by Jack Simmons in Arthur Helps, *The Life and Labours of Mr. Brassey*, p. viii.
11  Gourvish in *Mark Huish and the London & North Western Railway* (p. 23), says that the cost per mile for railways across Britain averaged £31,000 in 1846, double the cost in Belgium, where the state planned and specified the railway system. This was a period of very low or even at times negative inflation.
12  One estimate suggests that by 1900 Manchester's railways had displaced between 41,000 and 55,000 residents.
13  Steven Marchs in J. Dyos and Michael Wolff (eds), *The Victorian City: Images and Realities*, Routledge & Kegan Paul, 1973, p. 269.
14  Jack Simmons, *The Railway in Town & Country, 1830–1914*, David & Charles, 1986, p. 34.
15  Jack Simmons, *The Victorian Railway*, Thames and Hudson, 1991, p. 40.
16  Jack Simmons, *The Railway in England & Wales, 1830–1914*, Leicester University Press, 1978.

## SEVEN: The Agatha Christie Railway

1   Locomotive and coach wheels are usually fitted with tyres which rather like those on cars are replaced when worn out.
2   In *Small Talk at Wreyland*, Cambridge University Press, 1918.
3   David St John Thomas, *The Country Railway*, David & Charles, 1976, p. 26.
4   Detailed in Brian Hardy, *Tube trains on the Isle of Wight*, Capital, 2003. Remarkably a very heavily loss-making section of 8.5 miles between Shanklin and Ryde survives today, operated by six two-car former London

Underground Tube trains (dating back to 1938).

5    St John Thomas, *The Country Railway*, p. 85.

6    Michael Robbins, *The Railway Age*, Penguin Books, 1965, p. 63.

7    St John Thomas, *The Country Railway*, p. 28.

8    Ibid., p. 9.

9    See J. Horsley Denton, 'Private Stations', in H. A. Vallance (ed.), *The Railway Enthusiast's Bedside Book*, B. T. Batsford, 1966.

10   Another more recent example is in the 1996 cult film *Trainspotting*, where the group of misfits are bemused to find themselves in a totally remote station in the Scottish countryside.

11   The other four were the Caledonian, the Glasgow & South Western, the Highland and the Great North of Scotland.

12   In fact, many canals were bought up by the railways to kill any chance of competition.

13   St John Thomas, *The Country Railway*, p. 121.

14   Ibid., p. 125.

15   C. Hamilton Ellis, *The Midland Railway*, Ian Allan, 1953, p. 72.

16   Ibid., p. 74.

17   Later reduced to 2d: see Christian Wolmar, *The Subterranean Railway*, Atlantic Books, 2004, pp. 54–6, for a detailed account.

18   Sir William Acworth, *The Railways of England*, London, 1889, p. 412.

19   R. M. Robbins, quoted in H. P. White, *A Regional History of the Railways of Great Britain*, Vol. 13, *Greater London*, David & Charles, 1963.

20   See Wolmar, *The Subterranean Railway*, for this story.

21   F. M. L. Thompson, *The Rise of Suburbia*, Leicester University Press, 1982, p. 69.

22   C. Hamilton Ellis, *British Railway History 1877–1947*, George Allen & Unwin, 1959, p. 61.

23   As opposed to grade-separated junctions which use under- or over-passes to reduce conflicting movements.

24   Adrian Vaughan, *Railwaymen, Politics and Money*, John Murray, 1997, p. 240.

25   C. Hamilton Ellis, *British Railway History*, Vol. 1, *1830–1876*, George Allen & Unwin, 1954, p. 241.

26   Services to and from Kent will, of course, be greatly speeded up when domestic services on the high-speed line start operating in 2009.

27   They could not quite bring themselves to agree a full merger and still retained their individual identity as subsidiaries of a large grouping until the creation of the Big Four in 1923.

28   Their rivalry was fiercest on the Circle Line, which was operated jointly by the two companies: one company provided the clockwise trains and the other the anti-clockwise ones. They both insisted on having their own booking offices, whose clerks would try to maximize their own company's business,

irrespective of whether that was the best option for the passenger, and might send them the long way around.

29  John Betjeman, *London's Historic Railway Stations*, John Murray, 1972, p. 97.

30  Ibid., p. 99.

31  Jack Simmons, *The Railway in Town & Country, 1830–1914*, David & Charles, 1986, p. 47.

32  Walter Dexter, *The Letters of Charles Dickens*, vol. 3, Bloomsbury Nonesuch, 1938, p. 445.

## EIGHT: Danger and Exploitation on the Tracks

1  Dr Crippen, who had murdered his wife, was caught despite travelling to America on a ship, thanks to radio signals being sent across the Atlantic requesting his arrest, the first time radio had been used in that way.

2  See O. S. Nock, *Historic Railway Disasters*, Ian Allan, 1966, p. 28, for a discussion of this issue.

3  As mentioned in a previous footnote, the working timetable is the one that shows the precise times of all trains, including specials, locomotives, goods and excursions, and frequently has different timings from those in the official public timetable.

4  L. T. C. Rolt, *Red for Danger*, The Bodley Head, 1955, p. 130.

5  That is, if something fails, then it automatically goes into safe mode, the most notable example being a signal.

6  See Adrian Vaughan, *Railwaymen, Politics and Money*, John Murray, 1997, p. 255.

7  Ibid., p. 258.

8  Compulsory primary education was not introduced until 1880.

9  R. S. Joby, *The Railwaymen*, David & Charles, 1984, p. 184.

10  Helena Wojtczak, *Railwaywomen*, Hastings Press, 2005, p. 360.

11  Previously, the poor victim would have to pay not only for the doctor's call-out but also the splints and bandages, on the assumption that it was always their fault.

12  Joby, *The Railwaymen*, p. 184.

13  It was originally created as an offshoot of the Railway Clearing House and only assumed the name of Railway Companies Association in 1869.

14  Quoted in Michael Freeman, *Railways & Victorian Imagination*, Yale, 1999, p. 191.

15  Frank McKenna, *The Railway Workers 1840–1970*, Faber & Faber, 1980, p. 153.

16  One of the more obscure developments brought about by the railways was the change from drinking ale out of pewter tankards, which were more suitable for the capital's stouts, to glasses.

17 For the first time ever, this can be seen by passengers as that area is now open to the public as part of the refurbished international station at St Pancras.

18 C. Hamilton Ellis, *The Midland Railway*, Ian Allan, 1953 (paperback edition, 1966), p. 63.

19 Jack Simmons, *The Railway in England and Wales, 1830–1914*, Leicester University Press, 1978, p. 84.

## NINE: Speeding to Danger

1 O. S. Nock, *150 years of mainline Railways*, David & Charles, 1980, p. 89.

2 Stanley Hall, *Railway Milestones and Millstones*, Ian Allan, 2006, p. 27.

3 C. Hamilton Ellis, *British Railway History, 1877–1947*, George Allen & Unwin, 1959, p. 17.

4 Ibid.

5 Ibid.

6 The death toll of passengers from accidents in the 1870s was 394, beating even the 1910s, total of 391, even though it included the worst-ever accident, at Quintinshill, in which 227 perished.

7 Before the introduction of continuous brakes, long passenger trains would generally have more than one guard's brake van.

8 They work in similar ways. With vacuum brakes, the pressure in the pipes is maintained lower than atmospheric pressure and application of the valve allows air in, applying the brakes. Air brakes have a higher pressure, and the valve releases air, reducing pressure and applying the brakes. Both are fail-safe systems because when the line is broken, the brakes come on automatically.

9 O. S. Nock, *Historic Railway Disasters*, Ian Allan, 1966, p. 51.

10 L. T. C. Rolt, *Red for Danger*, 4th edn, David & Charles, 1982, p. 163.

11 Jack Simmons, *The Railways of Britain*, 2nd edn, Macmillan, 1968, p. 165.

12 For once, the railway is taken as the default means of travel, as the neighbouring bridge for motor vehicles is called the Forth Road Bridge.

13 Roger Fulford, 'Racing to Scotland', in Bryan Morgan (ed.), *The Railway-Lover's Companion*, Eyre & Spottiswoode, 1963, p. 104.

14 Ibid., p. 107.

15 Nock, *Historic Railway Disasters*, p. 78.

16 Adrian Vaughan, *Railwaymen, Politics and Money*, John Murray, 1997, p. 191.

17 It was an even greater achievement than the figure of 213 miles suggests, since there was nearly twice that amount of actual track involved. Nothing approaching this scale of operation could be carried out today even with the greatly increased level of mechanization.

18 With the exception, since its opening in 2007, of the twelve-mile-long tunnel on the Channel Tunnel Rail Link between St Pancras and Barking, which has a brief open section about halfway at Stratford.

19 Vaughan, *Railwaymen, Politics and Money*, p. 231.

20 Although some commentators feel the times were suspect and the locomotive only reached 99 mph.

21 As named by *The Times*, cited in Nock, *150 Years of Mainline Railways*, David & Charles, 1980, p. 84.

22 *The Times*, 14 September 1895.

23 Alan A. Jackson, *London Termini*, Pan Books, 1972, p. 225. The present lavish station was not opened until after the First World War.

24 Hamilton Ellis, *British Railway History, 1877–1947*, p. 16.

25 Nock, *Historic Railway Disasters*, p. 80.

26 Ibid., p. 84.


## TEN: The Only Way to Get There

1 Jack Simmons, *The Railway in England and Wales 1830–1914*, Leicester University Press, 1978, p. 93.

2 John Pendleton in 'The Last Main Line', in *Our Railways* in *The Railway-lover's Companion*, Eyre & Spottiswoode, 1963 p. 111.

3 Ibid., p. 113.

4 Simmons, *The Railway in England and Wales 1830–1914*, p. 93.

5 Although a few heavily used freight routes were built in the twentieth century and lines were being built right up to the 1960s to serve new collieries and ironstone quarries.

6 John Betjeman, *London's Historic Railway Stations*, John Murray, 1972, p. 177.

7 With the completion of the Piccadilly, Bakerloo and Hampstead railway in 1906–7, no further line was built in central London until the Victoria line opened in 1968 and the Jubilee line completed in 1999.

8 Today, they are not much faster: even using high-speed trains with a top speed of 125 mph, most services, which have slowed since privatization so that companies can avoid being penalized for lateness, take around an hour and three quarters, but this does include stops as there are virtually no long-distance direct trains.

9 Now that route is usually covered at a rate of 100 mph.

10 Philip Unwin, *Travelling by Train in the Edwardian Age*, George Allen & Unwin, 1979, p. 13.

11 As some trains do today, such as at Watford for long-distance services leaving Euston.

12 The Lancashire & Yorkshire alone used three different systems.

13 Cited in Roger Burdett Wilson, *Go Great Western*, David & Charles, 1970, p. 24.

14 David St John Thomas, *The Country Railway*, David & Charles, 1977, p. 113.

15  Ibid.

16  Ibid., p. 107.

17  Ibid., p. 116.

18  Simmons, *The Railway in England and Wales 1830–1914*, p. 110.

19  Jack Simmons, *The Railways of Britain*, 3rd edn, Macmillan, 1986, p. 31.

20  The main line railways each had between £30m and £200m of capital by the turn of the century. Terry Gourvish in *Railways and the British Economy 1830–1914*, Studies in Economic and Social History, Macmillan, 1980, p. 9, says the capital of the railways in 1913 was £1,330m, with income of around £140m.

21  Gourvish, *Railways and the British Economy 1830–1914*, p. 10.

22  The Amalgamated Society of Railway Servants, the Associated Society of Locomotive Engineers and Firemen, the General Railway Workers' Union and the United Pointsmen and Signalmen.


## ELEVEN: Fighting Together – Reluctantly

1  Actually forty-eight smaller companies, out of the total of 178, were left to their own devices.

2  Adrian Vaughan, *Railwaymen, Politics and Money*, John Murray, 1997, p. 302.

3  Suggesting there was a bit of padding in the timetable, although that is normal practice on many parts of the rail network today.

4  Quoted in Vaughan, *Railwaymen, Politics and Money*, p. 302.

5  Quoted in C. Hamilton Ellis, *British Railway History 1877–1947*, George Allen & Unwin, 1959, p. 301.

6  Vaughan, *Railwaymen, Politics and Money*, p. 301.

7  Jack Simmons, *The Railways of Britain*, 3rd edn, Macmillan, 1986, p. 34.

8  Ibid., p. 35.

9  According to the local LibDem MP John Thurso, although the road is also considerably shorter in distance.

10  Oddly, it was allowed twenty-two hours southbound.

11  Another was built at Southampton.

12  This number includes wounded German prisoners of war.

13  Vaughan, *Railwaymen, Politics and Money*, p. 306.

14  Ibid., p. 304.

15  Ibid., p. 303.

16  Quoted in Frank Ferneyhough, *The History of Railways in Britain*, Osprey Publishing, 1975, p. 162.

17  The points had to be within 250 yards of their lever and the signals no more than two miles away.

18  Vaughan, *Railwaymen, Politics and Money*, p. 310. In order to protect their workers from the criticism that they were dodging military service – many railwaymen were insulted in the streets or sent white feathers – the companies

in both wars produced badges carrying the words 'Railway Service' to show the men were not cowards.

19  Although they comprised 29 per cent of the workforce at the outbreak of the war.

20  Helena Wojtczak, *Railwaywomen*, Hastings Press, 2005, p. 44.

21  Although some women did clean engines during the war, a job which normally was the first step on the ladder to becoming a driver, they were all forced out of these jobs soon after the armistice.

22  According to John Westwood in *Railways at War*, Osprey Publishing, 1980, p. 170, by the end of the war, fifty-two restaurant car services, a seventh of the pre-war total, survived.

23  O. S. Nock, *Historic Railway Disasters*, Ian Allan, 1966, p. 107.

24  The cost of living was then 106 per cent higher than at the start of the war.

25  Westwood, *Railways at War*, p. 165.

26  The rail companies had to pay 25 per cent of the early war bonus but later the government covered all the increase.

27  Wojtczak, *Railwaywomen*, p. 117.

28  Edwin Pratt, *British Railways and the Great War*, Selwyn & Blount, 1921.

29  Hamilton Ellis, *British Railway History 1877–1947*, p. 304.

30  Michael Bonavia, *The Four Great Railways*, David & Charles, 1980, p. 9.

31  C. F. Klapper, *Sir Herbert Walker's Southern Railway*, Ian Allan, 1973, p. 12.

32  Ibid., p. 93.

33  Vaughan, *Railwaymen, Politics and Money*, p. 317.

## TWELVE: Compromise – The Big Four

1   Adrian Vaughan, *Railwaymen, Politics and Money*, John Murray, 1997, p. 315.

2   This was a locospotters' paradise as there were 404 different classes of locomotives!

3   A very early use of this American term in a UK business.

4   C. Hamilton Ellis, *British Railway History, 1877–1947*, George Allen & Unwin, 1959, p. 329.

5   The initials of the LMS and the LNER are used throughout this chapter as these companies were commonly known by their acronyms.

6   Michael Bonavia, *The Four Great Railways*, David & Charles, 1980, p. 34.

7   Ibid., p. 66.

8   Hamilton Ellis, *British Railway History 1877–1947*, p. 321.

9   Third-rail systems are powered by d.c. (direct current) while overhead systems can use either direct current or alternating current (a.c.).

10  This was a factor in the 1999 Ladbroke Grove train crash where it is thought the driver of the Thames train that went through a red light had difficulty seeing the signal because of relatively new gantries installed for Heathrow Express services.

11 Jack Simmons, *The Railways of Britain*, 2nd edn, Macmillan, 1968, p. 38.

12 Cited in Hamilton Ellis, *British Railway History, 1877–1947*, pp. 325–6.

13 Today, with around a third of route mileage, the electrified proportion of the British network is well below that of comparable European countries, which average at least half and in some cases far more.

14 The Southern did receive government help in 1935 with a £45m loan towards its electrification programme.

15 Bonavia, *The Four Great Railways*, p. 6.

16 The unions representing miners, railway workers and dockers had formed a triple alliance vowing to support each other in the event of industrial action.

17 Hamilton Ellis, *British Railway History, 1877–1947*, p. 340.

18 Interestingly, today's figures are similar with 1.1bn journeys in 2005 on a much smaller network but with a far bigger population – though there is some double counting as now journeys involving a change are counted as two, which they were not in the days of the Big Four.

19 Philip Unwin, *Travelling by Train in the 'Twenties and 'Thirties*, George Allen & Unwin, 1981, p. 59.

20 I remember travelling on these trains as a boy in the 1950s and being served teacakes and scones by incredibly friendly and efficient waiters.

21 Unwin, *Travelling by Train in the 'Twenties and 'Thirties*, p. 14.

22 Quoted in Bonavia, *The Four Great Railways*, p. 100.

23 Geoffrey Freeman Allen, *The Illustrated History of British Railways*, Basinghall Books, 1981, p. 116.

24 Bonavia, *The Four Great Railways*, p. 110.

25 It was the modern version of that train which was involved in the Ladbroke Grove train disaster in which thirty-one people were killed in October 1999.

26 Pacific is the name given to engines based on the wheel arrangement of 4-6-2, which means there are four bogie wheels, six large driving wheels, and two trailing wheels at the back. This very common type of locomotive was first developed by the Southern Pacific in the USA.

27 Today's schedules give a best service from London to Glasgow at just under four and a half hours.

28 Unwin, *Travelling by Train in the 'Twenties and 'Thirties*, p. 61.

29 Don Hale, *Mallard*, Aurum Press, 2005, p. 44.

30 It has some similarities with Johnston, the typeface designed for the precursor of London Underground in 1915, and which, slightly updated as New Johnston, is still in use today.

31 The history is set out in Roger Burdett Wilson, *Go Great Western*, David & Charles, 1970.

32 Long before the idea of 'integrated' transport became a politicians' catchword.

33 Simmons, *The Railways of Britain*, p. 41.

34 For more detail on London Transport's 1930s heyday, see Christian Wolmar,

*The Subterranean Railway*, Atlantic Books, 2004, chapter 13, pp. 254 ff.

35 Simmons, *The Railways of Britain*, p. 42.


## THIRTEEN: And Then There Was One

1 It was intended to mean that munitions trains should have priority!

2 Helena Wojtczak in *Railwaywomen: exploitation, betrayal and triumph in the workplace*, Hastings Press, 2005, p. 185, cites the case of a woman signal worker who was receiving £5 10s after deductions compared with just £1 10s as a teacher.

3 Reg Robertson, *Steaming through the war years*, Oakwood Press, 1996, p. 5.

4 David Wragg, *Signal Failure*, Sutton Publishing, 2004, p. 100. The Great Western had, in fact, supplied the least, just forty compared with Southern's fifty-five.

5 C. Hamilton Ellis, *British Railway History, 1877–1947*, George Allen & Unwin, 1959, p. 377.

6 'Knowing the road' is essential for safety as the driver needs to know all the features of a track, such as the position of signals, the gradients and the curves, to be able to operate safely and therefore a driver is not allowed to be in control of a train on tracks where he has not been before.

7 There is a fantastically detailed article on compiling timetables by G. E. Williams in H. A. Vallance (ed.), *The Railway Enthusiast's Bedside Book*, B. T. Batsford, 1966, p. 33. The diagram was often done with the help of weighted strings pinned to the top of a board with the $x$ axis as time, and the $y$ axis the route, a simple but time-consuming effort.

8 Wojtczak, *Railwaywomen*, p. 151.

9 This is virtually the same number as in 2006. As mentioned in the previous chapter, today's network is about two thirds the size, while the population is nearly double, and of course the market share of the railways is now far smaller.

10 O. S. Nock quotes this himself in his *150 Years of Mainline Railways*, David & Charles, 1980, p. 134.

11 The formula was based on pre-war revenues and ranged from 34.3 per cent for LMS and 23.6 per cent for LNER to 15.5 for Great Western, 15.4 per cent for Southern and 11.2 per cent for London Transport.

12 Terry Gourvish, *British Railways 1948–1973*, Cambridge University Press, 1986, p. 16.

13 These figures are from the official history of British Railways: Terry Gourvish's *British Railways 1948–1973*, p. 5.

14 According to Terry Gourvish, precise financial and usage details during this period are difficult to obtain because of the complex accounting arrangements established by the government.

15 *Hansard*, House of Commons, 17 December 1946, Vol. 439, col. 1809.

16 Gourvish, *British Railways 1948–1973*, p. 27.

17  In compensation for the forgone profits in the war, and the damage caused to the railways, British Railways was eventually given around £210m for investment.

18  The name British Railways had no official status until the 1960s as the organization was technically the Railways Executive of the BTC.

19  My personal copy of the ABC is dated 1963, when there were still thousands of steam locomotives and 'bunking' a shed with its engines in steam and the complete absence of security was a memorable experience.


## FOURTEEN: An Undeserved Reputation

1  This chapter and the next one are covered in greater detail in my book on rail privatization, *On the Wrong Line*, published by Aurum Press, 2005.

2  Horses were still commonplace in the 1950s; our milkman in Kensington, West London, used one until the end of that decade.

3  Terry Gourvish, *British Railways 1948–1973*, Cambridge University Press, 1986, p. 5.

4  Michael Bonavia, *British Rail, the first 25 years*, David & Charles, 1981, p. 61.

5  Conversation with author.

6  Email to author.

7  The normal sequence of signals is double yellow, yellow and red. The yellows in effect warn of an impending red signal.

8  As mentioned in Chapter 12, AWS was not made mandatory until after the 1997 Southall disaster, when a train with a failed AWS crashed into a freight service, killing seven people.

9  The exchange rate in the 1940s was $4 to the pound but was then fixed at $2.80 in September 1949, representing a 30 per cent devaluation and consequent increase in the cost of oil, which was priced in dollars.

10  David Henshaw, *The Great Railway Conspiracy*, Leading Edge, 1991, p. 54.

11  Henshaw quotes a figure for steam haulage of just under a shilling per mile compared with 3¾d for diesel.

12  Henshaw, *The Great Railway Conspiracy*, p. 51.

13  Gerard Fiennes, *Fiennes on Rails, fifty years of railways*, David & Charles, 1986, p. 49.

14  Bonavia, *British Rail, the first 25 years*, p. 52.

15  Quoted in Gourvish, *British Railways 1948–1973*, p. 270.

16  Calculated by the Central Statistical Office and quoted in Gourvish, *British Railways 1948–1973*, p. 68.

17  If the railways'contribution to the British Transport Commission's central charges are included, the loss for 1959 is doubled to £84m.

18  See also Chapter 13. Nearly all, about 1,000 miles, were kept open for freight.

19  Of course Marples divested his shares when he was Minister of Transport – to his wife.

20 Anthony Sampson, *Anatomy of Britain Today*, Hodder & Stoughton, 1965, p. 582.

21 Henshaw, *The Great Railway Conspiracy*, p. 117.

22 Ibid.

23 The Buchanan report on traffic, published in 1963, specifically warned that new roads would inevitably clog up. Ministry of Transport, *Traffic in Towns* (The Buchanan Report), HMSO, 1963.

24 I have happy memories of travelling as a child to Louth from London by train on this line.

25 Henshaw, *The Great Railway Conspiracy*, p. 232.

26 Gerard Fiennes, *I tried to run a railway*, Ian Allan, 1967.

27 Jack Simmons and Gordon Biddle (eds), *The Oxford Companion to British Railway History*, Oxford University Press, 1997, p. 29.

28 Hunter Davies, *A walk along the tracks*, Weidenfeld and Nicolson, 1982, p. 11.

29 British Railways Board, *The Development of the Major Trunk Routes*, British Railways Board, 1965.

30 The shorter name began to be used widely from 1965 and was virtually universally applied by 1970.

31 Interestingly, Birmingham was reached from Paddington and Manchester from St Pancras, completely different routes to the main ones used today.

32 It was originally known as Inter-City.

33 Terry Gourvish, *British Railways 1974–1997*, Oxford University Press, 2002, p. 2.

34 If the trains could not have braked so efficiently, then the intervals between signals would have had to be increased, reducing the capacity of the rail network.

35 She is reckoned to have used them once during her premiership, a trip on the Gatwick Express to take a plane.

36 The eventual cost for the total refurbishment of the line would eventually be £1bn (at 1990 prices) but this represented remarkably good value in relation to the cost, post-privatization, of the West Coast modernization whose bill came in at £10bn.

37 There is some debate about whether it was the cheapness of the work or the use of Eurostar trains on the line that exerted greater pressure on the wires that caused the difficulties.

38 The first chairman of that name as, confusingly, the next one was also Sir Bob Reid.

39 For example, the Southern Region extensively modernized the Exeter–Salisbury line, which provided a good secondary route between London and the West Country, with colour light signals during the early 1960s improving the line speed. As soon as it was transferred to the Western, the service started being run down and tragically large sections were turned

into a single track, greatly reducing its capacity and usefulness.

40 Since there were far fewer railway workers, the percentage of those killed per 1,000 staff went down only by a half in that period, from 0.32 to 0.15.

41 This is explained in Andrew Dow, *Dow's Dictionary of Railway Quotations*, Johns Hopkins University Press, 2006, p. 278.

42 Philip S. Bagwell, *The Railwaymen: the history of the National Union of Railwaymen*, Vol. 2, *The Beeching Era and After*, George Allen & Unwin, 1982, p. 3.

43 Terry Gourvish, *British Railways 1974–1997*, Oxford University Press, 2002, p. 450.

## FIFTEEN: The Future is Rail

1 For a full explanation of the structure of today's railway and the privatization which brought it about, see Christian Wolmar, *On the Wrong Line, how ideology and incompetence wrecked Britain's railways,* Aurum Press, 2005.

2 Apart from a residuary body which looked after some historical property rights and responsibilities.

3 *Independent*, 6 July 1995.

4 *Independent*, 13 October 2002.

5 Another, Grand Central, started operations in 2007 with just six daily services.

6 Including all the electric and diesel multiple units and a few locomotives used to haul passenger trains.

7 The distinction between renewal and maintenance was arbitrary, and depended on whether the length of track needing repair was more or less than 500 feet long, and this split was to cause endless bureaucratic hassles and much extra expense.

8 This was changed by the Labour government to 1 per cent above the rate of inflation in January 2004.

9 This is examined in detail in Wolmar, *On the Wrong Line.*

10 Between the Potters Bar accident in May 2002 and the derailment of a Virgin Pendolino train in Cumbria in February 2007, resulting in the death of one woman, there were no passenger fatalities in train accidents caused by industry error, the longest such period in the train's history. The only other deaths of passengers in an accident during this period were at Ufton Nervet near Newbury (in 2004), caused by a driver committing suicide by deliberately leaving his car on the line. The other fatal accident in the privatization period (not mentioned in the main text), at Great Heck in 2001, was also caused by a car on the line.

11 The old Southern zone, effectively the lines of the Southern Region, was the only exception to this. It was run by a knowledgeable railwayman, Michael Holden, who, unlike his colleagues, did not panic and therefore did not impose many speed restrictions.

12  See Wolmar, *On the Wrong Line*, p. 182.

13  This includes the extra money being borrowed annually by Network Rail which had debts of £18bn by the end of September 2006 and no prospect of ever paying them off. The burden will therefore be borne eventually by the taxpayer when it is written off. See Roger Ford, 'Informed Sources', in *Modern Railways*, November 2006.

14  For a full analysis, see Wolmar, *On the Wrong Line*, chapters 13–15.

15  For example, only some lines are electrified and there are two systems, third rail and overhead catenary, while different types of trains are required for long distance, regional, commuter and branch line services.

16  However, this seemed a case of trying to bolt the stable door too late. The contracts mostly had come up for renewal in 2004 and yet the Strategic Rail Authority sanctioned the new deals at the same high prices. See Wolmar, *On the Wrong Line*, pp. 275ff.

17  Interview with author, quoted in Wolmar, *On the Wrong* Line, p. 339.

18  David Willetts, a long-time senior Tory MP, admitted in a *Daily Telegraph* interview, 13 December 2003, that the privatization had been 'ideologically-driven' and a mistake. In 2006, the Shadow Transport Secretary, Chris Grayling, suggested that vertical integration – bringing back together operations and infrastructure – was the most desirable solution.

19  Though this is an area where the railways need to improve further as the technology has not kept pace with parallel developments in road transport. See, for example, Christian Wolmar, 'Rail needs to improve its efficiency', *Transport Times*, 10 November 2006.

20  Tyndall Centre for Climate Change, *Living within a Carbon Budget*, September 2006, executive summary, p. 9.

21  There is a debate about whether aviation is safer than trains, which rests on what assumptions are made and what factors are taken into account. Planes, for example, are most at risk on take-off and landing, and therefore air travel becomes statistically safer if long-haul journeys are considered. Moreover, on the railways, accidents to passengers falling down stairs at stations are included in statistics while the equivalent deaths at airports are not.

# FURTHER READING

As mentioned in the introduction, there are over 25,000 titles listed in George Ottley's *A Bibliography of British Railway History* and therefore this bibliography can only skim the surface of what is available. Even to list all the sources I have used to research the material in this book would take up rather too much space and therefore this list only includes those which were particularly useful or relevant.

I also made heavy use of the internet but I think it is futile to suggest any particular sites as most of the material can be found quickly via Google or Wikipedia. While the normal disclaimers concerning the internet apply, it is noticeable that these apply to books too, as on numerous occasions I found references that were contradictory or inaccurate – O. S. Nock in particular is a serial offender but he also provides much that is helpful. Like this book, my list focuses on the wider history of the railways which is likely to be of interest to the general reader rather than on technological developments or historical details that are mainly of interest to rail enthusiasts. This list also tries to avoid the coffee-table-type books which have more pictures than text and the histories of individual lines that often have a tendency to focus on technical detail rather than on the wider effect of their construction. In sum, therefore, this is very much a personal offering intended to stimulate interest in further reading rather than an attempt to be comprehensive.

In terms of a general history, there is no recent work, which is one of the reasons why this book has been written. There are a few older volumes that provide excellent outlines, notably several books by Jack Simmons. His *The Railways of Britain* (Macmillan, 1986) is an update of his 1961 book of the same title (published by Routledge & Paul) and his *The Victorian Railway* (Thames & Hudson, 1991) is a comprehensive account of how the railways influenced the Victorian era. Simmons also wrote *The Railway in England & Wales 1830–1914* (Leicester University Press, 1978), which curiously is listed as Volume one when no second volume ever appeared. He did, though, later produce *The Railway in Town & Country 1830–1914* (David & Charles, 1986), which again provides great detail on the effect of the railway throughout Britain. Simmons also co-edited, with Gordon Biddle, *The Oxford Companion to British Railway History* (Oxford University Press, 1997), which is a rather soulless but useful volume that has a relatively small number of longish entries that inevitably fail to be comprehensive but do provide very useful potted histories. Frank Ferneyhough, *The History of Railways in Britain* (Osprey Publishing, 1975) has many useful lists. The two volumes of C. Hamilton Ellis, *British Railway History* (George Allen & Unwin, 1954–9), are the most entertaining of these early histories and cover 1830–76 and 1877–1947 respectively. Among the numerous writings of O. S. Nock, there is *The Railways of Britain* (revised edition, B. T. Batsford, 1962) and *The Railway Enthusiast's Handbook* (Arrow Books, 1970), which contain a lot of basic information. Adrian Vaughan's *Railwaymen, Politics and Money* (John Murray, 1997) is a bold attempt at covering the great age of railways.

There are two books with similar titles which provide much of the wider context for the early railways: *The Railway Age* (Routledge & Kegan Paul, 1962; Penguin, 1965) by Michael Robbins, and Harold Perkin's *The Age of the Railway* (Panther, 1970). Nicholas Faith's *The World the Railways Made* (The Bodley Head, 1990) also looks at the effect of the railways on wider society as does Michael Freeman's particularly well-referenced *Railways and the Victorian Imagination* (Yale University, 1999).

The history of the Liverpool & Manchester Railway is well documented in *Liverpool & Manchester Railway 1830–1980* by Frank Ferneyhough (Robert Hale, 1980) and in Simon Garfield's elegant *The Last Journey of William Huskisson* (Faber & Faber, 2002). There are numerous accounts of the big companies that emerged in the later Victorian period, such as *The Midland Railway* by C. Hamilton Ellis

(Ian Allan, 1953) and Terry Gourvish's *Mark Huish and the London & North Western Railway: a study of management* (Leicester University Press, 1972). A series of books on 150 years of various lines was published by David & Charles, among them *LMS 150: The London Midland & Scottish Railway* written by Patrick Whitehouse and David St John Thomas (1987). Hunter Davies's entertaining *George Stephenson* (Weidenfeld & Nicholson, 1975) is one of the best railway biographies. Potted histories of many of the railway pioneers can be found in *50 Famous Railwaymen* by Chris de Winter Hebron (Silver Link, 2005). The development of Scottish railways is covered in *Battle for the North* by Charles McKean (Granta, 2006).

There is an entertaining series that shows what travelling on the railways was like in the pre-motor car age: *Travelling by Train in the Edwardian Age* (George Allen & Unwin, 1979) and *Travelling by Train in the 'Twenties and 'Thirties*(George Allen & Unwin, 1981), both by Philip Unwin. In this vein there is also *Victorian and Edwardian Railway Travel* by Jeoffry Spence (Fitzhouse, 1977).

The inter-war period is well covered by Michael Bonavia's *The Four Great Railways* (David & Charles, 1980) and there are various books on the individual companies such as *Sir Herbert Walker's Southern Railway* by C. F. Klapper (Ian Allan, 1973). The speeding up of the railway in this period is depicted well in *Mallard* (Aurum Press, 2005) by Don Hale. *Go Great Western* by Roger Burdett Wilson (David & Charles, 1970) is a rare account of a railway company's publicity machine.

Terry Gourvish has covered the business history of British Railways in two large thoroughly researched and official volumes, *British Railways, 1948–73: a business history* (1986) and *British Rail, 1974–97: from integration to privatization* (2002), which are published respectively by Cambridge and Oxford University Press. Gerard Fiennes wrote the classic *I tried to run a railway* about his career (Ian Allan, 1967) at British Railways (for which he was sacked) as well as the lesser-known but equally entertaining *Fiennes on Rails: fifty years of railways* (David & Charles, 1986). Michael Bonavia covers the early history of BR in *British Rail: the first 25 years* (David & Charles, 1981). The Beeching scandal is brilliantly exposed in *The Great Railway Conspiracy* by David Henshaw (Leading Edge, 1991).

My book, *On the Wrong Line: how ideology and incompetence wrecked Britain's Railways* (Aurum Press, 2005) details the story of privatization and its aftermath, and Nigel G. Harris and Ernest Godward's *The Privatisation of British Rail* (Railway Consultancy Press, 1997) has many useful figures. The rather more official version is provided in *All Change: British Railway Privatisation,* edited by Jon Shaw and Roger Freeman (McGraw Hill, 2000). *The InterCity Story* (Oxford Publishing, 1994), edited by Mike Vincent and Chris Green, outlines one of BR's great success stories. E. A. Gibbins has written several books on the unfairness of government policy towards the railways and BR in particular, including *Britain's Railways – The Reality* (Leisure Products, 2003), and while they are rather impenetrable, their wealth of information is invaluable. David Wragg's *Signal Failure: politics & Britain's railways* is another rare book on railway politics (Sutton Publishing, 2004) and he has also written a useful account, *Wartime on the Railways* (Sutton Publishing, 2006).

There is a huge literature on accidents of which the most famous is L. T. C. Rolt's *Red for Danger: a history of railway accidents and railway safety* (4th edn, David & Charles, 1982). There are eight volumes of a pictorial series on railway accidents entitled *Trains in Trouble* by various authors, published in the 1980s by Atlantic Books (not the current publisher), which is very comprehensive. Stanley Hall's *Danger Signals* (Ian Allan, 1987) and *Hidden Dangers* (Ian Allan, 1999) cover more recent disasters.

On the navvies, the lively *The Railway Navvies: a history of the men who made the railways* (Hutchinson, 1965, reprinted by Pimlico, 2000) by Terry Coleman remains the best account, but *The Railway Builders* by R. S. Joby (David & Charles, 1983) is also worth reading. Joby's *The Railwaymen* (David & Charles, 1984) provides background on the early workers in the industry and another good account is *The Railway Workers, 1840–1970* by Frank McKenna (Faber & Faber, 1980). The best biography of a contractor is the *Life and Labours of Mr. Brassey* by Sir Arthur Helps, originally published in 1872 and reprinted by Tempus Books in 2006.

The history of the unions can be found in the two volumes of *The Railwaymen: the history of the National Union of Railwaymen* by

Philip Bagwell (George Allen & Unwin, 1963 and 1982) and *ASLEF 1880–1980* by Brian Murphy, which was published by the union itself.

There are countless accounts of their life on the railway by staff of all grades. Those I enjoyed include *Tales of the Old Railwaymen* by Tom Quinn (David & Charles, 1998), which is a collection of over a dozen such lifetime stories, and *Small Coal and Smoke Rings* (John Murray, 1983), which is written by a Great Western fireman, Derek Brock, as is *Firing Days* by Harold Gasson (Oxford Publishing Company, 1973). *The Memories and Writings of a London Railwayman* is based partly on an oral history stretching back to the early twentieth century (edited by Alan Jackson, Railway & Canal Historical Society, 1993). John Farrington's *Life on the Lines* (Moorland Publishing, 1984) was compiled from a wide variety of conversations with railway workers, and Graham Zeitlin's *Staying on Track* (Scotforth Books, 2002) is a manager's account of life at BR. The previously neglected story of women in the railway industry has been covered comprehensively in the excellent *Railwaywomen: exploitation, betrayal and triumph in the workplace* by Helena Wojtczak (Hastings Press, 2005).

On stations, *London's Termini* by Alan A. Jackson (David & Charles, 1969) is a good start, while David St John Thomas evokes all the romanticism of rural railways and branch lines in *The Country Railway* (David & Charles, 1976). John Betjeman wrote the evocative *London's Historic Railway Stations* (John Murray, 1972). Two anthologies I stumbled upon are full of priceless detail and serendipity: *The Railway Enthusiast's Bedside Book*, edited by H. A. Vallance (Batsford, 1966) and *The Railway-Lovers Companion*, edited by Bryan Morgan (Eyre & Spottiswoode, 1963). Two more recent entertaining compilations of the good and the bad of the railway are: *Railway Blunders* by Adrian Vaughan (Ian Allan, 2003) and *Railway Milestones and Millstones* by Stanley Hall (Ian Allan, 2006).

For a wider history of transport, there is *British Transport: an economic survey from the seventeenth century to the twentieth* by H. J. Dyos and D. H. Aldcroft (Leicester University Press, 1969). The thorough *Dow's Dictionary of Railway Quotations* by Andrew Dow (Johns Hopkins University Press, 2006) is an indispensable reference book. Finally, for material written up to the late 1960s, the bibliography by E. T. Bryant, *Railways: A Readers' Guide* (Clive Bingley, 1968) is comprehensive and provides potted outlines of many of the books it lists. And obviously for anything missed out above, there is George Ottley, whose original work has been supplemented by a revised volume and two supplements: *A Bibliography of British Railway History* (George Allen & Unwin, 1965); *A Bibliography of British Railway History* (2nd edn, HMSO, 1983); *A Bibliography of British Railway History: Supplement: 7951–12956* (HMSO, 1988); *Ottley's Bibliography of British Railway History*; and *Second supplement 12957–19605* (National Railway Museum with Railway & Canal Historical Society, 1998).

# INDEX

ABC railway guide, 77
Aberayron & New Quay
   Light Railway, 226
Aberdeen, 81, 119, 128,
   230, 240, 270; and
   railway races, 173–5
Abergavenny, 129
Abergele, 151
accidents, 50–2, 138,
   147–52, 155, 265, 272,
   307–8, 337; Armagh,
   166–70; Tay Bridge,
   170–2; Preston, 175–7;
   Salisbury, 179–80;
   Quintinshill, 217–19;
   Southall, 235; and
   General Strike, 242;
   Harrow and
   Wealdstone, 272;
   Clapham Junction, 297;
   Hatfield, 307–8
Adley, Robert, 303
Advanced Passenger Train,
   291
aeroplanes and air
   transport, 198, 316,
   318
Agar Town, 117–18
Albert, Prince, 80–1, 112
Aldershot, 179, 208
Allan, Ian, 268
Allen, Cecil J., 244
Allen, Geoffrey Freeman,
   245

Allport, James, 132
Alton, 239
Amalgamated Society of
   Railway Servants
   (ASRS), 159–60, 200–1,
   204
Amalgamated Society of
   Railway Servants of
   Scotland, 199
ambulance trains, 210–11,
   214, 260
Amersham, 259
Annesley, 182
aqueducts, 63
Armagh accident, 147,
   166–70, 187
armoured trains, 260
*Arrow*, 38
Arundel, 236
Ashford, 136, 141
Ashton-under-Lyne, 86
Asquith, Herbert, 220
Associated Society of
   Locomotive Engineers
   and Fireman (ASLEF),
   160, 204, 215, 220–1,
   241, 254, 292, 294
Aston Hall, 62
*Athenaeum*, 75
atmospheric railways, 71,
   74
Attlee, Clement, 270, 276,
   282
Austria, 294

Automatic Train Control,
   235
Automatic Warning
   System, 235, 272
Avon, river, 35
Aylesbury, 182
Ayton, Richard, 8

Badminton station, 190
Baker, Benjamin, 172
Baker Street station, 183
Balaklava Railway, 206
Baldwin, Stanley, 241
Ballater, 81
balloons, 26, 74
Ballydehob, 131
Balmoral, 81–2, 171
Bank of England, 60, 105,
   144
banking system, 60–1, 144
Barlow, William, 120
Barnes, Alfred, 270
Barnsley, 163
Barrow-in-Furness, 120
Basingstoke, 73, 208, 297
Bass, Michael Thomas,
   159
Bath, 68, 104, 178
Batty Green, 163
BBC, 264
Beasley, Ammon, 201
Beaufort, Duke of, 190
Beckenham, 136
Beckton, 140

Bedford–St Pancras line, 294

Beeching, Richard, 282–4, 286, 316

Beeching cuts, 95, 124, 184, 196–7, 273–4, 277, 279, 282–8, 290, 294, 313

'Beer Trains', 234

Belfast, 130

Belgium, 60, 75, 194

Belmont station, 155

benevolent funds, 149

Benge, John, 150–1

Berkhamsted, 63

Berks & Hants line, 93, 190, 257

Berwick, 93, 128, 161

Bethnal Green, 261–2

Betjeman, John, 139–40, 185, 281

Bevan, Aneurin, 270

Bexleyheath, 238

Bickley loop, 190

Billingsgate Market, 141

Birkenhead, 177, 185

Birmingham, 67, 93, 108; railway connections, 56, 61–2, 64, 75, 111, 188; Curzon Street station, 62; New Street station, 62; London services, 76, 77, 110, 119, 188, 190, 216, 230, 288; and postal service, 83; fish deliveries, 84; suburban railways, 93; railway access, 117–18; workmen's trains, 134; and electrification, 279

Birmingham & Derby Junction Railway, 66, 75, 97

Bishop Auckland, 11

Bishop's Castle Railway, 197

Bishop's Stortford, 242

Bishopsgate station, 100

Blackfriars station, 139, 260, 324

Blair, Tony, 306

Blea Moor tunnel, 162

Blenkinsop, John, 13

Bletchley, 187

Bletchley flyover, 277

Blisworth, 95

Blitz, 258–9, 262

block working, 148–9, 152, 169–70

*Blucher*, 14

Blue Pullmans, 288, 291

Blumenfeld, R. D., 237

boat trains, 137, 150, 179–80

Bodmin, 57–8

Bodmin & Wadebridge Railway, 57–8, 76

Boer War, 206

boilers, 51; multi-tube, 37

Bolton, 42

Bolton & Leigh Railway, 56

*Bon Accord*, 270

Bonavia, Michael, 224, 234, 240, 275

Booth, Henry, 27, 104

Boston, 100, 285

Bouch, Thomas, 171–2

Boulogne, 80

Bournemouth, 178, 184

*Bournemouth Belle*, 244

Bourneville, 134

Boulton, Matthew, 3

Box tunnel, 68, 71

Bradford, 74, 132

Bradshaw, George, 77

Bradshaw, Robert, 24–6, 29

Bradshaw's rail guide, 77

braking systems, 167–70, 187

Branch Line Committee, 280

branch lines, 122–7,

194–7; closures, 215, 219, 250, 280–1, 283–6

Brassey, Thomas, 63, 115–16, 123

Brecon, 129

*Brentwood Gazette*, 255

Bridges, Frank, 262

Bridgwater, Duke of, 24, 29, 53

Bridgwater canal, 24, 53

Bridgwater, Frome & Central Somerset Railway, 95

Briggs, Asa, 22

Brighton, 28, 95, 280; London services, 76, 80, 136, 140, 178, 256, 270; electrification of line, 237–9

*Brighton Belle*, 244

Bristol, 56, 67, 93, 95, 102, 120, 257; time in, 104; London services, 179, 188, 230, 257, 289, 293, 295; Temple Meads station, 188; Parkway station, 190

Bristol & Exeter Railway, 93

British Electric Traction, 250

British Expeditionary Force, 206–7, 256

British Rail, 77, 108, 226, 241, 287–99, 308–9, 312–13; and Settle & Carlisle line, 161–2, 287–8; marketing, 289–90, 293; finances, 290–1, 294, 298; workforce, 292, 299; industrial relations, 295; reorganization, 296; safety record, 297; and privatization, 302–4

British Railways (BR), 240, 263–4, 269–87;

and horses, 232, 269;
interest payments, 267;
regions, 268–9, 273;
staff numbers, 269, 278;
and safety, 272–3;
switch from steam,
273–9, 286; freight
wagons, 275, 278; livery
and insignia, 275–6;
modernization
programme, 276–80,
283; finances, 280, 282;
route miles, 280; see
also British Rail
British Railways Board,
282, 294–5, 298
British Transport
Commission, 263,
266–7, 269, 273,
275–7, 280, 282, 292
British Transport Hotels,
120
Brixton, 191
broad gauge, 69–70, 77,
93, 108, 176; see also
standard gauge
Broad Street station, 188,
191
broccoli trains, 141
Bromley, 136
Brontë sisters, 105
Brookwood, 143
Broun, Sir Richard, 143
Brown, Ernest, 254
Brown, Patrick, 303
Broxbourne & Hertford
Railway, 124
Brunel, Isambard
Kingdom, 67–71, 77
Brunel, Marc, 67
Brussels, 8, 120, 315
Buchan, John, 128
Buckinghamshire, 133,
181
buffet cars, 184, 188; see
also dining (restaurant)
cars

Buntingford, 124
Burkhardt, Ed, 312
Burstall, Timothy, 37
buses, 165, 180, 185, 198,
253; alternative to
branch lines, 198, 283,
286; competition with
railways, 244–5, 315;
coordination with
railways, 249–51
Bushey, 183
butter, 85, 126
Buxton, Sidney, 204
Byers, Stephen, 308
by-laws, railway, 49

C2C, 300
cable operation, 27, 34–6,
57, 64, 66, 74, 191
Caledonian Railway, 155,
171; and railway races,
165–6; industrial
relations, 199; and
Quintinshill accident,
217–19; and
amalgamation, 227
Cambrian Railway, 160
Cambridge, 76, 124, 234;
see also Oxford–
Cambridge line
Cambridgeshire, 261
Camden Town, 66, 117
Camel, river, 58
Cameron Highlanders, 212
Cameroon, 294
Canada, 144
canals, 22–3, 29, 31, 35,
110, 129–30; and
opposition to railways,
24–6, 53; decline of,
53–4
Cannon Street station,
139, 272
Canterbury, 57, 136
Canterbury & Whitstable
Railway, 74
Capitals Limited, 270

Cardiff, 129, 190, 230
Cardwell, Edward, 114
Carlisle, 128, 161,
217–18; see also Settle
& Carlisle line
Carmarthenshire, 212
carriages, 44–5, 65–6, 70,
137–8, 164–5; first-
class, 44–5, 47, 65–6;
lighting, 47, 164–5,
188, 245, 257; second-
class, 48, 65, 132;
smoking, 48, 188, 244;
slam-door, 49; fourth-
class, 78; royal, 82;
building, 113, 233;
branch line, 126; third-
class, 132, 147; deluxe,
132–3; heating, 146,
165, 177, 245; sprung-
wheel, 163; corridors,
164–5, 177, 184,
187–8; toilets, 165, 188;
clerestory roofs, 177,
187; express, 187; and
wartime, 216–17; LMS,
233; Southern, 236,
239; women's, 239;
open-plan, 245; post-
war, 264–5; scrapped,
283; air-conditioning,
288, 293, 296, 317;
Marks 1 and 2, 289
cars, 3–5, 180, 228, 232,
251–3, 263; competition
with rail, 280, 292; age
of, 276, 289
Carstairs, 128
Carter Paterson, 250
Castle, Barbara, 287
Castle Cary, 190
Catch Me Who Can, 13
Catesby tunnel, 183
cattle, 72, 85, 278
cemeteries, 143
Central Electricity Board,
264

Chambers, Doctor, 38
Channel Islands, 179
Channel Tunnel, 107, 184, 314
Channel Tunnel Rail Link, 185, 314–15, 329
Charing Cross station, 139
chariots, 11
Charles II, King, 102
*Charlotte Dundas* (steam-powered boat), 3
Chartist disturbances, 83
Chat Moss, 25, 28, 33, 38, 52
Chatham, 94, 191, 239
cheese, 84, 86, 126
Cheltenham, 95
*Cheltenham Flyer*, 245
Chepstow, 93
Cheshire, 74, 84, 170
Cheshunt, 9
Chester, 76, 111, 129
Chester & Crewe Railway, 73
Chester & Holyhead Railway, 76
Chichester, 195, 236
Chigwell, 135
Chiltern, 296
Chippenham, 104
Chislehurst, 186, 191
cholera, 143
Christie, Agatha, 127
Church Fenton, 176
Churchill, Winston, 203, 224, 249, 276
Churchward, George, 178, 234
City & South London Railway, 173, 191
*City of Truro*, 178, 234, 247
Clapham, 186
Clapham Junction accident, 297
Clayton tunnel accident, 148–9

clergy, 91, 182
Clifton Suspension Bridge, 67
closures, 196–7, 250, 280–7; *see also* Beeching cuts
Clyde, river, 199
coaches, gas-powered, 26–7
coal, 43, 84, 266, 273, 312; prices, 9–10, 16, 24, 53, 125–6, 141; versus coke, 122; industry, 129, 231, 264; cheap or free, 154; and wartime, 210, 253; and strikes, 231, 242; and BR losses, 282
coal trains, 116, 141, 193, 274
coal wagons, 275, 283
Coalbrookdale, 4
Coalville, 57
Coghlan, Francis, 65–6
Colchester, 99
Coleman, Terry, 31
*Comet*, 248
commuter services, 27, 58, 108, 131–6, 140, 186, 280, 295–7; and electrification, 191, 235–9, 279; and Southern Railway, 234–5; and strikes, 292
Compagnie du Chemin de Fer du Nord, 112, 138
Connex, 309
Conservative Party, 276, 281, 290, 293–4; and privatization, 298, 301–3, 312–13
Conway, 129
Cook, Thomas, 79
Cooper, Sir Astley, 63
Co-operative Wholesale Society, 221
Corinth, Isthmus of, 1

Corn Laws, 41, 106–7
*Cornish Riviera*, 192
Cornwall, 2, 57, 93, 126, 141, 197, 258
*Coronation*, 247
*Coronation Scot*, 247
cottages, railway, 46, 153
cotton, 21–2, 57, 106
Coulsdon, 178
County Donegal Railways, 274
County Durham, 9, 16
courts of inquiry, 152
Covent Garden, 126
Coventry, 61
Craven Arms, 197
Creevey, Thomas, 28, 38, 53
Crewe, 73, 114, 174, 187
cricket, 182–3
Crimean War, 116, 206
Crippen, Dr, 148
Cromarty Firth, 208–9
Cromford & High Peak Railway, 35
cross-Channel steamers, 120, 150, 244
CrossCountry, 241
Crossrail, 316
Croydon, 7, 136; airport, 250
Croydon Tramlink, 319
Crystal Palace, 8, 112, 142, 238, 326
Cubitt, Lewis, 120
Cugnot, Nicolas, 3
Cumbria, 286
cut-offs, 190
*Cycloped*, 36

*Daily Telegraph*, 303
Dalhousie, Lord, 89–90
Dalton, Hugh, 266
Dandridge, Cecil, 248
dandy cars, 35
Darling, Alistair, 311
Darlington, Earl of, 10

Darlington, 11–12, 15–17, 76–7, 84, 188
Dartford, 238, 271
Dartmoor, 124
Dawlish, 285
Day Scotch Express, 166
Dee, river, 170
Deeside, 173
demolitions, 117–18, 133, 183, 187
Denison, Edmund, 96, 100
Denmark, 184
department stores, 142
Derby, Lord, 25, 28
Derby, 77, 79, 84, 97, 114; railway hotel, 120; workshops, 279, 292
Derbyshire, 126
Devil's Dyke line, 280
Devon, 126
Dickens, Charles, 109, 144; and Staplehurst accident, 147, 150–1
Didcot, 152
diesel multiple units, 274–5, 279, 281
Dingwall & Skye Railway, 128
dining (restaurant) cars, 69, 133, 164, 177, 187, 243, 269; withdrawn in wartime, 216, 258; see also buffet cars
Direct Northern Railway, 100
'direct' railways, 95
Disraeli, Benjamin, 144–5
doctors, 154
dogs, fares for, 65
Doncaster, 100, 268, 293; decoy goods yard, 260
Dorking, 238
Dorset, 207
double-decker trains, 271, 316
Dousland, 124
Dover, 136–8, 140, 210

Down Street station, 254
Drax power station, 312
Druimachdar Pass, 209
Dublin, 74, 130, 187
Dublin & Kingstown Railway, 57
Dundee, 57, 76, 171, 173
Dunkirk, 256
Dunrobin, 127
Durham, 24
Dutton viaduct, 63

Ealing, 135
Earls Court, 142
East Anglia, 99, 115, 233
East Coast main line, 76, 96, 99, 128, 163, 179, 233, 288, 295; and railway races, 165–6, 173–5; and accidents, 177, 308; expresses, 229, 242; publicity, 248; and wartime, 257, 260; electrification, 279, 289, 294–5; increased speeds, 289; high-speed trains introduced, 293
East India Company, 109
East Kent Railway, 136–7
East Lothian, 227
East Suffolk branch line, 285
Eastbourne, 80, 189, 238
Eastern Counties Railway, 76, 85, 99–100, 102, 131, 133; industrial relations, 157–8
Eastern Region, 277
Eastleigh, 141
Eccles, 40
Economist, The, 266–7
Eddington, Rod, 315
Edinburgh, 5, 21, 57, 74, 161; connection with Glasgow, 76, 82, 128, 199; suburban railways, 93, 128; London

services, 119, 166, 216, 230, 243, 246–7, 270, 289; and Forth Bridge, 172–3; accident, 242
Edinburgh & Berwick Railway, 99
Edinburgh & Glasgow Railway, 78, 83
Edinburgh Chronicle, 82
Edmondson, Thomas, 103–4
Edmonton, 134
Edward I, King, 129
Edward VII, King, 172
Eglinton, Lord, 83
Eiffel Tower, 142, 181, 184
Eldon, Lord, 10
electric telegraph, 102, 148
electrification, 191, 227, 231, 233, 264, 316–17; Southern Railway, 235–40, 244, 274; under BR, 274, 277, 294
Elgin, 128
Elizabethan, 270
Elliot, James, 168
Elliott, John Blumenfeld, 237
Ellis, Hamilton, 132, 136, 138, 162, 179, 236
Ely, 76, 100
emergency cords, 177
Employers' Liability Act, 159
Engine Drivers' and Firemen's United Society, 159
English Welsh and Scottish (EWS), 312
Epping, 186
Epsom, 158
Ericsson, John, 37
Esbjerg, 184
Essex marshes, 196

Eston, 133
Eton College, 68
European Commission, 317
Eurostar, 120, 315, 336
Eurotunnel, 185
Euston station, 13, 61, 77, 95, 99, 103, 108, 188, 216, 243–4; incline and cable operation, 64, 66; grandeur of old station, 66, 109, 185, 290; and Great Western Railway, 67–8; access to, 117; hotel, 119; and railway races, 166, 173–4; new layout, 187; military trains, 209; need for 'double headers', 232; compared with St Pancras, 240; smells, 240; rush-hour traffic, 272; rebuilding, 290
evacuations, wartime, 255–6
*Evening Standard*, 298
*Evening Star*, 273
excursion trains, 79–80, 112–13, 148, 216, 242–3; and Armagh accident, 168–9
Exeter, 5, 71, 177, 179, 285, 336; London services, 77, 93, 189, 230, 248
*Experiment*, 16
Express County Milk Supply Company, 141
express trains, 177, 187–8, 229, 293

Fairlop, 135
Faith, Nicholas, 54
Falkirk, 82
Falmouth, 93
fares, 44, 65, 82, 94, 242–3, 318; regulation,

78, 126, 131, 146, 202, 223, 228, 242; below-cost, 111; pooling system, 111; price competition, 112, 139, 146; cheap, 133–5; increases, 219, 223, 287, 291–3, 316; return, 242; passenger duty, 249; wartime, 257; income from, 283; and privatization, 306
farm removals, 287
Farnham, Lord and Lady, 151
Farrington, 133
Fay, Sam, 190, 192, 213
Fenchurch Street station, 230
Fenwick, Simon, 46
ferries, 137, 296
Ffestiniog Railway, 130, 194–5
Fiddlers Ferry power station, 274
Fiennes, Gerard, 275, 285–6, 289
Fife, 171–2
First World War (Great War), 123, 164, 245, 252; railways at outbreak, 127, 165, 180, 185–6, 188, 197, 202; impact on railways, 154, 205–19, 253, 255–6, 258, 260–1; armistice signed on train, 219; legacy for railways, 219–28, 263–4
fish, 84, 141, 193, 240, 278
Fleetwood, 80
Flint, 129
fly shunting, 125
*Flying Scotsman*, 234, 246–7
fog, 50, 266, 272

Folkestone, 76, 210; Pavilion Hotel, 120
food and drink, 243–4, 293, 298, 328
football, 142, 182
Forbes, James, 137–9, 142
Fort William, 226
Forth Bridge, 129, 166, 170, 172–3, 199
Fowler, Sir Henry, 232
fox-hunting, 10, 142
France, 67, 90, 147, 179, 194, 271; and First World War, 207, 210, 212, 219; high-speed network, 231, 314, 317; and Second World War, 259, 261; and electrification, 279
Fraser, Tom, 285
free trade, 18, 27
Freeman, Roger, 303
freight services, *see* goods services
French, Benjamin, 7
French, Sir John, 207
French Revolution, 41
Freud, Clement, 298
Frome, 95
fuel cells, 317
Furness Railway, 120
*Further North Express*, 248

Gallipoli, 218
Galloway, 128
Garnkirk & Glasgow Railway, 57
Garstang & Knott End Railway, 227
Gas Light & Coke Company, 140
Gatwick Express, 296, 336
Geddes, Sir Eric, 225, 227–8
General Railway Workers Union, 201, 204

General Strike, 241–2

George V, King, 247

Germany, 90, 206; and electrification, 279; ICE trains, 294; Maglev accident, 317

Gerrards Cross, 254

Gifford & Garvald Railway, 227

Giles, Frank, 73

Gill, Eric, 248

Gimbert, Ben, 261–2

Giza, Great Pyramid, 64

Gladstone, William, 78, 89, 114, 131, 223

Glamorgan, 129

Glasgow, 57, 74, 79; London services, 67, 119, 166, 174, 216, 247, 257, 270; connection with Edinburgh, 76, 82, 128, 199; suburban railways, 93, 128; workmen's trains, 134; evacuation, 256; port of, 256; and electrification, 279

Glasgow & South Western Railway, 199–200, 227

Glasgow, Paisley & Greenock Railway, 110

Glasgow–Stranraer branch line, 285

Glastonbury, 95

Gloucester, 70, 129, 190

GNER, 300

Godstone, 7

Golden Arrow, 244, 247

golf courses, 142

Golspie, 127

Gooch, Daniel, 72, 145, 158, 176–7

Gooch, John, 158

Gooch, Thomas, 30–1, 72

goods (freight) services, 84–6, 110, 125–7, 193, 233–4; number-takers,

103; separated from passenger services, 187; charges and receipts, 202, 231, 234, 252, 278; decline in, 231, 234, 278, 280, 282; average speeds, 251; and wartime, 258–9; scrapped, 283; and Settle & Carlisle line, 288; under privatization, 312–13

Gosport, 73–4, 76

Goswick accident, 265

Gourvish, Terry, 110, 270, 264, 298–9

Grace, W. G., 182

gramophone records, 247

Grand Junction Railway, 55, 59, 61–5, 73, 83, 97, 110; amalgamation, 96–7, 109

Grangemouth, 210, 218

Granite City, 270

Grantham, 285; accident, 180

Granville Express, 248

Gravesend, 238

Gravesend & Rochester Railway, 93–4

Gray, Thomas, 8–9, 23

Grayling, Chris, 338

Great Central Railway, 107, 163, 187, 219; creation of, 181–5; and cooperation, 190; publicity, 192; fish services, 193–4; and wartime, 213, 219; closure, 285

Great Eastern Railway, 115, 124, 134, 140, 142, 144, 186; maps, 193; and amalgamation, 227, 230; wine list, 243

Great Exhibition, 112–14, 142

Great Heck accident, 337

Great North of Scotland Railway, 128

Great North Road, 96

Great Northern Advertiser, 85

Great Northern Cemetery, 143

Great Northern Railway, 66, 95–6, 100–2, 109–10, 115, 117, 184, 193; route to Scotland and railway races, 96, 165–6, 172–5; costs, 100; track length, 101; topography, 109; enters price war, 112; and Midland Railway, 114, 116–17; introduces third class, 132; locomotive confiscated, 138; begins selling coal, 141; and amalgamation, 227, 233

Great Western Magazine, 262

Great Western Railway, 67–71, 74, 80, 119, 216, 273; gauge, 69–70, 77, 176–7; costs, 71; speeds, 77; and parliamentary trains, 78; and royal travel, 81–2; freight services, 84; track length, 97; time system, 104–5; expansion, 109; consolidation, 111, 114, 204; and Welsh lines, 129; and Irish services, 130; treatment of poorer passengers, 131; offers hunters' tickets, 142; financial difficulties, 145; accidents, 147, 150; telegraph system, 148;

wages and bonuses, 152, 154; industrial relations, 154, 160, 204; provident society, 156; working hours, 160; first corridor train, 164; and railway races, 176, 179; modernization and improvements, 177–8, 188; and cooperation, 190; publicity, 192–3, 245, 249, 256; loss-making services, 194; and Helston line, 197–8; compensation claim, 223; and amalgamation, 225–6, 231–2, 234–5; profitability, 235, 251, 266; introduces warning system, 235; livery, 240, 275; service improvements, 244; hundredth anniversary, 249; and wartime, 256–7, 263; workshops, 268; and diesels, 275

Greeks, ancient, 1
Green, Chris, 296
Greenwich, 136
Greenwich Mean Time, 104–5
Gresley, Nigel, 246–7, 315
Gretna Junction, 217–18
Grey, Earl, 41
Grimsby, 184, 193
'Grouse Traffic', 173
Guildford, 238
Gunnislake, 196

hackney cabs, 117
Hackworth, Timothy, 14, 17, 37
Halifax, 74
Hall, Stanley, 165
Hampshire, 141
Hampton Court, 237
Hardy, Thomas, 117

Harford, Edward, 200
Harrow, 65; accident, 219
Hartlepool, 217
Harwich, 95, 211
Hastings, 136, 189, 238
Hatfield, 100; accident, 304, 307–9
Heath, Edward, 290, 303
Heathrow Express, 332
Hedley, William, 14
Helmsdale, 127
Helston, 197–8
Henry, Thomas, 168
Henshaw, David, 273, 283, 285
Herapath, John, 91
Hereford, 113, 129
Hertfordshire, 63, 124, 135, 183
Hetton Colliery, 14
Hewitt, John, 157
High Speed One, 315, 318
High Speed Train (HST), 288, 291–3, 312
High Street Kensington station, 142
High Wycombe, 190
Highbridge, 95
Highland Railway, 127–8; wartime service, 208–10, 212
Highlands, 108, 127–8, 243, 286, 295
Hill, Rowland, 83
Hitchin, 115–16
Holborn Viaduct station, 324
Holden, Michael, 337
*Holiday Haunts*, 192
holiday trains, 189, 192, 207, 216, 219
Holland, 271, 323
Holyhead, 129, 187
hooliganism, 50
Hopton incline, 321
Hornsey, 135

horses, 19, 24, 35, 57, 199, 207, 269, 278; on Swansea & Mumbles Railway, 7–8; and railway gauge, 11–12; and Stockton & Darlington Railway, 15–17; and Liverpool & Manchester Railway, 27, 34; bolting, 52, 72; and trams, 185; and railway amalgamation, 232; under BR, 232, 269
hotels, 119–20, 234, 269, 296
Hounslow, 85
*Household Words*, 109
housing, 117–18, 133, 135, 183, 187
Howson, Martha, 17
Huddersfield, 184
Hudson, George, 97–103, 105, 108, 110, 114, 132, 181, 315
Hughes, Henry, 155
Huish, Captain Mark, 110–11, 113–14, 187
Hull, 57, 76, 80, 112, 163; Royal Station Hotel, 120; Paragon station, 120, 271
Hull & Barnsley Railway, 163, 192
Hull Trains, 304
Hundred of Manhood & Selsey Tramway, 195
Hunterston, 312
Huskisson, William, 33, 39–40, 42, 147
Hyde Park, 112

Immingham, 193
Imperial Airways, 228
India, 89, 294, 322
Ingleton, 161
innkeepers, 54

InterCity, 108, 288–91, 293–4, 296, 299
InterCity 225 trains, 295
interlocking, 122, 169
International Exhibition, 117, 139
Invergarry & Fort Augustus branch line, 280
Invergordon, 209
Inverness, 128, 199, 209, 212, 280
Ireland, 27, 32, 55, 225, 262, 274; first railways, 57, 76, 93; potato famine, 75, 130; steamer services, 129–30; railway network, 130–1; railway gauge, 130
Irish Mail, 129, 151, 244
Irish Sea, 130
*Iron Times*, 91
Irwell, river, 28, 41
Isle of Wight, 124, 179
Italy, 314

James, William, 9, 24–6, 28, 35
Japan, 135, 314, 322; bullet trains, 293
Jellicoe Specials, 210, 212, 218
Jessop, William, 8, 23
John O'Groats, 209
joint stock companies, 60
junctions, 11, 122, 187, 316; flat, 137

Kelly, Phil, 271
Kelvedon & Tollesbury Light Railway, 196
Kemble, Fanny, 52–3
Kent, 57, 136–8, 141, 150, 178, 236; and wartime, 210, 212, 215, 261

Kent & East Sussex Railway, 196
Kentish Town accident, 149, 152
Kenyon & Leigh Railway, 56
Kete, John, 68
Kew, 149
Killingworth Colliery, 14
Kilsby tunnel, 64, 72
King's Cross station, 66, 100, 109, 115–17, 193, 216, 270; Cambridge trains, 76; access to, 117; Great Northern Hotel, 117, 120; elegance, 120–1, 185; serves commuter lines, 135; cemetery services, 143; and railway races, 174; and 'Beer Trains', 234; smells, 240; LNER services, 243, 245–6
Kinnaber Junction, 174
Kitchener, Lord, 207

Labour Party, 200–1, 263–4, 276, 281, 284–5, 290, 298; and rail privatization, 300, 303, 306, 312
Ladbroke Grove accident, 307–8, 332–3
Laing, Samuel, 145
laissez-faire, 46, 83, 90, 149, 251–2
Lake District, 244
lamps, 50
Lancashire, 21–2, 32, 41, 50, 62, 74, 85, 227
Lancashire & Yorkshire Railway, 130, 161, 176, 191, 203, 227
Lancaster, 76
Land's End, 95
landowners, 9, 24–6, 28–9, 62–3, 68, 121–4,

129, 195, 197
Launceston, 124–5
Lawson, Nigel, 297
Lecount, Peter, 64
Lee Navigation, 9
Leeds, 8, 94; cotton industry, 57; London services, 67, 76, 139, 244, 270, 289; excursions, 80; investors, 92; railway access, 117–18; station refurbishment, 233; and electrification, 279
Leeds & Selby Railway, 57
Leeds Institute, 80
Leicester, 57, 74, 79, 115, 182–3, 241, 307
Leigh & Bolton Railway, 321
Letchworth Garden City, 234
level crossings, 30, 183; keepers, 154, 215
Lewisham, 136, 148; accident, 272
light railways, 194–6
Light Railways Act, 194–5, 197
Lightfoot brothers, 58
Lincoln, 100
Lincolnshire, 96, 108–9, 184, 193, 277, 285
liners, 176, 179, 262
liveries, 240, 275–6, 299
Liverpool, 52, 189; and building of Liverpool & Manchester Railway, 8, 21–3, 26, 43; population, 22; ban on locomotives, 29, 36; tunnel approach, 32–3; cable-operated approach, 35–6, 64; and opening of Liverpool & Manchester Railway, 38–40; railway

connections, 61, 67, 76–7, 111, 230; and horse-races, 79, 83; and postal service, 83; suburban railways, 93; workmen's trains, 134; viaduct bombed, 260; and electrification, 279

Liverpool & Manchester Railway, 2–3, 6, 9, 12, 17, 19–60, 72, 104, 162–3, 317–18; double track, 21, 30, 33, 42; surveys, 24–5, 62; costs, 26, 58; dividends and profits, 30, 54–6, 61; gauge, 33, 69; choice of steam power and Rainhill trials, 34–8; cable-operated section, 35–6, 64; opening, 38–43, 75, 113; passenger services, 43–54; tickets and fares, 43–4; carriages, 44–5; omnibus connections, 45; goods services, 55–6; mail services, 55, 83–4; track length, 57–8, 61, 65; excursions, 79; military transportation, 83; amalgamation, 109; telegraph system, 148; working conditions, 153; industrial relations, 157

Liverpool Courier, 39

Liverpool Mercury, 32, 37–8

Liverpool Overhead Railway, 191

Liverpool Street station, 188, 193, 196, 230; Cambridge trains, 76; building and cost, 134, 144; and electrification, 274; collaboration with

private sector, 299; and Crossrail scheme, 316

Liverpool Times, 56

Llanelli, 203

Llangynog-Llanrhaeadr-ym-Mochnant branch line, 280–1

Lloyd George, David, 202, 220

Locke, Joseph, 33, 36–7, 40, 73; and Grand Junction Railway, 61, 63–4

Locomotion, 15

Locomotion No. 1, 16

Locomotive Act (Red Flag Act), 5

Locomotive Exchanges, 273

locomotives: Duchess class, 66; coal-burning, 122; Crampton, 138; captured by other companies, 138–9; builders, 140–1; care of, 164; speed records, 178, 247; impact of war, 210, 213, 224; Royal Scots class, 232–3; Star and Saint classes, 234; King and Castle classes, 234, 246; Southern, 236; streamlining, 246–7; Pacific class, 246–8; investment in, 249; post-war, 264; private, 268; diesel, 268, 273–5, 277–9, 292; survival of steam, 268–9, 273–4, 276; electric, 273–4, 277–8, 292; Deltic diesels, 289

London: first railway, 57–9; first railway connections, 61, 64, 72–3; suburbs, 65; 134–5, 136; termini, 66,

90, 117, 139–40, 185, 260; growth in railway connections, 76–7, 84–6, 93, 95–102, 110, 138, 188; suburban and commuter railways, 76, 93, 108, 124, 133–6, 140, 185–6, 190–1, 233, 235–9, 279–80, 292, 296–7; and postal service, 83–4; time in, 104; exhibition traffic, 112–13, 117, 139; Midland Railway gains access, 114–17; impact of railways, 117–18, 140–2; workmen's trains, 133–4; population growth, 143; railway accidents, 148; and Great Central connections, 181–4; tramways, 186; and wartime, 206, 216–17, 256, 260, 263; and amalgamation, 225–6, 230; integrated transport system, 226, 251; wartime evacuation, 256; and electrification, 279

London & Birmingham Railway, 59, 61–6, 72, 97, 103, 117; surveys, 62; stagecoach connections, 64; fares, 65; investors, 74; and royal travel, 82; freight services, 84; amalgamation, 96–7, 109; departure times, 104; railway cottages, 153

London & Chatham Railway, 144, 178

London & Croydon Railway, 59

London & Greenwich Railway, 58–60; right-hand running, 59

London & North Eastern Railway (LNER), 225–6, 230, 232–3; network, 234; hotels, 234; livery, 240, 275; accidents, 242; rugby specials, 243; food and drink, 243; service improvements, 244–7; publicity, 245, 248–9; profitability, 251, 266; split at nationalization, 268; electrification, 274

London & North Western Railway (LNWR), 67, 97, 100, 109–14, 119, 190, 216; dominant position, 109–11; value and profitability, 109–11; enters price war, 112; and Midland Railway, 114–16; and Welsh lines, 129; and Irish services, 130; sells coal, 141; working hours, 160; and route to Scotland, 161; and railway races, 165–6; braking system, 168; Preston accident, 175; modernization and improvements, 186–9; *Sunny South Special* service, 189; electrification, 191; publicity, 192; compensation claim, 223; and amalgamation, 227, 232; livery, 275

London & South Western Railway, 72–4, 141, 143, 193–4; and railway races, 176, 179–80; reputation, 178–9;

electrification, 191, 237; consolidation, 204; wartime service, 208; and amalgamation, 226–7, 237

London & Southampton Railway, 72–4

London Bridge station, 59, 136, 191, 236

London, Brighton & South Coast Railway, 136, 139, 142, 178; collapse, 144–5; Clayton tunnel accident, 148–9; strike, 158; *Southern Belle* service, 188; electrification, 191, 237; and amalgamation, 226–7, 236–7

London, Chatham & Dover Railway, 137–9, 190, 324

London Electric Railway, 213, 228

London, Midland & Scottish Railway (LMS), 225, 227, 230, 234, 273; network and inventory, 232; livery, 240; service improvements, 244, 246–7; publicity, 248–9; workforce and repair facilities, 250; profitability, 251, 266; and wartime, 257, 260

London Midland Region, 277, 288

London Necropolis Railway, 143

London Passenger Transport Board, *see* London Transport

London Post Office, 6

London, Tilbury & Southend Railway, 230

London Transport, 226,

251, 253, 263–4; headquarters, 267

London Underground, 47–8, 137–40, 185, 188, 213, 228; Metropolitan Line, 90, 191; District Line, 90, 191; Circle Line, 140, 327; impact on shopping habits, 142; and electrification, 191; public relations, 193; and wartime, 211, 215, 217, 254, 262–3; women on, 215; Bakerloo Line, 215; Piccadilly Line, 254; increase in passengers, 312; overcrowding, 316; rails, 320; *see also* Metropolitan District Railway; Metropolitan Railway

London–York Direct Railway, 100

Londonderry, 130

looms, steam-powered, 3

Lord's cricket ground, 182

lorries, 180, 185, 228–9, 252–3, 269, 276, 278

Lossiemouth, 128

Loughborough, 79

Louis Philippe, King, 81

Louis XIV, 1

Ludgate Hill station, 324

Luton, 113

Lutterworth, 184

Macadam, John, 5, 42

Macclesfield, 290

MacDonald, Ramsay, 281

McGrath, Thomas, 168

MacGregor, John, 302, 304

Macmillan, Harold, 281

Maglev trains, 317

Maiden Lane station, 109–10
Maidenhead, 85
Maidenhead Bridge, 68
Maidstone, 94
mail order goods, 126
mail services, 55, 82–4, 110, 119, 126, 178
Major, John, 77, 299, 301–2
Mallaig, 226
*Mallard*, 247
Manchester, 38, 135, 181, 187, 244, 288; steam-powered looms, 3; and building of Liverpool & Manchester Railway, 8, 21–3; population, 22; indifference to railway, 40–1; weavers, 44; railway connections, 55, 61, 67, 76, 86, 93–4, 110, 114, 230, 274; investment in railways, 74; and excursions, 79–80, 83; railway access, 117–18; workmen's trains, 134; and railway races, 176; Great Central connections, 181, 184; and electrification, 279
Manchester & Birmingham Railway, 73
Manchester & Leeds Railway, 75, 78
Manchester & Sheffield Railway, 75
Manchester, Sheffield & Lincolnshire Railway, 146, 160, 167, 181, 183–4
Marlborough, 68
Marly, gardens of, 1
Marples, Ernest, 281–2, 285, 287

Marsh, Richard, 290, 294
marshalling yards, 278, 280–1
Marylebone Cricket Club, 182
Marylebone station, 183, 185, 187, 260, 267
Mayhew, Henry, 141
Meakin, George, 218–19
Mechanics' Institutes, 157
Mendips, 178
Merchant Navy, 152
*Mercury*, 51
Merstham, 7
Merthyr Tydfil, 129
Metroland, 135
Metropolitan District Railway, 135, 137, 139, 142
Metropolitan Railway, 8, 47, 135, 137, 139, 142; introduces Pullman service, 133; profitability, 133; and Great Central Railway, 181–3; and amalgamation, 228
middle classes, 105–6, 121, 131, 135, 146, 186, 242
Middlesbrough, 19, 73, 133, 260
Middlesex, 85, 135, 190
Middleton Colliery, 13
Mid-Kent Railway, 136
Midland Counties Railway, 75, 97
Midland Railway, 57, 79, 96–7, 99–101, 109, 184; enters price war, 112; access to London, 114–18; promotes third class, 121, 131–2; and Irish services, 130; Pullman service, 133; industrial relations, 159–60; and Settle &

Carlisle line, 160–3, 172, 287; braking system, 168; coal trains, 193; and wartime, 216, 219; and amalgamation, 227, 230, 232, 240
Milford Haven, 93
military trains, 83, 148, 206–19, 224, 256–9
milk, 84–5, 126, 141, 240
Milne, Sir James, 235
Milton Keynes, 285
mines, 1, 3, 7, 19, 57, 152–3
Molesworth, Sir William, 57
Monmouthshire, 129
Monmouthshire Railway and Canal Company, 129–30
monopolies, 18; Huish and, 110, 114; Victorian fear of, 220, 228; privatization and, 309
monorails, 9, 317
'monster trains', 79–80
Moon, Sir Richard, 165–6, 186–7
Morecambe Bay, 325
Moretonhampstead, 123
Moreton-in-the-Marsh, 35
*Morning Post*, 39
Morrison, Herbert, 264
Morton, Sir Alastair, 306
Motherwell, 199
motorways, 276, 278, 281, 284, 289
Mumbles, 7–8
munitions trains, 212, 214, 261–2
Myers Flat swamp, 15, 25

Napoleon Bonaparte, 41
narrow gauge railways, 130–1, 194–5, 212
National Rail Enquiry Service, 77, 307

National Union of Railwaymen (NUR), 160, 204, 207, 220–1, 225, 241

National Wages Board, 225

nationalization, 78, 107, 144–5, 170, 263–8, 300; opposition to, 156, 263, 265–8; and amalgamation, 223–5, 228, 231–2; and industrial relations, 291

navvies, 31–2, 123, 160–1, 183; deaths of, 64, 94, 162–3; shipped to Crimea, 206

Nesham's Colliery, 14

Network Rail, 77, 288, 302, 308–11

Network SouthEast, 226, 296, 299

New Southgate, 143

New Zealand, 294

Newbury, 194, 337

Newcastle, 99, 102, 295, 325; London services, 99, 184, 230, 245, 247, 293; Tyne bridges, 190; wartime evacuation, 256

Newcastle & Carlisle Railway, 35, 57, 68, 76; freight services, 84

Newcastle & Darlington Railway, 99

Newcastle Courant, 16

'Newcastle Roads', 2

Newcomen, John, 2–3

Newington Green, 186

Newport, 129

newspaper specials, 248

newspapers (press), 106, 126, 182, 215; and railway advertising, 90–1, 192; and railway races, 174; and rail strike, 221; Southern

Railway campaign, 236–7; opposition to nationalization, 266–7; switch to road haulage, 278; opposition to privatization, 303

Newton, 41, 79

Newton Abbot, 123, 179

Newtown, 113

night traffic, 110

Nightall, Jim, 261–2

Nock, O. S., 100, 168, 176, 179, 217

Norfolk, 85, 108, 141, 258, 263, 286

Normanton, 97, 120

North British Railway, 119, 129; route to Scotland and railway races, 161, 165–6, 171, 165–6, 172–5; industrial relations, 199; compensation claim, 223; and amalgamation, 233

North Devon & Cornwall Junction Light Railway, 195

North Eastern Railway, 115, 123, 190; industrial relations, 158–60; and railway races, 165–6, 172–6; electrification, 191; and wartime, 217; and amalgamation, 225, 227, 233

North London Railway, 149, 191

North Midland Railway, 66, 85, 97–8

North Staffordshire Railway, 114

Northampton, 72–3, 95

Northamptonshire, 183

Northern & Eastern Railway, 76

Northern Barrage, 209

Northern Ireland, 250

Northolt, 190

Northumberland, 265

Northwich, 65

Norway, 209

Norwich, 10, 76, 113, 289, 295–6

Nottingham, 56, 110, 138–9, 180, 182–3, 289

Nottinghamshire, 182

Novelty, 36

Nunhead–Lewisham loop, 272

Octuple agreement, 111–12

oil crisis, 290

Okehampton, 248

Old St Pancras churchyard, 117

Olive Mount cutting, 33, 52

Olympic Games, 315

omnibus connections, 45, 94; see also buses

One, 300

Orcadian, 248

Orkney, 209

Orpington, 136, 237–8

Oswestry, 129

Outram, Benjamin, 23

overcrowding, 312, 316

Overend Gurney collapse, 144

Overton, George, 12

Owen, Elizabeth Mary, 262

Oxford, 77, 93, 95

Oxford–Cambridge line, 277, 285

Oxford Companion to British Railway History, 286

Oxford, Worcester & Wolverhampton Railway, 93, 146

Paddington station, 78, 177, 188, 194, 248, 289; construction, 68, 71; Great Western Royal Hotel, 120; and electric telegraph, 148; smells, 240; and electrification, 279; and Crossrail scheme, 316
Paignton, 125
Paisley, 79
*Palatine*, 248
*Pall Mall Gazette*, 157
Palmer, Henry, 9
Papin, Denis, 2
Paris, 3, 81, 120, 135, 181, 184, 193, 244, 315
Parker, Peter, 42, 294–5
Parkinson, Cecil, 301
Parkside, 39
parliamentary trains, 78, 126, 131, 146
Pasenger's Charter, 77
Passchendaele, 212
Passenger Transport Executives, 287, 306
passengers, 48–9, 54, 127, 131–5, 186–7, 318; first services, 7–8; first-class, 44, 126, 130, 177, 184, 186, 288; second-class, 44, 121, 126, 165, 177, 288; third-class, 44, 78, 121, 132, 147, 177, 184, 245; riding on roofs, 48–50; VIPs, 49; deceased, 143; Atlantic, 176, 179; obstreperous, 215; luggage allowances, 216; decline in numbers, 230–1, 265, 280, 291, 297; dress, 243; increase in numbers, 290, 295, 312
*Patentee*, 51
Patricroft, 54
Peak District, 35

Pease, Edward, 10, 12, 19
Pease, Joseph, 10
Peckham, 191
Pembrey, 212
Pendleton, John, 181
Pendolino trains, 291, 307, 337
Penkridge viaduct, 63
Pennines, 94, 108, 274
penny post, 83
Pen-y-Darren, 4
Penzance, 93, 240
*Perseverance*, 37
Persia, ancient, 11
Perth, 128, 171, 199, 209, 272; marshalling yards, 278
Peru, 13
Peterborough, 95, 100, 138
Peterloo, 41
Peto, Sir Samuel, 116, 144
Peyton, Lord, 303
Pickford's, 34, 250
picnic baskets, 146
pigs, 55, 126
Plymouth, 71, 104, 124, 184, 196, 241, 285; wartime services, 208, 210, 257; London services, 178–80, 188–9, 204, 257; time in, 104; and Atlantic passengers, 176
points, 51, 122, 177
Pole, Sir Felix, 235
policemen, 49, 51, 66, 153, 155
Poole, 297
porters, 45, 58, 66, 70, 154–5, 159, 174, 189, 213
Portsmouth, 7, 72–4, 208, 236, 238–9
Post Office, 6, 55, 83, 125, 148
postcards, 192

posters, 248
Potters Bar accident, 307
pottery, 24, 55, 62
power supply debacle, 310
Pratt, Edwin, 222
Prescott, John, 306
press, *see* newspapers
Preston, 56, 166, 227; accident, 175–7, 179–80
Preston & Wyre Railway, 80
Preston Brook cutting, 63
Price, W. P., 161
Princetown, 124, 281
privatization, 297–311; costs of, 308–11
provident funds, 156–7
Provincial (later Regional) railways, 296
Public Service Obligation, 291
*Puffing Billy*, 14
Pullman, George, 133
Pullman cars, 133, 163, 188–9, 243–4, 271; *see also* Blue Pullmans
*Punch*, 70, 105, 237
Putney, 135

Quakers, 10, 17, 19, 103
*Quarterly Review*, 58
*Queen of Scots*, 270
Quintinshill accident, 210, 217–19, 265, 272

race trains, 79, 83, 142, 158
rack and pinion, 13
Radstock accident, 152
Rail, Marine and Transport Workers' Union (RMT), 160
railcards, 306
rails, 4, 6; L-shaped, 4, 7; wrought iron, 13; continuous welded, 292, 320

Railtrack, 77, 302, 304–9, 312–13
Railway Air Service, 250
Railway and Canal Traffic Act, 204
*Railway and Commercial Journal*, 91
Railway Clearing House, 103–5, 204
Railway Clerks Association, 158
Railway Companies Association, 156, 201, 225
railway companies:
  monopoly powers, 44, 53, 67, 89, 96, 98, 100, 110, 114, 180, 192, 198, 202, 231;
  profitability, 55, 186, 189–92, 202, 205, 220, 223, 231, 241, 251, 263, 265–6; joint stock and limited liability, 60–1; competition among, 79, 89, 110–11, 121, 129–30, 136, 138–9, 146, 161, 165, 188, 202, 220, 228;
  expansion of (railway mania), 86–107, 143–5;
  capital requirements, 88; share certificates, 90; advertising, 91, 191–3, 221, 248–9; investors, 91–2, 98, 146; and MPs, 92, 102; average costs, 93; dominance of large companies, 96–7, 108–21; mergers, 97–8, 108, 138, 225; requirement for accounts, 97; bubble collapses, 105–7; business model, 110, 187; improvement in public perception, 113–14; and hotels, 119–20; Scottish, 128–9; restrictions on housing development, 135; damage to reputation, 145–7; industrial relations, 154–60, 198–204, 220–1; cooperation and consolidation, 190, 204; public relations, 192–3; and closures, 197; and women's employment, 214–15; post-war compensation, 222–4, 228, 263–7; amalgamations, 224–32, 300, 313; valuation at nationalization, 266–7
Railway Development Association, 281
Railway Executive Committee, 206, 208, 210, 253–4, 267–9, 273, 276
railway inspectorate, 147, 149, 151, 311
railway journals, 91
railway mania, 75, 86–107, 109, 112, 121–2, 143–6
Railway Passenger Duty, 249
railway races, 165–6, 173–6, 188
Railway Regulation Acts, 78, 89, 169, 223
*Railway Ribaldry*, 249
*Railway Service Gazette*, 157
*Railway Times*, 91
railway workers, 45–7; fines, 45–6; working hours, 45, 152–3, 155–6, 160, 200–1, 204, 220–1, 223, 241; wages, 45–6, 152–3, 202–4, 213, 220–1, 223, 254–5, 292; sickness benefits, 46; deaths, 46, 152, 258, 265; recruitment, 153–4, 255; uniforms, 154; promotions, 155; industrial relations, 154–60, 198–204, 220–1, 241; size of workforce, 160, 292; enlistment and conscription, 212–15, 254–5; war bonuses, 220–1, 241; bravery awards, 262; under BR, 291–2
railwaywomen, 153–4, 214–15, 221–2, 254–5; wages, 254–5; numbers, 255
Rainhill, 50; trials, 36–8, 55
Ramsgate, 272
Rastrick, John, 94
Reading, 85, 95, 147, 151, 194, 293
recovery time, 323
Red Flag Act, *see* Locomotive Act
Redhill, 136, 178
Rednal, 150
Reform Bill, 56, 61–2
refreshments, 69, 71, 77, 119
Reid, Sir Bob, 295–7, 315
relief trains, 244
Rennie, George, 29–30
Rennie, John, 29–30
restaurant cars, *see* dining cars
Ribblehead viaduct, 162–3, 288
Richborough, 210
Richmond, 135, 191
Ridley, Nicholas, 295
Rifkind, Malcolm, 301

Rigby brothers, 71
roads, 3–6, 8, 22–5, 42,
    253, 265; steam vehicles
    on, 3, 5–6, 74, 180;
    Roman, 11; competition
    with railways, 55,
    228–30, 242, 249, 252,
    267, 278, 280, 318;
    deaths on, 249, 265,
    284; building, 281, 298;
    economics of, 283–4;
    and oil crisis, 290;
    congestion, 312, 314;
    environmental damage,
    316
Robbins, Michael, 69
Robertson, Reg, 255
Robertson, Sir William,
    212
Robinson, Heath, 249
Robson, Steve, 301
Rochester, 94
Rocket, 37, 40
rolling stock companies
    (roscos), 302, 304, 306,
    309
Rolt, L. T. C., 151
Romans, 4, 11
Rosslare, 262
rostering, flexible, 294
rotten boroughs, 41
Rouen, 81
Roulette, 1
Royal Commission on
    Metropolis Railway
    Termini, 90, 117, 140
Royal Engineers, 147
Royal George, 17
Royal Greenwich
    Observatory, 104
Royal Scots, 218
royal trains, 82
Rugby, 61, 66, 73, 79, 86,
    95, 97, 99–101, 116,
    182, 187, 244
rugby specials, 243
Runcorn, 56

running rights, 56, 101,
    108, 116
Russia, 27, 241, 322
Ryde, 326

Saatchi & Saatchi, 293
safety, 45, 51–2, 69,
    147–52, 156, 160, 166,
    175, 179–80; train
    protection systems, 235,
    308; under Big Four,
    265; under BR, 272–3,
    297; under
    privatization, 307–9,
    311; legislation, 317; see
    also accidents
sails, 7
St Helens, 42, 51, 56
St Mary Cray, 136
St Mungo, 270
St Pancras station, 102,
    107, 140, 161, 216,
    243, 289; construction,
    117; Gothic grandeur,
    120–1, 185; Midland
    Grand Hotel, 120;
    undercroft, 159;
    bombed, 217; compared
    with Euston, 240; see
    also Bedford–St Pancras
    line
St Patrick (liner), 262
Salford, 22
Salisbury, 208, 336;
    accident, 179–80
Salisbury Plain, 208
Salmon, Roger, 303
Sampson, Anthony, 282
Sandars, Joseph, 23–4,
    26–7
Sandwich, 210
Sandy Lodge (Moor Park)
    station, 142
Sankey viaduct, 33, 52
Sans Pareil, 37
Saturday-only services,
    244

Save Our Railways, 305
Saville, Jimmy, 293
Scapa Flow, 208–9
Scarborough, 80
Schull & Skibbereen
    Railway, 131
Schwarzenberg, Prince
    von, 3
Scotland, 32, 47, 109,
    188, 243, 280, 295,
    312; railway network,
    76, 127–9; connection
    with England, 93, 96,
    99, 165–6, 172–6; and
    Settle & Carlisle line,
    160–3, 172; labour
    conflict, 198–200; and
    amalgamation, 225–7,
    232; air service, 250;
    branch lines, 286
Scotrail, 48
Scots Fusiliers, 59
Scotsman, 38
Scott, Sir George Gilbert,
    120
Scott, Jane, 17
Scott, John, 155
Scottish Region, 128, 226
seaside holidays, 80
Sebastopol, fall of, 206
Second World War, 88,
    170, 213, 240, 245,
    308; impact on
    railways, 253–63; legacy
    for railways, 263–8, 270
Sefton, Lord, 25, 28, 38
Selby, 312
Selsey, 195
Serpell, Sir David, 294–5,
    316
Settle & Carlisle line,
    160–3, 172, 287–8;
    cost, 161; death toll,
    162–3
Severn tunnel, 177, 190
Shanklin, 326
Shap, 161

Sharland, Charles, 162
sheep, 72, 85
Sheffield, 135, 184, 187, 230, 274
*Sheffield and Rotherham Independent*, 85
Sheffield, Ashton-under-Lyne & Manchester Railway, 94
Shenfield, 254, 274
Shepperton, 237
Shepton Mallet, 95
ships, 131, 141, 189, 256; *see also* liners; steamships
Short, Clare, 306
Shrewsbury, 113
Shrewsbury & Chester Railway, 111, 129
Shropshire, 4, 150, 195
signalling, 49–50, 93, 122; and accidents, 148–9, 151–2, 217–19, 242; interlocking, 122, 169; and high-speed trains, 293, 295; radio, 295–6, 305, 317
signals passed at danger (SPADs), 308
Silver Jubilee, 247
Simmons, Jack, 79, 102, 121, 141, 163, 170; on Watkin, 181, 184; on Big Four, 250–1
Skerne, river, 15
Skibbereen, 131
Skipton, 108
Skye, 128
slave trade, 21–2
Sleaford, 285
sleeper services, 48, 65, 119, 163, 179–80, 216, 243, 245, 272
sleepers, 13, 50, 317
Slesser, Sir Henry, 281
Slough, 148
smallpox, 163

Smith, Adam, 18
Smith, Delia, 298
Smithfield, 85
Snailbeach District Railway, 195–6
'snow, wrong type of', 298
Snow Hill station, 260
Snowdon, 181
Soham, 261
Somers Town, 118
Somerset & Dorset line, 152, 178, 285
Somersetshire Midland Railway, 95
Sonning, 147
Souter, Brian, 315
South Africa, 206
South America, 17
South Croydon accident, 265
South Devon Railway, 71, 125
South Eastern & Chatham Railway, 193, 210, 223; and amalgamation, 226–7, 236, 238
South Eastern Railway, 80, 112, 120, 136–9, 141, 145, 178, 190; Staplehurst accident, 150–1; and Great Central Railway, 181; electrification, 191
South Kensington station, 138
South Korea, 314
South Sea Bubble, 61, 92
South West Trains, 300, 305
Southall, 85; accident, 235, 307
Southampton, 72–4, 76, 176, 178–9; and wartime, 206–8, 256
Southampton & Dorchester Railway, 93

Southampton Docks, 73, 179, 206, 208
Southend, 230, 232
Southern Railway, 191, 195, 208, 268; formation of, 226–7; electrification, 231, 235–40, 244, 274; commuter base, 234–5; public relations, 236–7; profitability, 238, 240, 251, 266; standardized running times, 239; livery, 240; food and drink, 243–4; service improvements, 244; platform lighting, 245; and wartime, 258, 260, 263; and diesels, 275
Southern Region, 271, 275, 337
Southgate, 135
Southport Chapel Street station, 271
Spain, 144, 294
'sparks effect', 238, 290
'Special Scotch Express', 166
specials, 82–3, 148, 268
Spence, Elizabeth Isabella, 8
Stafford, Marquess of, 29
Stafford, 290
Staffordshire, 61–3
Stagecoach, 305, 315
stagecoaches, 45, 48–9, 51, 58, 131; heyday of, 5–6; journey times, 22, 99, 104; decline of, 53–4; train connections, 64
Stamp, Joshua, 232–3, 251
standard gauge, 11–12, 33, 57, 69–70, 77, 130, 177, 195; half-standard gauge, 196; *see also* broad gauge

Stanier, William, 246–7
Stanley, Albert, 213, 220
Stanley Junction, 209
Staplehurst accident, 150–1
stations, 47, 66, 69, 93; private, 127, 190; closures, 215, 219, 283; refurbishment, 233, 235, 249, 271; lighting, 245; platform edges, 258; numbers of, 286; reopened, 288; platform extensions, 316
Statutes (Definition of Time) Act, 105
steam, high-pressure, 3–4
*Steam Horse*, 13
steamships, 67, 80, 112, 137, 187, 217
Stephens, Colonel Holman Fred, 195–6, 274
Stephenson, George, 2, 12–17, 67, 73, 97, 183, 315; and standard gauge, 12, 33, 57, 69; reputation, 12–14; and Liverpool & Manchester Railway, 25–6, 28–31, 36–40, 46, 55–6, 162–3, 318; salary, 30; described by Fanny Kemble, 52–3; and Midland railways, 61, 64, 66; Tyne bridge, 190
Stephenson, Robert, 17, 36–7, 56–7, 67–8, 97; and London & Birmingham Railway, 61–4, 72; bridge collapses, 170
Stirlingshire, 218
stock exchanges, 74, 92
Stockport, 86
Stockton, 9, 11, 15–17, 19
Stockton & Darlington Railway, 2, 9–12,

14–20, 21, 25, 30, 32, 37, 43, 96; origins and building, 9–11; gauge, 11–12, 33; horses on, 15–17, 35; opening, 15, 39, 157; passenger services, 16–17; economics, 17–18; single track, 18, 30; turnpike system, 18, 34; dividends, 19; carriages, 44–5; amalgamation, 115; workmen's trains, 133
Stoke, 114
Strategic Rail Authority, 306–7, 311, 313
Stratford & Moreton Railway, 35, 94
Stratford-on-Avon & Midland Junction Railway, 211
Stratford-upon-Avon, 184, 285
Strathmore, Earl of, 9
strikes, 155, 157–8, 199–201, 203–4; and wartime, 207–8, 254; post-war, 220–1; General Strike, 241–2; under BR, 292, 295
Stromeferry, 128
Strood, 94, 136
Submarine Railway Company, 184
subsidies, 194, 229, 290, 296–7, 300–1, 308–9, 314
suburbs, 65, 134–5, 233; and electrification, 191, 238–9
suffragettes, 214
Sunday services, 47, 125
Sunderland, 190
suppliers, to railways, 141
Surbiton, 189
Surrey, 143, 212, 236

Surrey Iron Railway, 7–8, 23
Sussex, 195
Sutherland, Duke of, 127
Swannington, 57
Swansea, 129, 190
Swansea & Mumbles Railway, 7–8
Swindon, 68, 71, 73, 77, 241, 245, 293; railway hotel, 120; workshops, 268, 273, 279
Swiss Cottage, 186
Szlumper, Gilbert S., 208

Taff Vale Railway, 200–1
Taiwan, 314
Taunton, 248
Tay Bridge, 170–3
Tebay, 161
Tees, river, 9
telephones, 193, 281
Telford, Thomas, 5
Telford, Tony, 271
Templecombe, 180
tenders, corridor, 246
Territorial Army, 207
TGV Est, 317
Thames, river, 9, 141, 211, 296; boat services, 58; tunnel, 67
Thames & Medway Canal Company, 93
Thatcher, Margaret, 91, 198, 233, 294–5, 301, 314
Thomas, David St John, 123, 130–1, 178, 196
Thomas, Jimmy, 221, 225
Thurso, 127–8, 209, 211
tickets, 43–4, 318; seat reservations, 44; through booking, 103; standardization of, 103–4; season, 135, 186, 236, 306; hunters', 142; interchangeable,

216; concessions scrapped, 219; excursion and tourist, 242, 257; cheap day, 257; and privatization, 306

Tilling, 250

tilting trains, 291

time, standardization of, 104–5

*Times, The*, 29, 40, 84, 178

timetables, 47, 77–8, 81–2, 165, 191, 289; and accidents, 148, 150; and railway races, 174; summer, 192; wartime, 207, 258; pre-war, 233–4, 244, 270; standardized running times, 239, 289; and high-speed trains, 293; under privatization, 311; working, 323

Tinsley, James, 218–19

Tiptree, 196

toilet breaks, 77, 119, 165–6

Tonbridge, 136, 237

Torquay, 80, 125

Torr, Cecil, 123

Tottenham, 134

TPOs, 84

Trades Union Congress, 200, 242

traffic management, 110

train paths, 259

Train Protection and Warning System (TPWS), 235, 308

trainspotting, 103, 192, 268

trams, 185–6, 191, 314

'tramways', 1

Transport Acts, 276, 290

travel agents, 79

travelcards, 296

Travellers Fare, 299

Trent Valley Railway, 67, 93

trespassers, 50

Trevithick, Richard, 3–4, 7, 13

troop trains, *see* military trains

tunnels, 32–3, 245

Turkey, 218

turkey specials, 141

turnpikes, 5–6, 18, 22

Tyndall Centre for Climate Change, 316

Tyne, river, 190

*Tyne Mercury*, 16

Tyneside, 1

typists, travelling, 188

U-boats, 210

Ufton Nervet accident, 337

unions, 156–7, 159–60, 183, 199–204; and wartime, 207, 214–15, 220, 154; and women's employment, 214–15, 222, 255; post-war position, 220–1; and nationalization, 224–5; and General Strike, 241–2; opposition to closures, 284; under BR, 291–2, 295

United Pointsmen and Signalmen, 204

United States of America, 3, 21–2, 27, 80, 132, 176

Unwin, Philip, 189, 244, 248

Usk valley, 129

Vaughan, Adrian, 30, 95, 152, 211

Vauxhall Bridge station, 68

Verney Junction, 133

Versailles, 147, 169

Victoria, Queen, 80–2, 105, 167, 171, 173, 185

Victoria station, 139–40, 236, 238

Vienna, 3

Vignoles, Charles, 28–30, 33

Virgin Trains, 291, 305–7

Voyager trains, 307

Waddington, David, 158

Wadebridge, 57

wagon ways, 1, 7–9, 11–13

Wales, 108, 113, 138, 160, 208, 211, 295; iron works, 4; railway network, 76, 93, 127, 129–30; coal, 200, 210, 226; and amalgamation, 226, 234; branch line, 280–1, 285–6

Walker, Sir Herbert, 208, 213, 227, 235–9

Walsall, 65

Walthamstow, 134

Wandle valley, 7

Wandsworth, 7

War Department railways, 213

Warburton, Ivor, 310

Ware, 124

Ware, Hadham & Buntingford Railway, 123–4

Wareham, 207

Warrenpoint, 168

Warrington, 61, 274

Warrington & Newton Railway, 56

Washington DC, 105

water troughs, 119

Waterloo & City Railway, 191

Waterloo Necropolis station, 143

Waterloo station, 178, 194, 235, 238, 248, 260
Watford, 61, 64, 191, 215
Watkin, Edward, 135, 137, 139, 142, 145, 167, 315; and Great Central Railway, 181–5; character, 181, 183; and Channel Tunnel, 184–5
Watt, James, 2–3
Watt, James (son), 62, 86
wayleave, 9–10
Wear, river, 14
Weaver, river, 63
Wellington, Duke of, 39–42
Welshpool, 113
Welwyn Garden City, 234
Wembley, 142, 181
West Coast main line, 76, 95–7, 109, 163, 179, 190, 216, 295, 310; and railway races, 165–6, 173–5; and accidents, 177, 308; expresses, 229, 247; electrification, 274, 277, 279, 288–90, 294; work stops, 282; tilting trains, 291; and privatization, 305–6
West End & Crystal Palace Railway, 136

West Highland Railway, 226
West Indies, 3
'West of England Express', 189
Western Region, 273, 288, 293
Westinghouse, George, 167–8
Weston, Clevedon & Portishead Railway, 274
Weston-super-Mare, 80
Weymouth, 93, 113
wheels, flanged, 6–7, 16; cogged, 13; steel tyres, 122
whistles, steam, 50
Whitelaw, William, 233
Whiteley, William, 142
Whitstable, 57
Wick, 127–8, 209
Wigan, 56; Wallgate station, 271
Wilkinson, Norman, 248
Willetts, David, 338
Wilson, Harold, 284–6, 290
Windsor, 81, 238
Wisonsin Central, 312
Wojtczak, Helena, 154, 214, 222, 262
Woking, 254

Wolverhampton, 65, 93
Wolverton, 153
Wood Green, 135
Woodhead tunnel, 94, 274
Woolwich, 9
workmen's trains, 131, 133–4
Worrall, Terry, 298
Wright brothers, 37
Wylam, 12

Yarmouth, 99
Yelverton, 124, 281
Yeovil, 93, 113
York, 103, 115, 166, 176, 188, 258; London services, 77, 85, 96–8, 100–1, 109, 193, 270, 293; and electrification, 279
York & North Midland Railway, 97–9, 101, 105
York, Newcastle & Berwick Railway, 99, 101–2
Yorkshire, 32, 85, 97, 105, 312; coal, 116, 141, 274
Ypres, 126

Zeppelins, 217